Pro Hyper-V

Harley Stagner

Pro Hyper-V

Copyright © 2009 by Harley Stagner

ISBN-13 (pbk): 978-1-4302-1908-8

ISBN-13 (electronic): 978-1-4302-1909-5

Lead Editor: Tony Campbell
Technical Reviewers: Jon Rolfe, Greg Shields
Editorial Board: Clay Andres, Steve Anglin, Mark Beckner, Ewan Buckingham, Tony Campbell,
    Gary Cornell, Jonathan Gennick, Jonathan Hassell, Michelle Lowman, Matthew Moodie,
    Duncan Parkes, Jeffrey Pepper, Frank Pohlmann, Douglas Pundick, Ben Renow-Clarke,
    Dominic Shakeshaft, Matt Wade, Tom Welsh
Project Manager: Beth Christmas
Copy Editor: Marilyn Smith
Associate Production Director: Kari Brooks-Copony
Production Editor: Laura Cheu
Compositor: Patrick Cunningham
Proofreader: Liz Welch
Indexer: Carol Burbo
Cover Designer: Kurt Krames
Manufacturing Director: Tom Debolski

Distributed to the book trade worldwide by Springer-Verlag New York, Inc., 233 Spring Street, 6th Floor, New York, NY 10013. Phone 1-800-SPRINGER, fax 201-348-4505, e-mail orders-ny@springer-sbm.com, or visit http://www.springeronline.com.

For information on translations, please contact Apress directly at 2855 Telegraph Avenue, Suite 600, Berkeley, CA 94705. Phone 510-549-5930, fax 510-549-5939, e-mail info@apress.com, or visit http://www.apress.com.

Apress and friends of ED books may be purchased in bulk for academic, corporate, or promotional use. eBook versions and licenses are also available for most titles. For more information, reference our Special Bulk Sales–eBook Licensing web page at http://www.apress.com/info/bulksales.

The source code for this book is available to readers at http://www.apress.com.

This book is dedicated to my amazing wife, Kimberly, and my three beautiful children, Bailey, Katelyn, and Madalyn. The successes in life are not as sweet without family to share them with.

Contents at a Glance

Contents

■CHAPTER 3   **Managing Virtualization with System Center Virtual Machine Manager 2008** 57

■CHAPTER 7   Creating Highly Available Hyper-V Systems 291

■CHAPTER 8   Protecting Your Virtual Machines 323

About the Author

HARLEY STAGNER is a seasoned IT professional who enjoys sharing his server virtualization experience through his writing. Currently, Harley is a Senior Systems Engineer for Bell Techlogix, an IT services firm in Richmond, Virginia. There, he specializes in designing and deploying IT life cycle solutions, including virtualization solutions, for the firm's many clients.

Harley graduated from ECPI Technical College with a BS degree in Management Information Systems, and later earned an MBA in Business Management from Strayer University. His industry certifications include Microsoft Certified System Engineer (MCSE) for Windows Server 2000 and 2003, VMware Certified Professional (VCP), and Microsoft Certified Technology Specialist (MCTS) in Windows Server Virtualization.

Harley has published many virtualization articles for the TechTarget network (http://www.techtarget.com) sites, including SearchSystemsChannel.com, SearchServerVirtualization.com, SearchVMware.com, and others. He also maintains his own blogs at HarleyStagner.com and SearchMarked.com.

In his free time, Harley can be found hanging out on Xbox Live, helping other virtualization users, or spending time with his friends and family.

About the Technical Reviewers

JON ROLFE has been an IT professional for more than 14 years. During that time, he has worked for some of the world's largest IT services companies. He is currently a Senior Technical Architect for one of Europe's leading IT services companies and specializes in designing secure Microsoft-based enterprise architectures for clients in the UK public sector and large blue-chip companies.

During the course of his career, Jon has gained extensive experience in all stages of the IT life cycle, including enterprise architecture design, software development, rapid system deployment, and large enterprise system support. Jon has also been awarded several professional qualifications, including Certified Information Systems Security Professional (CISSP), Certified Ethical Hacker (CEH), and Chartered IT Professional Membership of the British Computer Society (MBCS CITP).

When not working, Jon has an active interest in digital photography, follows motor sports, and enjoys mountain biking and skiing.

Jon can be contacted through his web site at `http://JonRolfe.com`.

GREG SHIELDS is a professional author, speaker, and IT consultant, with nearly 15 years experience in IT. He has worked extensively in systems administration, engineering, and architecture, specializing in remote application and virtualization technologies.

Greg is a columnist for *TechNet Magazine* and a former columnist for *Redmond Magazine* and *Virtualization Review*, and has authored or contributed to nine books. He serves as the Series Editor for Realtime Publishers, contributing to the Realtime Windows Server community and editing the *Windows Administration in Realtime* e-Journal. Greg is also an active instructor and speaker, presenting regularly at conferences like TechMentor events. Additionally, he produces computer-based training curriculum for companies like CBT Nuggets.

Greg is a recipient of Microsoft's Most Valuable Professional (MVP) award with a specialization in Windows Terminal Services, and of VMware's vExpert award.

Acknowledgments

Writing this book was a very ambitious project that I could not have accomplished without the support of many people. First, I would like to thank you, the reader. Without an audience, this book would not have been written. Thank you for your support in this endeavor.

Next, I would like to thank those who have supported me at home during this whole process, starting with my wife, Kimberly. She was there for me through the late night and daylong writing sessions. She took on the monumental task of balancing the care for our three children and supporting me as I worked on this project. Her patience and encouragement were a tremendous help as I worked through this book. I would also like to thank my son, Bailey, for showing genuine enthusiasm for everything that I do and helping me to learn how to share my experience with others. I'd like to thank my daughter Katelyn for her endless supply of energy and optimism. Her ability to cheer me up when I feel stressed is almost mystical. I'd also like to thank my youngest daughter, Madalyn, for showing me that big things can be accomplished with the support of your family and friends. I must also thank my mother, Linda Stagner, and my father, Ron Stagner, for giving me the support and education that made it possible for me to be in a position to write this book. They have also instilled the strong work ethic in me to tackle a project of this magnitude.

I would also like to thank my mentor, friend, and colleague, Chris Wolf, for being the catalyst for so many of my professional accomplishments.

The team at Apress was very dedicated to this book's success. I would like to thank my editor, Tony Campbell, who helped me maintain focus during this exciting project. Next, I would like to thank the project manager, Beth Christmas, for keeping the entire team focused and motivating me when I needed it most to be successful in this project. I must also thank Marilyn Smith for her detail-oriented approach to making this book a very enjoyable read. I would also like to thank my technical reviewers, Greg Shields and Jon Rolfe. Their dedication to the technical direction and success of this book was unparalleled. Their server virtualization, Windows, and PowerShell expertise, combined with their attention to detail, were instrumental in this project's success.

Finally, I would like to thank the Microsoft Virtualization Product team and several members of the virtualization community for their discussions and input on this dynamic topic. Thank you to Taylor Brown, Dung K. Hoang, Tony Soper, and Ben Armstrong (a.k.a. Virtual PC Guy) for your continued contributions to server virtualization technology and the evangelism of its many benefits.

Introduction

Server virtualization technology brings greater efficiency, flexibility, and mobility to your infrastructure. The abilities to run multiple virtual machines on a single host server, move those virtual machines between host servers, and recover those virtual machines quickly from a system failure have become standard in many datacenters.

The core component of server virtualization technology that makes it possible to run virtual machines is the *hypervisor*. The hypervisor software handles processor scheduling, memory management, and many other low-level system functions on behalf of the virtual machines it is hosting.

The most efficient method of running a hypervisor is on "bare-metal." This means the hypervisor is installed right on the server hardware, so that it has direct access to that underlying hardware. Up until recently, there have been only a few options for bare-metal hypervisors. Microsoft changed that with the release of Windows Server 2008. Microsoft customers who want a bare-metal hypervisor to host their virtual infrastructure will find one already built in as the Hyper-V role in Windows Server 2008.

Installing Hyper-V is a straightforward process. However, getting Hyper-V up and running is just the first step in your overall virtualization strategy. In this book, you will learn what you need to manage the life cycle of your Hyper-V virtual infrastructure. It explains how to handle the many aspects of this exciting new technology from Microsoft. The journey will start with automating the deployment of Hyper-V and take you to securing Hyper-V. Let's take a look at the contents of the chapters to see what's in store for you.

Chapter 1, Hyper-V and the Tools of the Trade: This chapter discusses what Hyper-V is and the requirements for getting started using this server virtualization technology. It covers some details, such as the anatomy of a Hyper-V virtual machine and how advanced networking like virtual local area networking (VLAN) trunking is handled by the Hyper-V host. It also introduces the tools that you will use throughout the book to assist in deploying, automating, managing, protecting, and securing your virtual infrastructure. These tools include Windows Deployment Services (WDS), Windows System Image Manager (SIM), PowerShell, Windows Management Instrumentation (WMI), and Scriptomatic. Having the right tools to accomplish a task is just as important as accomplishing the task.

Chapter 2, Automating Hyper-V Deployment: This chapter describes how to automate a Core installation of Windows Server 2008 with Hyper-V using WDS. You will learn the following:

- How to enable and configure the WDS role on Windows Server 2008

- How to configure boot and capture images for use with WDS

- How to capture an installation image for use with WDS to deploy Hyper-V

- How to use Windows SIM to create the answer files for automating the Hyper-V deployment with WDS

Chapter 3, Managing Virtualization with System Center Virtual Machine Manager 2008:
After you deploy Hyper-V, you need to manage it. You can manage a single Hyper-V
host at a time with the Hyper-V Manager tool. However, as your virtual infrastructure
grows, you need a more comprehensive management solution. That is why Microsoft has
released System Center Virtual Machine Manager (VMM) 2008. This chapter covers the
capabilities of VMM 2008 and how to take advantage of them to manage your virtual infrastructure. You will learn the following:

- How to install and configure VMM 2008 for your virtual infrastructure

- How to manage your Hyper-V hosts and virtual machines with VMM 2008

- How to integrate VMM 2008 with System Center Operations Manager (SCOM)
  2007 to take advantage of Performance and Resource Optimization (PRO) tips and
  enhanced virtual infrastructure reporting

Chapter 4, Migrating Physical and Virtual Machines to Hyper-V: Once you have deployed
and can manage your Hyper-V infrastructure, you need to actually run virtual machines
on your new virtual infrastructure. The quickest way to start consolidating some of your
workloads with Hyper-V is to convert physical and virtual machines (from other server virtualization vendors) to virtual machines that can run on Hyper-V. This chapter describes
how to perform this migration. You will learn the following:

- How to select and prepare your migration candidates by using free tools such as
  the Microsoft Assessment and Planning (MAP) toolkit

- How to migrate servers using VMM 2008

- How to migrate servers using free tools like VMware Converter and VMDK to VHD
  Converter

- How to automate migrations with PowerShell and VMM 2008

Chapter 5, Automating Hyper-V: Scripting is an excellent way to automate your Hyper-V
environment so you can save time and get consistent results with many of your virtual
infrastructure management tasks. This chapter shows you how to leverage PowerShell
with WMI and VMM 2008 to automate tasks in your virtual infrastructure. You will learn
the following:

- How to automate the configuration of Hyper-V servers with PowerShell and WMI,
  and with PowerShell and VMM 2008

- How to automate the configuration and creation of virtual machines with Power-
  Shell and WMI, and with PowerShell and VMM 2008

Chapter 6, Monitoring Hyper-V and VM Performance: This chapter covers performance monitoring, an important part of managing your virtual infrastructure. This is especially true with Hyper-V, since its ability to consolidate workloads while maintaining adequate system performance relies on regular performance monitoring. You will learn the following:

- How to monitor your virtual infrastructure with the Windows Reliability and Performance Monitor
- Some key metrics, thresholds, and special considerations for monitoring your virtual workloads
- How to collect baseline performance statistics for your virtual infrastructure
- How to automate the collection of performance statistics

Chapter 7, Creating Highly Available Hyper-V Systems: When consolidating your workloads with Hyper-V, you should consider your risk tolerance for a single point of failure in your virtual infrastructure. This chapter explains how to mitigate the impact or eliminate single points of failure in your virtual infrastructure. You will learn the following:

- Strategies for building and deploying your Hyper-V host server hardware with fault tolerance in mind
- Strategies for creating a fault-tolerant storage infrastructure for your Hyper-V hosts
- How to build Hyper-V failover clusters using Windows Server 2008
- How to design failover clusters in order to take advantage of Hyper-V "quick migration" for virtual machines
- Some considerations for building geographically dispersed multisite failover clusters for disaster recovery of your virtual infrastructure

Chapter 8, Protecting Your Virtual Machines: System availability is a concern for physical and virtual systems. Your business-critical data must be backed up so that it can be recovered in the event that data becomes lost or corrupt. Since virtual machines are just files, they must also be protected by a backup and recovery strategy. This chapter covers techniques for protecting your virtual machines. You will learn the following:

- How to use the tools that come with Hyper-V to back up and recover virtual machines
- How to mount virtual hard disk files to perform file-level recoveries
- How integrate the Microsoft Volume Shadow Copy Service and Windows Server Backup to back up running virtual machines on your Hyper-V hosts
- How to use Windows Server Backup to recover virtual machines
- How to use System Center Data Protection Manager 2007 (DPM 2007) to back up running virtual machines
- How to recover virtual machines using DPM 2007

Chapter 9, Securing Your Virtual Infrastructure: A Hyper-V host has a lot of your business-critical infrastructure hosted on it. Securing your virtual infrastructure from potential interruption of service or loss of data is very important. This chapter explains how to provide this security. You will learn the following:

- How to deploy and secure Hyper-V on a Windows Server 2008 Core installation

- Best practices and considerations for Hyper-V networking security

- How to enable role-based access security for virtual machines on Hyper-V using Hyper-V Manager, Authorization Manager (AzMan), and PowerShell with WMI

- How to enable role-based access security for virtual machines on Hyper-V using VMM 2008

Appendix, A Preview of Windows Server 2008 R2 Hyper-V with Live Migration: The appendix introduces some of the exciting new features in Hyper-V that are included in the upcoming Windows Server 2008 Release 2 (R2). Specifically, you will get a preview of the following features:

- Cluster Shared Volumes (CSV) used in Windows Server 2008 R2 failover clustering to allow multiple nodes access to the same volume simultaneously

- Hyper-V "live migration," which enables the migration of virtual machines to different nodes in a Windows Server 2008 R2 failover cluster without service interruption

- Some of the new PowerShell cmdlets available for managing Windows Server 2008 R2 failover clusters with PowerShell version 2

The learning does not stop for me or you after the final pages of this book are turned. I encourage you to continue the conversation on virtualization and related technology by visiting my web site/blog at http://www.harleystagner.com. You can also use the contact page there to contact me with any questions or discussion topics that you may have. I hope you will enjoy your educational journey through *Pro Hyper-V* as much as I have enjoyed writing it.

CHAPTER 1

■ ■ ■

Hyper-V and the Tools of the Trade

Our Age of Anxiety is, in great part, the result of trying to do today's jobs with yesterday's tools.

Marshall McLuhan

Hyper-V is an exciting new server virtualization product from Microsoft. It allows businesses to consolidate their server infrastructure, while making it more flexible at the same time. You can deploy Hyper-V as a Hyper-V role on Windows Server 2008 or as a stand-alone Hyper-V server. This book will focus on the version of Hyper-V that comes with Windows Server 2008.

To take full advantage of this technology, you must plan your deployment, management, and maintenance for your virtual infrastructure carefully. This chapter will introduce Hyper-V and the tools that you will use to set up and manage it.

Getting Started with Hyper-V

Unlike Microsoft's Virtual Server 2005 Release 2, Hyper-V is a bare-metal server virtualization product. This means that an operating system does not sit between the hardware and the hypervisor (the code that does the server virtualization). The hypervisor (Hyper-V) is installed directly on the server hardware. Even though Hyper-V can be deployed as a role on Windows Server 2008, it actually sits beneath the Windows Server 2008 operating system. When Hyper-V is enabled, Windows Server 2008 is known as the parent partition. It is more like a privileged guest virtual machine in that respect.

The parent partition and the hypervisor are the only items that get direct access to the underlying server hardware. The parent partition handles device drivers and some system memory for the hypervisor. The hypervisor arbitrates access for the rest of the hardware and divides the system into child partitions that the guest virtual machines use. So, while Windows Server 2008 is used for some system management functions, Hyper-V itself is actually installed directly on the server hardware.

The following hardware is required for deploying Hyper-V:

- The processor must be a 64-bit (x64) processor.

- The processor and motherboard BIOS must support hardware-assisted virtualization technology (AMD-V or Intel VT), and the feature must be enabled in the BIOS.

- The processor and motherboard BIOS must support hardware-enabled data execution prevention (DEP). This is the XD (execution disable) bit on Intel processors and the NX (no execution) bit on AMD processors. This feature must also be enabled in the system BIOS.

Once the hardware requirements have been met, enabling Hyper-V on your host machine can be accomplished with three general steps:

1. Install Windows Server 2008 and fully patch and configure it.

2. Enable the Hyper-V role using the Server Manager.

3. Configure your Hyper-V environment.

The recommended installation of Windows Server 2008 Core with Hyper-V is covered in Chapter 9. While enabling the Hyper-V role is fairly straightforward, configuring Hyper-V for your environment involves many considerations, such as backup and recovery, security, and high availability, to name a few. That is why this book focuses mainly on step 3, configuring your Hyper-V environment.

Virtualization with Hyper-V

Before you can begin exploring the many options available to you when configuring Hyper-V, you must understand some basic concepts about virtualization with Hyper-V and some of the supporting technology involved.

Components of a Virtual Machine

A physical server has many components that are put together to build a complete server. A virtual machine has many components as well. The components just exist in software, rather than hardware.

A virtual machine has the following basic components.

- A set of emulated hardware (motherboard, CPU, RAM, hard drive, DVD drive, and so on) defined by the configuration file

- A configuration file (*.xml) that details all of the hardware and virtual machine settings for the virtual machine

- A hard disk file (*.vhd)

The hardware settings for a virtual machine are defined when you create the virtual machine. They can be modified after you create the virtual machine by using graphical user interface (GUI) management tools or by scripting with a scripting language like PowerShell. This book will cover both methods.

Virtual Networking in Hyper-V

The concepts of networking are the same in a virtual machine and a physical machine. However, the way that networking is implemented on a Hyper-V host server is different from any other server that you are likely to have come across.

When a virtual network is created, a virtual switch is created for Hyper-V. The virtual switch is configured differently, depending on the type of virtual network.

Your first exposure to virtual networking is when you enable the Hyper-V role on your Windows Server 2008 server. You are asked to choose a network adapter to bind to an external network for use by your virtual machines. As a best practice, I suggest setting this up after the initial role installation.

Before you choose a network adapter, you should know what types of virtual networks are available in Hyper-V. You should also know what happens when you choose a physical network adapter to bind to a Hyper-V virtual network.

There are three basic types of virtual networks in Hyper-V:

External: A physical network interface card (NIC) is bound to this virtual network switch to allow the virtual machines to communicate with the parent partition, with each other, and with machines that are external to the Hyper-V host. Think of the physical NIC as the uplink port of the virtual switch that connects it to an external physical switch.

Internal: A virtual switch is created that is not bound to any physical NIC. The virtual machines on the host can communicate with each other, as well as with the parent partition.

Private: A virtual switch is created that is not bound to any physical NIC. However, only the virtual machines on the host can communicate with each other. They cannot communicate with the parent partition.

The external virtual network is likely to be the most common network type in your environment. When you create an external virtual network, a couple of things happen:

- The physical NIC becomes the uplink port for the virtual switch that connects the virtual switch to an external physical switch. This is evident by the addition of the Microsoft Virtual Network Switch Protocol to the physical NIC, as shown in Figure 1-1. All other bindings are disabled.

- A new NIC is created with whatever you have labeled the new virtual network. It is identified with "Virtual Network" at the end of its name, as shown in Figure 1-2. This new NIC gives the virtual machines access to the virtual switch.

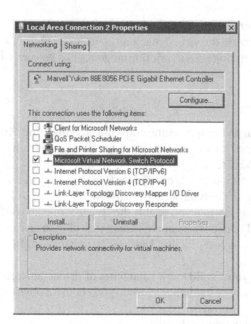

Figure 1-1. *The physical NIC is used as an uplink port by utilizing the Microsoft Virtual Network Switch Protocol.*

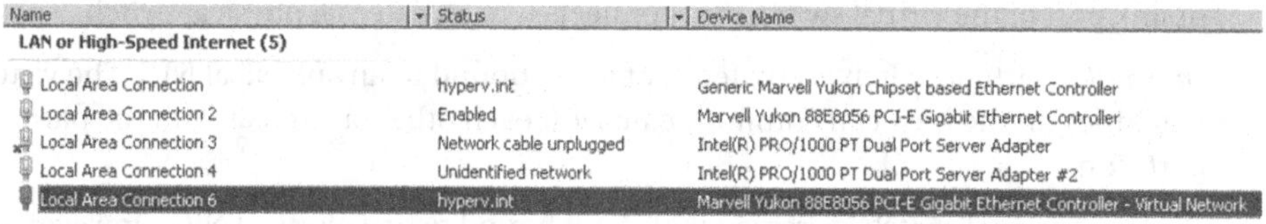

Name	Status	Device Name
LAN or High-Speed Internet (5)		
Local Area Connection	hyperv.int	Generic Marvell Yukon Chipset based Ethernet Controller
Local Area Connection 2	Enabled	Marvell Yukon 88E8056 PCI-E Gigabit Ethernet Controller
Local Area Connection 3	Network cable unplugged	Intel(R) PRO/1000 PT Dual Port Server Adapter
Local Area Connection 4	Unidentified network	Intel(R) PRO/1000 PT Dual Port Server Adapter #2
Local Area Connection 6	hyperv.int	Marvell Yukon 88E8056 PCI-E Gigabit Ethernet Controller - Virtual Network

Figure 1-2. *The new virtual NIC is created for the external virtual network.*

Along with this basic connectivity, there are some advanced virtual local area network (VLAN) options for external virtual networks.

VLAN Options for External Virtual Networks

As you may know, a VLAN is a way to separate broadcast traffic on a network and in a physical switch. Usually, VLANs allow you have a different subnet without needing to tie a separate physical switch to that subnet. You just divide the switch ports into multiple VLANs. This works quite well in a physical environment, where each server is usually a member of only a single VLAN. However, you may want to provide multiple VLANs for virtual machines that reside on a Hyper-V host. There are two basic ways to do this:

- Create a separate external virtual network for each VLAN and bind a separate physical NIC to each external virtual network.

- Create one external virtual network and use VLAN trunking to provide multiple VLANs over your physical NIC to your virtual machines.

Using separate external networks is the most straightforward method. Switches have two basic port modes: access port or trunk port. An access port is a member of a single VLAN. It behaves like a normal switch port, with a one-to-one mapping of a single VLAN to a single port. A trunk port multiplexes many VLANs on a single port. When using separate virtual networks for each VLAN, the bound physical NIC on the Hyper-V host is connected to an access port on an external physical switch that is a member of one VLAN. So, in order to provide access to multiple VLANs for your virtual machines using this method, you simply attach a separate physical NIC to a separate switch access port for each VLAN that you want available for your virtual machines.

As you can see, using separate virtual networks for each VLAN is not very scalable. If you want to provide access to four VLANs, you need four physical NICs dedicated to virtual machine traffic—one for each VLAN. Using VLAN trunking is a little more complicated, but it is a much more scalable solution.

With VLAN trunking, you can actually set a physical NIC that is bound to an external virtual network to act as a trunk port. This way, you can provide multiple VLANs to your virtual machines using a single physical NIC, which eliminates the need for a one-to-one mapping of physical NIC to VLAN. When you attach a virtual machine to the external virtual network that is using VLAN trunking, you just configure the VLAN ID for that virtual machine to designate which VLAN the virtual machine will be using for network traffic.

The easiest way to enable VLAN trunking for an external virtual network is by configuring it with System Center Virtual Machine Manager 2008 (VMM 2008), which is covered in detail in Chapter 3.

Managing Hyper-V with Hyper-V Manager

The Hyper-V Manager tool is built in to Windows Server 2008. It is available after you enable the Hyper-V role or by adding it as a feature under the Remote Server Administration Tools ➤ Role Administration Tools section.

Note The Hyper-V Manager tool is also available on Windows Vista SP1 when you download and install it. The Windows Vista 32-bit: version is available from `http://www.microsoft.com/downloads/details.aspx?FamilyId=A46D0047-E383-4688-9449-83373226126A&displaylang=en`. The 64-bit version is available from `http://www.microsoft.com/downloads/details.aspx?FamilyId=F10E848F-289C-4E04-8786-395371F083BF&displaylang=en`.

Launch Hyper-V Manager by choosing Start ➤ Administrative Tools ➤ Hyper-V Manager. You work with Hyper-V Manager through its three-pane interface. The left pane allows you to navigate your Hyper-V system, the middle pane shows the results of your current activity, and the right pane gives you access to the actions you can take.

Just click "Connect to server" in the Actions pane to manage a particular Hyper-V host server. Once you have connected to your Hyper-V host, it appears in the navigation pane, as shown in Figure 1-3. The results pane shows information about the virtual machines that you have on your Hyper-V host. The Actions pane shows you actions that you can perform on the Hyper-V host in the top section and actions that you can perform on the selected virtual machine in the bottom section.

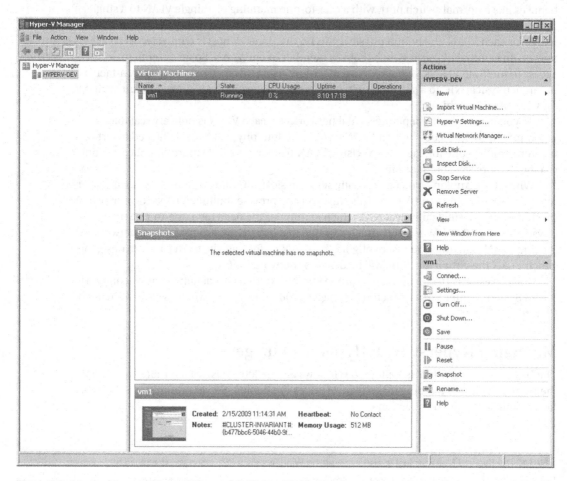

Figure 1-3. *Managing your Hyper-V host with Hyper-V Manager*

Hyper-V Host Actions

The following actions can be performed on the Hyper-V host (starting from the top of the Actions pane):

- Create a new virtual machine, virtual disk, or virtual floppy disk.

- Change the Hyper-V server settings such as the default paths for virtual machine and virtual disk files.

- Add or edit virtual networks and virtual network settings (choose the Virtual Network Manager selection).

- Edit a virtual disk by converting it from a dynamically expanding disk to a fixed-size disk and vice versa. You can also expand an existing virtual disk to add more space.

- Inspect a virtual disk to see its properties.

- Stop the Virtual Machine Management service.

- Remove the selected Hyper-V host serve from the management console.

- Refresh and customize your Hyper-V Manager console view.

- Access the Help menu for the host actions.

Virtual Machine Actions

Along with the Hyper-V host actions, you can perform the following actions on the selected virtual machine (starting from the top of the virtual machine section of the Actions pane):

- Connect to the virtual machine's console using VMConnect, as shown in Figure 1-4.

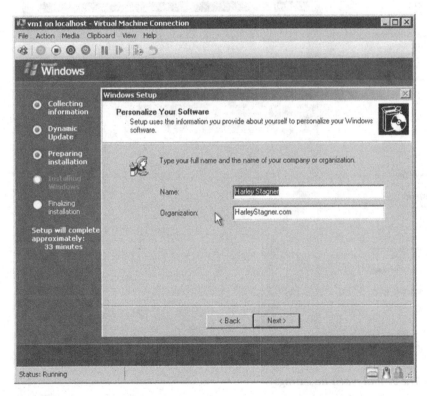

Figure 1-4. *Connecting to a virtual machine's console using VMConnect*

- Edit and view the virtual machine's hardware and management settings. These settings are discussed in more detail in the next sections.

- Turn off, shut down, or save the virtual machine state.

- Pause or reset the virtual machine.

- Take a snapshot or point-in-time copy of a virtual machine.

- Rename a virtual machine.

- Access the Help menu for virtual machine actions.

Virtual Machine Hardware Settings

When you choose Settings in the virtual machine section of the Actions pane, you are presented with a window that has both hardware settings and management settings for the virtual machine, as shown in Figure 1-5.

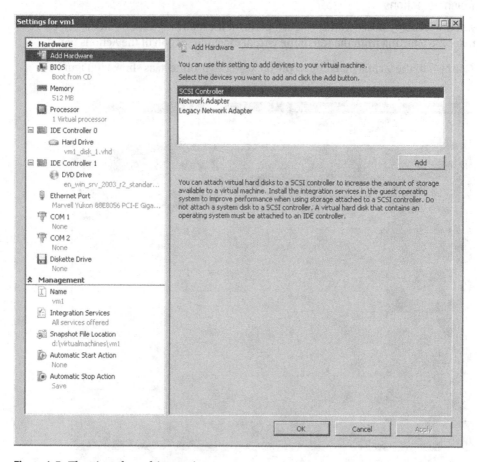

Figure 1-5. *The virtual machine settings*

Just as a physical server has many hardware components that make up the whole server, a virtual machine is made up of many emulated hardware components. Every virtual machine has the following hardware components:

- Motherboard

- RAM (up to the amount available on the Hyper-V host)

- CPU (up to four if the Hyper-V host has that many available)
- Two IDE controllers
- Two COM ports (named pipe, not physical)
- A diskette drive (floppy drive)

In addition to the base hardware, a virtual machine can, and will likely, have the following hardware, which you can add and remove through the virtual machine settings:

- Network adapter (legacy or default)

Note The legacy adapter may be slower, but it is available when the virtual machine boots. The default network adapter requires that Integration Services be installed on the virtual machine, so it is not available until the operating system boots.

- SCSI controller
- Hard drive (IDE or SCSI)
- DVD drive (using the physical Hyper-V host drive or an ISO image)

When you select the Processor item in the virtual machine hardware settings, you will see some options listed under "Resource control" in the right pane, as shown in Figure 1-6. These options give you a bit more flexibility when assigning processor resources for a particular virtual machine:

Virtual machine reserve (percentage): This is the percentage of the total CPU resources on the host server that you want to reserve for the selected virtual machine. This percentage is relative to the number of virtual CPUs that are assigned to the virtual machine. For example, on a single processor virtual machine that is hosted on a dual-processor host, if you reserve 50% of the CPU, you will be reserving 25% of the physical host's CPU resources.

Virtual machine limit (percentage): This is the maximum percentage of the total CPU resources assigned to the virtual machine that the selected virtual machine can use. This is also relative to the number of virtual CPUs assigned to the virtual machine.

Relative weight: This value is used when there is resource contention between two or more virtual machines, and determines how Hyper-V will allocate resources. For example, if virtual machine A has a relative weight of 100 and virtual machine B has a relative weight of 200, virtual machine B will have a higher priority than virtual machine A when CPU resources are allocated.

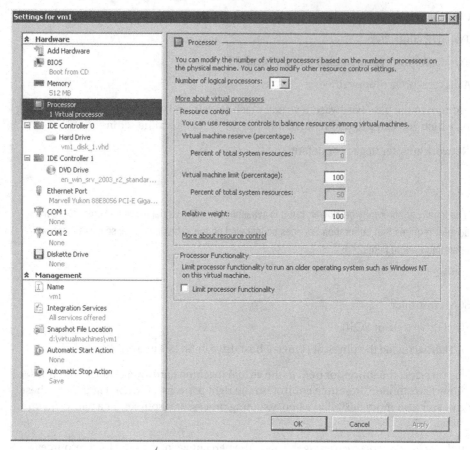

Figure 1-6. *Virtual machine processor resource control options*

The final option in the Processor section is to limit processor functionality. This hides some newer processor features so that virtual machines that are running legacy operating systems like Windows NT will function correctly.

Virtual Machine Management Settings

The following management settings are available for a virtual machine (see Figure 1-6):

- Name
- Integration Services
- Snapshot File Location
- Automatic Start Action
- Automatic Stop Action

As their names suggest, using these options, you can name your virtual machine, choose the snapshot file location, and set actions to occur automatically upon virtual machine startup and shutdown.

When you select the Integration Services option, you will see the window shown in Figure 1-7.

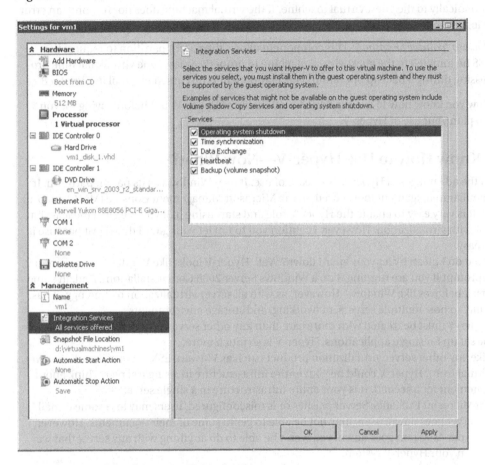

Figure 1-7. *Virtual machine Integration Services options*

Five components can be enabled for Integration Services if the guest operating system supports the component and Integration Services is installed on the guest operating system. For example, the Backup (volume snapshot) component will work only with Windows guests, since it uses Windows Volume Shadow Copy Services (VSS). The following components are included in Integration Services:

Operating system shutdown: This will gracefully shut down the guest operating system.

Time synchronization: This will synchronize the guest operating system time with the Hyper-V host time.

Data Exchange: This is a means for the guest virtual machine to share data about itself with the parent partition and third-party management tools. By default, the guest virtual machine (Windows) shares the information located in the HKLM\Software\Microsoft\ Virtual Machine\Auto registry key, if this component is selected.

Heartbeat: This is a mechanism that the parent partition uses to determine if a virtual machine has become unresponsive. The parent partition will send out a heartbeat signal periodically to the guest virtual machine. If the virtual machine does not respond, an error is logged in the event log.

Backup (volume snapshot): This component allows the parent partition to request that VSS be initiated in the guest virtual machine to properly quiesce the virtual machine processing during a backup operation. This component is discussed in detail in Chapter 8.

Now you know how to use the basic functionality of Hyper-V. But before diving in, you need to plan your use of Hyper-V.

You Know How to Use Hyper-V—Now What?

One of the advantages of Hyper-V is its ease of use. It uses Windows as its parent partition. It uses familiar management tools based on the Microsoft Management Console (MMC) snap-in model. It is very easy to enable the Hyper-V role and start using it, if you are even the least bit familiar with virtualization. However, I caution you to not let your guard down just because it seems easy.

What do I mean by let your guard down? Well, Hyper-V looks like Windows (or a command prompt if you are running it on a Windows Server 2008 Core installation). And, in some aspects, it behaves like Windows. However, as with all server virtualization technology, it has the ability to host multiple servers, networking, and storage environments.

Hyper-V must be treated with more care than any other server system. While other servers may be set up for single applications, Hyper-V is so much more.

Like any other server virtualization product (such as VMware ESX Server, Citrix XenServer, and Virtual Iron), Hyper-V could be your entire infrastructure in a single server. Think about that statement for a second. It is your entire infrastructure in a single server!

If a Microsoft Exchange Server crashes or is misconfigured, users may lose some e-mail. If a file server goes down, users may not be able to get to some of their documents. However, if your Hyper-V system goes down, you won't be able to do anything with any server that was running on your Hyper-V system.

I'm not trying to discourage you from enjoying the benefits that virtualization offers. I'm just making a point. Hyper-V cannot be treated like any x64 server that has been installed in the past. Misconfiguration, improper planning, and hardware failures in a virtualized environment could have disastrous consequences. This is why, now more than ever, you need to establish policies and procedures for building consistent, virtualized systems based on Hyper-V. In other words, you need to plan your work and work your plan.

When working your plan, you should strive for consistent results. One of the best ways to achieve consistent results is through automation.

Every task requires tools. Painters have brushes, carpenters have levels, and scripting guru's have their languages. Automating Hyper-V is no different. It requires tools. From automating Hyper-V deployment to managing complex tasks, having a good set of tools available is the key to working your plan. The next sections introduce these tools.

Deployment Automation: Windows Deployment Services and System Image Manager

Windows Deployment Services (WDS) is the predecessor to Remote Installation Services (RIS). It will allow you to PXE-boot a server and deploy an image to it automatically after some preparatory work.

■**Note** PXE stands for Preboot Execution Environment. PXE-boot is a method to boot a server from the network into an operating environment. In the case of WDS, PXE-boot is used to boot the server into a Windows Preinstallation Environment (WinPE), which is like a mini-Windows operating environment. WinPE is used to install the image that is being copied from the WDS server.

For automating the deployment of Hyper-V installations, WDS offers machine-independent image formats and automation capabilities for unattended installations. Some server vendors may offer their own deployment tools, or your company may use certain third-party deployment tools for automating server installations. However, the advantage of WDS is that it can be used for free in any environment that will support it.

WDS comes with Windows Server 2003 Service Pack 2 (SP2) and Windows Server 2008. In Windows Server 2003, you install it via Add/Remove Programs as a Windows component. In Windows Server 2008, you enable the Windows Deployment Services role. After WDS is installed, you administer it through the WDS MMC snap-in.

There are three general steps involved in deploying Hyper-V (or any other system) using WDS:

- Configure WDS for your environment.

- Install, prepare, and capture your deployment image on the WDS server.

- Deploy the image to your Hyper-V servers via PXE-boot.

This process allows you to control your Hyper-V deployment process. It essentially captures your operating system and Hyper-V installation best practices once and allows you to deploy that same image consistently across your enterprise. As you will see in Chapter 9, there are many steps involved with deploying a properly secured Hyper-V installation on a Windows Server 2008 Core system. If you can capture as much of the configuration as possible in the installation image, it can be applied consistently every time using WDS.

Windows System Image Manager (SIM) is the companion to WDS that helps you to create the answer files that are necessary to automate the Windows operating system deployment. Answer files are small XML files that will answer all those annoying deployment questions for you, such as how to partition the hard drives and what your license key is. (Who has time to type in license keys, anyway? We have virtual machines to create!)

Windows SIM comes in the Windows Automated Installation Kit (available from http://www.microsoft.com/downloads/details.aspx?FamilyID=94bb6e34-d890-4932-81a5-5b50c657de08&DisplayLang=en).

Chapter 2 details the steps involved in the WDS deployment process, including configuring just the options that you need to successfully automate a Windows Server 2008 with Hyper-V deployment using the answer files that Windows SIM creates.

Management Automation: PowerShell, WMI, and Other Goodies

One of the main complaints that Windows administrators have had is the lack of a powerful shell, such as Bash in Linux. The Windows command shell (cmd.exe) has been sufficient for simple automation tasks using batch files. However, if you wanted to do anything more advanced, such as query Active Directory or use complex conditional output, you needed to use a scripting language like VBScript or Perl.

I have many fond memories of writing reams of VBScript, trying to perfect whatever task I was automating, only to discover while running the script that I had left out some obscure semicolon or period. The Windows Script Host would then promptly give an equally obscure error code, and I would be off to Google to research what had happened to my scripting opus. Then, once I found the problem, I would correct it, save the script, and run it again. Inevitably, it would throw another error at me, because VBScript is an interpreted language. It is interpreted line by painful line. This vicious cycle would continue until I had ironed out the kinks, and my script was finally ready for testing.

So why am I taking you down memory lane with my scripting horror story? I wanted to let you know that there is a better way, which comes in the form of PowerShell. PowerShell is the new optional shell environment for Windows. PowerShell can be used on Windows XP SP2, Windows Vista (all versions), Windows Server 2003 (all versions), and Windows Server 2008 (all versions except for Core installations).

Why all the fuss over PowerShell? Well, PowerShell can be used for scripting, just as you can write shell scripts in a Unix or Linux shell. You can think of PowerShell as a more flexible batch file. This is because PowerShell is object-oriented and has the .NET programming environment at its disposal. So, simple one-line commands can do very complex tasks. However, since PowerShell is a shell environment, commands can be run interactively at the shell prompt so you can test them line by line. No more write, save, error, Google, repeat.

PowerShell Installation and Use

If you want to start using PowerShell on Windows XP, Windows Vista, or Windows Server 2003, you just need to download it (from http://www.microsoft.com/windowsserver2003/technologies/management/PowerShell/download.mspx) and install it. The installation is pretty straightforward. Once PowerShell is downloaded, just run the installation file and follow the wizard's instructions. You'll be interacting with PowerShell in no time.

If you want to use PowerShell on Windows Server 2008, you need to enable it as an optional component. This can be accomplished with the following steps.

1. Open the Server Manager tool by selecting Start ➤ Administrative Tools ➤ Server Manager.

2. Select Features in the left pane and click the Add Features link in the Features Summary section in the right pane, as shown in Figure 1-8.

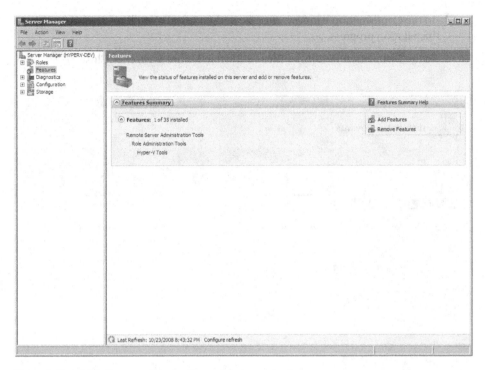

Figure 1-8. *Add features using the Server Manager tool.*

3. When the Add Features Wizard starts, scroll down to the bottom of the window and select Windows PowerShell, as shown in Figure 1-9. Click Next to continue.

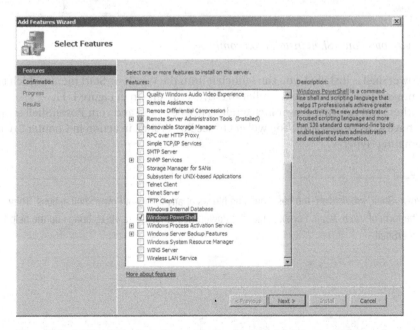

Figure 1-9. *Adding Windows PowerShell using the Add Featuress Wizard*

4. In the Confirmation window, click Next, then Install. You'll see a window showing the installation progress.

5. In the Installation Results window, shown in Figure 1-10, click Close.

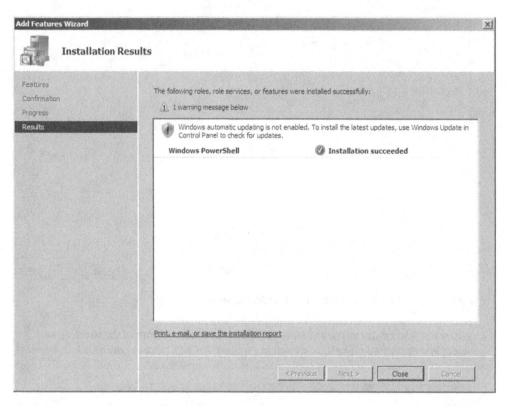

Figure 1-10. *Windows PowerShell installation complete*

Once PowerShell is installed, you can launch it from the Windows Start menu, which takes you to a command prompt that looks similar to cmd.exe, as shown in Figure 1-11.

This is where you run your PowerShell cmdlets like Get-Help and your PowerShell script files (which have a .ps1 extension). You will get to see PowerShell in action in Chapter 5, which covers automating Hyper-V.

■Note In PowerShell, *cmdlets* are the basic building blocks of any series of PowerShell actions. They usually take the form of *Verb-Noun*. For example, the PowerShell cmdlet Get-Help brings up the help functionality in PowerShell.

Figure 1-11. *The PowerShell console*

Here are some things you should keep in mind when using PowerShell:

- PowerShell scripts cannot be run by default. To enable PowerShell scripts to run, type `Set-ExecutionPolicy RemoteSigned` at the command prompt. This tells PowerShell that it is OK to run local PowerShell script files. PowerShell script files that have been downloaded from the Internet need to be digitally signed. The other execution policies include `Restricted` (no scripts run), `AllSigned` (all scripts must be digitally signed), and `Unrestricted` (all scripts can run).

- In order to run a PowerShell script at the PowerShell prompt, you must type the full path to the script every time you want to run it (`C:\yourdirectory\yourscript.ps1`). If you are in the same directory as the script, you can also use `.\yourscript.ps1` to run the script.

- You can call PowerShell scripts from a batch file (`*.bat` or `*.cmd`) by adding `powershell C:\yourdirectory\yourscript.ps1` to the batch file. This can be very useful for scheduling PowerShell scripts to run with the Windows Task Scheduler.

WMI Crash Course

Windows Management Instrumentation (WMI) is still here. WMI is the interface for managing the different aspects of the Windows operating system and its services. Now that includes Hyper-V. WMI is used when you want to do remote management of a Hyper-V server and you do not have VMM 2008, because PowerShell 1.0 does not have remote capabilities.

In case you aren't familiar with WMI, I'll give you a crash course to get you started. This is not meant to be an exhaustive resource on the subject. There are whole books written on WMI, regardless of the scripting language.

Many scripting books start with a Hello World example that shows you how to accomplish something simple, like printing "Hello World" to the screen with the chosen scripting language. With that said, here is a Hello VM example of what can be done with PowerShell and WMI:

```
$Server = "YourRemoteHyperVServer"

$VM_Service = get-wmiobject -computername $server ➥
-namespace root\virtualization Msvm_VirtualSystemManagementService

$VM_Service.DefineVirtualSystem()
```

Those three little lines will create a new virtual machine on your Hyper-V server. Nifty, huh?

Now, let's take a quick look at how WMI works. WMI is split into three main sections or layers: consumers, WMI infrastructure, and managed resources.

Consumers

In WMI, a *consumer* is the component that is asking for something. That component could be asking for anything about a Windows system—from the operating system version to performance statistics. Any data that WMI can provide about a Windows machine is what the consumer is after.

If you want to know if a process on a system (local or remote) is using above 60% of the total processor available, you just ask WMI using a script. So, a WMI script is the consumer, and the WMI query (question) contained in the script is what WMI needs in order to give the script the data that it requested. Scripts are the type of WMI consumer that we will deal with in this book.

WMI Infrastructure

The WMI infrastructure layer is made up of the rules and services associated with WMI. Four basic parts are sitting in the WMI infrastructure layer: the WMI scripting library, the WMI service (Common Information Model Object Manager), the WMI provider, and the WMI repository (Common Information Model repository).

The WMI scripting library sets the ground rules for talking to WMI. Interpreters are provided in the form of the WMI scripting library. So, you have a way to query WMI in VBScript, PowerShell, or even Perl, JavaScript, or Ruby—it doesn't really matter which language you use. The WMI scripting library (interpreter) will ensure that the question (query) is received properly by WMI.

The job of the WMI service is to answer requests from WMI consumers (scripts). The actual WMI service runs on Windows systems to make sure that the consumers (scripts) can ask questions (queries) and get the data that they need.

The WMI scripting library (interpreter) is there to ensure the script knows how to get what it wants. The WMI service is running. There is just one more small detail. How does the script know which details are available for the Windows system in question? This is provided by the Common Information Model (CIM) repository.

The CIM repository is a schema that defines which classes of WMI objects are available to the script (the consumer), so it acts like a catalog. It doesn't store the objects, but it does define the types of WMI objects that are available. These objects could be anything, such as the Windows Event log or Windows processes. As you will see later in the book, you will be mostly concerned with virtualization objects. Just as a store catalog has categories (housewares, gardening, tools, and so on), the CIM repository has groupings (called namespaces). The virtualization objects just happen to be stored in the root\virtualization namespace.

Scripting with WMI

Now take another look at the sample script, and you might see something that looks familiar.

```
$Server = "YourRemoteHyperVServer"

$VM_Service = get-wmiobject -computername $server ➡
-namespace root\virtualization Msvm_VirtualSystemManagementService

$VM_Service.DefineVirtualSystem()
```

The first line sets the $Server variable to the server on which you will be using WMI. As long as the WMI service is running on that server, it is ready to accept WMI queries.

The $VM_Service variable is defined on the second line. You are defining this variable with what you want from the YourRemoteHyperVServer server. This portion:

```
get-wmiobject –computername $server
```

is saying that you would like to get a WMI object from the YourHyperVServer server. Lucky for you, YourHyperVServer's WMI service is running. But what does YourHyperVServer have available in its CIM repository (catalog)? Does it have a virtualization namespace?

```
-namespace root\virtualization
```

This is saying that you would like something from the virtualization namespace (root\virtualization). OK, so what do you want?

```
Msvm_VirtualSystemManagementService
```

The Msvm_VirtualSystemManagementService just happens to be the WMI object that can manage virtual machines on a Hyper-V server.

To recap, your script is the consumer. It wants something from the YourRemoteHyperVServer WMI service.

```
$Server = "YourRemoteHyperVServer"
```

The WMI service is running on YourRemoteHyperVServer. The script (consumer) is looking for a specific WMI object:

```
$VM_Service = get-wmiobject -computername $server ➡
-namespace root\virtualization Msvm_VirtualSystemManagementService
```

Now all that's left is to do something with the Msvm_VirtualSystemManagementService object that the script just received from the store:

```
$VM_Service.DefineVirtualSystem()
```

The script can use the `Msvm_VirtualSystemManagementService` object to do all kinds of virtual machine-related tasks. In this case, the script just made a shiny, new virtual machine using the `Msvm_VirtualSystemManagementService` object that it received from the `YourRemoteHyperVServer` WMI service.

The WMI syntax can be tricky to master. However, WMI can be really powerful. Once you become familiar with the basic syntax for WMI, you can easily figure out how to use WMI in your scripts. The scripts that use WMI usually have the same general format:

- Set up the hostname and the namespace on that host as variables that can be used for WMI queries later in the script.

- Get an instance of a WMI class (type) object, such as `Msvm_VirtualSystemManagementService`.

- Define some parameters that will be used by a method (action) of the WMI class that you are using.

- Use a method (action) of the WMI class that you are using to do something given specific parameters.

When you do more WMI scripting, you will start to see this general pattern emerge.

In Chapter 5, we will go over some WMI examples for managing Hyper-V. (For those who have VMM 2008, we will also look at using pure PowerShell to manage Hyper-V.) The main work of the scripts that use WMI will be in the sections that define the parameters that will be used by the WMI class methods in the script. This is where the majority of the WMI queries will happen. The following is one example that we will explore in Chapter 5. (Don't worry if the syntax looks unfamiliar now; by the end of this book, you will understand what is going on in this line and many others like it.)

```
$VirtualSwitchQuery.SetupSwitch($ExternalSwitchPort, $InternalSwitchPort, ➥
$ExternalNic, [guid]::NewGuid().ToString(), "Hyper-V Internal Ethernet Port")
```

This example is taken from the last line of a script. It is using a method, called `SetupSwitch`, to set up a switch for an external virtual network on a Hyper-V host. This method takes five parameters (located in the parentheses following the `SetupSwitch` method statement). One of those parameters is the external NIC that the virtual switch will use for its external uplink port. This is defined by the `$ExternalNic` variable. So, what is stored in that `$ExternalNic` variable? Let's take a look at the line that defines that.

```
$ExternalNic = Get-WmiObject -Class "Msvm_ExternalEthernetPort" ➥
-Namespace $Namespace | ➥
Where-Object -FilterScript ➥
{$_.ElementName -eq "Marvell Yukon 88E8056 PCI-E Gigabit Ethernet Controller"}
```

The first part of this line should look familiar from the Hello VM example presented earlier. It is getting an instance of the WMI class object, MSVM_ExternalEthernetPort. The trick is that you need to tell WMI which instance of the MSVM_ExternalEthernetPort object you want. After all, there may be several network adapters on your Hyper-V host server. That is where WMI filtering is useful. Notice that the first part of the query:

```
$ExternalNic = Get-WmiObject -Class "Msvm_ExternalEthernetPort" ➥
-Namespace $Namespace
```

is piped (|) into this line:

```
Where-Object -FilterScript ➥
{$_.ElementName -eq "Marvell Yukon 88E8056 PCI-E Gigabit Ethernet Controller"}
```

Where-Object -FilterScript {} filters the results of anything that came before the pipe symbol (|) using the parameters that are given in the brackets ({}). In this case, the ElementName property of the Msvm_ExternalEthernetPort class object is used to do the filtering. A method of an object is an action that the object can perform. A property of an object is a distinguishing characteristic about the object. For this example, we want the Msvm_ExternalEthernetPort object that has an ElementName of Marvell Yukon 88E8056 PCI-E Gigabit Ethernet Controller. That sufficiently narrows down our choices to that particular network adapter. The result of this particular query is stored in the $ExternalNic variable so that it can be used as a parameter at the end of the script.

Queries like the one shown here serve as fundamental building blocks for scripts that use WMI. Filtering using Where-Object is a very common way to get exactly the WMI class object that you are looking for in a query. It is used in scripts throughout this book.

Scriptomatic for PowerShell

Scriptomatic was a fantastic tool for creating VBScripts that used WMI. The Scriptomatic GUI would allow you to choose some WMI objects, and the Scriptomatic tool would output the VBScript to perform the selected WMI query for you. You chose a WMI namespace and WMI class. The Scriptomatic tool would translate those selections into a VBScript WMI query. It was an excellent learning tool to master the WMI syntax.

Well, the same folks who brought us Scriptomatic for VBScript have made a similar tool for PowerShell called Windows PowerShell Scriptomatic (go figure). This tool will let you select some WMI objects and then output PowerShell code for you. You can download Scriptomatic for PowerShell from http://www.microsoft.com/downloads/details.aspx?FamilyID=d87daf50-e487-4b0b-995c-f36a2855016e&displaylang=en.

Using Scriptomatic is pretty straightforward. As shown in Figure 1-12, the user interface is divided into four main sections: the WMI section at the top, the script section (a blank text area) below the WMI section, the Control Pad section to the right, and the Target Computers section at the bottom.

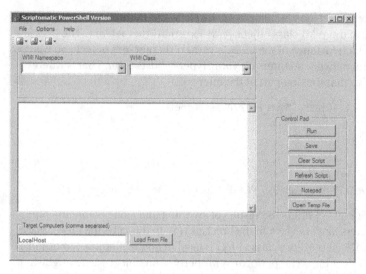

Figure 1-12. *The Scriptomatic for PowerShell user interface*

You choose an available WMI namespace and a WMI class from the drop-down lists at the top of the window. Then a script shows up in the script section, as shown in Figure 1-13.

```
$computer = "LocalHost"
$namespace = "root\virtualization"
Get-WmiObject -class Msvm_ComputerSystem -computername $computer -namespace
$namespace
```

Figure 1-13. *A sample script created by Scriptomatic*

The cool thing about Scriptomatic is that you can test the script that it creates by clicking Run in the Control Pad section. You can even run the script against a single computer or multiple remote computers by using the Target Computers section. You will be using the Windows PowerShell Scriptomatic tool to create some WMI queries in Chapter 5, which covers automating Hyper-V management.

Summary

As you saw in this chapter, getting started with Hyper-V is not difficult. However, as you begin to plan your larger virtual infrastructure, items like security, automation, backup, recovery, and high availability need to be considered. The rest of this book exposes you to tools and techniques that will help you tackle those aspects when you are designing your virtual infrastructure.

Automation can help with deployment, management, and maintenance by reducing the chance for human error when deciding on standard best practices for your virtual infrastructure. The tools outlined in this chapter will help you as you move from deploying Hyper-V to securing, protecting, and maintaining Hyper-V. Along your journey through this book, you will become more proficient with tools such as PowerShell and WMI. This proficiency will allow you to. better manage Hyper-V and apply what you learn to other scripting problems using the same techniques.

CHAPTER 2

∎∎∎

Automating Hyper-V Deployment

A virtual infrastructure cannot exist without the most basic component: the host server. Deploying the Hyper-V host server is one of the first steps that you will take when building your infrastructure. Choosing the initial deployment settings for your Hyper-V hosts will involve careful planning. You will be considering industry best practices and your company's policies. Once you have decided on the appropriate installation settings for your environment, you should ensure that these settings are applied consistently whenever you deploy a new Hyper-V host.

As stated in Chapter 1, you should try to reduce the potential for errors as much as possible when deploying your virtual infrastructure. Even if your installation settings are well documented and a step-by-step procedure is available, there is still room for human error. Therefore, to make sure you have a consistent and error-free deployment of your Hyper-V hosts from the beginning, you should automate the installation.

This chapter focuses on the steps necessary to deploy a Windows Server 2008 Core installation with the Hyper-V role using Windows Deployment Services (WDS). This will give you the benefit of configuring your installation settings once and applying them whenever you deploy a Hyper-V host. The chapter will guide you through installing and configuring WDS on Windows Server 2008, and then capturing an installation image of Windows Server 2008 with the Hyper-V role enabled. Finally, you will learn how to create an answer file so that you can perform an unattended installation of your Hyper-V host.

Installing WDS for HyperV

WDS, Microsoft's new replacement for Remote Installation Services (RIS), enables you to boot a server from the network via a PXE-boot and install an image on that server. In the example used in this chapter, that image will be a Windows Server 2008 Enterprise Core installation, with the Hyper-V role set up on it.

WDS Prerequisites

Before installing WDS, make sure your environment is set up to support WDS. Your system must meet the following prerequisites:

Active Directory: You need an Active Directory domain to deploy images using WDS. If you don't already have Active Directory deployed, you will need to create a new domain for WDS. However, since you are reading this book, you must be into virtualization. You can just create a WDS domain using a Windows Server 2008 Standard virtual machine as the domain controller, if you don't already have an Active Directory domain.

Dynamic Host Configuration Protocol (DHCP): Since WDS uses PXE-boot (which relies on DHCP addressing) to deploy images to systems, you will need an active DHCP server. This book uses a Windows Server 2008 DHCP server.

Domain Name Service (DNS): You must have a functioning DNS server on the network.

An NTFS partition: WDS requires an NTFS partition to store the images.

Credentials: To install WDS, you must be a member of the Administrators group on the WDS server. To install an image, you must be a member of the Domain Users group.

The following is a checklist to help you collect the information you'll need before you begin the installation and configuration of WDS:

- Active Directory domain name
- DHCP server hostname or IP address
- Name of account with administrator rights on the proposed WDS server
- Drive letter of the NTFS partition (such as D:\ or E:\) where the WDS images will be stored

Adding the WDS Role

Once the prerequisites are met, you can install WDS. This example outlines how to add the Windows Deployment Services role on Windows Server 2008.

1. Select Start ➤ Administrative Tools ➤ Server Manager to open Server Manager.

2. Select Add Roles in the Roles section of the Server Manager window, and then click Next in the first Add Roles Wizard window.

3. In the Server Roles window, select Windows Deployment Services, and then click Next.

4. The introduction to Windows Deployment Services window will tell you about some of the prerequisites discussed earlier, as shown in Figure 2-1. Click Next to proceed.

5. In the Select Role Services window, leave the Deployment Server and Transport Server check boxes selected, as shown in Figure 2-2. The deployment server includes all of the WDS functionality that you will need, and it depends on the transport server components. The transport server includes only a subset of WDS services that can be used for multicasting images. It does not include a PXE server component, so it should be used if you will provide your own PXE server. Click Next.

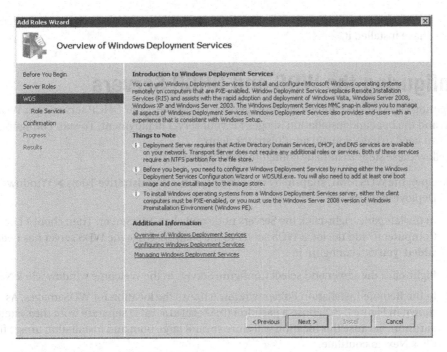

Figure 2-1. *WDS prerequisite overview*

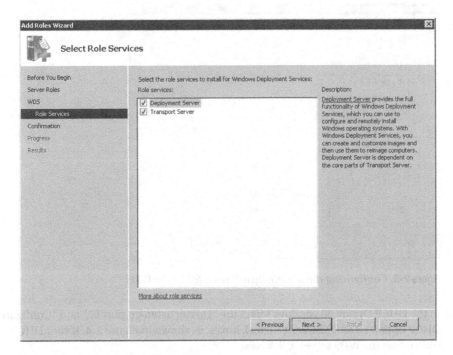

Figure 2-2. *Choosing the WDS role services*

6. In the Confirmation window, click Install. When the installation completes, click Finish to exit.

As you've seen, installing the role is straightforward. All the work is in configuring WDS after you have installed it.

Configuring the WDS and DHCP Servers

Configuring WDS means configuring three general categories: your DHCP server, your WDS server, and the boot and installation images for your server deployment. To start configuring WDS, you need to have domain administrator rights.

Follow these steps to initially configure your servers:

1. Open the WDS MMC snap-in by selecting Start ➤ Administrative Tools ➤ Windows Deployment Services.

2. In the left pane, right-click the Servers node and click Add Server. Then choose Local Computer to add the local WDS server to the snap-in. Once the WDS server has been added, you can configure it.

3. Right-click the server and select Configure Server. In the Welcome window, click Next.

4. In the Remote Installation Folder window, choose the location for WDS images. As shown in Figure 2-3, I chose a partition (D:\RemoteInstall) separate from the system partition, because this location will store several large boot and installation image files. Click Next to continue.

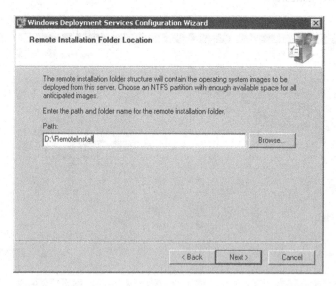

Figure 2-3. *Configuring the remote installation folder for WDS*

5. In the DHCP Option 60 window, select the "Do not listen on port 67" and "Configure DHCP option 60 to 'PXEClient'" check boxes, as shown in Figure 2-4, if your DHCP server is on the WDS server. Click Next.

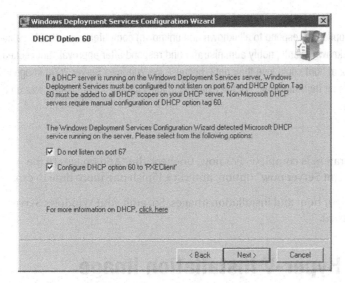

Figure 2-4. *Setting the DHCP options for WDS*

6. In the PXE Server Initial Settings window, you can select how you want the server to respond to clients. Known client computers are computers that have been prestaged with computer accounts in Active Directory. In this example, I selected the option to "Respond to all (known and unknown) computers" to automate the deployment as much as possible, as shown in Figure 2-5. Click Finish.

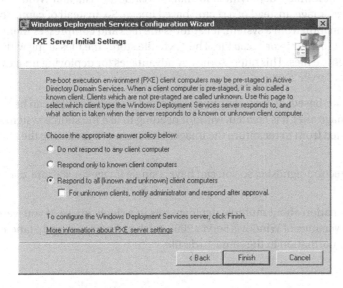

Figure 2-5. *Setting the PXE server settings for WDS*

■**Caution** If you select the option to respond to all (known and unknown) computers, you should be careful if you leave the option "For unknown clients, notify administrator and respond after approval" unchecked. If you do, users who press F12 at boot could lose their data, because the Windows Server 2008 image will overwrite the operating system on their machine. For the example in this chapter, I made sure I was on a separate deployment network.

---

7. The initial configuration is complete. For now, uncheck the "Add images to the Windows Deployment Server now" option, and click Finish one more time to exit.

Now it's time to add your boot and installation images. So, grab your Windows Server 2008 DVD and let's get started.

Preparing the Hyper-V Installation Image

Now that you have your initial WDS server configuration, it's time to add the boot and installation image to your WDS server. The boot image will boot the target Hyper-V server so that you can install the image. The first boot image that you will make is a standard boot image. You will use this image to make a special boot image called a *capture image*. This will allow you to capture an installation of Hyper-V on a Windows Server 2008 Core system that you have run through Sysprep for later deployment.

The boot image, capture image, and final captured image will be stored in the Windows Image format, which is the new image deployment format for Windows Vista and Windows Server 2008. It is a file-based image, instead of a sector-based image. So, instead of capturing sector-based volume information from a system, it captures the files and compresses them in a `*.wim` file, which is similar to a `*.zip` or `*.cab` file. The `*.wim` file stores the files along with the metadata associated with those files. This offers some key advantages for deploying images of Windows Vista or Windows Server 2008:

- Since the image is file-based, drivers, scripts, patches and many other files can be injected into the image after it is created, without needing to use the source system that the image was created from to recapture the image. This makes maintaining the image much easier.

- The image is architecture-agnostic, so you can have a single image for x86 and x64 deployments.

- You can store information about multiple deployments in a single image. If you want to deploy different versions of Windows Server 2008 (such as Enterprise and Standard), you can store that information in the same `*.wim` file.

In this chapter, you will learn how to create an image from a source machine so you can deploy a Core installation of Windows Server 2008 Enterprise with the Hyper-V role. So, you will not be changing the image after it is captured. However, the capture process described in this chapter can be used for any other system that you want to deploy.

Let's start by creating the boot image.

Creating the Boot Image

Follow these steps to create a standard boot image:

1. Select Start ➤ Administrative Tools ➤ Windows Deployment Services to open the WDS MMC snap-in.

2. Expand your WDS server (or add it if it is not visible) and select the Boot Images folder.

3. Put your Windows Server 2008 installation DVD into the WDS server's DVD drive.

4. Right-click the Boot Images folder and select Add Boot Image.

5. In the Image File window, browse to the \Sources directory of the Windows Server 2008 DVD and select the file called boot.wim, as shown in Figure 2-6. The boot.wim file will be used to boot your source and final systems into Windows Preinstallation Environment (WinPE), so the image can be either captured from the source system or installed on the final system. Click Next.

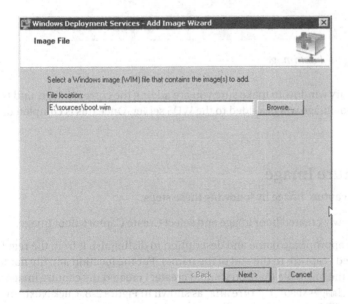

Figure 2-6. *Selecting the boot image*

6. In the Image Metadata window, name your image appropriately and give it a description, as shown in Figure 2-7. Click Next.

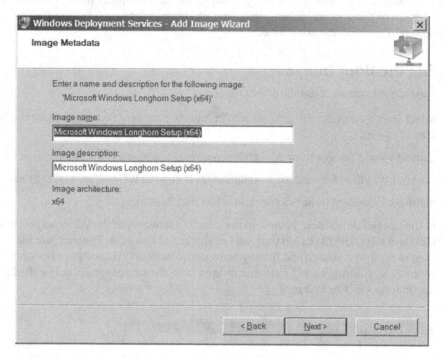

Figure 2-7. *Naming the boot image*

7. Review the Summary window to make sure you are adding the correct image, and then click Next. The boot image will be added to the WDS server. Once this is completed, click Finish.

Creating the Capture Image

Now you can create your capture image by following these steps.

1. Right-click your newly created boot image and select Create Capture Boot Image.

2. Give the image an appropriate name and description to distinguish it from the regular boot image (I added -capture to the end of the name). For the location and file name, enter the name of the *.wim file that you want to create. I created my capture image as D:\RemoteInstall\Images\boot-capture.wim, as shown in Figure 2-8. Click Next, and the capture image will be created.

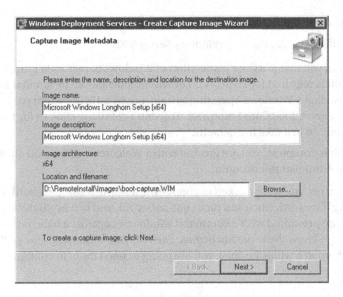

Figure 2-8. *Creating the capture image*

3. Once you have created the boot capture image, add it to your WDS server boot images by right-clicking Boot Images and selecting Add Boot Image. Browse to the location where you stored your capture boot image and select it. The process is the same as adding the original boot.wim image, outlined in the previous section.

That's it for your boot images. You should now have a boot image that is used to boot into the WinPE environment. You should also have a capture image that is a derivative of the boot image that you can use to capture your installation image.

Creating the Install Image Group

You need to take one more step before you can create an install image: create an install image group. An install image group is used to logically separate your installation images. It is needed when you capture and deploy your installation image.

To create an install image group, right-click the Install Images folder and select Add Image Group. In the text box, type an appropriate name (like Hyper-V) for the image group.

Creating the Installation Image

Now it's time to create the custom installation image. To do that, you must first install and configure Windows Server 2008 manually (but only once).

Installing and Configuring Windows Server 2008

Here are the steps for installing and configuring Windows Server 2008:

1. For this example, you will install a Core installation of Windows Server 2008 Enterprise Edition 64-bit (64-bit is required for Hyper-V). The installation should be familiar to anyone who has installed a Windows operating system. I used a 15GB system partition and chose to install Server 2008 Core Enterprise. You don't get many choices for the rest of the installation, so just take the defaults.

2. After the installation is complete, you are greeted with a Welcome window. Go ahead and log on with the Administrator account.

3. The first time you log on, you will be asked to change the administrator password. Pick a moderately strong password. Once you pick your password, you will begin the logon process. Next, you are presented with a command window set against a blue back-drop—awe inspiring, I know. Now the fun begins. Dust off your command-line skills if you haven't used them in a while, because you are going to need them to configure this server for Hyper-V.

Note The Core installation steps shown here will install a functioning Hyper-V server that you can deploy to your Hyper-V hosts. However, there are some additional security features that you may want to put in place before you create your first installation image, as discussed in Chapter 9. Either way, the procedure described in this chapter for capturing the installation image will be the same.

---

4. Enable Remote Administration:

```
netsh advfirewall firewall set rule group="Remote Administration" ➡
new enable=yes
```

5. Enable Remote Desktop (if you wish):

```
cscript \windows\system32\scregedit.wsf /ar 0
cscript \windows\system32\scregedit.wsf /cs 0
```

Note The line cscript \windows\system32\scregedit.wsf /cs 0 will enable Remote Desktop connections for clients with operating systems earlier than Windows Vista and Windows Server 2008. It is needed only if you will connect to your Hyper-V host server using the Remote Desktop client from one of these earlier operating systems.

---

6. Download any Hyper-V updates that you want to apply to this image to an accessible network share.

7. Map the network share:

```
net use <DriveLetter> \\<ServerName>\<ShareName>
```

8. Apply the update. Just execute the *.msu update files by navigating to their directory
   (cd) and typing the name of the file.

Tip If you do not want to search for and install any updates that you may need individually, there is
an easier solution available on the Microsoft MSDN site. Copy the script that is available at http://msdn.
microsoft.com/en-us/library/aa387102(VS.85).aspx. Then paste the script text into Notepad and
name the file WUA_SearchDownloadInstall.vbs. This script will search for, download, and let you apply
any new updates that are applicable to your Windows Server 2008 installation. Just copy the script to your
Windows Server 2008 Core installation and run it from the command line by typing cscript WUA_
SearchDownloadInstall.vbs.

---

9. Enable the Hyper-V role (this command is case-sensitive):

```
start /w ocsetup Microsoft-Hyper-V
```

Enabling the Hyper-V role will require a reboot.

These few configuration items will allow you to remotely administer your Hyper-V server
once you deploy it through WDS.

Preparing the System for Installation

Now it's time to run this installation through Sysprep, so you can capture it as an installation
image. You need to do this so you will be able to generate a new security identifier (SID) for the
installation when you deploy it. This also generalizes the installation so that it can be deployed
to multiple systems.

Navigate to the sysprep directory:

```
C:\
cd %systemroot%\system32\sysprep
```

Run Sysprep with the options to use the Windows Welcome process and remove system-
specific information such as the SID:

```
sysprep /oobe /generalize /reboot
```

where:

- /oobe ensures that the image will run the "out-of-box" experience when it boots for the
  first time. This includes the Windows Welcome process.

- /generalize strips system-specific information, such as the SID and hardware-specific
  information from the image.

- /reboot tells the system to reboot after Sysprep runs.

Capturing the Image

When your reference system reboots, make sure that you set the BIOS or use the boot menu to PXE-boot before anything else. If your WDS server is working properly, you should see a DHCP address message, followed by "copying Boot\x64\pxeboot.com."

If you do not see this screen, shut down your reference system to avoid the Sysprep version being ruined. Run the following command on your WDS server:

```
wdsutil /set-server /architecturediscovery:yes
```

This command uses the command-line WDS utility (wdsutil) to enable the option to turn on the WDS architecture discovery. This enables your WDS server to know the system that is booting is an x64 system. This is the only option that applies to WDS in this book. (For more information about wdsutil, see http://technet.microsoft.com/es-es/library/cc771206.aspx.)

Next, follow these steps to capture the image:

1. Press F12 to continue the network boot. In the boot menu, select the capture image that you created. In the Volume to Capture drop-down list, select the appropriate volume (your Sysprepped system volume). Also, enter a name and description for the image.

■Note If you do not see any volumes, something went wrong with the Sysprep operation, or you forgot to perform the Sysprep.

---

2. On the Image Capture Destination screen, choose either a local drive or a mapped network drive to temporarily store the image before it is copied to the WDS server. I chose the remaining space on the C:\ drive. Since this is a Windows Image format file, and not a sector-based hard drive image, the image file itself will not appear on your final image. This is because the capture process captures only the boot sector along with individual files. The *.wim file itself is not included in those individual files that the image process captures.

3. In the file name box, type an appropriate file name for the image (this will become a *.wim file).

4. Click Upload image to WDS Server. Type the name of your WDS server in the box, and then click Connect.

5. Provide the administrator credentials for your WDS server when you are prompted.

6. In the Image Group drop-down list, choose the Hyper-V image group that you set up earlier.

7. Click Finish, and the image will be captured.

When it is complete, the image will be ready for installation to your Hyper-V servers. However, you don't want to manually go through the installation process, do you? In the next section, you'll see how to automate much of the process.

Creating Answer Files

Now that you have your boot and installation images ready to go, you could just PXE-boot your target server and fill in all the installation question bits until you are done. But that wouldn't be any fun, would it? Clever administrators answer questions only once. Since you're reading this book, you must be a clever administrator. So, let's automate this installation by using answer files, which you will generate with Windows System Image Manager (SIM), a graphical tool for this purpose.

You'll create two answer files. Why do you need two of these files for a single installation? Well, you need one answer file (called WDSClientUnattend.xml) for the initial WDS client setup phase, to respond to questions like which image and partitioning scheme to use. The other answer file (called ImageUnattend.xml) is for the rest of the Windows installation.

These answer files could be created without Windows SIM, because they are just XML files. However, Windows SIM allows you to see, graphically, each setting in the answer file that corresponds to a certain Windows configuration pass. A *configuration pass* is an individual phase of a Windows setup. You can apply settings to a Windows setup during a configuration pass. Subsequently, you can provide settings in an unattended installation answer file for each configuration pass. Table 2-1 lists the valid configuration passes.

Table 2-1. *Windows Setup Configuration Passes*

Pass	Description
windowsPE	Applies basic Windows setup options. These may include, but are not limited to, user interface settings, product key settings, and disk setup options.
offlineServicing	Applies updates (security patches, packages, language packs, drivers, and so on) to the Windows image.
specialize	Applies system-specific settings to the Windows installation. Examples of this might include network settings, domain settings, language settings, and so on.
generalize	Runs only when the sysprep /generalize command is run on the source image. This strips out system-specific information from the image (SID and hardware-specific information).
auditSystem	Applies settings before a user logs on to the system in audit mode. This pass runs only if you boot the system into audit mode. Audit mode is usually used by original equipment manufacturers (OEMs) to make configuration changes and customizations to a Windows image without needing to go through the full out-of-box experience (OOBE) that includes the Windows Welcome steps.
auditUser	Applies settings after a user logs on to the system in audit mode. This pass runs only if you boot the system into audit mode.
oobeSystem	Applies settings to the system before the Windows Welcome screen appears.

■**Note** For the scenario discussed in this chapter, you will be applying settings only in the windowsPE and specialize configuration passes. The windowsPE configuration pass applies to the WDSClientUnattend. xml file, and the specialize configuration pass applies to the ImageUnattend.xml file.

In addition to the ability to graphically see the settings for each configuration pass, Windows SIM lets you validate an answer file. This is useful if you need to troubleshoot deployment problems.

Installing the Windows Automated Installation Kit

You'll need to get a copy of the Windows Automated Installation Kit, which includes Windows SIM, and install it on a workstation so you can create the answer files. The Windows Automated Installation Kit can be downloaded from http://www.microsoft.com/downloads/details.aspx?FamilyID=94bb6e34-d890-4932-81a5-5b50c657de08&DisplayLang=en.

Note Pay close attention to the system requirements for Windows SIM listed at the bottom of the download page. If you are going to use anything other than Windows Vista or Windows Server 2008, there are specific service pack and patch requirements.

After you've downloaded the Windows Automated Installation Kit, follow the wizard's instructions to install it.

Using Windows SIM

After you've installed the Windows Automated Installation Kit, open Windows SIM by selecting Start ➤ All Programs ➤ Windows Automated Installation Kit ➤ Windows System Image Manager. You'll see the Windows SIM window, as shown in Figure 2-9.

The Windows SIM interface is split into five panes:

Distribution Share: This pane is where you can define a distribution share. A distribution share is a folder where you can store third-party drivers, Microsoft patches, and other files that you need in your imaging process.

Windows Image: This pane is where you open a Windows Image (*.wim) or catalog (*.clg) file, which supplies the appropriate components to add to your answer file.

Answer File: This pane is where you open an existing answer file or create a new one. Once a base answer file is created, this is where you will be adding components to each configuration pass in the answer file.

Properties: This pane is where you adjust the settings of each component that you add to the answer file.

Messages: This pane is where you will view any XML, validation, or configuration set error or warning messages. It will display the output of an answer file validation.

The Windows Image pane on the left is where you will get the components to add to the Answer File pane on the right.

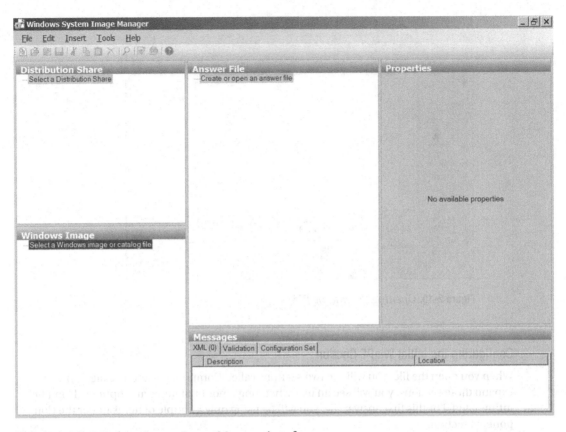

Figure 2-9. *The Windows System Image Manager interface*

Creating the Windows Deployment Answer File

The first file you will make is the WDSClientUnattend.xml file. This will automate the WDS client setup portion of the installation. To start the process, you'll need the Windows Server 2008 DVD. To begin, follow these steps.

1. Browse to the root of the DVD and copy the Sources\install_Windows Longhorn SERVERENTERPRISECORE.clg file to the hard drive on your Windows SIM workstation. The *.clg file is a catalog file. It will be used to set the properties in your WDSClientUnattend.xml file.

2. Navigate to the Windows Image section of the Windows SIM interface. Right-click "Select a Windows image or catalog file" and select Select Windows Image.

3. In the browse window, navigate to where you saved the install_Windows Longhorn SERVERENTERPRISECORE.clg file, as shown in Figure 2-10. Select the file and click Open.

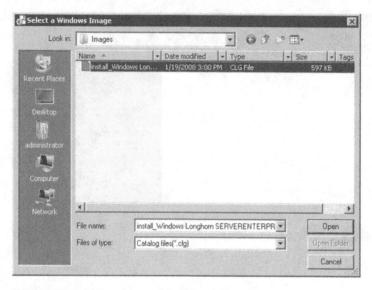

Figure 2-10. *Opening the catalog file*

Configuring the initial WinPE Section

When you open the file, you will see two sections called Components and Packages. If you expand these sections, you will see an overwhelming amount of items and options. Don't be intimidated. For this first answer file, you will be using only a couple of items under the Components section.

As stated earlier, when you initially boot using WDS, you boot into WinPE. So, one of the components for the WDSClientUnattend.xml file will be the amd64_Microsoft-Windows-International-Core-WinPE_6.0.6001.18000_neutral component. This will allow you to configure a couple user interface options that apply specifically to the initial WinPE portion of the installation: the user interface language and when to show the user interface.

Choose File ➤ New Answer File to start creating a new answer file. Then navigate to the amd64_Microsoft-Windows-International-Core-WinPE_6.0.6001.18000_neutral component in the Windows Image pane, right-click it, and select the Add Setting to Pass 1 windowsPE option. The component now appears in the Answer File pane, under the Components/windowsPE section, as shown in Figure 2-11. This is where you will be applying the options for the WinPE portion of the installation.

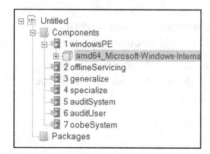

Figure 2-11. *Adding the WinPE component to the answer file*

The root and Setup components have the following settings:

- *UILanguage*: This sets the language for the user interface. You will set it to en-US for this example.

- *WillShowUI*: If this is set to onError, the user interface for WinPE will be shown if there is an error during the installation.

Select each component in the Answer File pane and adjust its settings in the Properties pane as shown in Table 2-2. Figure 2-12 shows the settings for the UILanguage component under amd64_Microsoft-Windows-International-Core-WinPE_6.0.6001.18000_neutral.

Table 2-2. *WinPE UI Settings for the WDSClientUnattend.xml File*

Component	Setting	Value
Root	UILanguage	en-US
Root/SetupUILanguage	UILanguage	en-US
Root/SetupUILanguage	WillShowUI	OnError

Figure 2-12. *Configuring the UILanguage component*

That's it for the WinPE component.

Adding the Windows Setup Components

Now you'll answer the rest of the WDS client setup questions with the amd64_Microsoft-Windows-Setup_6.0.6001.18000_neutral component. This component is used in the windowsPE installation section to configure some preinstallation options like disk partitioning. Here, you will use only the DiskConfiguration and WindowsDeploymentServices subcomponents.

For this example, you will be creating two partitions: one for the system volume and one for your virtual machines (which takes up the remainder of the disk). To accomplish this, you need to tell the WinPE portion of the installation to create some partitions, and then modify the partitions that were created. This will be reflected in the answer file settings.

Follow these steps to add the appropriate CreatePartition, ModifyPartition, and Windows-DeploymentServices components to the answer file:

1. Select the DiskConfiguration component. Right-click it and select the Add Setting to Pass 1 windowsPE option. It will be added to the Answer File pane.

2. Navigate to the Disk component directly beneath the DiskConfiguration component in the Windows Image pane. Right-click it and select the Add Setting to Pass 1 windowsPE option.

3. Right-click the CreatePartition component two levels down under the Disk component and select the Add Setting to Pass 1 windowsPE option.

4. Repeat step 3 two more times for a total of three CreatePartition components. Your Answer File pane should now look like Figure 2-13.

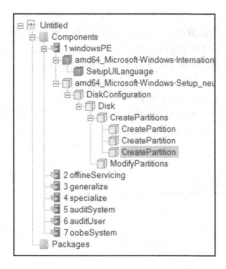

Figure 2-13. *Adding the disk and partition components to the answer file*

■**Note** The three CreatePartition components added will allow you to create the two partitions for this example (one partition for the system volume and one for the virtual machines). You can adjust the partition scheme according to your environment once you see how creating partitions in this answer file works.

---

5. In the Windows Image pane, navigate to DiskConfiguration/Disk/ModifyPartitions and select ModifyPartition.

6. Right-click ModifyPartition and select the Add Setting to Pass 1 windowsPE option.

7. Repeat step 6. The expanded DiskConfiguration component in the Answer File pane should now look like Figure 2-14.

8. In the Windows Image pane, navigate to WindowsDeploymentServices and select it.

9. Right-click it and select the Add Setting to Pass 1 windowsPE option. Now you should see the WindowsDeploymentServices component in the Answer File pane.

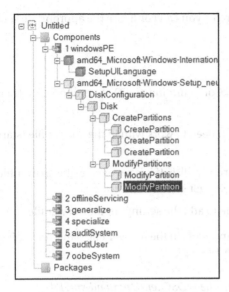

Figure 2-14. *Adding the ModifyPartition components to the answer file*

Under the WindowsDeploymentServices component, you will see subcomponents called ImageSelection and Login. Each of these has its own subcomponents with settings. The ImageSelection component will be used to define the installation image name (as named on the WDS server) and the image installation location.

With all of the components expanded in the Answer File pane, it should look like Figure 2-15.

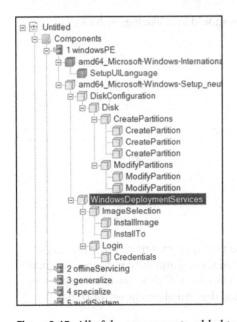

Figure 2-15. *All of the components added to the answer file*

Now that you've set up the complete hierarchy, you can configure the appropriate settings for the components.

Configuring the Disk Settings

First, you need to adjust the settings for the DiskConfiguration and Disk components. These components have the following settings:

- *DiskID*: This is the ID for the disk that you need to work with in the answer file (starting with a first disk ID of 0).

- *WillWipeDisk*: This can have a value of true or false. If it is set to true, the answer file is set so that it can overwrite the disk in the target system.

- *AddListItem*: This just tells the answer file to add the settings to the answer file.

Select the DiskConfiguration and Disk components in the Answer File pane, and adjust their settings in the Properties pane as shown in Table 2-3.

Table 2-3. *DiskConfiguration and Disk Settings for the WDSClientUnattend.xml File*

Component	Setting	Value
DiskConfiguration	WillShowUI	OnError
DiskConfiguration/Disk	DiskID	0
DiskConfiguration/Disk	WillWipeDisk	true
DiskConfiguration/Disk	Action	AddListItem

When you are finished, the Settings section values should look like Figure 2-16.

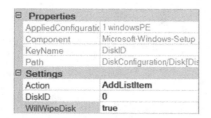

Figure 2-16. *Configuring the disk settings*

Configuring the Create Partition Settings

Now, you can move on to the individual CreatePartition component settings. The first partition, for the system volume, will be 15GB. The combined second and third partitions will make up a logical partition that will take up the rest of your disk (the total disk space on the machine in this example is 250GB). This logical partition will hold the virtual machines for Hyper-V.

The CreatePartition component has the following settings:

- *Extend*: This can be true or false. If it is set to true, the partition extends to the size of the rest of the disk. If it is set to false, you need to set a size for the partition.

- *Order*: This is the order that the partition takes on the disk.

- *Size*: This is the size of the partition in megabytes.

- *Type*: This is the partition type, which can be Primary, Logical, or Extended.

Select each CreatePartition component in the Answer File pane, and adjust the settings in the Properties pane as listed in Tables 2-4, 2-5, and 2-6. Figures 2-17, 2-18, and 2-19 show how the settings for each CreatePartition component should look when you are finished.

Table 2-4. *First CreatePartition Component Settings for the WDSClientUnattend.xml File*

Component	Setting	Value
DiskConfiguration/Disk/CreatePartitions/CreatePartition	Extend	false
DiskConfiguration/Disk/CreatePartitions/CreatePartition	Order	1
DiskConfiguration/Disk/CreatePartitions/CreatePartition	Size	15360
DiskConfiguration/Disk/CreatePartitions/CreatePartition	Type	Primary
DiskConfiguration/Disk/CreatePartitions/CreatePartition	Action	AddListItem

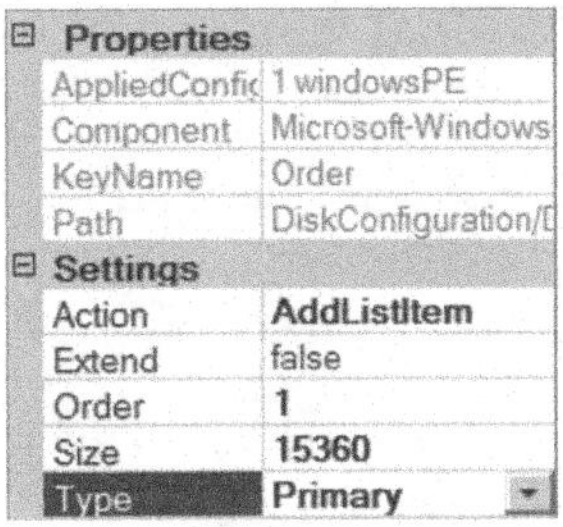

Figure 2-17. *Configuring the first partition*

Table 2-5. *Second CreatePartition Component Settings for the WDSClientUnattend.xml File*

Component	Setting	Value
DiskConfiguration/Disk/CreatePartitions/CreatePartition	Extend	true
DiskConfiguration/Disk/CreatePartitions/CreatePartition	Order	2
DiskConfiguration/Disk/CreatePartitions/CreatePartition	Size	
DiskConfiguration/Disk/CreatePartitions/CreatePartition	Type	Extended
DiskConfiguration/Disk/CreatePartitions/CreatePartition	Action	AddListItem

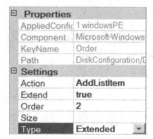

Figure 2-18. *Configuring the second partition*

Table 2-6. *Third CreatePartition Component Settings for the WDSClientUnattend.xml File*

Component	Setting	Value
DiskConfiguration/Disk/CreatePartitions/CreatePartition	Extend	true
DiskConfiguration/Disk/CreatePartitions/CreatePartition	Order	3
DiskConfiguration/Disk/CreatePartitions/CreatePartition	Size	
DiskConfiguration/Disk/CreatePartitions/CreatePartition	Type	Logical
DiskConfiguration/Disk/CreatePartitions/CreatePartition	Action	AddListItem

⊟ **Properties**	
AppliedConfig	1 windowsPE
Component	Microsoft-Windows
KeyName	Order
Path	DiskConfiguration/D
⊟ **Settings**	
Action	**AddListItem**
Extend	**true**
Order	**3**
Size	
Type	**Logical**

Figure 2-19. *Configuring the third partition*

Now that the partition settings have been created, you just need to modify the partitions so that they are formatted for you.

Configuring the Modify Partition Settings

The first ModifyPartition component will be used to format the system partition. The second ModifyPartition component will be used to format the virtual machine (data) partition. Both will be NTFS partitions.

The ModifyPartition component has the following settings:

- *Active*: This can be set to true or false. If it is set to true, that partition is the active boot partition. If it is false, it is not an active boot partition.

- *Extend*: This can be set to true or false. If it is set to true, the partition is extended to take up the remainder of the disk space. If it is set to false, it stays the same size.

- *Format*: This can be NTFS, FAT, or FAT32. You will be using the NTFS format in the majority of cases.

- *Label*: This is the friendly name that you want to give to the partition. For this example, you'll use the labels OSDisk for the system volume partition and VM for the virtual machine partition.

- *Letter*: This is the drive letter that you want to assign to the partition.

- *Order*: This is the order that the partition will be placed on the disk.

- *PartitionID*: This is the ID that you give to the partition (starting with 1).

Select each ModifyPartition component in the Answer File pane and adjust the settings for these components in the Properties pane as listed in Tables 2-7 and 2-8. Figures 2-20 and 2-21 show how the settings for each ModifyPartition component should look after you've finished.

Table 2-7. *First ModifyPartition Component Settings for the WDSClientUnattend.xml File*

Component	Setting	Value
DiskConfiguration/Disk/ModifyPartitions/ModifyPartition	Active	true
DiskConfiguration/Disk/ModifyPartitions/ModifyPartition	Extend	false
DiskConfiguration/Disk/ModifyPartitions/ModifyPartition	Format	NTFS
DiskConfiguration/Disk/ModifyPartitions/ModifyPartition	Label	OSDisk
DiskConfiguration/Disk/ModifyPartitions/ModifyPartition	Letter	C
DiskConfiguration/Disk/ModifyPartitions/ModifyPartition	Order	1
DiskConfiguration/Disk/ModifyPartitions/ModifyPartition	PartitionID	1
DiskConfiguration/Disk/ModifyPartitions/ModifyPartition	Action	AddListItem

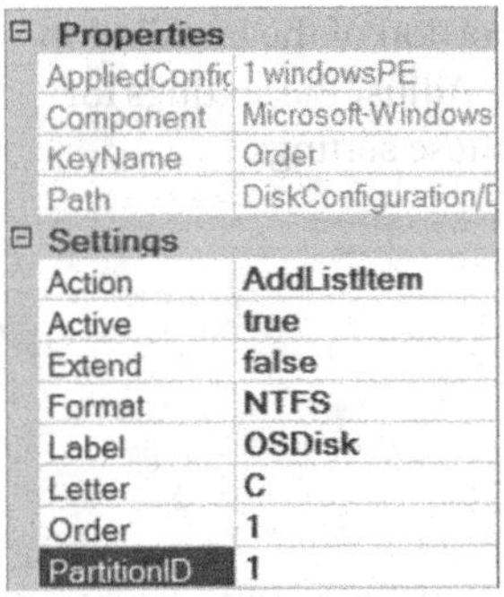

Figure 2-20. *Modifying the first partition*

Table 2-8. *Second ModifyPartition Component Settings for the WDSClientUnattend.xml File*

Component	Setting	Value
DiskConfiguration/Disk/ModifyPartitions/ModifyPartition	Active	false
DiskConfiguration/Disk/ModifyPartitions/ModifyPartition	Extend	false
DiskConfiguration/Disk/ModifyPartitions/ModifyPartition	Format	NTFS
DiskConfiguration/Disk/ModifyPartitions/ModifyPartition	Label	VM
DiskConfiguration/Disk/ModifyPartitions/ModifyPartition	Letter	D
DiskConfiguration/Disk/ModifyPartitions/ModifyPartition	Order	2
DiskConfiguration/Disk/ModifyPartitions/ModifyPartition	PartitionID	2
DiskConfiguration/Disk/ModifyPartitions/ModifyPartition	Action	AddListItem

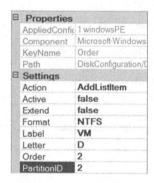

Figure 2-21. *Modifying the second partition*

Configuring the WDS Settings

That just leaves the WindowsDeploymentServices component section for the initial WinPE configuration portion of the installation.

The InstallImage component settings are Filename, ImageGroup, and ImageName. The settings for your own answer files depend on the file name, group name, and image name that you configure for your WDS Hyper-V deployment. The InstallTo component has DiskID and PartitionID settings. For this example, you will tell the initial WinPE portion of the installation process to install the image to Disk0, Partition1 (the system partition). Adjust the settings for these components as listed in Table 2-9. Figures 2-22 and 2-23 show these settings.

Table 2-9. *ImageSelection, InstallImage, and InstallTo Component Settings for the WDSClientUnattend.xml File*

Component	Setting	Value
Root/WindowsDeploymentServices/ImageSelection	WillShowUI	OnError
Root/WindowsDeploymentServices/ImageSelection/ InstallImage	Filename	ServerCore-HyperV.wim
Root/WindowsDeploymentServices/ImageSelection/ InstallImage	ImageGroup	HyperV
Root/WindowsDeploymentServices/ImageSelection/ InstallImage	ImageName	Server2008EntCore-HyperV
Root/WindowsDeploymentServices/ImageSelection/ InstallTo	DiskID	0
Root/WindowsDeploymentServices/ImageSelection/ InstallTo	PartitionID	1

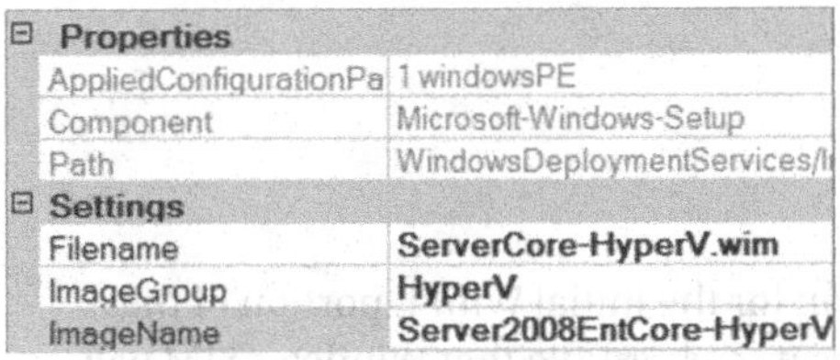

Figure 2-22. *Configuring the InstallImage component*

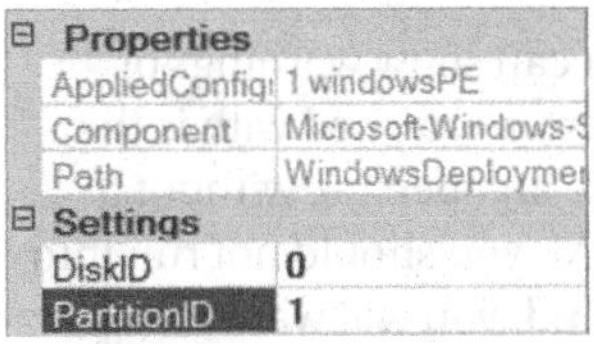

Figure 2-23. *Configuring the InstallTo component*

Finally, you need to configure the Login and Credentials components. For the Login component, WillShowUI should be set to OnError. The Credentials component, under the Login component, is where you provide the credentials that the answer file will use to establish a connection with the WDS server.

Caution Since the Credentials component settings will be readable in the answer file, be sure to protect this answer file with the appropriate Windows folder/file permissions. Also, you should use a user account that has only administrator access on the WDS server, and disable that account when you are not using it for deployment.

Adjust the settings for the Login and Credentials components as shown in Table 2-10. Figure 2-24 shows the settings for the Credentials component.

Table 2-10. *Login and Credentials Component Settings for the WDSClientUnattend.xml File*

Component	Setting	Value
Root /WindowsDeploymentServices/Login	WillShowUI	OnError
Root /WindowsDeploymentServices/Login/Credentials	Domain	HyperV.int
Root /WindowsDeploymentServices/Login/Credentials	Password	P@55w0rD
Root /WindowsDeploymentServices/Login/Credentials	Username	administrator

Figure 2-24. *Configuring the Credentials component*

Now you have completed the entire configuration for the initial WinPE portion of the installation. This will be contained in the WDSClientUnattend.xml file that Windows SIM will create. However, before you save the file, let's take a look at the Messages pane.

Validating and Saving the Answer File

The Messages pane of the Windows SIM window has three tabs that can show warnings or errors: XML, Validation, and Configuration Set. The main area you are concerned with is the Validation tab. This just validates the XML file to check for errors like an open tag without a matching closing tag. If you are generating the file with Windows SIM, you should not run into these problems. However, if you later edit an existing XML file by hand, you will want to validate your file.

To validate the answer file that is open in Windows SIM, select Tools ➤ Validate Answer File. Make sure you don't see any errors or warnings in the Validation or Configuration Set tabs of the Messages pane.

■**Note** You may see a warning in the XML tab that says "Cannot find Windows image information in answer file." I have confirmed that the answer file will still work despite this warning, so it is harmless, and you can proceed with creating the file.

After confirming that you have no serious errors with your answer file, you should save it. To save the answer file you just created, select File ➤ Save Answer File As. In the Save As dialog box, choose a location for your answer file. I chose D:\RemoteInstall\WdsClientUnattend\ WDSClientUnattend.xml. Make sure the file name is WDSClientUnattend.xml.

Congratulations! You just created an unattended answer file for the WDS portion of the setup. Now you can move on to the Windows installation image unattended answer file.

Creating the Windows Installation Answer File

Now you need to automate the Windows installation portion of the setup. Here, you can create an answer file to fill in information like the Windows product key, screen resolution, IP settings, and so on. Since the majority of your customization comes from the Sysprepped image, you are concerned with only the following in this example:

- Entering the product key

- Entering the computer name

- Possibly joining the server to the domain

As you can tell, this answer file, which will be named ImageUnattend.xml, will be a lot less complicated than your WDSClientUnattend.xml file.

To begin, from the Windows SIM window, right-click in the Windows Image pane and browse to the SERVERENTERPRISECORE.clg file, which you saved to the hard drive earlier. Then choose File ➤ New Answer File to start creating a new answer file.

Entering the Product Key

First, add the ProductKey component. Within amd64_Microsoft-Windows-Setup_6.0.6001. 18000_neutral, under UserData, you'll find ProductKey. Right-click it and select Add Setting to Pass 1 windowsPE.

After you add the component, highlight the UserData component. You'll see that it has AcceptEula, FullName, and Organization settings. If AcceptEula is set to true, the End User License Agreement (EULA) is accepted for you automatically. If it is set to false, you must accept the EULA manually. The ProductKey component setting is the value for your 29-character (including dashes) Windows product key.

Select the UserData and ProductKeys components in the Answer File pane and adjust their settings in the Properties pane as shown in Table 2-11. (Of course, you can enter anything you like for the name and organization values.) Figures 2-25 and 2-26 show these settings.

Table 2-11. *UserData and ProductKey Component Settings for the ImageUnattend.xml File*

Component	Setting	Value
Root Component/UserData	AcceptEula	true
Root Component/UserData	FullName	Harley Stagner
Root Component/UserData	Organization	harleystagner.com
Root Component/UserData/ProductKey	WillShowUI	OnError
Root Component/UserData/ProductKey	Key	Your 29-character product key

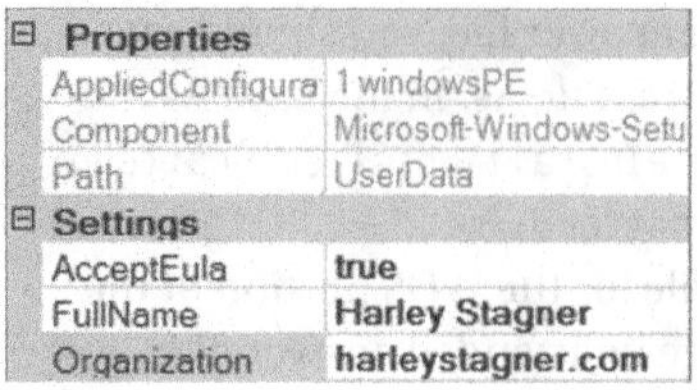

⊟ **Properties**	
AppliedConfigura	1 windowsPE
Component	Microsoft-Windows-Setu
Path	UserData
⊟ **Settings**	
AcceptEula	**true**
FullName	**Harley Stagner**
Organization	**harleystagner.com**

Figure 2-25. *Configuring the UserData component*

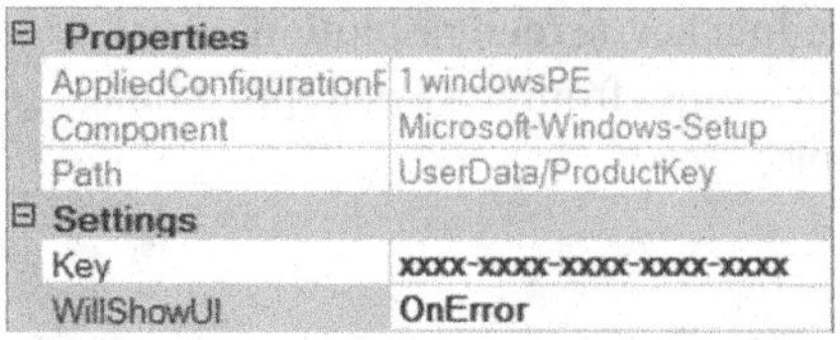

⊟ **Properties**	
AppliedConfigurationF	1 windowsPE
Component	Microsoft-Windows-Setup
Path	UserData/ProductKey
⊟ **Settings**	
Key	**XXXX-XXXX-XXXX-XXXX-XXXX**
WillShowUI	**OnError**

Figure 2-26. *Configuring the ProductKey component*

Entering the Computer Name

Next, you will configure settings for the specialize portion of the Windows installation. The first setting will be the server's computer name.

Select the amd64_Microsoft-Windows-Shell-Setup_6.0.6001.18000_neutral component, right-click it, and select Add Setting to Pass 4 specialize. The only value that you will change for this computer is the ComputerName setting. Set it to an asterisk (*), so that a random computer name will be generated, as shown in Figure 2-27. This will be useful if you are deploying multiple HyperV servers that you would like to join to a domain.

⊟ **Properties**	
AppliedConfigure	4 specialize
Enabled	True
⊞ Id	amd64_Microsoft-Windo
⊟ **Settings**	
BluetoothTaskbe	
ComputerName	*
CopyProfile	
DisableAutoDayl	
DoNotCleanTask	
ProductKey	
RegisteredOrgar	Microsoft
RegisteredOwne	AutoBVT
ShowWindowsLiv	
StartPanelOff	
TimeZone	

Figure 2-27. *Setting the computer name in the answer file*

Joining a Domain

Finally, if you want to automatically join this computer to the domain, you need to add the Identification component. Within amd64_Microsoft-Windows-UnattendedJoin_6.0.6001.18000_neutral, under Identification, you'll find Credentials. Right-click it and select Add Setting to Pass 4 specialize.

In the Answer File pane, select the Identification component. You'll see that it has several settings. Here, you are concerned with just three:

- *JoinDomain*: This is the domain that you want to join automatically.

- *MachineObjectOU*: This is the organizational unit (OU) where you want to place the computer account once it has joined to the domain.

- *UnsecureJoin*: This may sound unsettling, but for Windows Server 2008, setting it to true just means that a shared computer account password will be used to join the computer to the domain without credentials. A computer account password will be dynamically generated by WDS and applied to the computer when it is joined to the domain. The UnsecureJoin option must be used for Windows Server 2008.

Adjust the Identification component settings as shown in Table 2-12 and Figure 2-28.

Table 2-12. *Identification Component Settings for the ImageUnattend.xml File*

Component	Setting	Value
Root /Identification	JoinDomain	HyperV
Root /Identification	MachineObjectOU	OU=MyOu,DC=MyDom,DC=MyCompany,DC=com
Root /Identification	UnsecureJoin	true

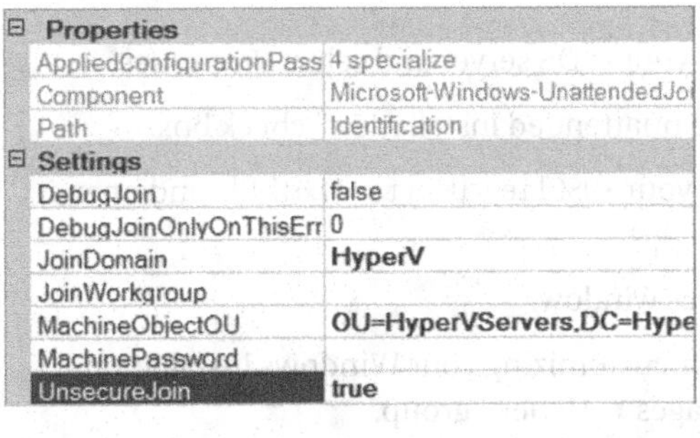

Properties	
AppliedConfigurationPass	4 specialize
Component	Microsoft-Windows-UnattendedJo
Path	Identification
Settings	
DebugJoin	false
DebugJoinOnlyOnThisErr	0
JoinDomain	**HyperV**
JoinWorkgroup	
MachineObjectOU	**OU=HyperVServers,DC=Hype**
MachinePassword	
UnsecureJoin	**true**

Figure 2-28. *Configuring the server to automatically join the domain*

Completing the Answer File

Now, you can clean up the answer file by deleting any subcomponents that are not being used. Your clean Answer File pane should look like Figure 2-29.

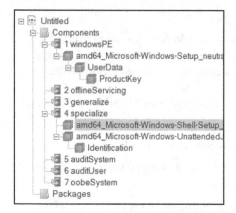

Figure 2-29. *The final ImageUnattend.xml answer file*

Validate the answer file before you save it by choosing to Tools ➤ Validate Answer File. You should not see any errors or warnings in the Messages pane. Save the file as ImageUnattend. xml (I saved my file to D:\RemoteInstall\WdsClientUnattend\ImageUnattend.xml).

Now that both of your answer files are created, all you need to do is configure WDS to use them. This will allow you to PXE-boot your target server and deploy the Hyper-V image to it automatically.

Configuring WDS to Use the Answer Files

You are almost ready to deploy your Hyper-V image via WDS. First, you need to configure WDS to use your answer files by following these steps:

1. Open the WDS MMC snap-in (Start ➤ Administrative Tools ➤ Windows Deployment Services).

2. In the left pane, under Servers, right-click your WDS server and select Properties.

3. Click the Client tab and select the "Enable unattended installation" check box.

4. In the x64 architecture section, browse to your WDSClientUnattend.xml file and open it, as shown in Figure 2-30.

5. Click OK to close the WDS server Properties window.

6. Next, you need to specify an answer file for customizing your Windows installation. In the left pane, navigate to the Install Images ➤ HyperV group.

7. Select the HyperV image that you created. Right-click it and select Properties.

8. On the General tab, select the "Allow image to install in unattended mode" check box.

9. Click Select File. Click Browse to open your ImageUnattend.xml file. Click OK twice to exit.

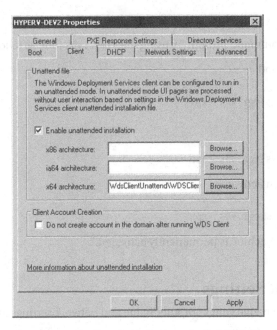

Figure 2-30. *Configuring WDS to use the WDSClientUnattend.xml answer file*

Deploying the Hyper-V Image

Now, you are ready to deploy your Hyper-V image. Make sure your target server is set to boot from the network using PXE by adjusting the BIOS settings appropriately. Follow these steps to deploy the Hyper-V image:

1. Boot your target server.

2. Look for a DHCP address message, followed by "copying Boot\x64\pxeboot.com."

3. Press F12 when you are prompted, to continue the network boot.

4. In the boot menu, select the normal boot image (not the capture image) that you created.

From this point on, the setup should run automatically. You just need to wait for it to complete. After the setup is complete, you are presented with the Windows logon screen. You will be prompted to change the administrator password. Go ahead and change it to whatever you would like. When you log on, you just need to activate Windows and do a little bit of network and boot configuration.

Activating Windows

You can activate Windows from the command prompt by using the `slmgr.vbs` tool, as follows:

1. View your activation grace period:

```
cscript c:\windows\system32\slmgr.vbs -xpr
```

2. Activate Windows:

```
cscript c:\windows\system32\slmgr.vbs -ato
```

3. Verify that the product has been activated:

```
c:\windows\system32\cscript slmgr.vbs -xpr
```

   You should see message "The machine is permanently activated."

Configuring Network Boot Settings

From the command prompt, you can change your computer name and network settings as necessary.

To rename the computer, use the following command:

```
netdom renamecomputer %computername% /Newname:YourNewName
```

Before you can change the IP address and DNS settings, you need to show the interfaces on your server and their unique IDs, as follows:

```
netsh interface ipv4 show interfaces
```

Note the `Name` and `Idx` fields for each interface.

To change the IP version 4 settings on any one interface, type the following:

```
netsh interface ipv4 set address name=<YourNicID> ➥
source=static address=<YourStaticIPAddress> ➥
mask=<YourSubnetMask> gateway=<YourDefaultGateway>
```

`<YourNicID>` is the `Idx` number for the NIC you are configuring.

You can configure a primary and secondary DNS address with this command:

```
netsh interface ipv4 add dnsserver name=<YourNicID> address=<YourDNSIP> index=1
```

For a secondary address, use the same command, but increment the index by one.

Configuring Boot Settings

You need to add the Hyper-V launch directive back to the Boot Configuration Database (BCD) so that the Hyper-V hypervisor will properly launch on the server. The BCD is read when the system boots to provide boot configuration settings for the operating system environment. The Hyper-V launch directive is stripped out of the BCD when you generalize the image with Sysprep, because the image is supposed to be hardware-independent. However, Hyper-V uses certain aspects of the system hardware to function (x64, virtualization extensions, and data execution prevention).

To add the launch directive back in once the system has booted, type the following at the command prompt:

```
bcdedit /set hypervisorlaunchtype auto
```

Finally, you can reboot your Hyper-V host server after these changes by typing the following command at the command prompt:

```
shutdown /r /t 0
```

Congratulations, you have just deployed your Hyper-V server with WDS.

Summary

The Hyper-V host server is the foundation for your virtual infrastructure. Best practices and policies for the installation should be applied to this installation in a consistent, repeatable manner. WDS can help you achieve that consistency by capturing your installation settings once and applying them whenever you need to deploy a Hyper-V host server. Automation using WDS can be achieved with these general steps:

1. Install the WDS server.

2. Configure the WDS server.

3. Create your boot and capture images.

4. Capture your installation image.

5. Create the WDSUnattend.xml and ImageUnattend.xml answer files to automate the installation. You can use Windows SIM for this.

6. Configure WDS to use the two answer files.

7. Deploy your unattended image by PXE-booting your target server.

8. Perform a few necessary postinstallation steps on your deployed Hyper-V host.

After your Hyper-V hosts have been deployed, you can start to configure and manage them. You can manage them individually using Hyper-V Manager. However, as you deploy more Hyper-V hosts to grow your virtual infrastructure, you may want to consider managing your virtual infrastructure with Windows System Center Virtual Machine Manager 2008. This single tool will help you manage your entire virtual infrastructure from a single interface. In Chapter 3, you will learn about the benefits of this application, how to deploy it, and how to get the most out of the many features that System Center Virtual Machine Manager 2008 has to offer.

CHAPTER 3

■■■

Managing Virtualization with System Center Virtual Machine Manager 2008

When you are just managing a single Hyper-V server, using the Hyper-V Manager tool may fit your needs. However, if you are planning on deploying a larger environment consisting of several Hyper-V servers, you should consider using System Center Virtual Machine Manager (VMM) 2008. VMM is Microsoft's newest management product in the System Center line of products. Here are some of its key benefits:

- Provides a single management console for multiple servers in your virtual environment
- Allows you to manage VMware ESX hosts
- Integrates with System Center Operations Manager
- Monitors and reports on your virtual environment
- Allows easy automation through PowerShell cmdlets
- Supplies wizard-guided physical-to-virtual conversions
- Supports optimizing the load on your hosts
- Allows you to delegate administrative tasks to defined roles
- Provides improved Hyper-V failover cluster management

This chapter introduces VMM. It covers installing the VMM components, using the Administrator console, and performing common tasks. You'll learn about physical-to-virtual conversions in Chapter 4, automating Hyper-V Management in Chapter 5, and configuring failover clustering in Chapter 7.

VMM Components

Your first consideration when planning for your VMM deployment is where you will install all of the VMM components. There are five server components to consider:

- SQL Server
- VMM server
- Administrator console
- Self-Service Portal
- Library server

For the highest degree of scalability, these components should be installed on separate computers. For example, you might collocate the Self-Service Portal on an existing Internet Information Services (IIS) server, the library server on an existing file server, and the Administrator console on your management desktop. The Administrator console should be installed on the same server as SCOM 2007 in order to enable reporting. It can also be installed on an administrator's workstation for remote connectivity.

The following sections discuss installing each of these components.

SQL Server

Most management products require a database to function. VMM is no different. If you do not already have SQL Server set up to use in your environment, you will need to install and configure it. VMM comes with SQL Server 2005 Express Edition. However, this should be used only in small environments (a few servers with no reporting) due to the following limitations:

- A database size limit of 4GB
- Ability to use only 1GB of RAM
- Ability to use only a single processor
- Unavailability of VMM reporting

Another reason to consider using SQL Server 2005 Standard or Enterprise Edition is System Center Operations Manager (SCOM), which will not work with SQL Server 2005 Express Edition. (VMM can also use SQL Server 2008, but SCOM 2007 will not work with that version of SQL Server.) If you want the ability to get Performance and Resource Optimization (PRO) alerts and recommendations (also called *PRO tips*) with VMM, you will need to integrate it with SCOM 2007.

Note PRO tips are a functionality that comes with VMM when it is integrated with SCOM 2007. These tips will warn you about items like a lack of resources on your Hyper-V host servers. In some cases, the PRO tip will suggest an action to take manually or automatically to correct the perceived problem. More information about PRO tips can be found in the "Enabling PRO Tips and Reporting" section later in the chapter.

Here, we will walk through the steps for installing SQL Server 2005 Standard Edition Service Pack 2 (SP2) x64, which will allow you to take advantage of everything that VMM has to offer. For scalability, you should also install the database server on a different server than the one that will run the VMM server.

SQL Server 2005 Standard Edition Requirements

In general, the system requirements for SQL Server 2005 Standard are either an x86 or x64 processor of 1 GHz or higher and 1GB or more of RAM. The system requirements for SQL Server 2005 Standard Edition specifically for VMM vary depending on the number of hosts you will be managing. Table 3-1 shows the requirements for 5 to 10 hosts, Table 3-2 shows the requirements for 11 or more hosts, and Table 3-3 shows the requirements for more than 150 hosts.

Table 3-1. *SQL Server Hardware Requirements for Five to Ten Hosts*

Hardware Component	Minimum	Recommended
Processor	Pentium 4, 2 GHz	Dual-core Pentium 4, 2 GHz or greater
RAM	2GB	2GB
Hard disk space	10GB	40GB

Table 3-2. *SQL Server Hardware Requirements for 11 or More Hosts*

Hardware Component	Minimum	Recommended
Processor	Pentium 4, 2 GHz	Dual-core Pentium 4, 2 GHz or greater
RAM	2GB	4GB
Hard disk space	10GB	50GB

Table 3-3. *SQL Server Hardware Requirements for More Than 150 Hosts*

Hardware Component	Minimum	Recommended
Processor	Pentium 4, 2 GHz (x64)	Dual-core Pentium 4, 2 GHz (x64) or greater
RAM	4GB	8GB
Hard disk space	10GB	50GB

In addition to the hardware requirements, some software requirements must be met in order to take advantage of the advanced SQL Server 2005 features, like reporting, as listed in Table 3-4.

Table 3-4. *SQL Server Software Requirements*

Component	Folder
Static Content	Common HTTP Features
Default Document	Common HTTP Features
HTTP Redirection	Common HTTP Features
Directory Browsing	Common HTTP Features
ASP.NET	Application Development
ISAPI Extension	Application Development
ISAPI Filters	Application Development
Windows Authentication	Security
IIS Metabase	Management Tools
IIS 6 WMI	Management Tools

To add these IIS prerequisites to the Windows Server 2008 server, follow these steps:

1. Select Start ➤ Administrative Tools ➤ Server Administrator.

2. In the navigation pane on the left, select Roles, as shown in Figure 3-1. On the right, select Add Roles, and then click Next.

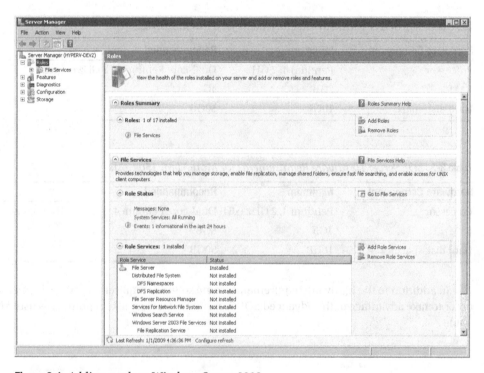

Figure 3-1. *Adding a role to Windows Server 2008*

3. In the Server Roles window, select Web Server (IIS). Click Next to continue.

4. In the Web Server (IIS) window, click Next to continue.

5. In the Role Services window, make sure all of the prerequisites listed in Table 3-4 are checked. Click Next to continue to the Confirmation window.

6. Click Install when you are ready to add the role to your server. If the installation was successful, click Close in the Results window.

SQL Server 2005 Standard Installation

After you have made sure your system meets the requirements, you can install SQL Server 2005 Standard. Before you begin the installation, make sure you have downloaded SQL Server 2005 SP2. You can get it here:

```
http://www.microsoft.com/downloads/details.aspx?familyid=AE7387C3-
348C-4FAA-8AE5-949FDFBE59C4&displaylang=en
```

Install SQL Server as follows:

1. Click Setup from the SQL Server installation CD or directory.

2. Read and accept the license agreement.

3. Click Install to install the SQL Server native client and setup support files. Click Next to continue. Click Next in the Welcome window.

4. In the System Configuration Check window, make sure that all of the prerequisites are configured. If they are not, review the previous section regarding SQL Server requirements and check for anything that may be missing. Click Next to continue.

5. In the Registration Information window, enter an appropriate name and company. Click Next to continue.

6. In the Components to Install window, select all of the components. If you want to selectively install components or choose a different installation directory for some of the components, click the Advanced button. Click Next.

7. In the Instance Name window, you can either choose a name for the SQL Server instance or choose a default instance (MSSQLSERVER). Click Next to continue.

8. In the Service Account window, you can either choose a domain account for all the SQL Server services, specify the local system account for all the SQL Server services, or define a separate account for each SQL Server service. You can also choose which services to start at the end of setup. Click Next after making your selections.

9. In the Authentication Mode window, choose either Windows Authentication or Mixed (SQL Server and Windows Authentication). Windows Authentication is recommended for the best security. Click Next to continue.

10. In the Collation Settings window, click Next to accept the default settings.

11. In the Report Server Installation window, choose to use the default installation so that SQL Server Reporting Services will be ready to use after the installation. Click Next to continue.

12. Review the components that will be installed, and then click Install to continue. Once all of the selected components have a green check beside them, indicating that they have been installed successfully, click Next.

13. Review the information in the Completing Microsoft SQL Server 2005 Setup window. Click Finish to complete the installation.

SQL Server SP3 Installation

After the initial installation of SQL Server 2005 Standard SP2, install SP3 as follows:

1. Click the setup file for SP3. In the Welcome window, click Next.

2. Read and accept the license agreement, and then click Next.

3. Click Next to accept the default settings in the Feature Update window.

4. In the Authentication window, leave the box checked to "Apply to all instances" and click the Test button to test authentication. Click Next to continue.

5. If you do not want to participate in Microsoft Error Reporting, leave the defaults and click Next.

6. If the Running Processes window reports any locked files, you have the opportunity to stop any services (like the MSSQLSERVER) to avoid a reboot of the server. Click the Refresh button to check for locked files again once you have stopped any necessary services. When you are satisfied, click Next to continue.

7. In the Ready to Install window, click Install. When all of the components are finished installing, click Next to continue.

8. In the Installation Complete window, click the View Summary button to see the summary, if you would like. Then click Next to continue.

9. In the Additional Information window, click Finish to launch the SQL Server 2005 User Provisioning Tool for Windows Vista (needed for Windows Server 2008 as well), as shown in Figure 3-2.

10. Use the double arrows to select both permissions. Make sure any SQL Server services you stopped at the beginning of the installation are started again. Click OK when you are finished.

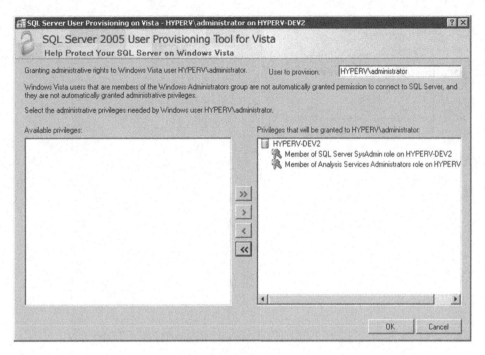

Figure 3-2. *Setting up user permissions with the User Provisioning Tool for Vista*

SQL Server Reporting Services Setup

If you try to test Reporting Services by opening Internet Explorer and going to `http://localhost/reportserver`, you will probably get a 403.1 Forbidden error. One last item needs to be taken care of before Reporting Services will work on Windows Server 2008. Take the following steps:

1. Open the IIS administration console by selecting Start ➤ Run and typing in `inetmgr`.

2. In the Connections pane, select the `ReportServer` virtual directory that is listed under the default web site. Double-click Handler Mappings under the IIS section of the middle pane.

3. In the pane on the right, click "Edit feature permissions." Make sure script is selected, and then click OK.

Now if you try `http://localhost/reportserver` again, you should get a Reporting Services web page, as shown in Figure 3-3.

You should also be able to access the SQL Server Reporting Services home page by going to `http://localhost/reports`, as shown in Figure 3-4.

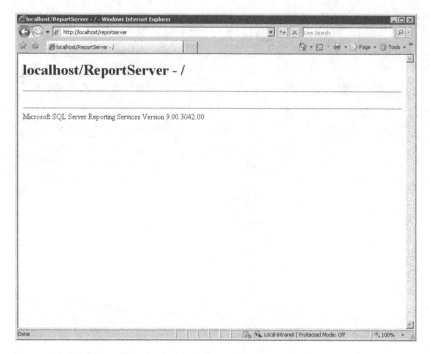

Figure 3-3. *Verifying that the ReportServer page is working*

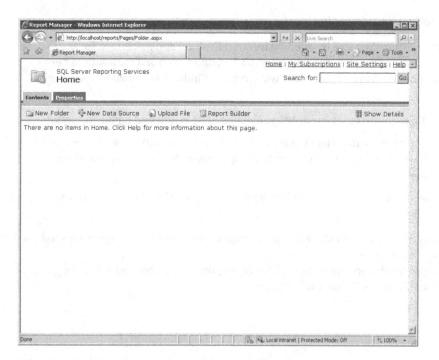

Figure 3-4. *Verifying that the reports page is working for reporting services*

The SQL Server portion of your setup is now complete.

VMM Server

Once you have your database set up, you can proceed with the VMM server installation.

VMM Server Requirements

The system requirements for the VMM server component will vary depending on the number of hosts you will be managing. Table 3-5 lists the requirements for up to 150 hosts, and Table 3-6 lists those for more than 150 hosts.

Table 3-5. *VMM Server Hardware Requirements for Up to 150 Hosts*

Hardware Component	Minimum	Recommended
Processor	Pentium 4, 2 GHz (x64)	Dual-core Pentium 4, 2 GHz (x64) or greater
RAM	2GB	4GB
Hard disk space	10GB	50GB

Table 3-6. *VMM Server Hardware Requirements for More Than 150 Hosts*

Hardware Component	Minimum	Recommended
Processor	Pentium 4, 2 GHz (x64)	Dual-core Pentium 4, 2 GHz (x64) or greater
RAM	4GB	8GB
Hard disk space	10GB	50GB

The VMM server can be installed only on Windows Server 2008 Standard, Enterprise, and Datacenter 64-bit editions. In addition, there are several other software requirements:

- Windows Remote Management (WinRM) (installed by default)

- Microsoft .NET Framework 3.0 (will be installed by the Setup wizard if it is not present)

- Windows Automated Installation Kit (WAIK) 1.1 (automatically installed by the Setup wizard)

VMM Server Installation

Follow these steps to install the VMM server:

1. Launch the setup file. You will see the main setup menu. Select VMM Server.

2. Read and accept the license agreement, and then click Next to continue.

3. In the Microsoft Update window, choose if you would like to use Windows Update when checking for VMM updates. Click Next to continue.

4. In the Customer Experience Improvement Program window, choose if you would like to participate in this program. Click Next.

5. In the Product Registration window, fill in the appropriate details for name and company. Click Next.

6. In the Prerequisites Check window, if all of the prerequisites mentioned in the preceding section have been met, the hardware and software requirements should be OK. Click Next to continue.

7. In the Installation Location window, either accept the default installation location or choose an alternative location. Click Next to continue.

8. In the SQL Server Settings window, you can either have the Setup wizard install SQL Server 2005 Express or you can use another supported instance of SQL Server that has been preinstalled. If you choose to use another supported instance and this is the first installation of VMM, select the check box to create a new database, as shown in Figure 3-5. If you are not logged on to the system with an account that has the rights to create a new database on SQL Server, you can also choose to use different credentials. Click Next to continue.

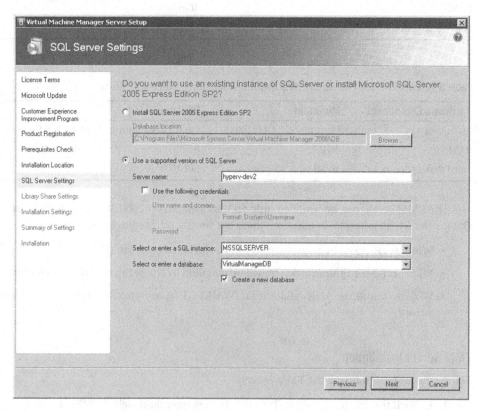

Figure 3-5. *Using an existing SQL Server instance for VMM*

9. In the Library Share Settings window, shown in Figure 3-6, you can create a new share on the VMM server to be the VMM library (the default), or you can use an existing share as the library share. Click Next after making your selection.

Caution You cannot delete or move the default library share once the VMM server has been installed. Be sure to carefully consider where you would like to host your library items (virtual disks, templates, profiles, and so on).

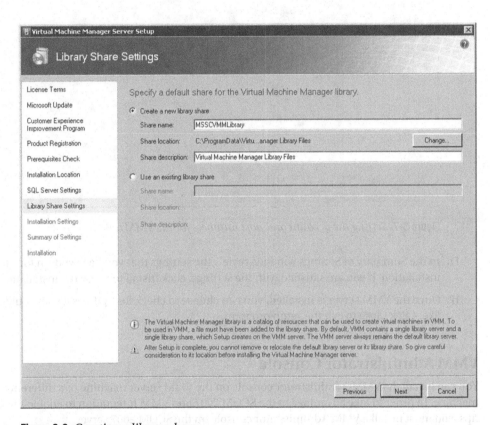

Figure 3-6. *Creating a library share*

10. In the Installation Settings window, shown in Figure 3-7, you can change the ports that are used for VMM Administrator console, host agent, and library server communication, as well as the port used for file transfers to host agents and library servers. You can also choose an account to use for the VMM service if you do not want to use the local system account. Click Next after making your selections.

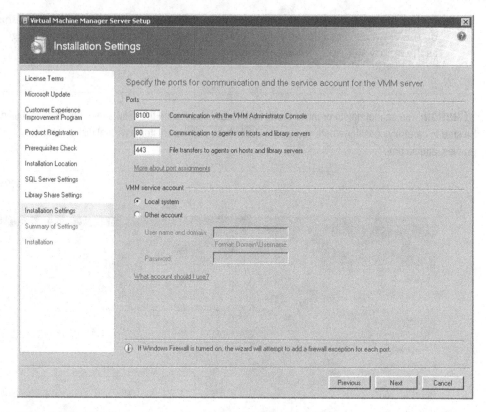

Figure 3-7. *Setting the account and port numbers for the VMM server*

11. In the Summary of Settings window, review the settings that you have chosen for this installation. If you are satisfied with the settings, click Install to begin the installation.

12. Once the VMM server is installed, you can choose to check for updates if you would like. Click Close to exit the setup program.

VMM Administrator Console

You can install the VMM Administrator console on the VMM server machine or a different machine. In order to take advantage of the SCOM 2007 and VMM integration to enable PRO tips, you must install a VMM Administrator console on the SCOM 2007 server.

The VMM Administrator console component can be installed on the following operating systems:

- Windows Server 2008 Standard, Enterprise, and Datacenter 32-bit and 64-bit (excluding Window Server 2008 Core)

- Windows Server 2003 Standard, Enterprise, and Datacenter 32-bit and 64-bit with SP2 (R2 with SP2 is included as well)

- Windows Vista with SP1
- Windows XP Professional 32-bit with SP2 or SP3
- Windows XP Professional 64-bit with SP2

The VMM Administrator console component requires Windows PowerShell 1.0, which will be installed by the Setup wizard if it is not present.

To install the Administrator console, follow these steps:

1. Launch the setup file. You will see the main setup menu. Select VMM Administrator Console.

2. Read and accept the license agreement, and then click Next to continue.

3. Click Next in the Customer Experience Improvement Program window.

4. If the Prerequisite Check window reports that everything is OK, click Next to continue.

5. In the Installation Location window, accept the default installation location or choose an alternative location. Click Next.

6. In the Port Assignment window, if you changed the default port of 8100 for VMM Administrator console communication when you installed the VMM server, change the port number here to match it. Click Next.

7. If the settings in the Summary Settings window are acceptable, click Install to install the Administrator console. .NET 3.0 and PowerShell 1.0 will be added if they were not installed previously.

8. When the installation is complete, you can choose to check for updates. Click Close to exit the setup program.

VMM Self-Service Web Portal

The VMM Self-Service Portal allows users to create and manage their own virtual machines. Its use is discussed in the "Using the VMM Self-Service Portal" section later in the chapter. This section describes installing the portal.

VMM Self-Service Portal Requirements

The system requirements for the VMM Self-Service Portal component are listed in Table 3-7.

Table 3-7. *Self-Service Portal Requirements*

Hardware Component	Minimum	Recommended
Processor	Pentium 4, 2.8 GHz	Pentium 4, 2.8 GHz; dual-core 64-bit 3.2 GHz or greater for more than 10 concurrent connections
RAM	2GB	2GB
Hard disk space	1GB	1GB

The Self-Service Portal can be installed on the following operating systems:

- Windows Server 2008 Standard, Enterprise, and Datacenter 32-bit and 64-bit (excluding Windows Server 2008 Core)

- Windows Web Server 2008

- Windows Server 2003 Standard, Enterprise, and Datacenter 32-bit and 64-bit with SP2 (R2 with SP2 is included as well)

The Self-Service Portal also has the following software requirements:

- Windows PowerShell 1.0 (comes with Windows Server 2008)

- IIS 6.0 or IIS 7.0

- Microsoft .NET Framework 2.0 (installed by the Setup wizard if not present)

- Microsoft .NET Framework 3.0 (installed by the Setup wizard if not present)

If you are installing the Self-Service Portal on a Windows Server 2008 system, the following IIS 7.0 components are needed:

- IIS 6 Management Compatibility
  - IIS 6 Metabase Compatibility
  - IIS 6 WMI Compatibility
- Common HTTP Features
  - Static Content
  - Default Document
  - Directory Browsing
  - HTTP Errors
- Application Development
  - ASP.NET
  - .NET Extensibility
  - ISAPI Extensions
  - ISAPI Filters
- Security
  - Request Filtering

VMM Self-Service Portal Installation

Follow these steps to install the Self-Service Portal:

1. Launch the setup file. You will see the main setup menu. Select VMM Self-Service Portal.

2. Read and accept the license agreement, and then click Next to continue.

3. If your system passes the prerequisites check, click Next to continue. Otherwise, review the prerequisites in the previous section to make sure you have met them.

4. In the Installation Location window, accept the default installation location or choose an alternative location. Click Next.

5. The Web Server Settings window appears, as shown in Figure 3-8. If this will be the only web site on the server, then just keep the default settings. If it will share the IP address with other sites on the same server, you need to either specify a different port or a host header. Click Next to continue.

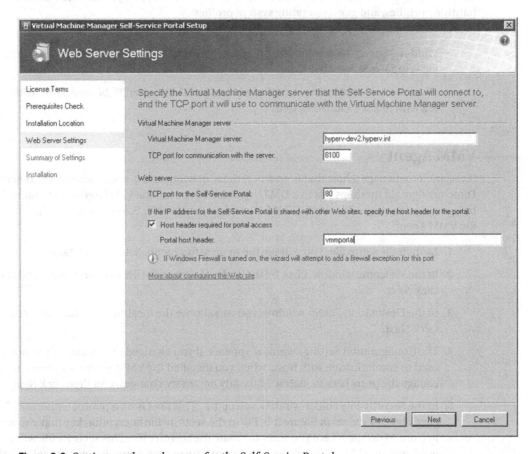

Figure 3-8. *Setting up the web server for the Self-Service Portal*

Note If you use a host header for the Self-Service Portal, you need to make sure to register the host header name in DNS with the appropriate IP address.

6. Review the settings in the Summary Settings window. If everything looks OK, click Install to begin the installation.

7. When the installation is complete, you can choose to check for updates. Click Close to exit the Setup wizard.

VMM Library Server

A VMM library server is just a Windows file server with a share to use as the VMM library storage. It is used for storing items like ISO images, virtual machine templates, virtual hard drives, hardware profiles, and guest operating system profiles.

The following operating systems can be used as library servers:

- Windows Server 2008 Standard, Enterprise, and Datacenter 32-bit and 64-bit (including Windows Server 2008 Core)

- Windows Server 2003 Standard, Enterprise, and Datacenter 32-bit and 64-bit with SP2 (R2 with SP2 is included as well)

VMM Agent

If you want to manage a host that is on a perimeter network and is not a member of an Active Directory domain (perhaps it is in a DMZ), you need to install the VMM Agent on it manually before you attempt to add it to the VMM Administrator console. Follow these steps to install the VMM Agent:

1. Launch the setup file. You will see the main setup menu. Select Local Agent.

2. In the Welcome window, click Next. Read and accept the license agreement, and then click Next.

3. In the Destination Folder window, you can choose the location to install the agent. Click Next.

4. The Configuration Settings window appears. If you changed any of the default ports used to communicate with hosts when you installed the VMM server, you need to change the ports here to match. Make any necessary changes, and then click Next.

5. In the Security File Folder window, select the "This host is on a perimeter network" check box, as shown in Figure 3-9. Fill in the security file encryption key that you want to use and decide where you want to create the security file. This security file will be used later to add this host to your VMM server using the Administrator console. Click Next to continue.

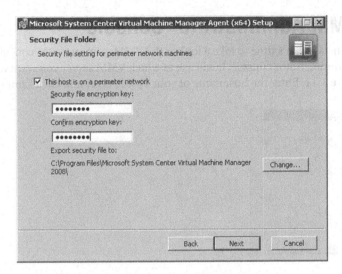

Figure 3-9. *Creating the security file for perimeter hosts*

6. In the Host Network Name window, choose the host computer name if you will have name resolution available for this host. If not, choose Use IP address, as shown in Figure 3-10. Click Next.

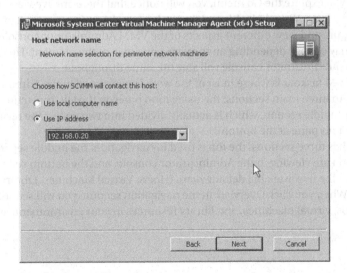

Figure 3-10. *Setting how the perimeter host will be contacted by VMM*

7. The agent will be installed. Click Finish when the installation is complete.

Touring the VMM Administrator Console

Now that you have VMM installed, it's time to take a look at the VMM Administrator console. When you first open the Administrator console, it will ask to which VMM server you want to connect, as shown in Figure 3-11. Enter the host name of your VMM server and click Connect.

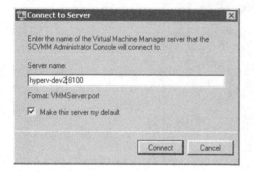

Figure 3-11. *Connecting to the VMM Administrator console for the first time*

When the Administrator console opens, take a moment to explore its interface, shown in Figure 3-12. At the top of the console is the menu bar with File, View, Go, Actions, and Help options. The File menu lets you open a new connection to another VMM server or exits the Administrator console. If you explore the Go menu, you will notice that there are five views in the Administrator console: Hosts, Virtual Machines, Library, Jobs, and Administration. Each of these views lets you configure and view different aspects of the VMM Administrator console. The menus and options may change depending on the view you are in at the moment. However, the mechanics of the Administrator console will stay the same throughout.

The area below the VMM taskbar is where most of the work is performed in the Administrator console. It is split into three main sections: the navigation pane on the left, the Actions pane on the right, and the middle section, which is actually divided into two panes: the results pane at the top and the details pane at the bottom.

The navigation pane has three sections: the top is used for navigation, the middle section allows you to filter what you are viewing in the Administrator console, and the bottom section is where you choose one of the five available default views (Hosts, Virtual Machines, Library, Jobs, or Administration). When you click Overview in the navigation section, you will see some graphs of hosts, recent jobs, virtual machines, and library resources in your environment, as shown in Figure 3-13.

Note The Reporting view shown in Figure 3-12 is available only if reporting integration with SCOM 2007 has been enabled. SCOM integration is discussed in the "Enabling PRO Tips and Reporting" section later in this chapter.

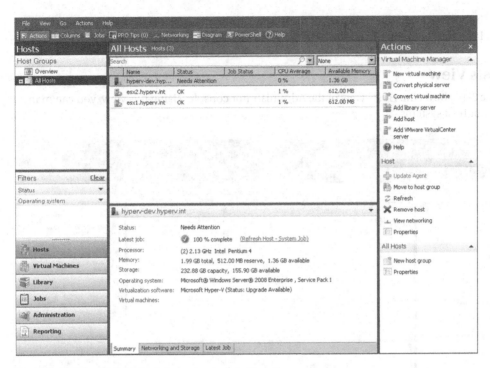

Figure 3-12. *The VMM Administrator console interface*

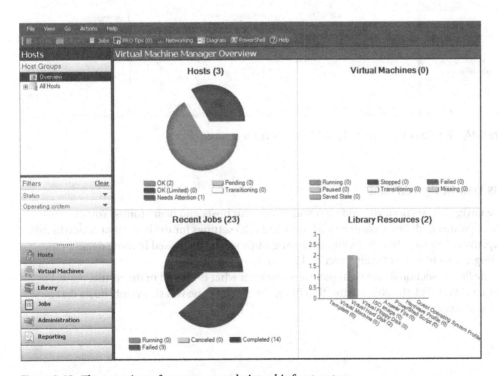

Figure 3-13. *The overview of your managed virtual infrastructure*

The options available in the rest of the Administrator console interface depend on the view. Let's start with the Hosts view.

Hosts View

Figure 3-14 shows the Hosts view of the Administrator console. Using this view, you can manage your host systems.

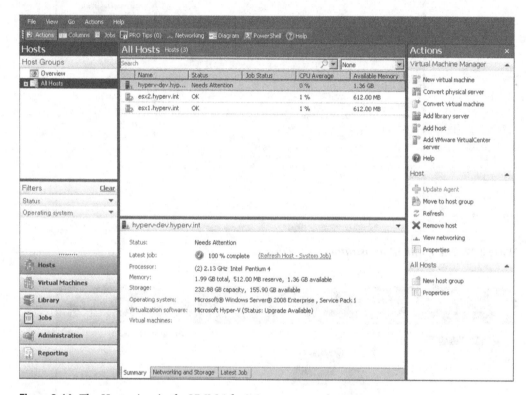

Figure 3-14. *The Hosts view in the VMM Administrator console*

Hosts View Navigation Pane

In the navigation section, you can view and select your hosts and host groups. You can create host groups to define resource utilization and PRO settings for the hosts that reside in that group, instead of each host individually. Host groups will be discussed in more detail in the "Adding a Host to a Host Group" section later in this chapter.

The Filters section in the right pane lets you filter what is viewed in the results pane. For example, if you click the Needs Attention filter, the results pane will show only hosts that have a status of Needs Attention.

Hosts View Results and Details Panes

When you select a host in the results pane, the details pane is populated with three tabs at the bottom:

- *Summary*: This tab show general information about the selected host (see Figure 3-14).

- *Networking and Storage*: This tab gives you a snapshot of how many virtual networks are configured on the selected host, as shown in Figure 3-15. You can also see how much free space is on each of the host's disks.

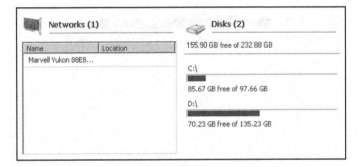

Figure 3-15. *The networking and storage details for the selected host*

- *Latest Job*: This tab is a good place to start if you are troubleshooting a particular host and need to find out if any changes were made recently. Here, you can see what command was last performed on the host and when it was performed, as shown in Figure 3-16. The right side of this screen will show you which properties, if any, were changed by the command.

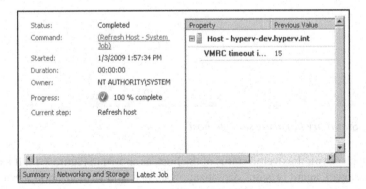

Figure 3-16. *The Latest Job tab can be useful for troubleshooting host problems.*

Hosts View Actions Pane

The top of the Actions pane will always be populated with the actions that can be performed with the Administrator console. The sections below the top section are context- sensitive. They will change depending on which one of the five views you are in at the time.

In Hosts view, click the Properties action. You will see a new window that lets you view and adjust the host's properties. Several tabs are available for host properties:

- *Summary*: This tab gives you a good idea of what resources are available to the host, as shown in Figure 3-17. Also, you can add a description of the selected host.

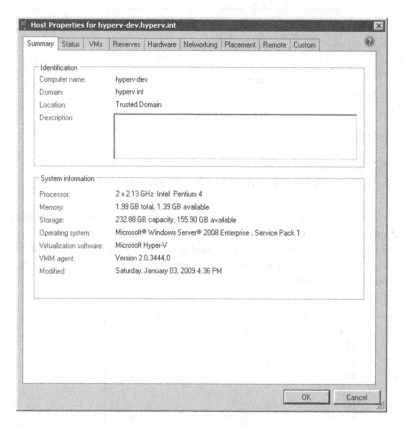

Figure 3-17. *The Summary tab of the selected host*

- *Status*: This tab gives you the overall status of the host, as shown in Figure 3-18. It lists the connection, agent, agent version, virtualization service, and virtualization service version status. You can also choose if this host will be available for virtual machine placement. If you are having any trouble with your host, this is a good place to start troubleshooting.

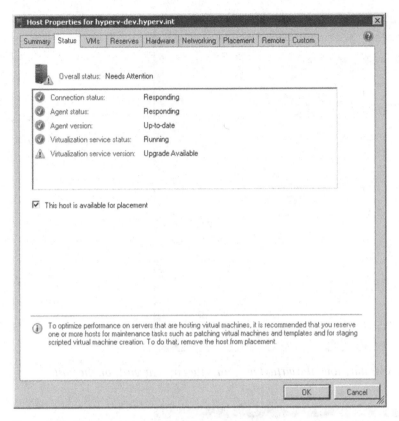

Figure 3-18. *The Status tab of the selected host can also be used for troubleshooting.*

- *VMs*: This tab shows any virtual machines that are hosted by this host, along with their status, as shown in Figure 3-19. You can also register new virtual machines by browsing for them.

- *Reserves*: Using this tab, you can set aside resources for the host operating system, as shown in Figure 3-20. You can adjust the CPU percentage, memory, disk space, disk I/O, and network capacity percentage for an operating system on the host. This lets you guarantee a certain amount of resources for use by the host operating system (Windows Server 2008), so the virtual machines will not consume resources the host needs to operate.

■**Note** You should need to adjust the settings on the Reserves tab only if you will be opening multiple management consoles or other applications on the Hyper-V host machine, or if you will be running other Microsoft or third-party services on the Hyper-V host that require extra resources. Both of those situations are against the best practice of deploying Hyper-V on a Windows Server 2008 Core installation. Also, once the Hyper-V role has been enabled, Windows Server 2008 becomes like a privileged virtual machine running on the Hyper-V hypervisor. Since the hypervisor is responsible for things like resource allocation, there is little danger of the hypervisor running out of resources under normal operating circumstances.

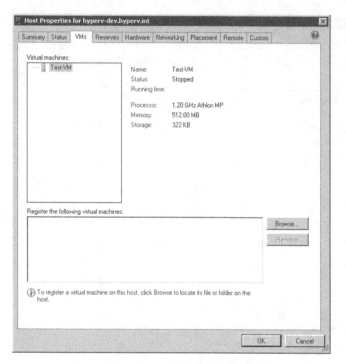

Figure 3-19. *The VMs tab shows the virtual machines that are currently on the host.*

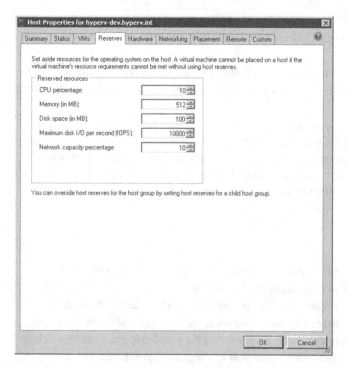

Figure 3-20. *The Reserves tab is used to guarantee resources for the host.*

- *Hardware*: This tab lists the hardware that is available for the host, as shown in Figure 3-21. There is not much you can do on this tab. However, if you click any of the storage disks, you can select if you want that disk available for the placement of virtual machines.

Figure 3-21. *The Hardware tab gives an overview of the hardware available on the host.*

- *Networking*: This tab is where you can add or remove virtual networks for a host, as shown in Figure 3-22. You can also adjust the properties of an existing virtual network.

- *Placement*: This tab lets you specify the default path for virtual machine placement on the host, as shown in Figure 3-23. You can also add or remove paths from the host. Note that you must have at least one path for the host.

Figure 3-22. *The Networking tab gives an overview of the available virtual networks for the host.*

Figure 3-23. *The Placement tab is where you can specify paths for virtual machines.*

- *Remote*: On this tab, you can set the remote connection port for the host. The default port number is 2179, as shown in Figure 3-24.

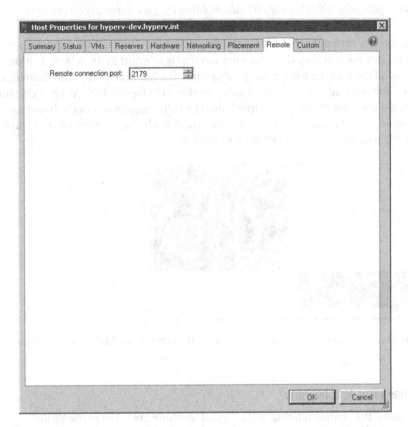

Figure 3-24. *You can change the default remote connection port on the Remote tab.*

- *Custom*: On this tab, you can define up to ten custom attributes for the host. This may be useful for filtering the view or scripting.

Virtual Machines View

Now, let's take a look at the Virtual Machines view. As you would expect, this allows you to manage your virtual machines.

Virtual Machines View Navigation, Results, and Details Panes

In the navigation section on the left, you can select a host or host group. When you select the host or host group, the results pane will be populated with the virtual machines that are on the host or hosts, as shown in Figure 3-25.

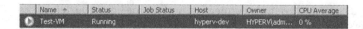

Name ▲	Status	Job Status	Host	Owner	CPU Average
▶ Test-VM	Running		hyperv-dev	HYPERV\adm...	0 %

Figure 3-25. *The results pane showing the virtual machines that are currently on the host*

When you select a virtual machine, the details pane has the same tabs that appear at the bottom of the Hosts view, but they show information that is relevant to the selected virtual machine, instead of the host. One interesting thing about the Summary tab is the thumbnail that is visible on the right side of that tab's display, as shown in Figure 3-26. At a glance, you can see what is going on inside the virtual machine. The CPU usage graph at the bottom is also useful for troubleshooting a situation where a virtual machine has an "out-of-control" process that is taking CPU resources from other virtual machines.

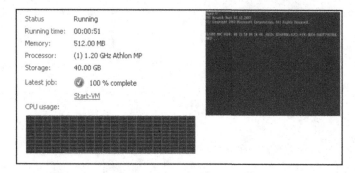

Figure 3-26. *The Summary tab gives a quick overview of the virtual machine's current state.*

Virtual Machines View Actions Pane

In the Actions pane, the actions relating to the virtual machine are listed in the Virtual Machine section, which is divided into three subsections. Altogether, these three subsections offer the following actions:

- Start a virtual machine
- Stop a virtual machine
- Pause a virtual machine
- Save the state of a virtual machine
- Discard the saved state of a virtual machine
- Shut down a virtual machine
- Connect to a virtual machine's console
- Migrate the virtual machine to another host
- Create a new checkpoint (a point-in-time snapshot of the virtual machine)
- Manage existing checkpoints
- Disable undo disks (these were used in Microsoft Virtual Server instead of checkpoints)

- Repair the virtual machine (if it is left in a failed state after a particular job)

- Install guest services in the virtual machine

- Create a new template from the virtual machine

- Clone the virtual machine

- Store the virtual machine in the library

- Delete the virtual machine

- View the graphical representation of the virtual machine's networking

- View the virtual machine's properties

If you click Properties, you will see a new window displaying the virtual machine's properties. This window has the following tabs:

- *General:* This tab displays some general information for the virtual machine, as shown in Figure 3-27. Here, you can adjust the name, description, owner, cost center (useful for calculating chargeback if you are using chargeback accounting), tag (used for filtering the view), and operating system of the virtual machine.

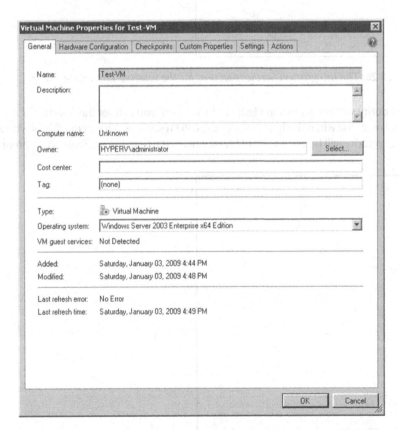

Figure 3-27. *The General tab of the selected virtual machine's Properties window*

- *Hardware Configuration*: This tab lets you view, add, or modify hardware settings for the virtual machine. The Advanced section has three settings areas:
  - The Integration Services section lets you choose which Integration Services will be offered to the virtual machine, as shown in Figure 3-28.

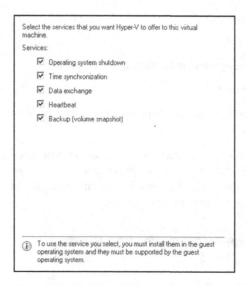

Figure 3-28. *The Integration Services section for the selected virtual machine*

  - The Priority section, shown in Figure 3-29, is where you can set the priority for the virtual machine when the host is assigning CPU resources. Virtual machines with a higher priority will be assigned CPU resources first when there is resource contention.

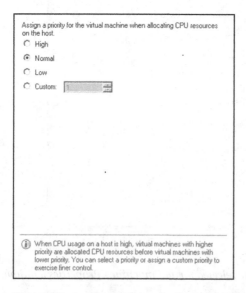

Figure 3-29. *Set the CPU priority higher for those virtual machines that need it.*

- The Availability section lets you choose to make the virtual machine highly available. If that option is selected, VMM will attempt to place the virtual machine in a group of clustered host servers.

- *Checkpoints*: On this tab, you can manage the checkpoints for a virtual machine, as shown in Figure 3-30. You can create new checkpoints, remove existing checkpoints, restore a virtual machine to a past checkpoint, and view the properties of an existing checkpoint. If you click the Properties button on the Checkpoints tab, you'll see a window with two tabs:

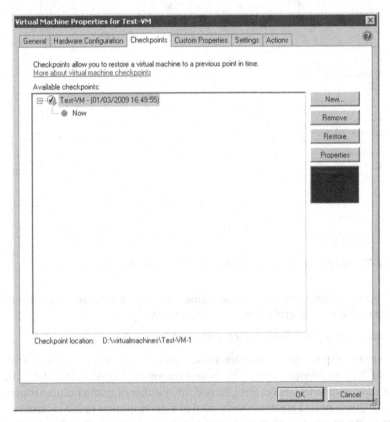

Figure 3-30. *The available checkpoints for the selected virtual machine*

- The General tab shows when the checkpoint was created. This is useful if you want to revert a virtual machine back to a specific checkpoint.

- The Hardware Configuration tab shows more information about the hardware state of the particular checkpoint, as shown in Figure 3-31.

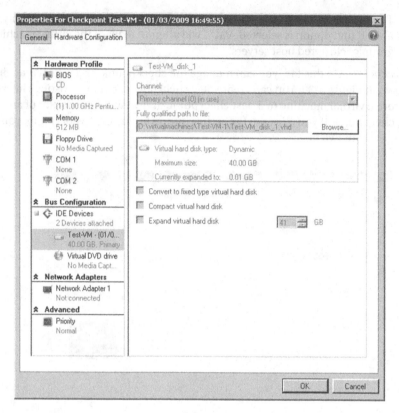

Figure 3-31. *The hardware configuration for the selected checkpoint*

- *Custom Properties*: This tab allows you to define up to ten custom properties for a virtual machine. These are useful for filtering views and scripting.

- *Settings*: This tab lets you adjust two settings (see Figure 3-32):

  - The number of quota points that are associated with the virtual machine. This is used for the Self-Service user role to control the amount of virtual machines that a user can provision. Users cannot exceed the number of quota points assigned to them. Quota points are commonly used in a development or lab environment. Quota points are discussed in more detail in the "Creating the Self-Service User Role" section later in the chapter.

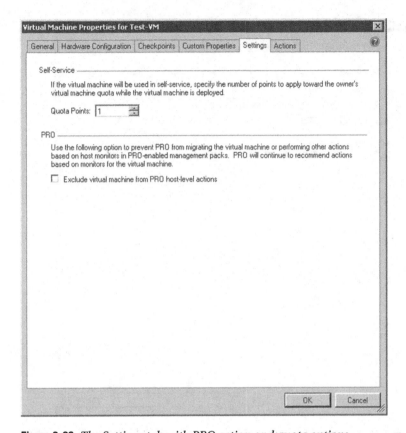

Figure 3-32. *The Settings tab with PRO action and quota options*

- Whether the virtual machine will participate in PRO host-level actions. You may want to override PRO settings if you do not want a particular virtual machine to migrate from the host. This is useful for keeping redundant virtual machines like domain controllers or cluster nodes on different host servers. When PRO is enabled for VMM, it can be set to automatically take certain actions (like migrating a virtual machine to another host). This setting overrides the PRO actions.

- *Actions*: On this tab, you can define actions for the virtual machine when the physical host server starts and stops, as shown in Figure 3-33. You can also set the delay (in seconds) for the virtual machine to start. This may be useful for staggering the startup of systems that depend on each other. A common example would be a three-tiered (application, database, and web) application. The application server depends on the database server. The web server uses components from the application server. So, you will want to stagger the startup of servers appropriately.

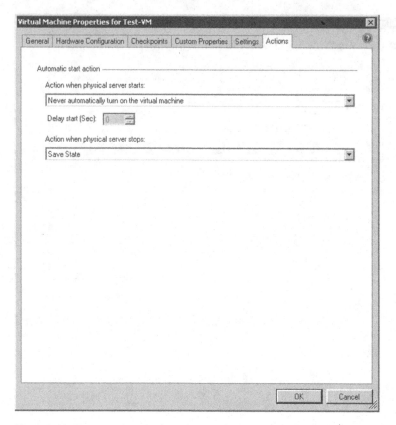

Figure 3-33. *You can stagger the startup of virtual machines in the Actions tab.*

Library View

The Library view is where you can view and modify all of your library resources and settings. The navigation section lets you navigate to your library servers and view the library resources (*.vhd files, templates, hardware profiles, and guest operating system profiles) that are in your library.

If you select any of the items in the results pane as you are navigating the Library view, the details pane will be populated with a Summary tab and Latest Job tab, as shown in Figure 3-34. The Summary tab gives you some basic information about the item, and the Latest Job tab shows some information about the last job to run on the particular item.

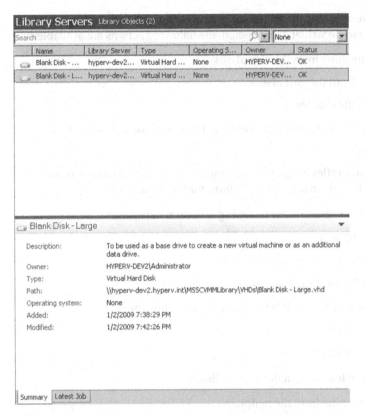

Figure 3-34. *The Summary tab of a *.vhd file in the VMM library*

The Filters section lets you filter your view of the items in your library. If you have selected the Library Servers item in the navigation section, you will see Library Actions options in the Actions pane. These actions include creating a new template, hardware profile, or guest operating system profile. You can also view the library settings, as shown in Figure 3-35. The only setting for a library is the refresh interval, which is how often the library server will be scanned for new items (set in hours).

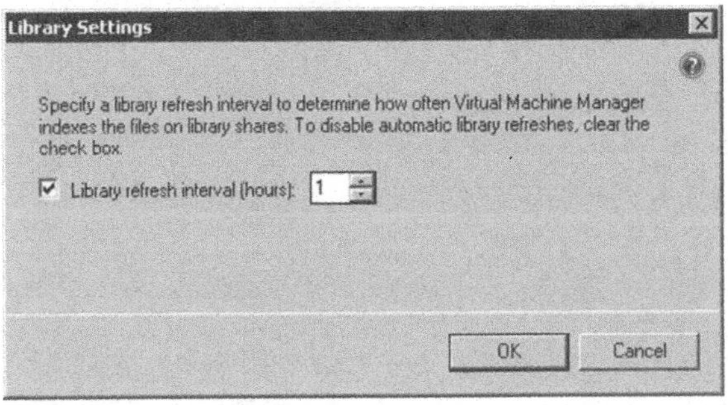

Figure 3-35. *You can adjust the automatic library refresh interval.*

The other actions that are available in the Actions pane depend on which item you have selected in the library. If you have a virtual disk selected, the following actions are available:

- Create a new virtual machine from the virtual disk
- Create a new template from the virtual disk
- Open the virtual disk's file location
- Disable the virtual disk so that it is not available for use in new virtual machines
- Remove the virtual disk
- View the virtual disk properties where you can adjust the name, description, owner, path, operating system, and virtualization platform for the virtual disk

If you have a virtual machine selected, the following actions are available:

- Deploy the virtual machine
- Repair the virtual machine
- Open the file location for the virtual machine
- Disable the virtual machine so that it is not available for deployment
- Remove the virtual machine
- View the virtual machine's properties

If you select a template, the following actions are available:

- Create a new virtual machine from the template
- Create a new template from the template
- Repair the template
- Disable the template so that it is not available for virtual machine creation
- Remove the template
- View the template's properties

If you select a guest operating system or hardware profile, the following actions are available:

- Copy the profile
- Remove the profile
- View the properties of the profile

Jobs View

In the Jobs view, the results pane shows the jobs that are in progress or have completed. If you selected a job, the details pane will be populated with three tabs:

- *Summary*: This tab gives you some general information about the job. including what properties were changed by the job, as shown in Figure 3-36.

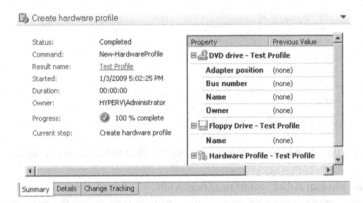

Figure 3-36. *The Summary tab for a job gives an overview of the selected job.*

- *Details*: This tab shows the steps involved in the particular job, along with the start and end time, as shown in Figure 3-37.

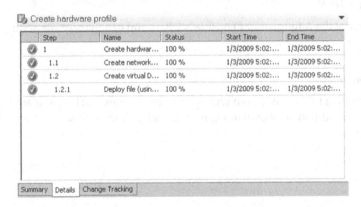

Figure 3-37. *If you want to see the steps involved in a selected job, view the Details tab.*

- *Change Tracking*: This tab shows you any changes that occurred to an item as a result of the job, as shown in Figure 3-38.

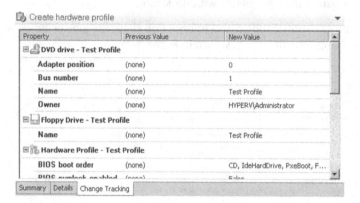

Figure 3-38. *The Change Tracking tab shows any changes that the selected job made.*

In the Actions pane, you can either restart or cancel a job.

The Jobs view is very useful for troubleshooting and auditing. It gives you the exact details that you need to assess if something has changed anywhere in your virtual infrastructure. You can see the steps involved with the change, what was changed, how long the change took, and when the change happened.

Administration View

The Administration view of the Administrator console is where you can manage the settings for VMM.

General Administration Items

If you select the General item in the navigation section, the results pane will be populated with several items that can be modified, as shown in Figure 3-39. Select one of these items and click Modify in the Actions pane.

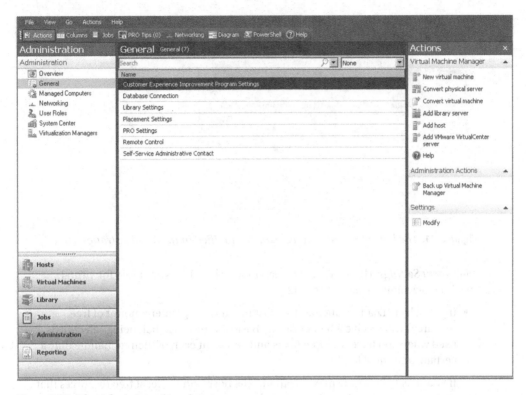

Figure 3-39. *The Administration view*

- *Customer Experience Improvement Program Settings*: Here, you can decide if you want to send information to the Microsoft Customer Experience Improvement Program.

- *Database Connection*: When you choose this and click Modify in the Actions pane, you will see database connection information, as shown in Figure 3-40. These settings cannot be modified.

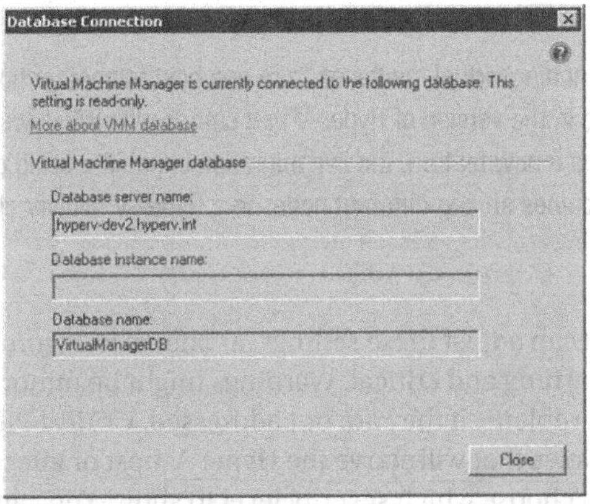

Figure 3-40. *You can see your VMM database details in the Database Connection section.*

- *Library Settings*: Here, you can modify the refresh interval for library items, as shown in Figure 3-41.

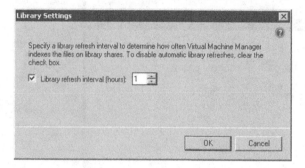

Figure 3-41. *The library refresh interval can be modified in the Administration view.*

- *Placement Settings*: This is where you can modify how hosts are rated for virtual machine placement (see Figure 3-42):

  - If you select "Load balancing" the host that has the greater amount of free resources will receive a higher rating. Basically, the Load balancing selection is used when you have multiple hosts and you want each of them to handle only a certain amount of load.

  - If you select "Resource maximization," the host with the least free resources that still meets the virtual machine's requirements will receive a higher rating. The "Resource maximization" option attempts to use all the available resources that it can for your Hyper-V hosts. You can use the sliders to give more weight to any of the four core resources: processor, memory, disk, and network utilization. If you have fewer hosts, you may want to choose "Resource maximization" to get the most out of your host's resources. This is an important distinction, because Hyper-V does not yet support a live migration feature to be able to load balance the virtual machines on different hosts dynamically without service interruption.

■**Note** Live migration, or the ability to migrate running virtual machines from one host to another host without any service interruption, will be supported in the version of Hyper-V that comes with Windows Server 2008 Release 2. Although not specifically stated as a new feature, the live migration capability could potentially allow dynamically load balancing virtual machines among different nodes in a Hyper-V failover cluster.

- *PRO Settings*: If PRO is enabled, you can adjust these settings, as shown in Figure 3-43. PRO tips have two severity levels: warning and critical. Warnings might be minor issues that may cause system availability problems if they are not addressed. Critical PRO tips are generally severe performance issues that will starve the Hyper-V host or guest virtual machines of resources. You can choose which severity level to show. You can also decide if you would like any PRO tips (such as a quick migration of a virtual machine to another host) to be implemented automatically.

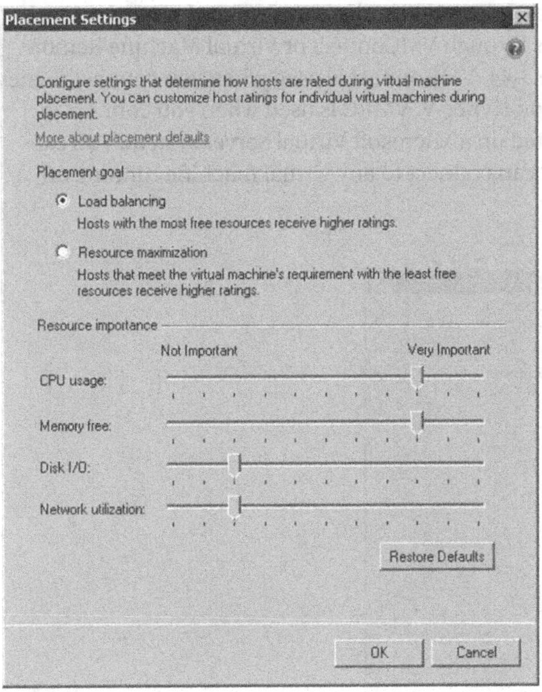

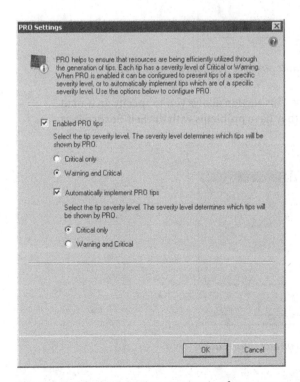

Figure 3-42. *You can adjust how your hosts are rated for virtual machine placement.*

Figure 3-43. *The PRO Settings section is where you can choose your options for PRO tips.*

- *Remote Control*: This section will allow you to adjust the port settings for connecting remotely to virtual machine consoles through VMConnect or Virtual Machine Remote Console (VMRC), as shown in Figure 3-44. VMConnect is used when you connect to the console of a virtual machine hosted on Hyper-V. VMRC is used when you connect to the console of a virtual machine hosted on a Microsoft Virtual Server system. You can also add VMRC access accounts that can connect to any virtual machine running on Virtual Server.

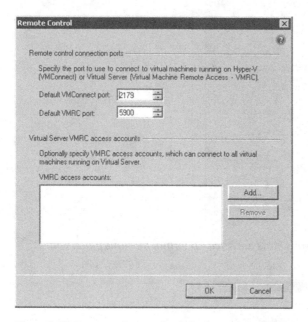

Figure 3-44. *You can change the default ports for VMConnect and VMRC.*

- *Self-Service Administrative Contact*: This section allows you to specify an e-mail address for users to contact when they have problems with the Self-Service Portal, as shown in Figure 3-45.

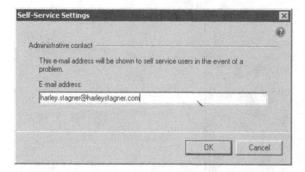

Figure 3-45. *Setting the Self-Service contact information*

Managed Computers Administration Items

In the navigation section of the Administration view, the Managed Computers section lets you update the agent, reassociate, or remove any computers that are managed by VMM (typically library and host servers). Figure 3-46 shows the list of managed computers.

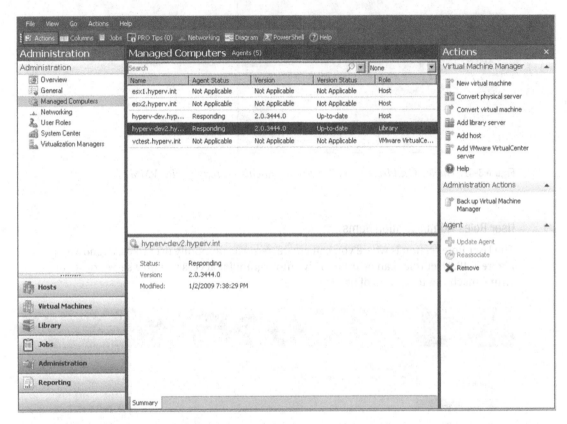

Figure 3-46. *Showing the computers that are currently managed by VMM*

Networking Administration Items

The Networking section contains the Global MAC Address Range item. This is the range of MAC addresses that are assigned to virtual machines when they are created. To modify this range, select the item and click Modify in the Actions pane. You will see the dialog box shown in Figure 3-47.

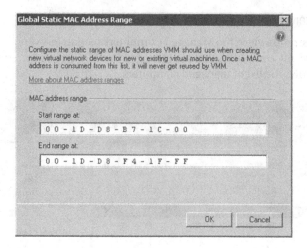

Figure 3-47. *The MAC address range for virtual machines created with VMM*

User Roles Administration Items

The User Role section is where you can create, remove, or modify user roles, as shown in
Figure 3-48. User roles can be used to give more granular access to a host server or set of
virtual machines to a group of users.

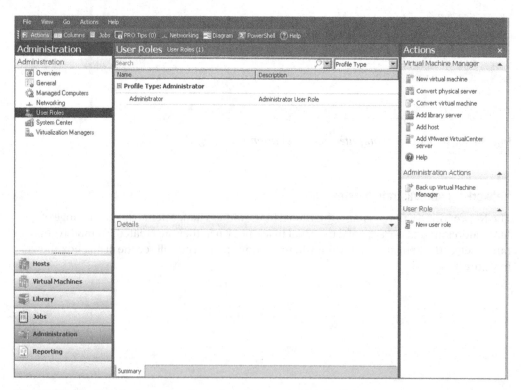

Figure 3-48. *The User Roles section is used to create user roles for delegation.*

System Center Administration Items

The System Center section is where you can define the SCOM server name and SCOM reporting server URL if you want to enable SCOM 2007 integration. Figure 3-49 shows these items listed in the results pane.

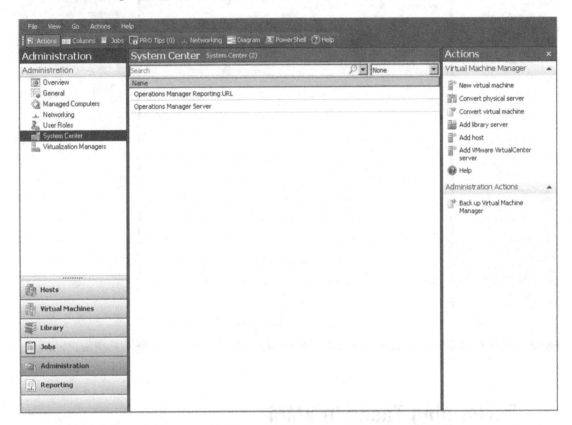

Figure 3-49. *The System Center section is where you enable SCOM 2007 integration for PRO.*

Virtualization Managers Administration Items

The Virtualization Managers section is where you can view and modify the properties of any third-party virtualization manager, such as VMware vCenter. Figure 3-50 shows an example of this section.

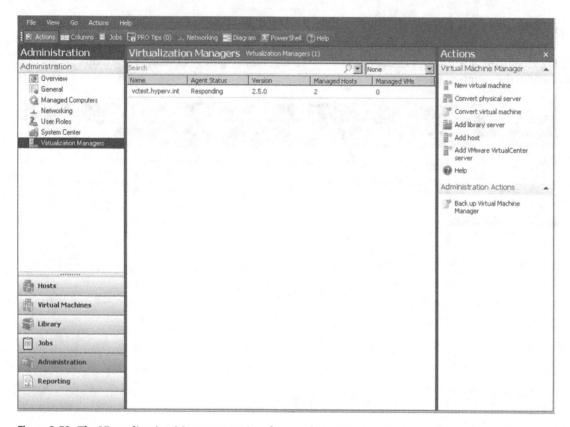

Figure 3-50. *The Virtualization Managers section shows other virtualization managers such as vCenter.*

Performing Tasks in VMM

Now that you are familiar with the VMM Administrator console, it's time to start using it. The first order of business after a fresh installation of VMM is to add a host.

Adding a Host

In the Actions pane, under Virtual Machine Manager, click Add Host. This will bring up the Add Hosts wizard. The first window prompts you to select the host location. This can be a Hyper-V or Virtual Server host that is a member of an Active Directory domain, a host that is on a perimeter network (such as a DMZ), or a VMware ESX host.

Adding an Active Directory Member Host

To add an Active Directory member host, follow these steps:

1. From the Add Hosts wizard's Select Host Location window, select "Windows Server-based host on an Active Directory Domain," and fill in the appropriate administrative credentials to connect to the host, as shown in Figure 3-51. Click Next.

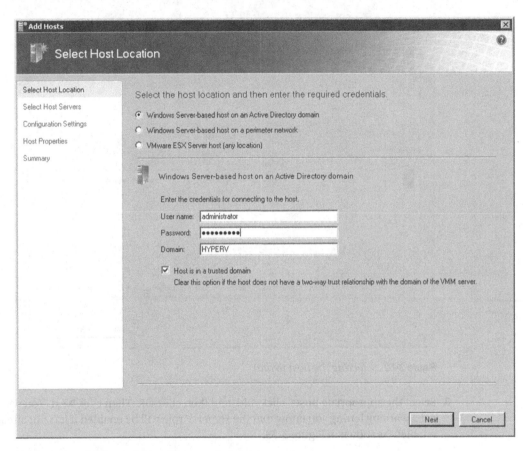

Figure 3-51. *Adding an Active Directory host*

2. The next window is where you select your host servers. You can either enter the computer names manually or search for them. To search for them, click the Search button. In the Computer Search window, select the Hyper-V option. This will limit the search to Hyper-V servers. Click Search in this window, and all of your Hyper-V servers in the domain should be listed, as shown in Figure 3-52.

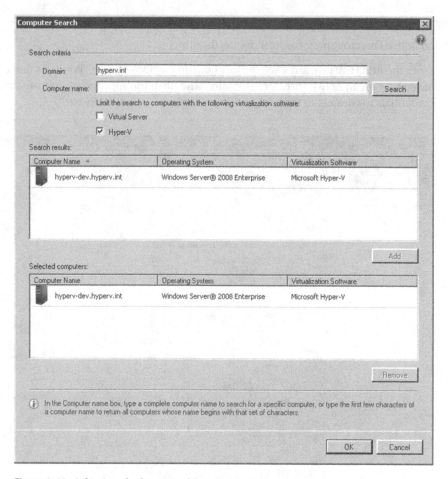

Figure 3-52. *Selecting the host to add*

3. Select the appropriate hosts, click Add, and then click OK. Then click Next. You will get a warning letting you know that the Hyper-V role will be enabled if it is not already enabled, as shown in Figure 3-53.

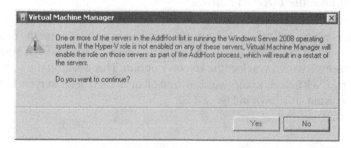

Figure 3-53. *If the Windows Server 2008 host does not have the Hyper-V role, it will be set up.*

4. In the Configuration Settings window, you can assign a host to a certain host group by selecting one from the drop-down list, as shown in Figure 3-54. You can also reassociate the host if it is being managed by another VMM server. Make your selections, and then click Next to continue.

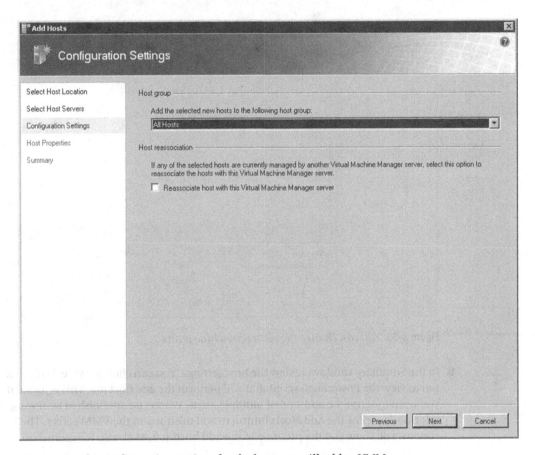

Figure 3-54. *The configuration settings for the host you will add to VMM*

5. In the Host Properties window, you can define default paths to use as virtual machine file storage paths. You can also change the port number for using VMConnect to connect to virtual machine consoles. The default is 2179, as shown in Figure 3-55. Click Next to continue.

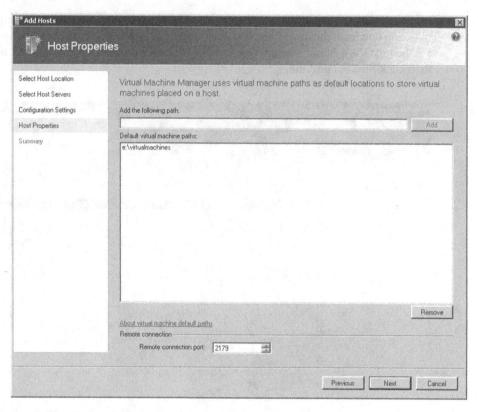

Figure 3-55. *You can change the virtual machine paths.*

6. In the Summary window, review the host settings. You can click the View Script button to view the PowerShell script that will perform the add host job. This is useful if you want to script the addition of multiple hosts. When you are finished reviewing this information, click the Add Hosts button to add the hosts to the VMM server. The Jobs window will show you the progress of the add hosts job, as shown in Figure 3-56.

Note You may notice that after you add a fully patched (through Windows Update) Hyper-V host to the VMM server, it still has the Needs Attention status. If you investigate the status, it will say "Upgrade Available" for the Virtualization Service version. There are two updates that were not available through Windows Update at the time of this writing that need to be applied to the Hyper-V host. One is for Hyper-V (http://www.microsoft.com/downloads/details.aspx?FamilyID=FD44B4E3-2DCC-4299-B345-BC09A9A37B60&displaylang=en) and the other is for BITS (http://www.microsoft.com/downloads/details.aspx?familyid=9EC9DBB9-82AD-4D34-9267-76A0126A8F18&displaylang=en).

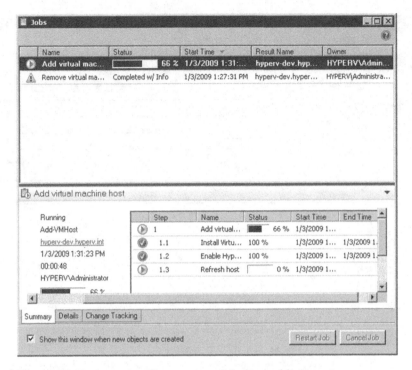

Figure 3-56. *You can view the progress of the host addition.*

Adding a Perimeter Host

A *perimeter host* is a host that is not a member of Active Directory. This may be a host that is in a workgroup or a host that resides in your network's demilitarized zone (DMZ), such as a host that has company web servers as virtual machine guests.

Before you can add the perimeter host, you need to install the VMM Agent manually on the host and generate a security file for the host in the process. To install the VMM Agent, follow the instructions in the "VMM Agent" section earlier in this chapter. Then copy the security file that is generated to a location that the VMM server can access.

After installing the VMM Agent, choose the "Windows Server-based host on a perimeter network" option from the Add Hosts wizard's Select Host Location window. Fill in the computer name or IP address, and the encryption key that you defined when you installed the VMM Agent and created the security file. You also need to type in or browse to the security file that you created, as shown in the example in Figure 3-57. Then click Add to add the appropriate host to the Selected hosts section. The rest of the process is the same as adding an Active Directory member host, as described in the previous section.

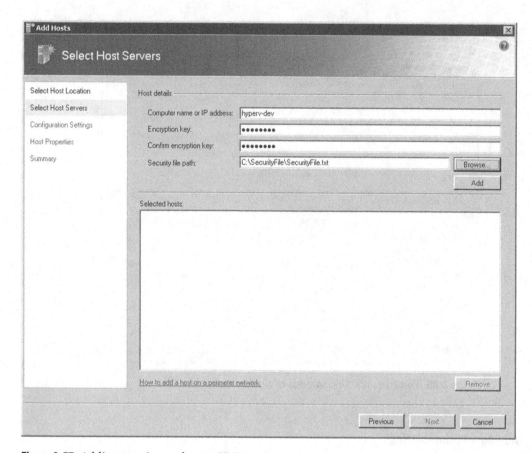

Figure 3-57. *Adding a perimeter host to VMM*

Adding a VMware ESX Host

Before you can add a VMware ESX host to VMM, you need to add the VirtualCenter server that is managing the ESX host. Follow these steps to add this server, and then add the host:

1. Select Add VMware VirtualCenter Server from the Virtual Machine Manager section of the Actions pane.

2. In the Add VMware VirtualCenter Server window, fill in the appropriate credentials and clear the "Communicate with VMware ESX Server hosts in secure mode" check box if you want to require only credentials to communicate with VMware ESX servers, as shown in Figure 3-58. Click OK.

3. You will be prompted to import the VirtualCenter machine's security certificate into the VMM server's certificate store to continue importing the VirtualCenter machine, as shown in Figure 3-59. Click Import.

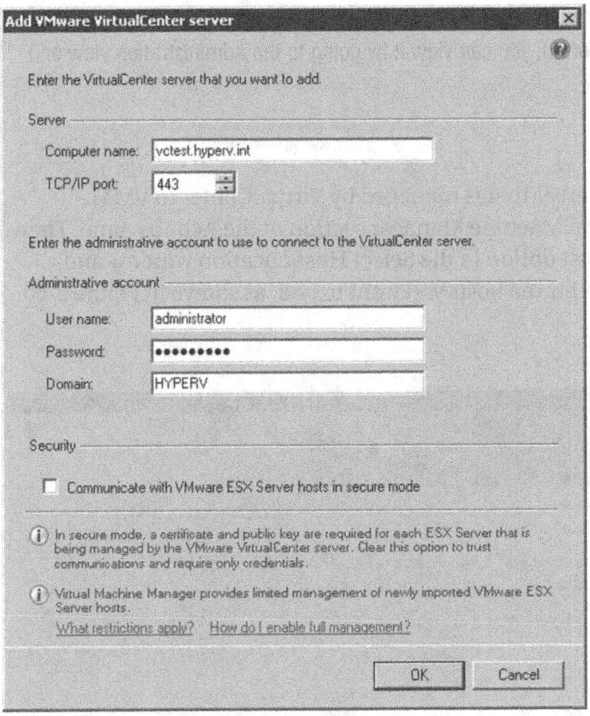

Figure 3-58. *Adding the vCenter server to VMM*

To verify the identity of the VMware VirtualCenter server, Virtual Machine Manager must import the server's security certificate into the local machine certificate store.

⊗ Hide Certificate

▭ Certificate Information

This CA Root certificate is not trusted. To enable trust, install this certificate in the Trusted Root Certification Authorities Store.

Issued to:	VMware
Issued by:	VMware
Valid from:	1/3/2009 to 1/3/2011
Serial number:	00A8BE3A3AA90DB505
Public key:	30 81 89 02 81 81 00 f3 c5 2c 2a a3 f2 98 27 de 7c 94 50 a9 c5 8f 9d 68 93 63 13 83 51 fd f5 7e 89 63 1d 3c e6 5b 02 5b 95 4a f6 e0 a4 a7 51 e4 46 6f 60 03 fa d4 e6 68 48 4e 09 08 65 4a 0f 47 bf 60 1e 02 cb be 96 29 37 c4 7f 89 2b 10 bd df 6b 98 fd 73 48 82 27 da c4 e7 ef 1e e0 f0 58 3e e9 8f cb 3b 04 2e 4e 91 f5 24 8c 82 4b 98 3a 2f 15 e4 94 15 dd 33 93 91 cc f1 4b 08 78 91 1d 7b 84 6a de da 77 ce 13 02 03 01 00 01
Thumbprint:	C4596E121AE89DBE3B3544D80C64F1C82D160F02

ⓘ If you do not import the certificate, Virtual Machine Manager will not add the VMware VirtualCenter server.

Import   Cancel

Figure 3-59. *Importing the VirtualCenter server's security certificate*

Note Once the VirtualCenter server is imported, you can view it by going to the Administration view and selecting Virtualization Managers.

4. Now you can add the ESX host server that is managed by VirtualCenter to VMM. Choose Add Host from the Virtual Machine Manager section of the Actions pane. Then select the VMware ESX Server host option in the Select Host Location window and enter the appropriate credentials for the hosts you want to add, as shown in Figure 3-60. Click Next to continue.

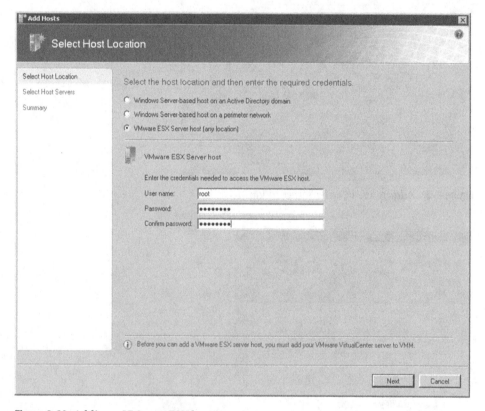

Figure 3-60. *Adding a VMware ESX host server*

5. In the Select Host Servers window, enter the appropriate hostname or IP address for the ESX hosts that you want to add. Click the Add button for each host you want to add. Click Next to continue.

6. In the Summary window, review the settings, and then click the Add Hosts button to add the VMware ESX hosts. You can view the status of the add ESX hosts job in the Jobs window.

When the ESX hosts are added, they will show up in the Hosts view. You will notice that they have a status of OK (Limited), as shown in Figure 3-61. When the hosts have the OK (Limited) status, you will be able to perform only the following VMware virtual machine operations:

- Start

- Stop

- Pause

- Modify properties

- Create a new checkpoint

- Manage checkpoints

- Remove

- Migrate with VMware VMotion

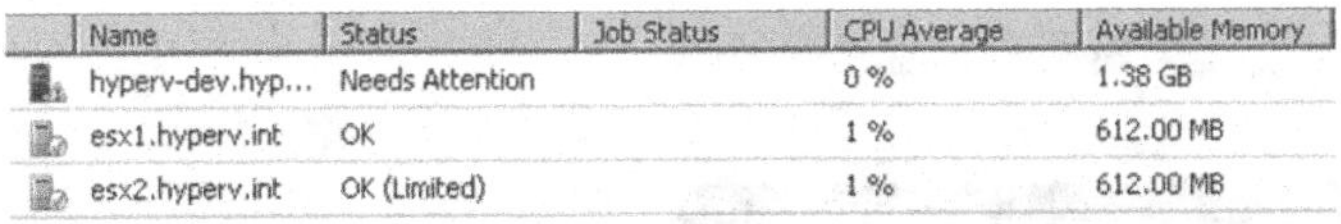

Name	Status	Job Status	CPU Average	Available Memory
hyperv-dev.hyp...	Needs Attention		0 %	1.38 GB
esx1.hyperv.int	OK		1 %	612.00 MB
esx2.hyperv.int	OK (Limited)		1 %	612.00 MB

Figure 3-61. *The ESX hosts have a status of OK (Limited) when they are first added.*

To change the status to OK, right-click the ESX host, choose Properties, and select the Security tab. Fill in the appropriate administrative credentials for the ESX host, as shown in Figure 3-62, and then click OK.

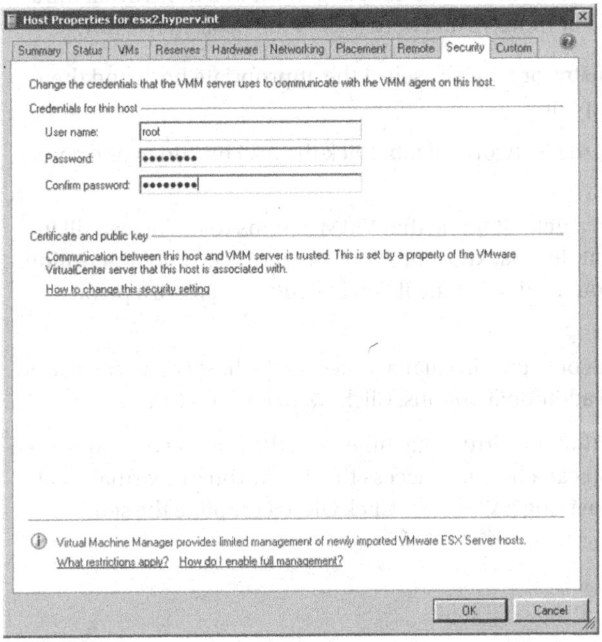

Figure 3-62. *Setting up the appropriate credentials for the ESX host*

After this is complete, the ESX host will be listed with a status of OK, as shown in Figure 3-63. Now you can perform the following operations in addition to the ones previously listed:

- Save state

- Discard saved state

- Migrate across VirtualCenter server

- Store in the VMM library

- Clone within the same VirtualCenter

- Clone on the same ESX server host

- Perform virtual-to-virtual (V2V) conversion

- Create from a VMM template

- Create from a blank disk

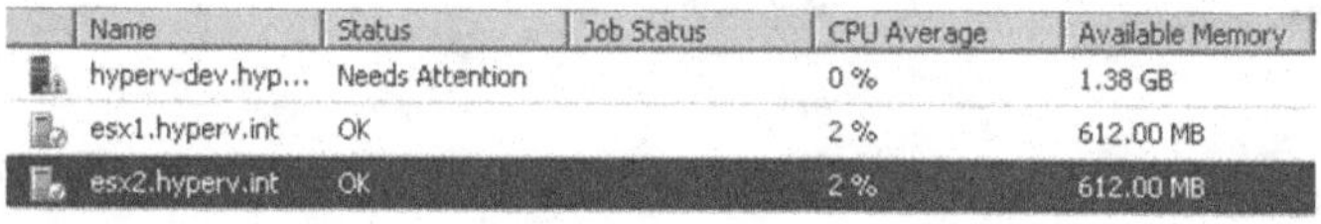

Name	Status	Job Status	CPU Average	Available Memory
hyperv-dev.hyp...	Needs Attention		0 %	1.38 GB
esx1.hyperv.int	OK		2 %	612.00 MB
esx2.hyperv.int	OK		2 %	612.00 MB

Figure 3-63. *The ESX host with a status of OK after the credentials were entered*

Adding Networking to a Host

One of the first tasks you will want to do after the host is added to VMM in a new virtual infra-structure implementation is to add one or more virtual networks to the host. Here's how:

1. In the Hosts view in the Administrator console, select the appropriate host, and then select Properties in the Actions pane.

2. In the Properties window, click the Networking tab. Click the Add button to add a new virtual network.

3. The network will be added with a default name that VMM assigns to it. You can fill in the name, network tag (for example, "Backup" for a backup network), and description for the virtual network. Then you need to decide if you are going to create a private, internal, or external network.

   - A private network is one that only the virtual machines on the host server can access. The private network has no additional options. Click OK to complete the setup.

   - An internal network is one that the virtual machines and the host server can access. If you select this option, you can choose to access the host through a virtual local area network (VLAN) by providing a VLAN ID. Click OK to complete the setup.

- An external network is bound to a physical network adapter, and it enables the virtual machines to access the network outside the Hyper-V host server. If you want to create an external network, select the "Physical network adapter" option. You are presented with several options, as shown in Figure 3-64. Continue with the following steps.

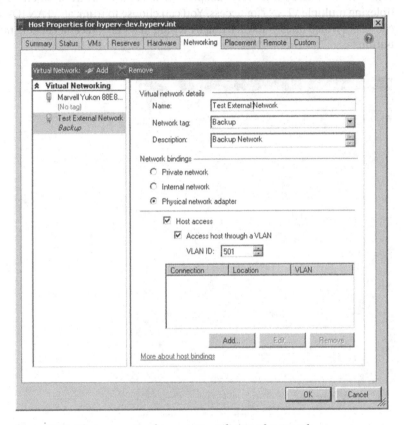

Figure 3-64. *The properties for an external virtual network*

4. By default, the virtual machines on the host can access the host through the physical network adapter. If you do not want to allow this, clear the Host access check box. If you need the virtual machines to access the host through a VLAN, check the "Access host through a VLAN" box and select the appropriate VLAN ID.

5. You need to add a physical network adapter. To do this, click the Add button at the bottom of the window.

6. In the Switch Binding window, select the host network adapter from the drop-down list, as shown in Figure 3-65. If you want to enable VLANs on the network adapter, select the "Enable VLANs on this connection" box. Two VLAN modes are possible:

- Access mode, where the network card is accessing only a single VLAN.

- Trunk mode, where the network adapter will act as a VLAN trunk when it is multiplexing multiple VLANs for access. You can choose to trunk all VLAN IDs, or you can select which ones you will trunk by typing in a VLAN ID and clicking the Add button.

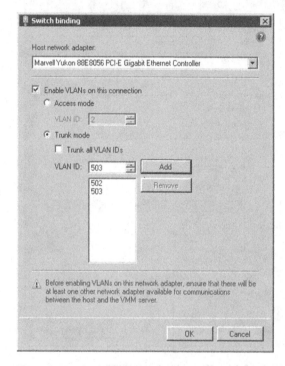

Figure 3-65. *The VLAN settings for your external virtual network*

7. Click OK in the Switch Binding window, and then click OK in the Networking tab.

Adjusting Host Server Reserves

The other host properties settings you might be interested in are on the Reserves tab of the Properties window. Here, you can reserve a certain amount of resources for the host operating system, as shown in Figure 3-66. You can adjust the CPU percentage, memory (in megabytes), disk space (in megabytes), maximum disk I/O per second, and network capacity percentage.

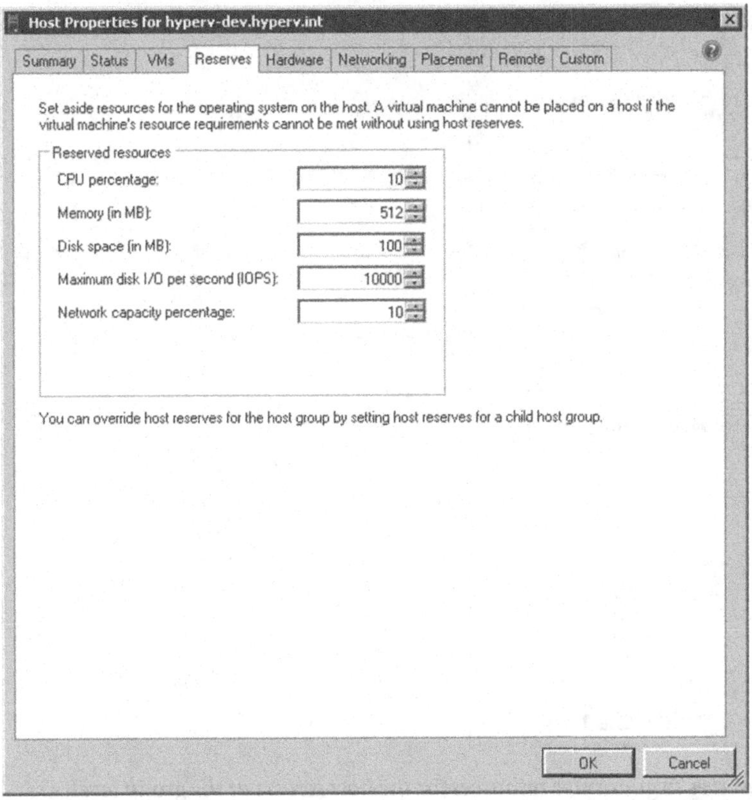

Figure 3-66. *Setting the reserves to guarantee resources for the host operating system*

Again, these settings allow you to guarantee that the operating system (Windows Server 2008) in the parent partition has a certain amount of resources available to it. This will ensure that the guests residing on the host do not consume resources that the host operating system needs to function properly.

Adding a Host to a Host Group

Host groups form a hierarchy that allows you to delegate permissions to the hosts contained in the group. This makes it much easier for administrators to manage the Hyper-V host servers as one group instead of individually. Host groups are also used with the Self-Service Portal to define which hosts a particular user role may access.

To create a host group, select All Hosts in the navigation pane and click "New host group" in the Actions pane. When the host group shows up in the navigation pane, give it a name.

You can set Reserves properties for the host group by selecting the group in the navigation pane and clicking Properties in the Actions pane. Click the Host Reserves tab and adjust the settings as desired, as shown in Figure 3-67.

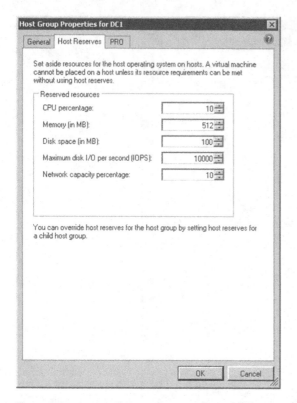

Figure 3-67. *Setting the reserves to guarantee resources for the host servers at the group level*

If you have enabled SCOM 2007 integration, you can also adjust the PRO settings for the host group. Select the host group in the navigation pane, click Properties in the Actions pane, and click the PRO tab, as shown in Figure 3-68. Here, you can choose to inherit the PRO settings from the parent host group (the very top host group will always be identified as All Hosts). You can also choose to override the settings inherited from the parent host group. You can enable PRO tips and choose the tip severity level (critical only or warning and critical). You can also choose to automatically implement PRO tips on the host group for critical or warning and critical PRO tips. This gives you more control over the PRO tips that you want VMM to automatically implement. Some PRO tips may suggest that a "quick migration" be performed for a virtual machine to migrate from one host to another. This may not be ideal situation during business hours, because a quick migration causes the virtual machine to be unavailable for a short time.

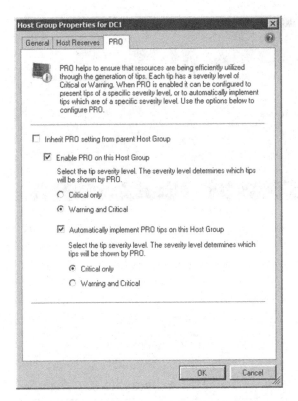

Figure 3-68. *Setting the PRO options for the host group*

Adding a Library Server

A library server is just a file share that has been added to VMM 2008. Library servers are used to store items like ISO images, virtual machine templates, hardware and guest operating system profiles, and virtual machines. They are a central repository for these items to make it easier for a Hyper-V administrator to access them when a virtual machine needs to be deployed or modified. The library server enables the Hyper-V administrator to deploy a virtual machine using the files stored in the library server to any host that can also access the library share.

By default, the server that the VMM server component is installed on is also a library server. However, you may want to add more library servers. To add a new library server, follow these steps:

1. Click Add Library Server under Virtual Machine Manager in the Actions pane.

2. In the first Add Library Server wizard window, enter the administrative credentials you will use to communicate with the library server, and then click Next.

3. In the Select Library Servers window, shown in Figure 3-69, you can either type in the computer name of the library server you want to add or search for it in Active Directory. Once you have selected the library server, click the Add button. Then click Next.

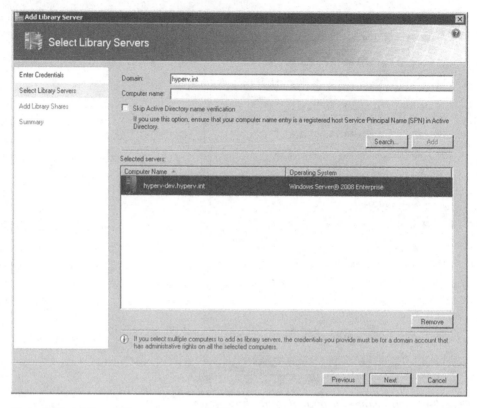

Figure 3-69. *Adding a library server to VMM*

4. The Add Library Shares window will enumerate any shares that are on the target server. Select the shares that you would like to be library shares, and then click Next.

5. In the Summary window, click the Add Library Servers button.

Creating a Hardware Profile

Hardware profiles are used to predefine hardware settings for a virtual machine. Hardware profiles are useful when you want to use a particular set of hardware settings for a virtual machine, and you do not want to configure these manually for each new virtual machine that is created.

For example, if you know that every database server that you deploy will require 2GB of memory and a 20GB virtual hard disk, and each IT management server that you deploy will require only 1GB of memory and a 13GB virtual hard disk, you could create two hardware profiles: one to use to deploy your database servers (with 2GB of memory and a 20GB virtual hard disk) and another to deploy your IT management servers (with 1GB of memory and a 13GB virtual hard disk). This lets you configure the hardware once and apply it to many virtual machine deployments, even if those deployments will be using different operating systems.

To create a new hardware profile, go to the Library view in the Administrator console, and click "New hardware profile" in the Actions pane. In the New Hardware Profile window's General tab, give the hardware profile a name, description, and owner (by default, the owner is the user who is creating the hardware profile). Click the Hardware Settings tab, and adjust the hardware settings and add any new hardware that you would like, as shown in Figure 3-70.

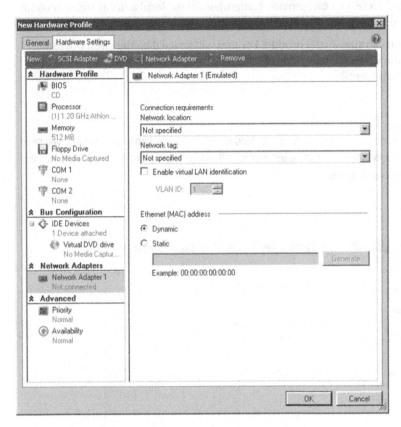

Figure 3-70. *The hardware settings for your hardware profile*

After you've completed the hardware profile, it will be listed in the results pane of the Library view when Profiles is selected.

Creating a Guest Operating System Profile

Creating a guest operating system profile allows you to automate some of the settings for a Windows guest operating system so that you do not need to do this manually every time a new virtual machine is created.

To create a guest operating system profile, go to the Library view in the Administrator console and click "New guest OS profile" in the Actions pane. On the General tab of the New Guest OS Profile window, give the guest operating system profile a name, description, and owner (by default, the owner is the user who is creating the guest operating system profile).

On the Guest OS tab, you can adjust the guest operating settings. This tab is divided into three main parts: General Settings, Networking, and Scripts.

Under General Settings, set the following:

- *Identity Information*: Specify the computer name, full name, and organization name that you would like to use. If you leave an asterisk in the Computer Name field, a random computer name will be generated.

- *Admin Password*: Here, you can provide credentials for the local administrator account that will be used in the guest operating installation.

- *Product Key*: You can specify the product key that will be used by the guest operating system installation, as shown in Figure 3-71. You can also specify that the product key is defined in an answer file.

Note Answer files are used to automate the setup of Windows operating systems. Any item that you need to provide information for during the setup can be automated with an answer file that is used during an unattended installation of the operating system.

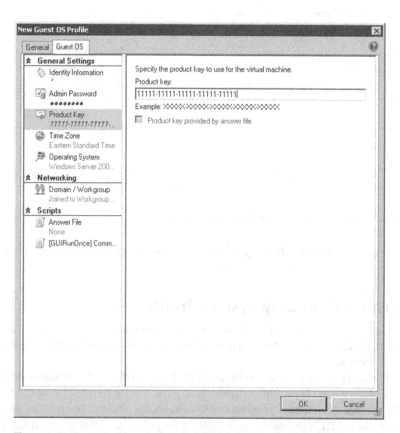

Figure 3-71. *Entering the product key for your Windows installation*

- *Time Zone*: Select the appropriate time zone.

- *Operating System*: Select the appropriate operating system, as shown in Figure 3-72.

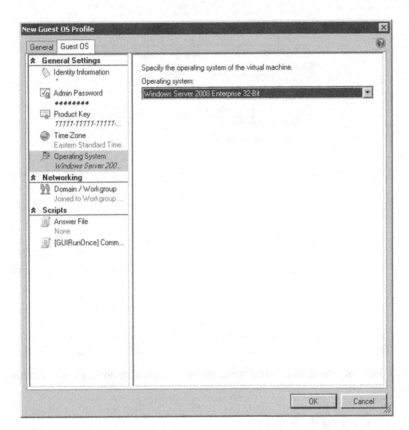

Figure 3-72. *Choosing the operating system version for your guest operating system profile*

Under Networking, select the Domain/Workgroup item, as shown in Figure 3-73. Here, you can choose to leave the guest operating system in a workgroup or join the guest to a domain and provide credentials for joining the domain.

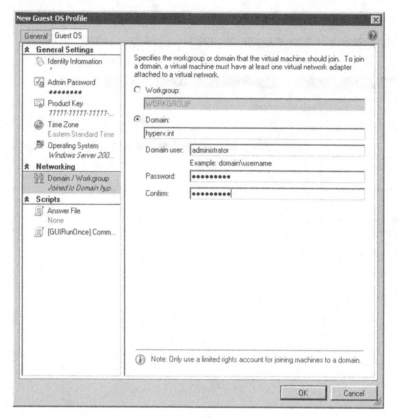

Figure 3-73. *Entering the domain credentials to join the guest operating system to the domain*

Under Scripts, you can set the following:

- *Answer File*: You can provide an answer file to automate the installation of the guest operating system (sysprep.inf for Windows XP/Windows Server 2003 guests and unattended.xml for Windows Vista/Windows Server 2008 guests), as shown in Figure 3-74. (See Chapter 2 for details about the format and use of an unattended.xml file for use with Windows Deployment Services.)

- *[GUIRUNONCE] Commands*: Here, you can specify a command to run the first time a user logs on. Figure 3-75 shows an example of adding the gpupdate /force command, which will make sure that group policies that need to be applied to the operating system are applied immediately after the first logon. You may want to use GUIRUNONCE commands to perform any cleanup tasks that you need to do after deployment, such as ensuring that group policies are applied to the operating system.

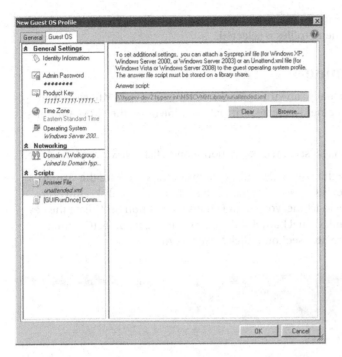

Figure 3-74. *Setting the location of any answer file that you need to automate the guest operating system installation*

Figure 3-75. *You can set commands to run once when a user first logs in to the guest operating system.*

When you have completed your new guest operating system profile, it will be listed in the results pane of the Library view when Profiles is selected.

Creating a Virtual Machine

At some point, you will want to actually run virtual machines on your Hyper-V hosts. To do this, you must create a virtual machine. To create a virtual machine using the VMM Administrator console, follow these steps:

1. In the Virtual Machine Manager section of the Actions pane, click "New virtual machine."

2. In the first New Virtual Machine wizard window, choose your source for the virtual machine. You can use an existing virtual machine, template, or hard disk. However, since this is the first virtual machine, you should choose the option to "Create the new virtual machine with a blank virtual hard disk," as shown in Figure 3-76. (Creating a template is discussed in the next section.) Click Next to continue.

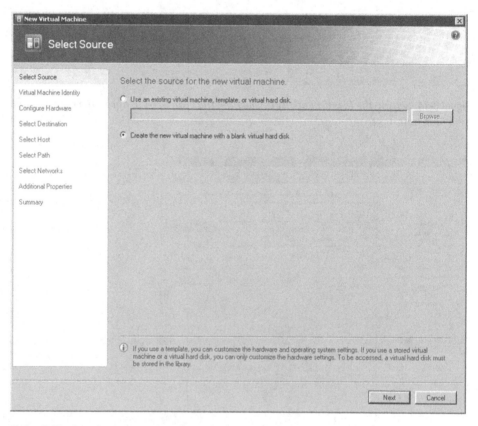

Figure 3-76. *Creating a new virtual machine*

3. In the Virtual Machine Identity window, you can give the virtual machine a name, description, and owner (by default, this is the user who is creating the virtual machine), as shown in Figure 3-77. Fill in the information, and then click Next.

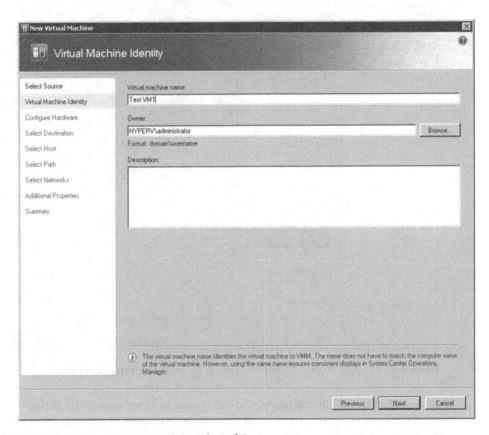

Figure 3-77. *Naming your new virtual machine*

4. In the Configure Hardware window, you can adjust the hardware settings of the virtual machine, as shown in Figure 3-78. You can either adjust the hardware settings manually (creating a new hardware profile) or choose an existing hardware profile from the drop-down list at the top of the window. Click Next when you are ready to continue.

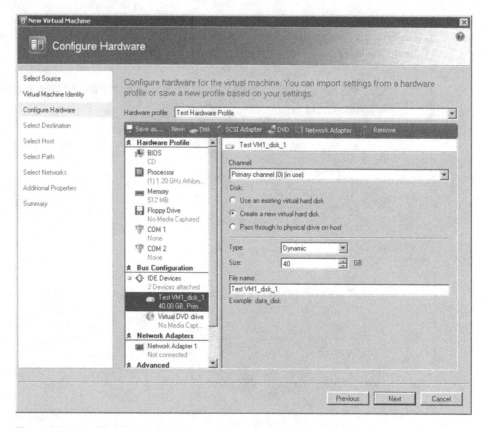

Figure 3-78. *Configuring the hardware settings for your new virtual machine*

5. In the Select Destination window, you can choose to either deploy the virtual machine to a host or store it in the library. Since this virtual machine is using a blank hard disk, it won't do you much good in the library. Go ahead and choose the option to "Place the virtual machine on a host," as shown in Figure 3-79. Then click Next.

6. In the Select Host window, select the host server that will host the new virtual machine, as shown in Figure 3-80. You will see a list of all the hosts managed by VMM, along with a rating for each one, ranging from one to five stars. The aim of the ratings is to help you determine the best host for the new virtual machine based on some parameters. To see the parameters used for this rating, click the Customize Ratings button.

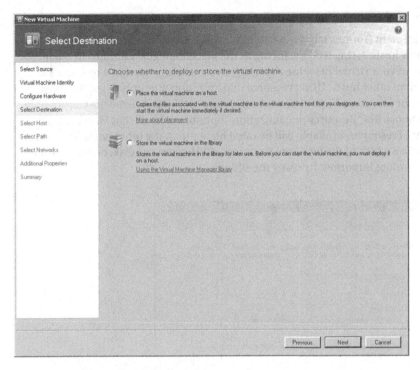

Figure 3-79. *Placing the virtual machine on a host*

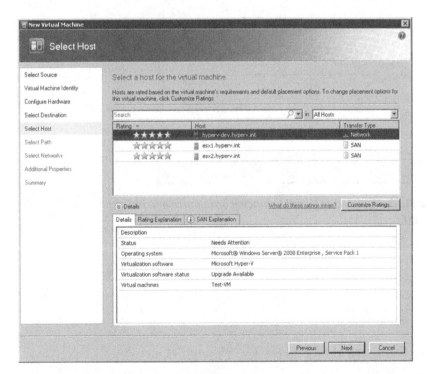

Figure 3-80. *Host ratings help you determine a host's suitability for virtual machine placement.*

7. You will see the Customize Ratings window, which has two tabs:

- The Placement Options tab, shown in Figure 3-81, lets you customize how VMM rates your hosts. Using load balancing as the placement goal attempts to balance the load of your virtual machines by rating hosts with the most free resources higher than other hosts. Using resource maximization attempts to get the most out of your resources by putting as many virtual machines on one host as possible. If you choose the "Resource maximization" option, the hosts that have the least amount of resources available will be rated higher than the other hosts. You can also choose which of the four core resources (CPU, memory, disk, or network utilization) is more important by using the sliders.

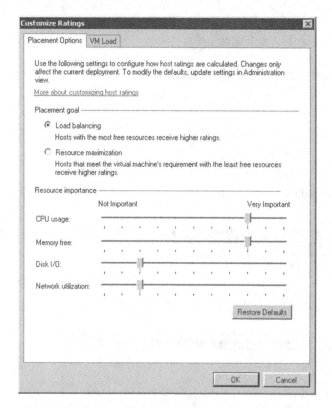

Figure 3-81. *You can decide if load balancing or resource maximization is more important.*

- The VM Load tab, shown in Figure 3-82, lets you predict how much CPU, disk, and network resources the new virtual machine will be using. Then the rating for a particular host is adjusted accordingly.

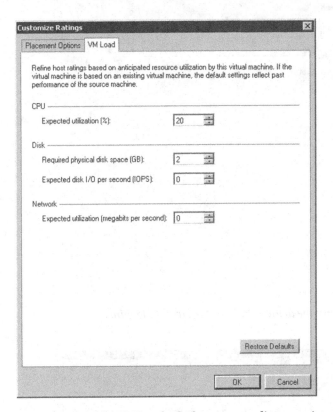

Figure 3-82. *Use the VM Load tab if you can predict your virtual machine's resource needs.*

8. After you are finished adjusting your ratings, click OK in the Customize Ratings window to return to the Select Host window. Choose your host, and then click Next to continue.

9. In the Select Path window, choose the path where the new virtual machine files will be stored, as shown in Figure 3-83. Click Next to continue.

10. In the Select Networks window, use the drop-down list under Virtual Network to select the virtual network location for each of the virtual network adapters that are assigned to the new virtual machine, as shown in Figure 3-84. Click Next.

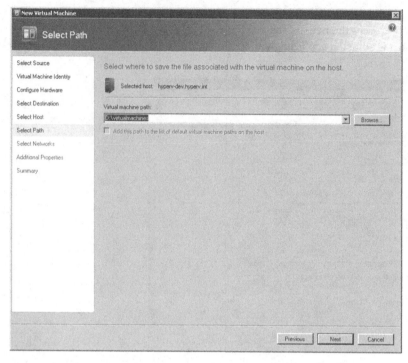

Figure 3-83. *You can change the default path for the virtual machine.*

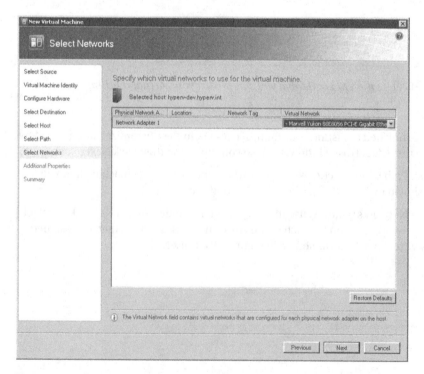

Figure 3-84. *Choosing the virtual networks for your new virtual machine*

11. In the Additional Properties window, you can choose from the following actions for when the host machine starts:

- Never automatically turn on the virtual machine.

- Always automatically turn on the virtual machine.

- Automatically turn on the virtual machine if it was running when the physical server stopped.

If you choose one of the options to automatically turn on the virtual machine, you can set the delay (in seconds) for the virtual machine to start.

12. Choose from the following three options for when the physical server stops:

- Save state, which saves the current state of the virtual machine

- Turn off virtual machine, which is like pulling the plug on a physical machine

- Shut down guest OS, which gracefully shuts down the guest operating system

13. Choose the operating system that you will be installing on the machine from the drop-down list at the bottom of the window, as shown in Figure 3-85. Click Next to continue.

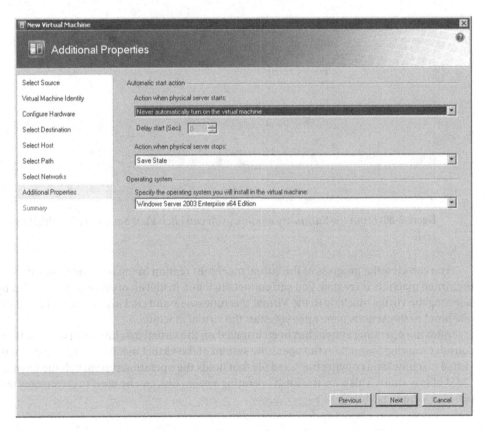

Figure 3-85. *Choosing the startup, shutdown, and operating system options*

14. In the Summary window, shown in Figure 3-86, you can click the View Script button if you want to see the PowerShell script that will perform the virtual machine creation job. If you are satisfied with the settings listed in the Summary window, click the Create button to create the new virtual machine.

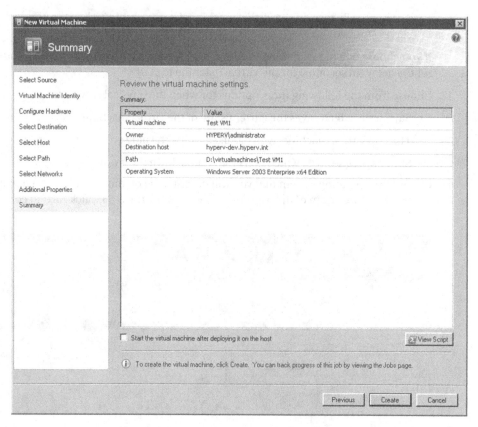

Figure 3-86. *From the Summary window, you can click View Script to view the PowerShell code.*

You can view the progress of the virtual machine creation in the Jobs window. Once the virtual machine is created, you can connect to it and install an operating system on it by selecting the virtual machine in the Virtual Machines view and clicking "Connect to virtual machine" in the Actions pane after you start the virtual machine.

After the operating system has been installed on the virtual machine, you may want to consider running Sysprep on the operating system of the virtual machine, shutting down the virtual machine, and copying the *.vhd file that holds the operating system volume to your VMM library share. This way, the fresh operating system disk can be used to create new templates or virtual machines.

Creating a Template

You will eventually want to create templates for common virtual machine images (like a fresh installation of an operating system). To create a template from an existing virtual machine, follow these steps:

1. Select the virtual machine (make sure you have already run Sysprep on it) and choose New template in the Actions pane. You will see a warning letting you know that creating a new template from the virtual machine will destroy the source virtual machine, as shown in Figure 3-87. If you want to go ahead and create the template, click Yes to continue.

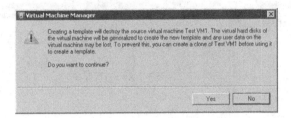

Figure 3-87. *Be sure you don't need the virtual machine before creating a template from it.*

2. The New Template Wizard starts, as shown in Figure 3-88. In the Template Identity window, give the template an appropriate name, description, and owner (this is the user who is creating the template, by default). Click Next.

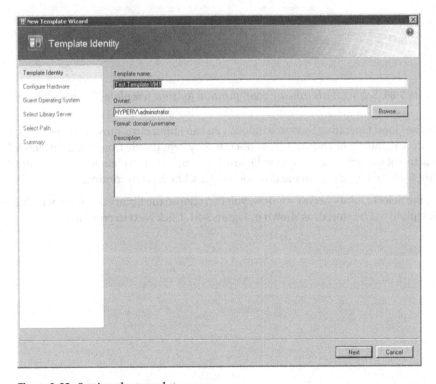

Figure 3-88. *Setting the template name*

3. In the Configure Hardware window, you can either choose a hardware profile or configure the hardware manually, as shown in Figure 3-89. Click Next to continue.

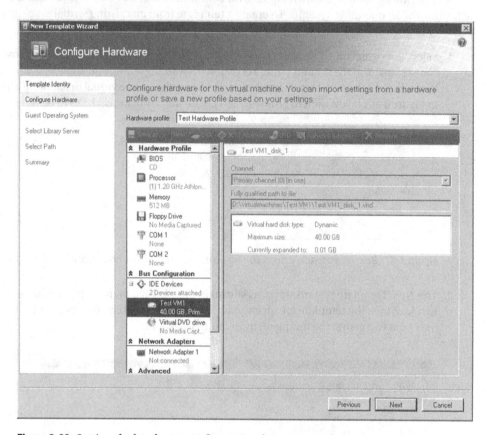

Figure 3-89. *Setting the hardware configuration for your template virtual machine*

4. In the Guest Operating System window, you can either customize the guest operating system manually or choose a guest operating system profile from the drop-down list at the top of the screen, as shown in Figure 3-90. You can also choose the Customization Not Required option from the drop-down list. Click Next to continue.

5. In the Select Library Server window, you can choose the library server on which the template will be stored, as shown in Figure 3-91. Click Next to continue.

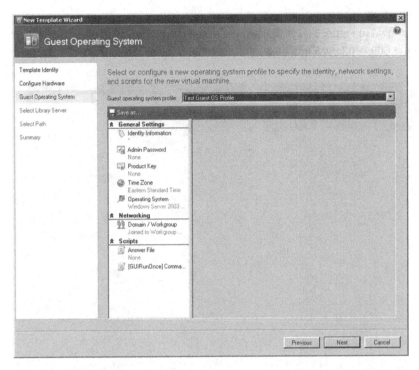

Figure 3-90. *Setting the guest operating system options for your virtual machine template*

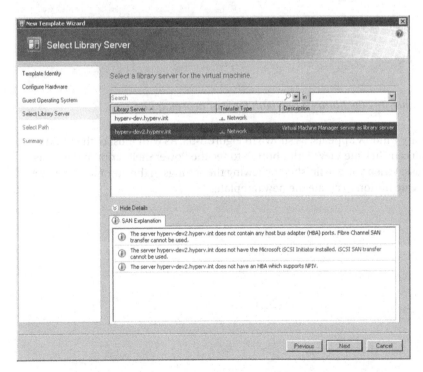

Figure 3-91. *Selecting the library server where the template will be stored*

6. In the Select Path window, choose the share on the library server on which to store the template, as shown in Figure 3-92. Click Browse to select from the available shares. Click Next after choosing the share location.

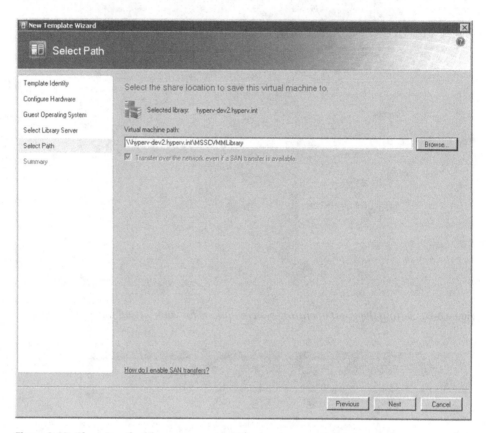

Figure 3-92. *Choosing the library server path for your new template*

7. The Summary window appears, as shown in Figure 3-93. As with most of the VMM actions, you can click the View Script button to see the PowerShell script that will perform this task. When you are finished reviewing the settings in the Summary window, click the Create button to create the new template.

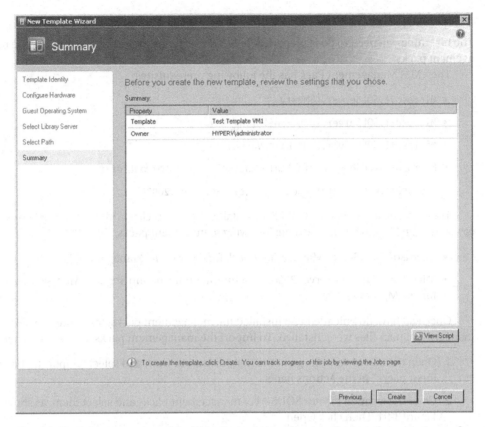

Figure 3-93. *Take advantage of the View Script button to view the template creation code.*

You can view the template creation process in the Jobs window.

Enabling PRO Tips and Reporting

PRO tips are recommendations for your virtual environment based on the monitoring that integrating SCOM with VMM enables. If you want to enable PRO tips in VMM, you need to integrate VMM with SCOM. If you already have a SCOM environment set up, then most of the work is done. However, if you don't, you will need to invest in SCOM 2007. A detailed reference guide for SCOM can be found at http://technet.microsoft.com/en-us/library/bb310604.aspx.

Note If you are just starting out with your virtual environment and do not already have a SCOM server, you may want to consider purchasing Microsoft's System Center Server Management Suite Enterprise. This bundle includes SCOM 2007, System Center Configuration Manager 2007 Release 2, System Center Data Protection Manager 2007 (discussed in Chapter 8), and VMM 2008. For more information, visit http://www.microsoft.com/systemcenter/en/us/management-suites.aspx.

Preparing the SCOM Server

The first thing you need to do is prepare your SCOM server by importing the appropriate management packs.

The VMM Management Pack has the following prerequisites:

- `Microsoft.SQLServer.Library`

- `Microsoft.SQLServer.2005.Monitoring`

- `Microsoft.SQLServer.2005.Discovery`

- `Microsoft.Windows.InternetInformationServices.CommonLibrary`

- `Microsoft.Windows.InternetInformationServices.2003`

These can be found in the SCOM 2007 Catalog (`http://technet.microsoft.com/en-us/opsmgr/cc539535.aspx`). Download the following management packs:

- Microsoft SQL Server Management Pack for Operations Manager 2007

- Microsoft Windows Server 2000/2003 Internet Information Services Management Pack for OpsMgr 2007

Once you have downloaded and installed the management packs, take note of where the management pack files were installed. To import the management packs, follow these steps:

1. Open the SCOM console, go to the Administration view, and select "Import management packs" in the Actions panel.

2. Go to the location of your SQL Server management packs and select them, as shown in Figure 3-94. Then click Open.

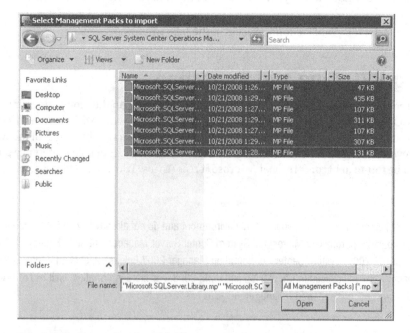

Figure 3-94. *Importing the SQL Server management packs for SCOM 2007*

3. The Import Management Packs window appears, as shown in Figure 3-95. Click the Import button to import the management packs. When the import is finished, click Close.

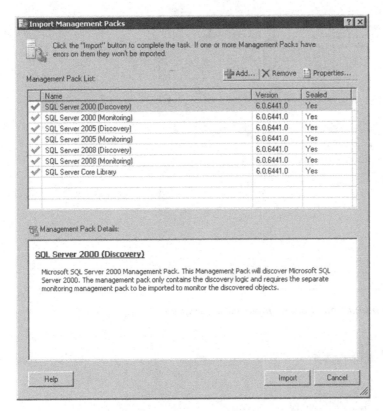

Figure 3-95. *The SQL Server management packs imported successfully.*

4. Repeat steps 1 through 4 to import the Microsoft Windows Server 2000/2003 Internet Information Services Management Pack for OpsMgr 2007, as shown in Figure 3-96.

5. Now you need to run the VMM setup on the SCOM 2007 root management server. Choose Configure Operations Manager from the Setup options, as shown in Figure 3-97.

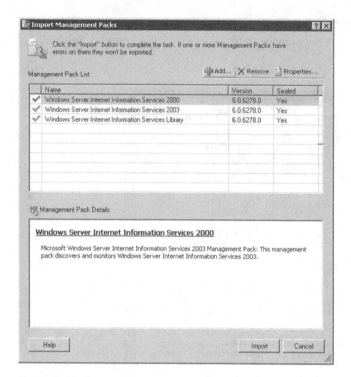

Figure 3-96. *The IIS management packs imported successfully.*

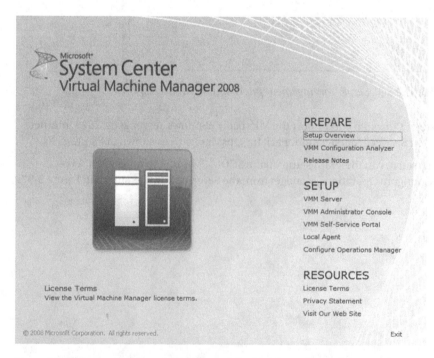

Figure 3-97. *Choose Configure Operations Manager from the VMM 2008 setup menu.*

6. When the Setup wizard starts, read and accept the license agreement, and then click Next.

7. In the Customer Experience Improvement Program window, click Next.

8. The Prerequisites Check window appears, as shown in Figure 3-98. If everything is OK, click Next.

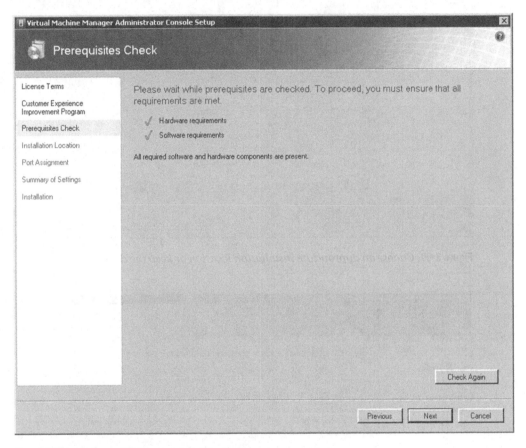

Figure 3-98. *A successful prerequisite check*

9. In the Installation Location window, choose an appropriate installation location, as shown in Figure 3-99. Click Next to continue.

10. In the Port Assignment window, enter the appropriate VMM server, as shown in Figure 3-100. If you changed the default port of 8100 for communications when you set up your VMM server, you need to change the port number here to match. Click Next.

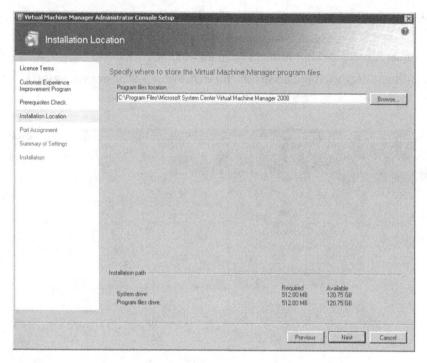

Figure 3-99. *Choose an appropriate installation location or keep the default.*

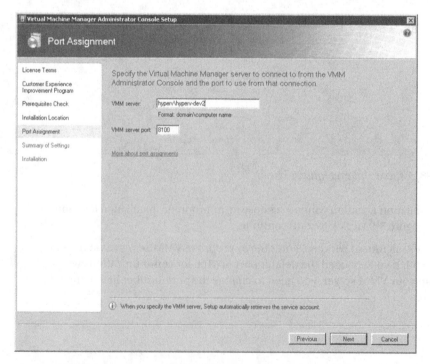

Figure 3-100. *If you changed your VMM server port, you will need to change it in this window.*

11. Review the settings in the Summary window, as shown in Figure 3-101. If everything looks good, click Install.

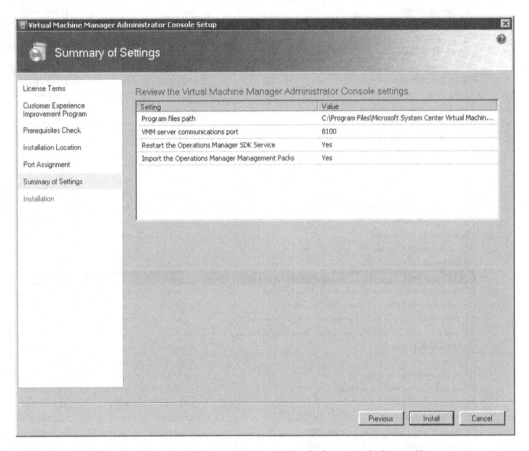

Figure 3-101. *Check the settings in the Summary window before you click Install.*

Once the installation is complete, verify that the VMM management packs were installed. Open the SCOM console, go to the Administration view, and select Management Packs in the navigation pane. In the results pane, scroll down until you see that the following management packs are installed (see Figure 3-102):

- System Center Virtual Machine Manager 2008
- System Center Virtual Machine Manager 2008 PRO Host Performance
- System Center Virtual Machine Manager 2008 PRO Library
- System Center Virtual Machine Manager 2008 Virtual Machine Right-Sizing
- System Center Virtual Machine Manager 2008 VMware Host Performance

Name	Version	Sealed	Date Created
Notifications Internal Library	6.0.6278.0		1/3/2009 1:53:3
Notifications Library	6.0.9010.0	Yes	1/3/2009 1:53:2
Operations Manager 2007	6.0.6278.0	Yes	1/3/2009 1:52:5
Operations Manager Agent Management Library	6.0.6278.0	Yes	1/3/2009 1:53:3
Operations Manager Internal Library	6.0.6278.0	Yes	1/3/2009 1:52:5
Performance Library	6.0.6278.0	Yes	1/3/2009 1:52:0
SNMP Library	6.0.6278.0	Yes	1/3/2009 1:51:2
SQL Server 2000 (Discovery)	6.0.6441.0	Yes	1/3/2009 3:05:3
SQL Server 2000 (Monitoring)	6.0.6441.0	Yes	1/3/2009 3:05:4
SQL Server 2005 (Discovery)	6.0.6441.0	Yes	1/3/2009 3:05:4
SQL Server 2005 (Monitoring)	6.0.6441.0	Yes	1/3/2009 3:05:5
SQL Server 2008 (Discovery)	6.0.6441.0	Yes	1/3/2009 3:06:0
SQL Server 2008 (Monitoring)	6.0.6441.0	Yes	1/3/2009 3:06:0
SQL Server Core Library	6.0.6441.0	Yes	1/3/2009 3:05:3
Synthetic Transactions Library	6.0.6278.0	Yes	1/3/2009 1:53:1
System Center Core Library	6.0.6278.0	Yes	1/3/2009 1:52:2
System Center Core Monitoring	6.0.6278.0	Yes	1/3/2009 1:52:4
System Center Internal Library	6.0.6278.0	Yes	1/3/2009 1:52:4
System Center Rule Templates	6.0.6278.0	Yes	1/3/2009 1:53:3
System Center Task Templates	6.0.6278.0	Yes	1/3/2009 1:53:3
System Center UI Executed Tasks	6.0.6278.0	Yes	1/3/2009 1:53:3
System Center Virtual Machine Manager 2008	2.0.3444.0	Yes	1/3/2009 3:19:3
System Center Virtual Machine Manager 2008 PRO Host Performance	2.0.3444.0	Yes	1/3/2009 3:19:4
System Center Virtual Machine Manager 2008 PRO Library	2.0.3444.0	Yes	1/3/2009 3:19:3
System Center Virtual Machine Manager 2008 PRO Virtual Machine Right-Sizing	2.0.3444.0	Yes	1/3/2009 3:19:4
System Center Virtual Machine Manager 2008 PRO VMware Host Performance	2.0.3444.0	Yes	1/3/2009 3:19:4
System Hardware Library	6.0.6278.0	Yes	1/3/2009 1:53:3
System Library	6.0.6278.0	Yes	1/3/2009 1:51:1
Web Application Monitoring Library	6.0.6278.0	Yes	1/3/2009 1:53:0
Windows Client Operating Systems Library	6.0.6278.0	Yes	1/3/2009 1:53:3
Windows Cluster Library	6.0.6278.0	Yes	1/3/2009 1:53:0
Windows Core Library	6.0.6278.0	Yes	1/3/2009 1:52:0
Windows Server Internet Information Services 2000	6.0.6278.0	Yes	1/3/2009 3:11:0
Windows Server Internet Information Services 2003	6.0.6278.0	Yes	1/3/2009 3:11:1
Windows Server Internet Information Services Library	6.0.6278.0	Yes	1/3/2009 3:10:5
Windows Service Library	6.0.6278.0	Yes	1/3/2009 1:52:3
WS-Management Library	6.0.6278.0	Yes	1/3/2009 1:53:3

Figure 3-102. *Verify that the VMM 2008 management packs are installed.*

■**Note** At the time of this writing, you may need to download the updated VMM 2008 Management Pack
for SCOM 2007 (http://www.microsoft.com/downloads/details.aspx?familyid=D6D5CDDD-4EC8-
4E3C-8AB1-102EC99C257F&displaylang=en) in order to get the reports management pack. To install it,
you must remove the old VMM 2008 management packs in the Management Packs section of the Administration view in SCOM 2007. Then you can install and import the management packs (follow the same
procedure as outlined here for installing the IIS and SQL Server management packs).

Enabling Reporting

To enable reporting, you need to add the appropriate users to the Report Operator role in SCOM. Follow these steps to enable reporting:

1. In the SCOM console, go to the Administration view and select User Roles under Security in the navigation pane.

2. In the results pane, select Operations Manager Report Operators, as shown in Figure 3-103. Then select Properties from the Actions pane.

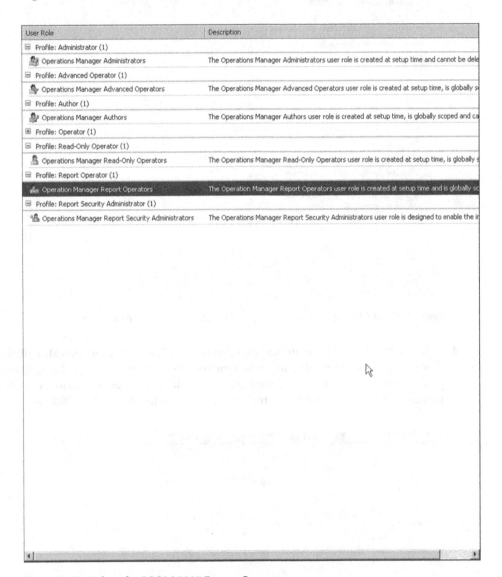

Figure 3-103. *Select the SCOM 2007 Report Operators group.*

3. In the Properties window, click Add and add the appropriate user names, as shown in Figure 3-104. Click OK when you are finished.

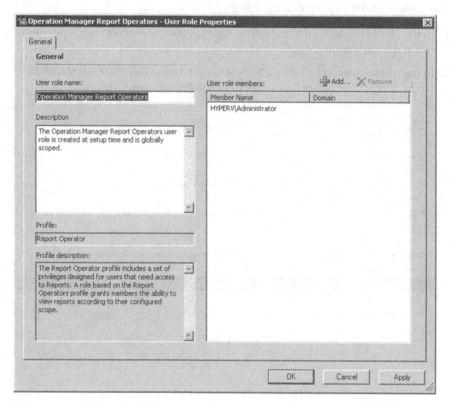

Figure 3-104. *Adding members to the SCOM 2007 Report Operators group*

4. To let the VMM server know the location of your SCOM services, open the VMM Administrator console. Go to the Administration view and select System Center in the navigation pane. In the results pane, double-click Operations Manager Server and fill in the appropriate server name for your SCOM root server, as shown in Figure 3-105. Click OK.

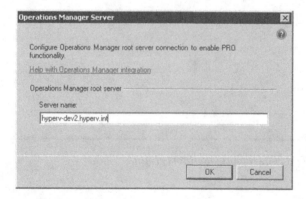

Figure 3-105. *Configuring SCOM 2007 integration for PRO Tips*

5. To enable reporting, double-click Operations Manager Reporting URL. Click the check box to enable reporting and fill in the appropriate reporting server URL, as shown in Figure 3-106. Click OK.

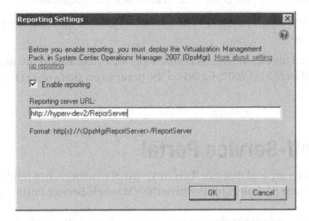

Figure 3-106. *Configuring SCOM 2007 integration for reporting*

You should now have a Reporting view in the VMM Administrator console. In order to start reporting on your Hyper-V hosts and other systems, they must be managed by SCOM 2007. You can add systems in the SCOM 2007 console by going to the Administration view and clicking "Configure computers and devices to manage" in the Actions pane on the right. The following reports are available:

- *Host Utilization*: This report shows the utilization of the four core resources (processor, memory, network, and disk) for a host or group of hosts. Figure 3-107 shows an example of the Host Utilization report.

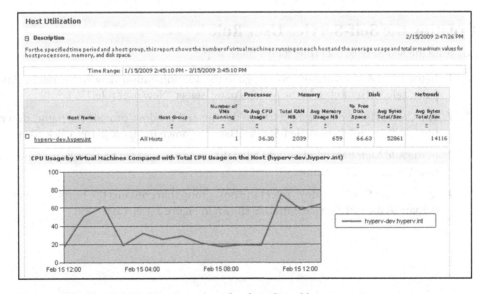

Figure 3-107. *The Host Utilization report for the selected host*

- *Host Utilization Growth*: This report is useful for trending the growth of host utilization over time.

- *Virtual Machine Allocation*: This report shows how each of the four core resources is allocated to each virtual machine. This is very useful for chargeback scenarios.

- *Virtual Machine Utilization*: This report shows how much of the four core resources each virtual machine is using.

- *Virtualization Candidates*: This report suggests candidates for virtualization (for any systems that are managed by SCOM 2007) based on the parameters that you set up in the report.

Using the VMM Self-Service Portal

You may want users to be able to create and manage their own virtual machines, but not have access to the full VMM Administrator console. This is where the VMM Self-Service Portal can be used.

Once you have installed the Self-Service Portal properly, as described earlier in the chapter, you need to do the following before users can start using it:

- Create a host group that will contain the hosts that will be used in the Self-Service Portal. Then move any hosts that you want to participate in the Self-Service Portal into the host group that you created.

- Create templates for the users of the Self-Service Portal to use to create new virtual machines.

- Create a Self-Service user role and populate it with your Self-Service Portal users.

Host groups and templates were covered earlier in the chapter. That leaves the creation of the Self-Service user role.

Creating the Self-Service User Role

To create the Self-Service user role, follow these steps:

1. In the VMM Administrator console, go to the Administration view. In the navigation pane, select User Roles. In the Actions pane, select "New user role."

2. The Create User Role wizard starts. In the General window, provide the name, description, and user role type of Self-Service User, as shown in Figure 3-108. Click Next.

3. In the Add Members window, add all of the users you want to be members of this user role. Click Next to continue.

4. In the Select Scope window, select the host group that contains the hosts that will participate in the Self-Service Portal, as shown in Figure 3-109. Click Next.

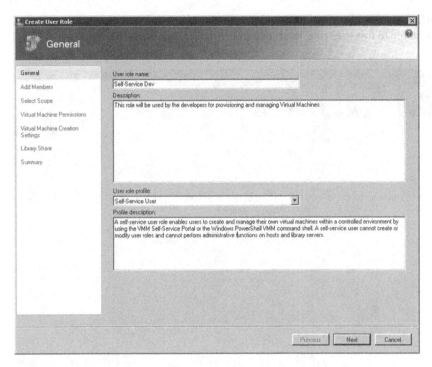

Figure 3-108. *Naming the Self-Service user role*

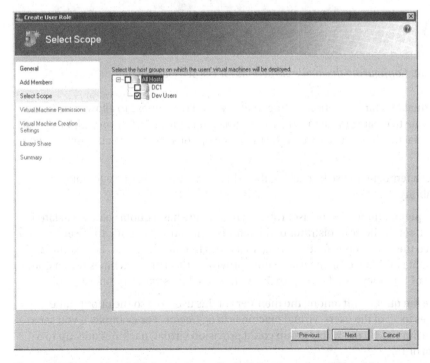

Figure 3-109. *Decide which host groups the Self-Service user will be able to access.*

5. In the Virtual Machine Permissions window, choose the virtual machine actions that will be available to this user role, as shown in Figure 3-110. Click Next.

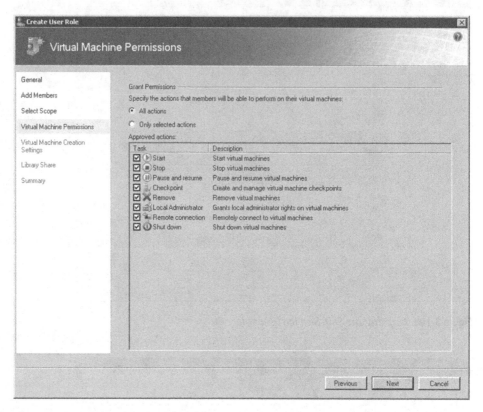

Figure 3-110. *Configuring the available actions for the Self-Service role*

6. In the Virtual Machine Creation Settings window, you can choose to allow members of this user role to create virtual machines, as shown in Figure 3-111. If you want them to create virtual machines, you can set the following options (click Next after making your choices):

- Select a template to use by clicking the Add button and choosing a template from the library.

- Set a quota number for the user role. Each template has a quota value associated with it, set by the administrator of the template. If you set a quota, the users cannot exceed the quota value for the virtual machines that are deployed. For example, if the quota limit were 10, the users could provision 10 virtual machines with a quota value of 1, or they could provision five virtual machines with a quota value of 2.

- Share the quota limit among the members of this user role so the quota value applies to all of the users' virtual machines in aggregate. For example, if you set a quota limit of 10, the whole group could provision virtual machines only up to a quota of 10.

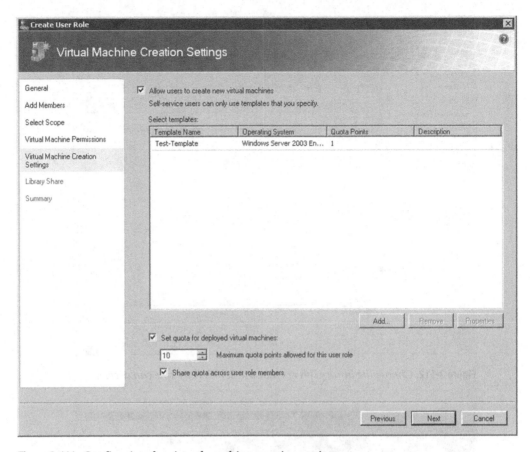

Figure 3-111. *Configuring the virtual machine creation settings*

7. In the Library Share window, you can choose to allow users in this user role to be able to store virtual machines in the library. If you check this option, then select the appropriate library server and path (if you want to limit it to a certain path), as shown in Figure 3-112. Click Next to continue.

8. The Summary window appears, as shown in Figure 3-113. Click the Create button to create the user role.

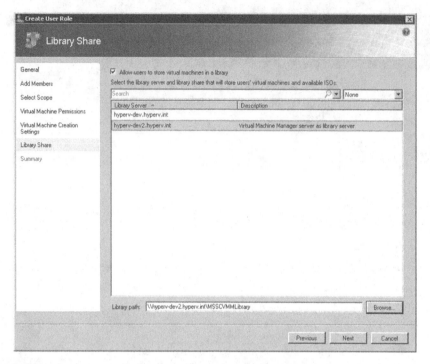

Figure 3-112. *Choose the library servers that the Self-Service role can access.*

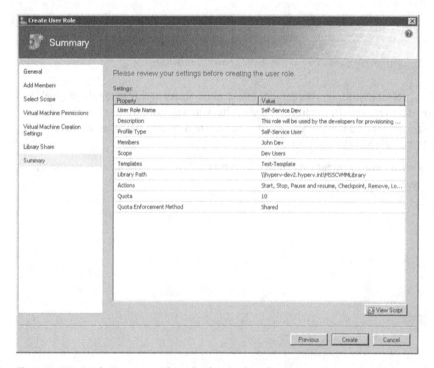

Figure 3-113. *Make sure everything looks good in the Summary window before clicking Create.*

Creating Virtual Machines with the Self-Service Portal

After you've taken care of all the prerequisites for the Self-Service Portal, distribute the URL of the Self-Service Portal to the users who need it.

When users log in, they should be able to create new virtual machines by clicking New Computer in the Create section, as shown in Figure 3-114. This brings up the New Virtual Machine page. The user just needs to fill in the appropriate information for the new virtual machine, as shown in Figure 3-115, and then click the Create button. The virtual machine should show up in the list of computers on the main Self-Service Portal page, as shown in Figure 3-116.

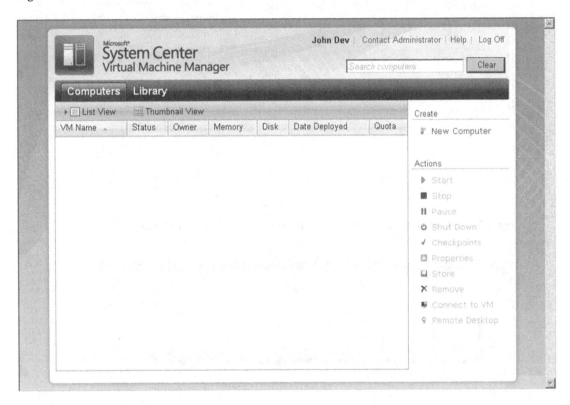

Figure 3-114. *The Self-Service Portal menu*

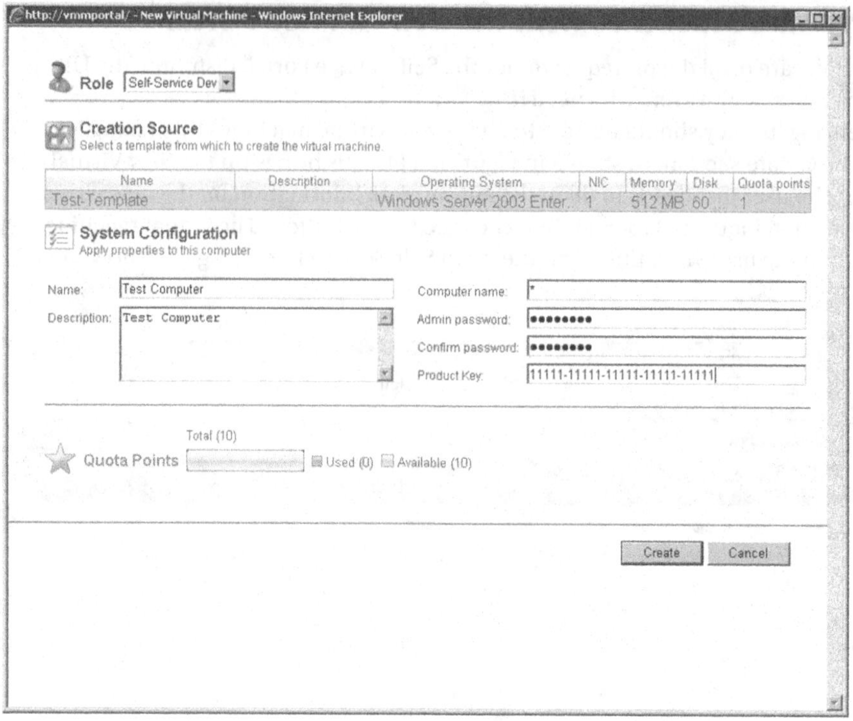

Figure 3-115. *Creating a new virtual machine using the Self-Service Portal*

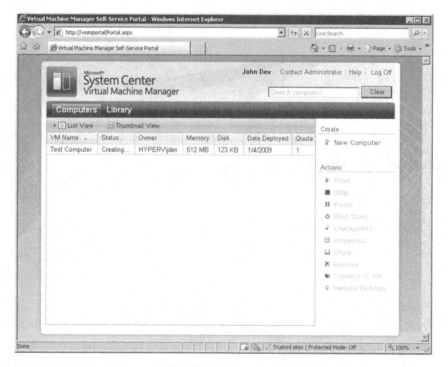

Figure 3-116. *The newly created virtual machine is listed in the Self-Service Portal.*

Summary

This chapter covered a lot of ground. VMM is a comprehensive management solution for your virtual environment. It is best to dedicate systems for the different components for maximum scalability. The components can be broken down into mandatory components, optional components, and components that are prerequisites for both mandatory and optional components, as shown in Table 3-8.

Table 3-8. *The VMM Components*

Prerequisite Components	Mandatory Components	Optional Components
SQL Server	Hyper-V host	VMM Self-Service Portal
IIS 6.0 or 7.0	VMM server	VMM PRO integration
SCOM 2007	VMM Administrator console	VMM reporting
Windows Server 2008 64-bit (Standard, Enterprise, Datacenter)	VMM library server	VMM database

All of the work put into designing and deploying VMM is worth it. You can take advantage of the PowerShell scripting environment to quickly automate your business processes related to virtualization. You can also manage a heterogeneous virtual environment by taking advantage of the ability to manage your VMware virtual infrastructure using the same VMM Administrator console. As you begin to place more emphasis on virtualization in your infrastructure, having a solid management solution for your virtual environment becomes crucial. VMM fits this role nicely.

CHAPTER 4

■ ■ ■

Migrating Physical and Virtual Machines to Hyper-V

Virtual machines make life much easier for system administrators. One day, servers will start life as virtual machines by default. However, until then, we still must deal with some physical machines. Fortunately, we can convert physical machines to virtual machines. This is known as a physical-to-virtual (P2V) migration. You may even need to migrate virtual machines from other platforms to Hyper-V. This is known as a virtual-to-virtual (V2V) migration.

As you'll learn in this chapter, you can accomplish P2V migration in several ways. But before you perform the migration, you need to decide which physical machines will make good candidates for virtualization.

Selecting Migration Candidates

How do you select which machines would make good candidates for virtualization? The general wisdom says to grab the low-hanging fruit first. These are systems that are not very resource-intensive. Some examples might be Dynamic Host Configuration Protocol (DHCP), Windows Internet Name Service (WINS), or print servers. For more resource-intensive systems, you need to gather some performance data to assess their virtualization readiness. A good place to start is with the Microsoft Assessment and Planning (MAP) toolkit.

Downloading and Installing the MAP Toolkit

The MAP toolkit will collect performance metrics on your potential virtualization targets, store the results in a database, and create readiness reports for you to use for your virtualization target assessment. The MAP toolkit can also be used to collect a hardware inventory and perform operating system compatibility checks for your infrastructure.

You can download the MAP toolkit from Microsoft at the following URL:

```
http://www.microsoft.com/downloads/details.aspx?FamilyID=
67240b76-3148-4e49-943d-4d9ea7f77730&displaylang=en
```

To use the MAP toolkit, the system on which you will install MAP must have the following installed:

- .NET Framework version 3.5 Service Pack (SP) 1 (http://www.microsoft.com/downloads/details.aspx?FamilyId=AB99342F-5D1A-413D-8319-81DA479AB0D7&displaylang=en)

- Windows Installer version 4.5 (http://www.microsoft.com/downloads/details.aspx?FamilyId=5A58B56F-60B6-4412-95B9-54D056D6F9F4&displaylang=en)

- Word 2007 or Word 2003 SP2

- Excel 2007 or Excel 2003 SP2

- Microsoft Office primary interop assemblies

Note The Microsoft Office primary interop assemblies will be installed with MAP for Office 2003. If you are using Office 2007, you will need to install them from the Office 2007 setup files.

In addition to these prerequisites, you will need to have access to a SQL Server instance that will be used for the MAP toolkit. MAP will download and install SQL Server 2008 Express by default. If you would like to use an existing SQL Server 2005 or SQL Server 2008 server, you just need to create an instance named MAPS.

More information about the prerequisites for the MAP toolkit can be found at http://www.microsoft.com/map.

Once all of the prerequisites have been met, you can install the MAP toolkit by following the Setup Wizard's instructions. In the portion of the wizard that asks you about the SQL database, either choose an existing database or let the Setup Wizard download and install a copy of SQL Server 2008 Express edition.

Gathering Performance Data

Before you run MAP's Performance Metrics Wizard to gather performance data, you need to create a simple text file that lists the computer names you will be targeting for virtualization. The text file should have one computer name listed per line. Make a note of where you save this text file.

Also, make sure the Remote Registry service is running on the systems that are listed in this text file. It needs to be running in order for the MAP toolkit to collect performance metric data. You should also open the following ports on any firewall (including the Windows Firewall) that may be in the communication path between the MAP toolkit server and your target servers:

- TCP port 135 for remote administration

- TCP ports 139 and 445 for file and printer sharing

- UDP ports 137 and 138 for file and printer sharing

Then you can follow these steps to gather performance data for the computers under consideration for virtualization:

1. Launch the MAP toolkit. You will be presented with the main window, as shown in Figure 4-1.

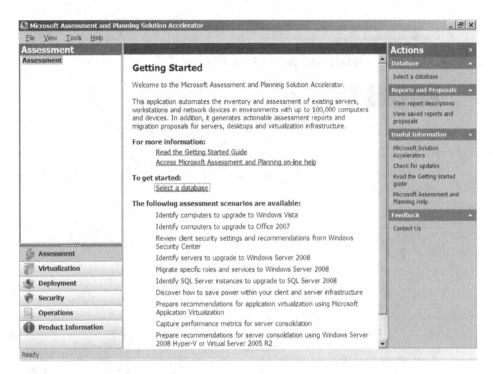

Figure 4-1. *The MAP main window*

2. Click the Select a database link in the Actions pane on the right side of the screen. In the dialog box that appears, either choose an existing database or fill in a database name to create a new database, as shown in Figure 4-2. Then click OK.

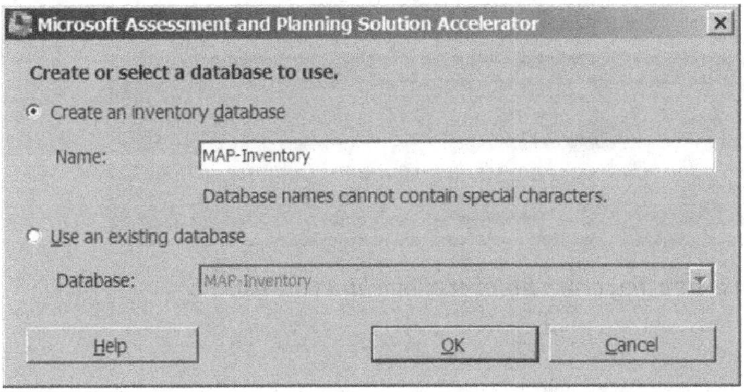

Figure 4-2. *Creating the MAP database*

3. Select Gather Performance Metrics in the Actions pane on the right. This will launch the Performance Metrics Wizard. The first thing it will ask for is a list of computers that will be imported into the inventory. These are the computers on which the performance metrics will be gathered. Browse to the text file you created previously and select it, as shown in Figure 4-3. Then click Next.

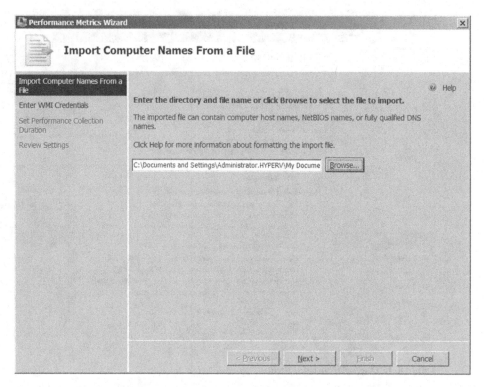

Figure 4-3. *Choosing the text file that MAP will use to gather the inventory*

4. A confirmation dialog box will pop up, telling you how many computers will be added to the inventory, as shown in Figure 4-4. Make sure it matches your expectations, and then click OK.

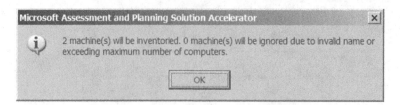

Figure 4-4. *Make sure the correct number of machines are listed.*

5. The next screen will ask for the credentials that you will be using to gather the performance metrics. Click New.

6. In the Inventory Account dialog box, enter the details for an account that has administrator access to the machines that you will be targeting. In the example in Figure 4-5, I used the Administrator account in the hyperv.int domain. If you will be using the same account for all of the computers, select "Use on all computers." If you will be using different accounts for your computers, select "Use only on the following computer" and type in the computer name. If you are using different accounts, you will need to create a new credential for each account using the same process. Click Save, or click Save and New if you need to create another account.

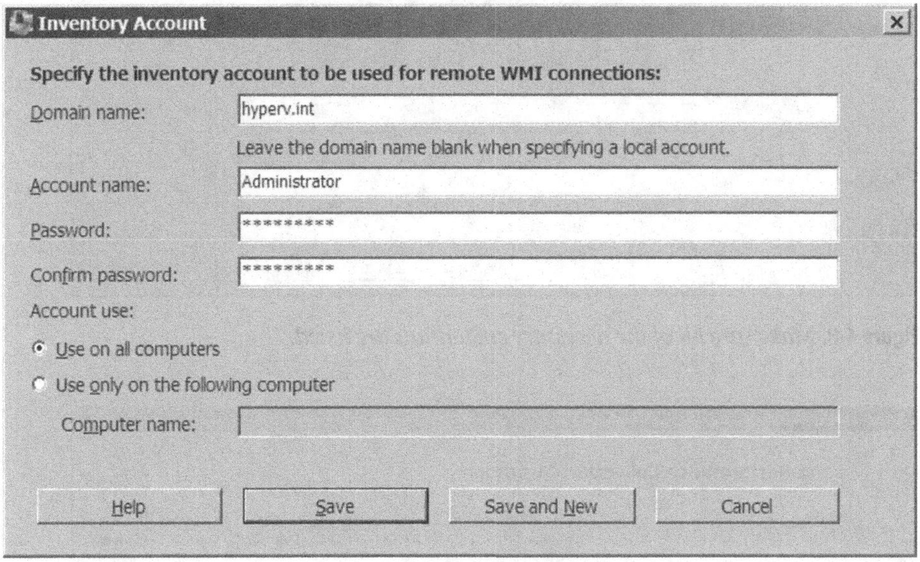

Figure 4-5. *The administrator credentials needed for WMI*

7. Make sure all of the credentials you need are listed in the Enter WMI Credentials window, as shown in Figure 4-6. Then click Next to continue.

8. The next item to configure is the performance collection duration. In order for the MAP toolkit to make any virtualization recommendations, it needs to gather performance metrics data for at least 24 hours. However, you may want to gather the metrics for a week or more to measure the server activity over an entire business cycle. With that in mind, set an appropriate end time, as shown in Figure 4-7. Then click Next.

9. In the next window, review your settings to make sure they are correct, and then click Finish.

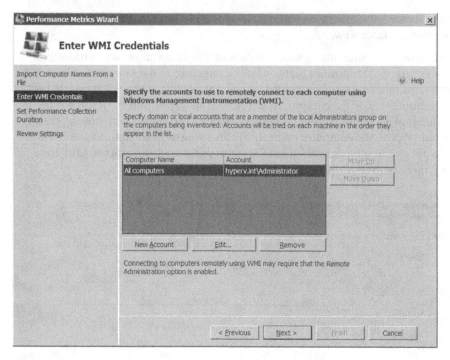

Figure 4-6. *Make sure all of the necessary credentials are listed.*

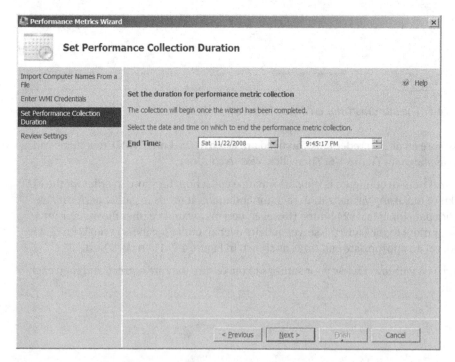

Figure 4-7. *At least 24 hours is needed for MAP to make virtualization recommendations.*

After you click Finish, you will see the Status window, which will let you know what is going on in the process of gathering performance metric data, as shown in Figure 4-8. Just keep this screen up until the gathering process is complete.

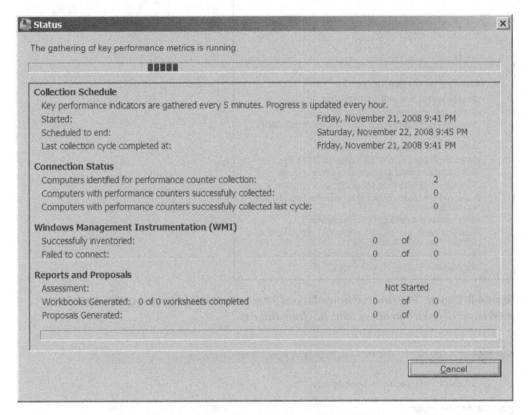

Figure 4-8. *There will be 24 hours of data collection. You can watch the progress if you want.*

Running a Server Consolidation Recommendation Report

After the performance data has been gathered, you can run a report that will give you recommendations for server consolidation using Microsoft Virtual Server or Hyper-V. Obviously, you will be interested in the Hyper-V option. Follow these steps to run the report:

1. From the MAP main window, click the "Prepare recommendations for server consolidation using Windows Server 2008 Hyper-V or Virtual Server 2005 R2" link, as shown in Figure 4-9. This will launch the Server Virtualization and Consolidation Wizard.

2. Choose the Hyper-V option, as shown in Figure 4-10. Then click Next.

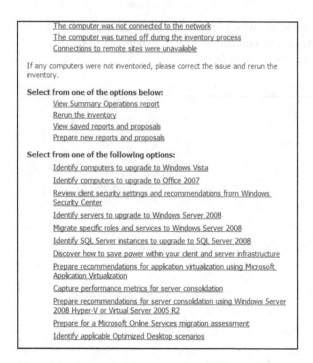

The computer was not connected to the network
The computer was turned off during the inventory process
Connections to remote sites were unavailable

If any computers were not inventoried, please correct the issue and rerun the inventory.

Select from one of the options below:
View Summary Operations report
Rerun the inventory
View saved reports and proposals
Prepare new reports and proposals

Select from one of the following options:
Identify computers to upgrade to Windows Vista
Identify computers to upgrade to Office 2007
Review client security settings and recommendations from Windows Security Center
Identify servers to upgrade to Windows Server 2008
Migrate specific roles and services to Windows Server 2008
Identify SQL Server instances to upgrade to SQL Server 2008
Discover how to save power within your client and server infrastructure
Prepare recommendations for application virtualization using Microsoft Application Virtualization
Capture performance metrics for server consolidation
Prepare recommendations for server consolidation using Windows Server 2008 Hyper-V or Virtual Server 2005 R2
Prepare for a Microsoft Online Services migration assessment
Identify applicable Optimized Desktop scenarios

Figure 4-9. *Choose "Prepare recommendations for server consolidation using Windows Server 2008 Hyper-V or Virtual Server 2005 R2" from this list.*

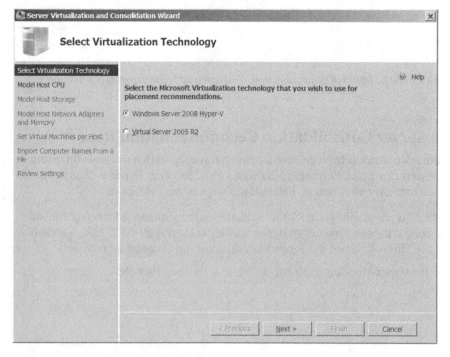

Figure 4-10. *Choose the Hyper-V option.*

3. In the Model Host CPU window, fill in the appropriate information for your Hyper-V host or the Hyper-V host that you plan to purchase (MAP can be used for modeling purposes as well), as shown in Figure 4-11. Then click Next.

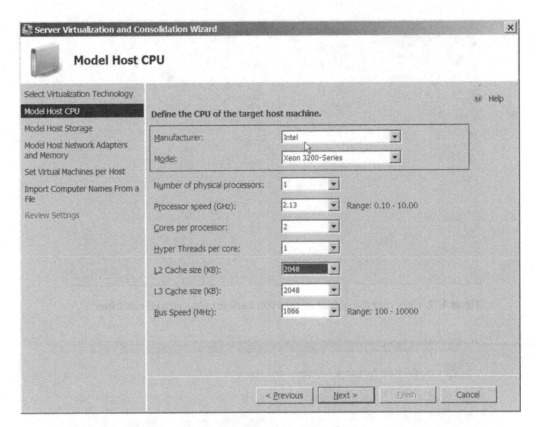

Figure 4-11. *Choosing the type of processor your Hyper-V host has*

4. In the Model Host Storage window, fill in the appropriate information for the storage that will hold your virtual machines on your Hyper-V host, as shown in Figure 4-12. Click Next to continue.

5. At this point, you will notice a pattern emerging. The Server Virtualization and Consolidation Wizard is asking for information about the four core resources (processor, disk, network, and memory). In the Model Host Network Adapters and Memory window, fill in the appropriate memory and network adapter information for your Hyper-V host, as shown in Figure 4-13. Click Next.

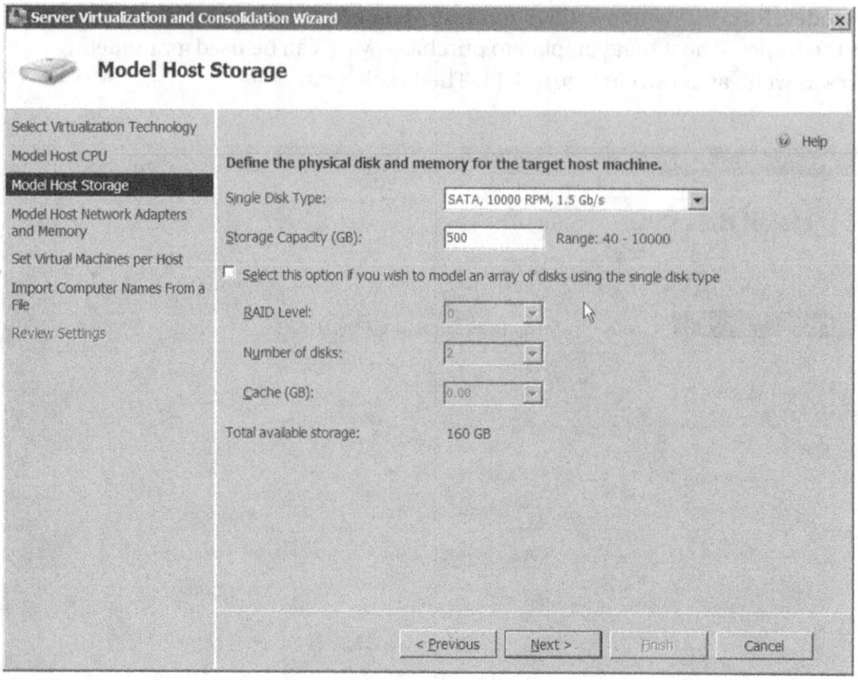

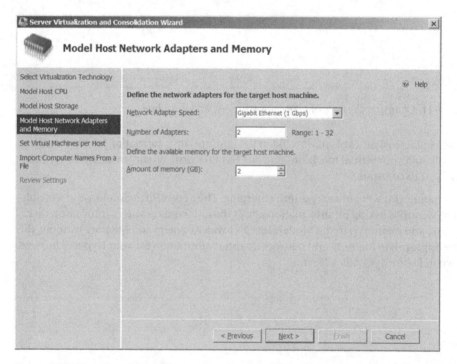

Figure 4-12. *Choosing the type of storage you have for your virtual machines*

Figure 4-13. *Choosing the speed, number of network interface cards, and the amount of memory on your Hyper-V host*

6. In the Set Virtual Machines per Host window, choose how many virtual machines you think you will run on your Hyper-V system simultaneously, as shown in Figure 4-14. Click Next.

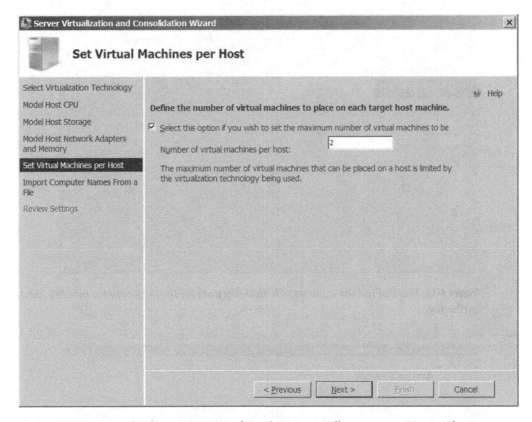

Figure 4-14. *Try to predict how many virtual machines you will run on your Hyper-V host.*

7. The next window asks you to import the computer names that you are considering for conversion to Hyper-V, as shown in Figure 4-15. You can use the same text file that you used for the performance metric data gathering. Click Next to continue.

8. The next window displays a summary of your settings, as shown in Figure 4-16. Review your settings to make sure everything looks correct, and then click Finish. A status window will appear, so you can view the progress of the reports that are being generated.

9. When the reports are finished, you will be back at the main MAP window. Click the "View saved reports and proposals" link to go to your new reports.

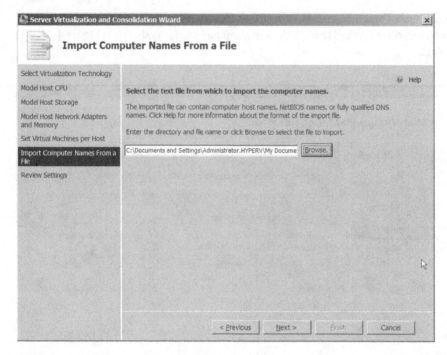

Figure 4-15. *You can use the same text file that you used for the performance monitor metric gathering.*

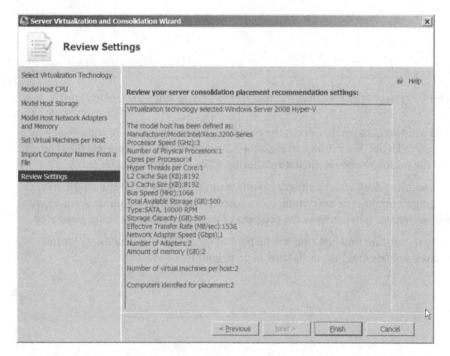

Figure 4-16. *Make sure all the settings look correct before clicking Finish.*

You will find that MAP has created two documents. One is an Excel spreadsheet that contains technical details, such as utilization of the four core resources before and after consolidation, to help you in assessing the impact that virtualization will have on your systems. The other document is a nicely formatted Word file. This Word document includes graphs that depict the information contained in the Excel spreadsheet, along with some text about the benefits of consolidation with Hyper-V, as shown in Figure 4-17. For you *Dilbert* fans, you can think of the Word document as the report to hand to your pointy-haired boss. If you are not a fan of *Dilbert*, then the Word document is a nice report to hand to your nontechnical manager. These files will be saved in `%userprofile%\my documents\map\map-inventory`.

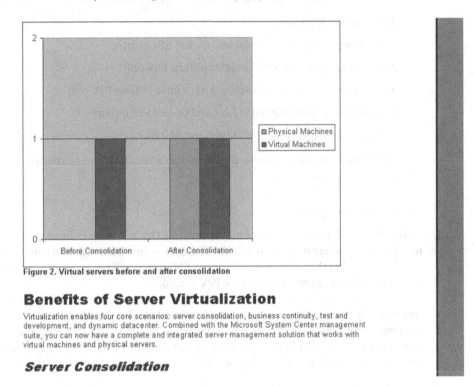

Figure 2. Virtual servers before and after consolidation

Benefits of Server Virtualization

Virtualization enables four core scenarios: server consolidation, business continuity, test and development, and dynamic datacenter. Combined with the Microsoft System Center management suite, you can now have a complete and integrated server management solution that works with virtual machines and physical servers.

Server Consolidation

Figure 4-17. *When it is finished, MAP will give you a spreadsheet and Word document with some good information to help you consolidate.*

Migrating Physical Servers

Now that you have selected your migration candidates, it's time to actually migrate them. As stated earlier, there are several ways to accomplish this. However, the only official Microsoft way is to use System Center Virtual Machine Manager (VMM) 2008 to migrate your physical machines to virtual machines, and we will look at that approach first. Then we will look at an alternative method for performing P2V migrations, in case you are not ready to deploy VMM 2008 yet. In either case, make sure you perform the following tasks on your servers before you convert them:

- Install the latest patches and service packs on your target physical servers.

- Check the disks on the target physical servers for errors.

- Defragment the disks on the target physical servers.

Migrating Physical Servers Manually Using VMM 2008

VMM 2008 can be used to convert physical machines to virtual machines on any host that VMM 2008 controls. The following systems are supported by Microsoft for P2V migrations:

- Windows Server 2008

- Windows Server 2003 (32-bit and 64-bit) SP1 or later

- Windows 2000 Server SP4 or later (offline P2V only)

- Windows 2000 Advanced Server SP4 or later (offline P2V only)

- Windows XP Professional (32-bit and 64-bit) SP2 or later

- Windows Vista SP1 or later (32-bit and 64-bit)

A P2V migration should not be performed on a Windows Server 2008 machine with the Hyper-V role enabled.

Running the Conversion

By default, VMM 2008 does an online conversion. This will work in most cases. However, you may find that you are having a hard time doing an online conversion of some machines. In this case, either the conversion will fail or VMM 2008 will warn you that an offline conversion is recommended at the end of the P2V wizard.

An offline conversion will copy a customized image of Windows PE 2.0 to the physical machine. Then it will reboot the physical machine into the Windows PE 2.0 environment. The data from the physical disks is then transferred to the target Hyper-V server and put into the virtual hard disk (*.vhd) format. If you are going to perform an offline P2V conversion, the target server must have at least 512MB of RAM.

Caution An offline P2V conversion will involve some extended downtime for the target physical server. Make sure you are prepared for this downtime.

Follow these steps to run the P2V conversion:

1. Start VMM and click Convert physical server in the Actions pane. This will launch the Convert Physical Server (P2V) Wizard.

2. Select the source machine that you want to convert and provide administrator credentials for that machine, as shown in Figure 4-18. Click Next.

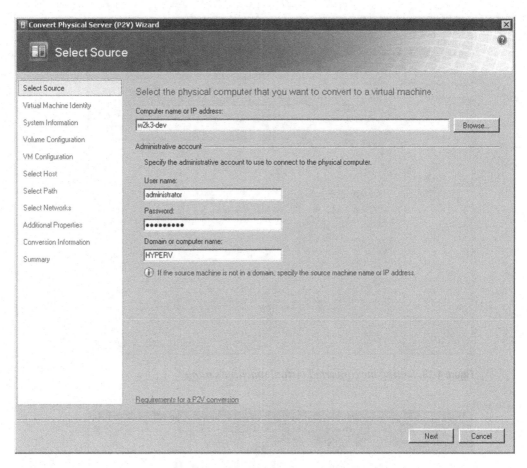

Figure 4-18. *Choosing your source physical machine to convert*

3. In the Virtual Machine Identity window, shown in Figure 4-19, name the virtual machine, assign it an owner, and enter any description details that you want for this virtual machine. The virtual machine name that you define here is what will appear in Hyper-V. This does not necessarily need to match the computer name. However, for clarity, it is generally a good practice to make them match. Once you are finished filling in the information, click Next.

4. In the System Information window, shown in Figure 4-20, click the Scan System button to let VMM 2008 collect the necessary information from the physical machine that VMM 2008 needs to continue. This process might take a few minutes, as indicated by the blue progress bar. Click Next when it's complete.

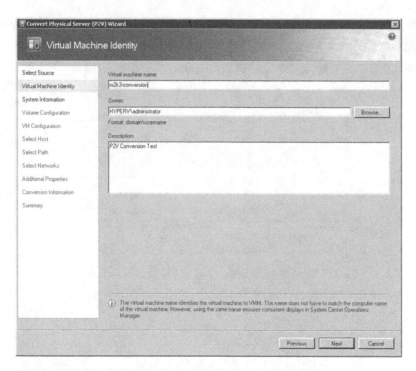

Figure 4-19. *Setting the converted virtual machine's name*

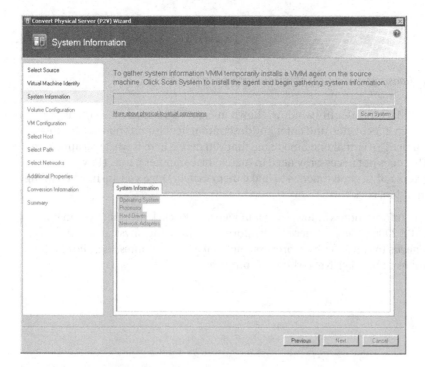

Figure 4-20. *Scanning for the physical machine's system information*

5. In the Volume Configuration window, specify which volumes you are going to convert and whether they will be dynamic or fixed disks.

6. At the bottom of the Volume Configuration window, click Conversion Options. This will reveal a few options, as shown in Figure 4-21. As noted, by default, VMM 2008 does an online conversion. If you select to do an offline conversion, you will see the Offline Conversion Options window, as shown in Figure 4-22. Here, you set up your IP address options for the physical machine that is being converted. You can choose an IPv6, a static IPv4, or a DHCP address. You can also choose which network adapter to bind the IP to by choosing a MAC address in the drop-down list. Click Next to continue.

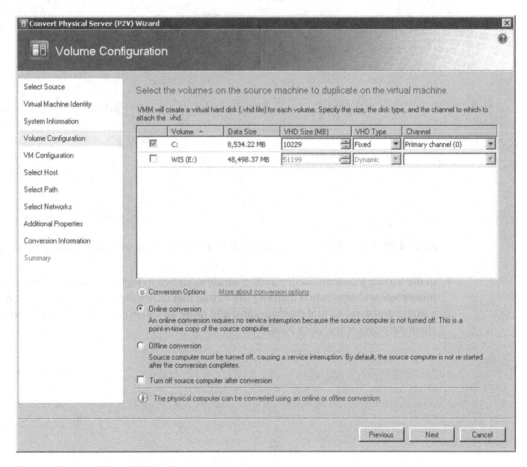

Figure 4-21. *Deciding which volumes to convert*

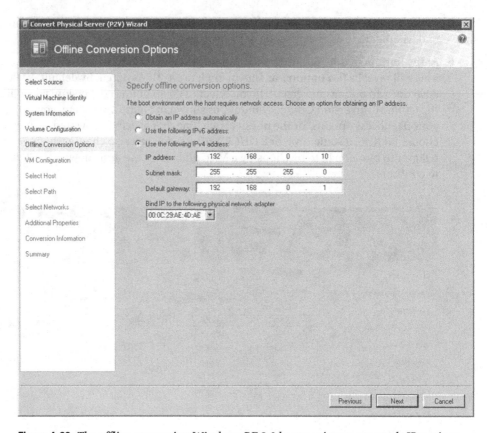

Figure 4-22. *The offline conversion Windows PE 2.0 boot environment needs IP settings.*

7. In the Virtual Machine Configuration window, shown in Figure 4-23, choose how many processors and how much memory the virtual machine will get. You should start with a single processor virtual machine, and add more virtual processors only if they are absolutely necessary. Click Next.

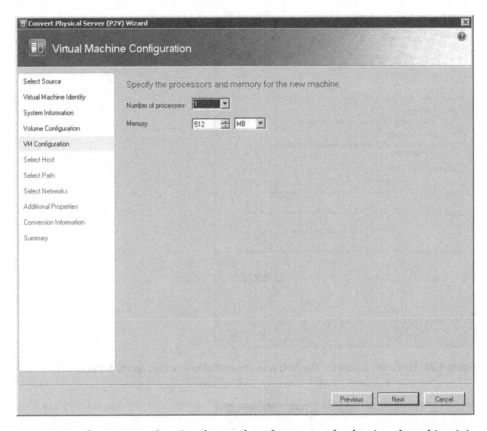

Figure 4-23. *When you are choosing the number of processors for the virtual machine, it is usually best to start with one processor.*

8. In the Host Selection window, choose a host. You will notice a recommendation rating from 0 to 5 stars. This recommendation is based on an algorithm that VMM 2008 uses to place guest machines. You can customize the recommendation settings by clicking the Customize Recommendation Settings button. The Customize Ratings dialog box has two tabs:

- On the Placement Options tab, there are two general options, as shown in Figure 4-24. If you select Load balancing, the host that has the greater amount of free resources will receive a higher rating. If you select Resource maximization, the host with the least free resources that still meets the virtual machine's requirements will receive a higher rating. The Resource maximization option attempts to use all the available resources that it can for your Hyper-V hosts. You can use the sliders to give more weight to any of the four core resources.

- On the VM Load tab, shown in Figure 4-25, you can refine the ratings if you choose the anticipated resource needs of the virtual machine. This will help determine the host assignment of the virtual machine. On this tab, three of the four core resources are taken into consideration: CPU, disk, and network utilization.

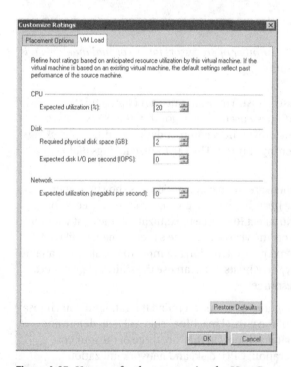

Figure 4-24. *You can customize the host recommendation ratings using these metrics.*

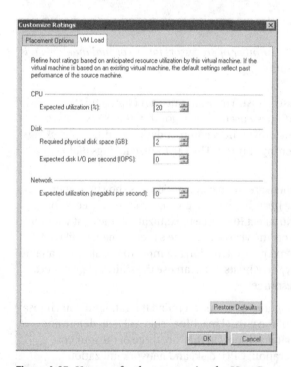

Figure 4-25. *You can further customize the Host Recommendation ratings by indicating your new virtual machine's CPU, disk, and network utilization.*

9. Click OK in the Customize Ratings dialog box, and then click Next to continue.

10. In the Select Path window, shown in Figure 4-26, choose the path where your newly converted virtual machine will be stored. Click Next.

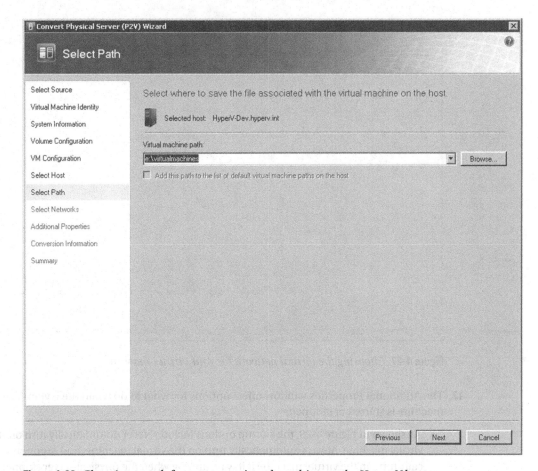

Figure 4-26. *Choosing a path for your new virtual machine on the Hyper-V host*

11. In the Select Networks window, shown in Figure 4-27, specify to which virtual network your newly converted virtual machine will be attached. Just select any preconfigured virtual network from the drop-down list, and then click Next.

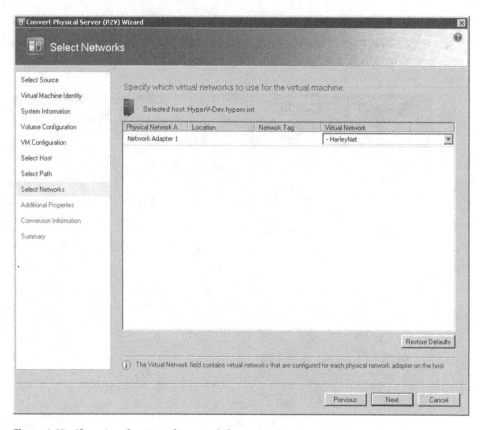

Figure 4-27. *Choosing the virtual network for your virtual machine*

12. The Additional Properties window offers options for what to do when the Hyper-V host machine is started or stopped:

  • As shown in Figure 4-28, the startup options include Never automatically turn on the virtual machine, Always automatically turn on the virtual machine, and Automatically turn on the virtual machine if it was running when the physical server stopped.

  • As shown in Figure 4-29, the options for when the Hyper-V host is stopped include Save state, Turn off virtual machine, and Shut down guest OS. A saved state for a virtual machine is a point-in-time copy of the running state of that virtual machine. It is similar to a snapshot. However, a saved state can be applied to a virtual machine only once, and it must be taken when the virtual machine is running.

  Make your selections, and then click Next.

Note When choosing the host start and stop actions for your virtual machines, you may want to consider which virtual machines may depend on other virtual machines. The virtual machines that are running services that the other virtual machines depend on should start first. You may also want to stagger the startup of your virtual machines to ease the load on the host server as the virtual machines are booting.

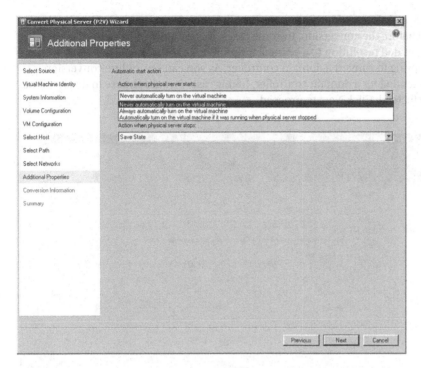

Figure 4-28. *Setting the host start action for the virtual machine*

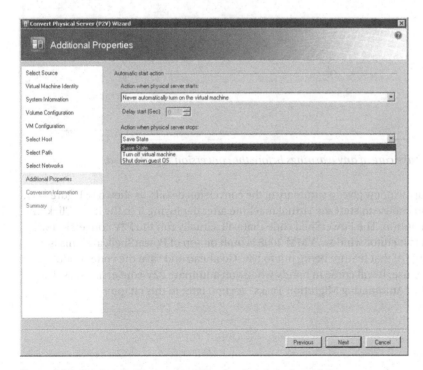

Figure 4-29. *Setting the host stop action for the virtual machine*

13. The Conversion Information window will let you know about any issues that need to be resolved before the conversion. In some cases, this window will also let you know the recommended resolution to a particular problem. In the example in Figure 4-30, I was attempting to convert a domain controller. As you can see, online conversion is not recommended for a domain controller. In this case, I would choose to do an offline conversion instead. Click Next to proceed.

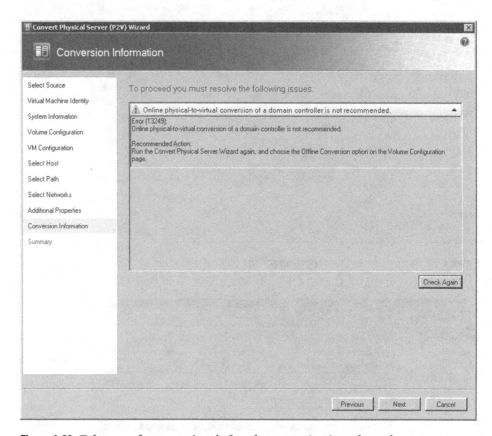

Figure 4-30. *Take care of any warnings before the conversion is performed.*

14. The Summary window gives a summary of the conversion details, as shown in Figure 4-31. You can also choose to start the virtual machine after deploying it to the host. Click the View Script button. The PowerShell code that will actually run the P2V conversion will appear in a text editor window. VMM 2008 is built on top of PowerShell, and this is a good example of that feature being put to use. Go ahead and save the code produced here for later use. It will come in handy when you automate P2V conversions, as discussed in the "Automating Migration Tasks" section later in this chapter.

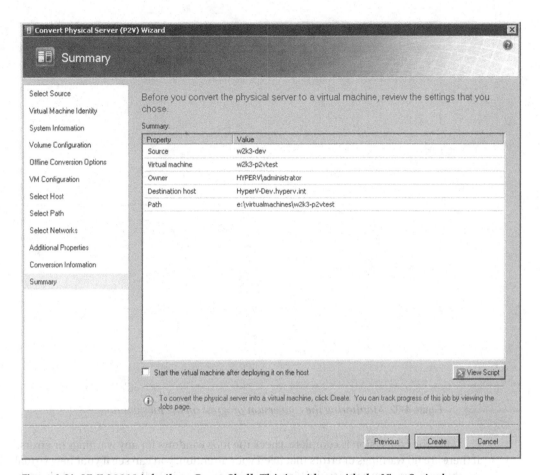

Figure 4-31. *VMM 2008 is built on PowerShell. This is evident with the View Script button.*

15. Click the Create button in the Summary window when you are ready to perform the conversion. A Jobs window appears, in which you can monitor the progress of the conversion, as shown in Figure 4-32.

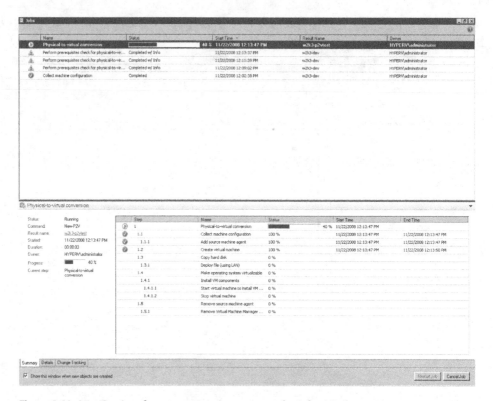

Figure 4-32. *Monitoring the conversion progress on the Jobs window*

After the conversion is complete, check the Jobs windows for any warnings or errors. If there are no warnings or errors that need your attention, you can see if your new virtual machine will boot by going to the Virtual Machine section in VMM 2008, right-clicking the virtual machine, and choosing Start. You can also connect to the virtual machine from here to watch it boot.

Cleaning Up After Conversion

Go ahead and log in to your new virtual machine. You will want to do some cleanup after the conversion. The first item on your list should be to make sure that the Hyper-V integration components are installed. These should be listed in Add/Remove Programs.

You should also uninstall any hidden drivers that may be left over from the physical machine. To do this, open a command prompt on your newly converted virtual machine and type in the following:

```
set DEVMGR_SHOW_NONPRESENT_DEVICES=1
```

Then type in `DEVMGMT.MSC` and select Show hidden devices, as shown in Figure 4-33.

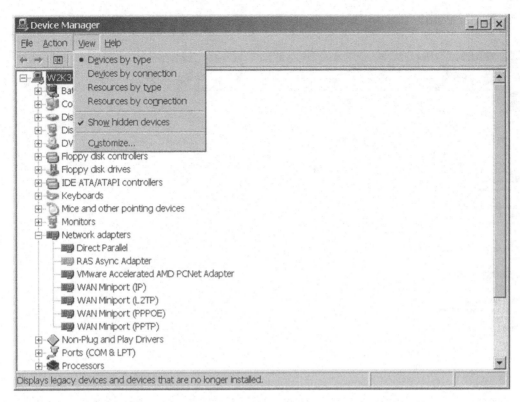

Figure 4-33. *Showing hidden devices in Device Manager*

You can now uninstall any grayed-out or old hidden devices. In the example shown in Figure 4-34, a virtual machine from another virtualization technology was used as the conversion target. Can you guess which one? To Hyper-V, this was simply another physical machine to convert.

Next, go to Add/Remove Programs and remove any vendor-specific or hardware-specific applications. Some examples might be HP or Dell management agents and server utilities that might be installed. Also, look for any management tools that may have been installed for the storage or network cards that were on the physical server.

If you did not perform these cleanup tasks, the virtual machine would probably still function. However, you are trying to achieve maximum performance and efficiency for the virtual machines on your Hyper-V hosts. This cleanup is a necessary step to achieve that goal. You should now have a much more stable converted virtual machine.

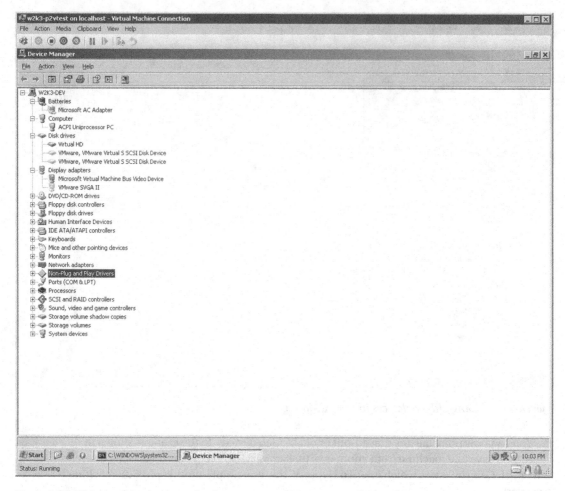

Figure 4-34. *This machine happened to be a converted VMware machine. Those drivers will be removed.*

Installing Single CPU Drivers

One other item to consider is the Hardware Abstraction Layer (HAL) drivers that are installed for the new virtual machine. On any Windows server machine after Windows Server 2003, if you go from a single CPU to multiple CPUs, the HAL will automatically be upgraded on the first boot. On Windows 2000, a reinstallation of the operating system is recommended. However, if you go from multiple CPUs to a single CPU, some work must be done to ensure the proper HAL drivers are used.

Remember that it is best practice to use a single CPU in a virtual machine, unless it is absolutely necessary to use multiple CPUs. However, the physical machine you converted may have had multiple CPUs, so the HAL will be a multi-CPU HAL when it is converted. The virtual machine will still run, but it will be wasting processor time polling for another CPU. In a virtual environment, making the most efficient use of your resources is highly recommended. So, you need to change the HAL driver on the converted virtual machine if you went from a multi-CPU physical machine to a single-CPU virtual machine.

To change the HAL driver, follow these steps:

1. Open Device Manager and expand the Computer node.

2. Under Computer, you will see something like ACPI Multiprocessor PC if the machine is using the multi-CPU HAL. Right-click this entry and select Update driver. This launches the Hardware Update Wizard.

3. In the first wizard window, select "No, not this time," as shown in Figure 4-35, and then click Next.

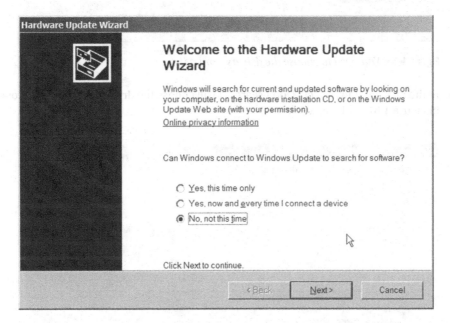

Figure 4-35. *Make sure you do not automatically search for software.*

4. In the next window, select "Install from a list or specific location (Advanced)," as shown in Figure 4-36, and then click Next.

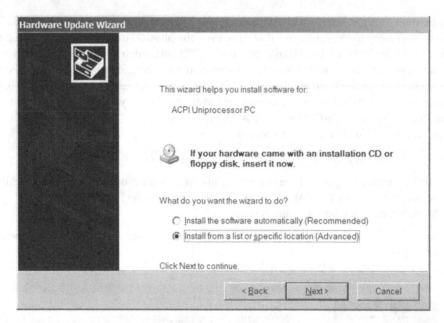

Figure 4-36. *You need to choose the drivers from a list.*

5. In the next window, select "Don't search. I will choose the driver to install," as shown in Figure 4-37, and then click Next.

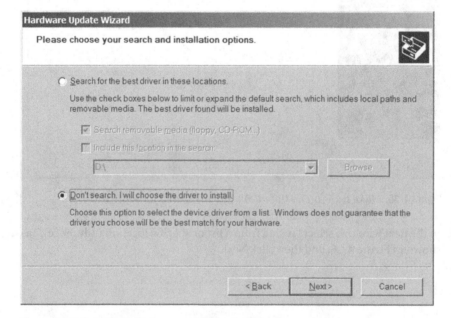

Figure 4-37. *Don't let Windows search for drivers.*

6. In the next window, make sure that the "Show compatible hardware" box is checked. Now, instead of ACPI Multiprocessor PC, choose ACPI Uniprocessor PC, as shown in Figure 4-38. Click Next, and the driver will be installed, as shown in Figure 4-39.

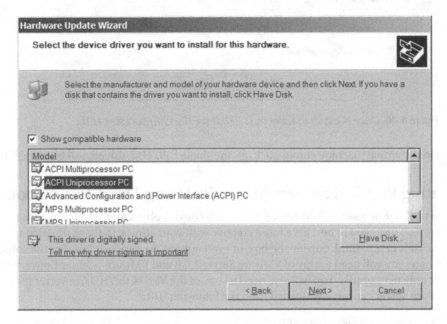

Figure 4-38. *Selecting the Uniprocessor driver*

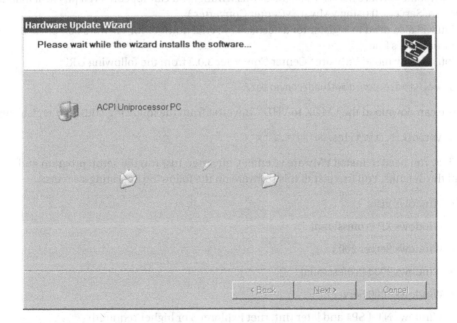

Figure 4-39. *It will only take a few seconds to install the Uniprocessor driver.*

7. Click Finish, and the system will ask for a reboot, as shown in Figure 4-40.

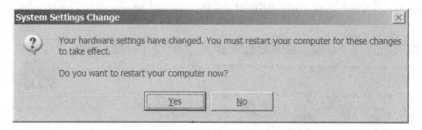

Figure 4-40. *Once the system reboots, it will have the Uniprocessor HAL.*

When the virtual machine comes back up, the single CPU HAL drivers will be installed.

Migrating Physical Servers Manually Using Third-Party Tools

If you do not have access to VMM 2008, you can still convert physical machines to virtual machines. You just need to be a little more creative with your efforts. In these situations, sometimes it is best to think outside the box, or even outside the vendor's box. For the solution detailed here, you will need a copy of VMware Server 1.0.8 and VMware vCenter Converter 3.0.3, but only temporarily. You will also need a copy of the VMDK to VHD Converter tool.

VMware Server can be downloaded from the following URL:

`http://www.vmware.com/download/server/`

Download VMware Server 1.0.8. (As of this writing, you cannot convert a physical machine to VMware Server 2.0 using VMware vCenter Converter.)

You will also need to register for a license key serial number for VMware Server 1.0.8. Don't worry—it's free.

You can download VMware vCenter Converter 3.0.3 from the following URL:

`http://www.vmware.com/download/converter/`

You can download the VMDK to VHD Converter from the following URL after registering:

`http://vmtoolkit.com/files/default.aspx`

First, you need to install VMware vCenter Converter. Just run the setup program and accept the defaults. You can install this software on the following operating systems:

- Windows Vista

- Windows XP Professional

- Windows Server 2003

- Windows 2000 Professional

- Windows 2000 Server

- Windows NT 4 SP4 and later (Internet Explorer 5 or higher required)

When you are finished installing VMware vCenter Converter, go ahead and install VMware Server 1.0.8. Again, just run the setup program and accept the default settings. You will not need it to run a virtual machine for long.

■**Note** Make sure the system on which you are installing VMware Server 1.0.8 has enough resources to run the virtual machine that you will be converting.

This migration will be a three-step process. You will convert the physical machine to a VMware virtual machine. Then you will convert the virtual hard disk (*.vmdk) of that virtual machine to a *.vhd file and copy it to your Hyper-V server. Finally, you will create a new Hyper-V virtual machine and attach the converted *.vhd file to the new virtual machine.

Converting to a VMware Virtual Machine

After downloading and installing the conversion tools, follow these steps to convert the physical machine to a VMware virtual machine:

1. Launch VMware vCenter Converter 3.0.3. When you first launch it, you will get a message about the software being unlicensed, as shown in Figure 4-41. Click the Continue in Starter Mode button.

■**Note** Before proceeding, make sure you know the local administrator password for the physical system you are going to convert. You will need it after the conversion.

Figure 4-41. *The free version of VMware vCenter Converter runs in Starter mode.*

2. You will be presented with the main window, as shown in Figure 4-42. Click Convert Machine along the top left of the window to get started with the Conversion Wizard. Click Next in the first wizard window.

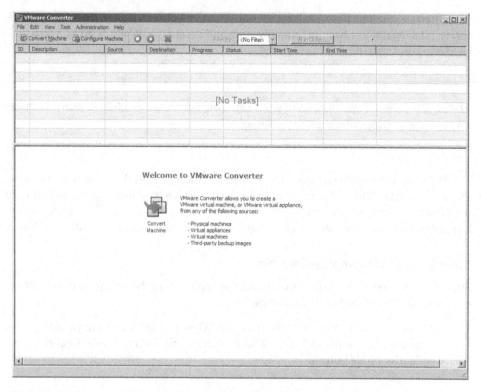

Figure 4-42. *The main VMware vCenter Converter window*

3. This will bring you to the first step of the process, in which you define the source machine, as shown in Figure 4-43. Click Next.

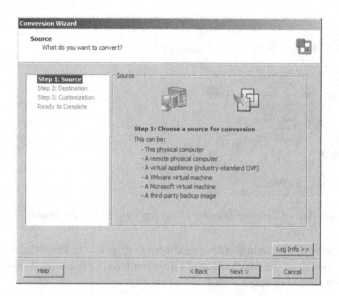

Figure 4-43. *Setting up your source machine is the first step.*

4. In the next window, you select the type of source you will be converting. As shown in Figure 4-44, you have four choices. Choose Physical Computer, and then click Next.

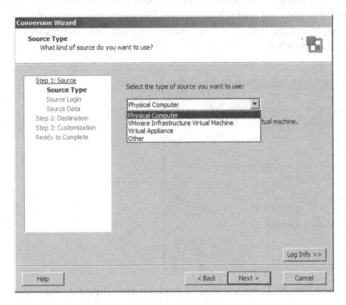

Figure 4-44. *You will be converting a physical computer.*

5. In the next window, shown in Figure 4-45, you need to enter a name or IP address for the source physical machine. You also need to provide credentials that have administrator privileges on the source physical machine. Enter the information, and then click Next.

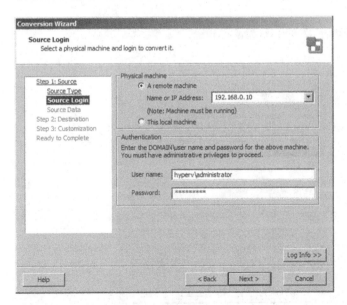

Figure 4-45. *Administrator credentials must be provided to perform the conversion on the source machine.*

6. You will be presented with a warning, as shown in Figure 4-46. This is just telling you that a remote installation of the VMware Converter Agent is required. If the system you are converting is Windows NT or Windows 2000, the agent installation will cause a reboot. If the system you are converting is any newer Windows version, a reboot is not required. In any case, select the option to "Automatically uninstall the files when conversion succeed." Then click Yes.

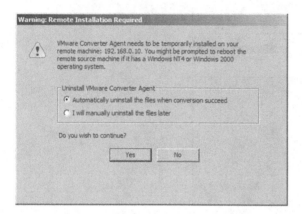

Figure 4-46. *Windows Server 2003 will not require a reboot after the agent installation.*

7. Once the agent finishes installing, you will be at the Source Data window of the Conversion Wizard, as shown in Figure 4-47. Here, you choose which volumes need to be converted and whether you want to maintain their size or resize them. In this example, only the C: drive is being converted, and the size of C: is being maintained. Everything else is left at the default settings. Make your source selections and click Next to continue.

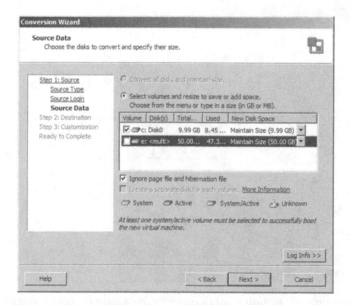

Figure 4-47. *Choosing which volumes to convert*

8. Now you will be at step 2 of the wizard, in which you set the destination settings, as shown in Figure 4-48. Click Next.

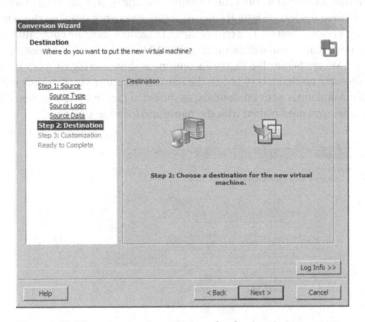

Figure 4-48. *The next step is setting up the destination parameters.*

9. In the Destination Type window, you have only one choice in Starter (unlicensed) mode: Other Virtual Machine, as shown in Figure 4-49. Click Next to proceed.

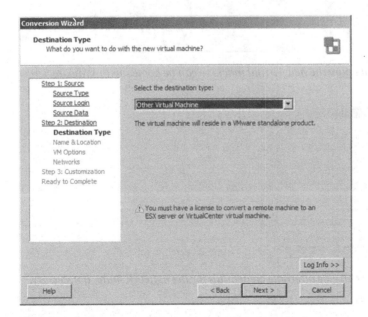

Figure 4-49. *Other Virtual Machine should be the only choice.*

10. In the next window, you need to set the name and location for the virtual machine. You also need to set the type of virtual machine you want to create. The location must be a network share that both the converter machine and the source physical machine can access. It will save some time later if you just create a network share on the same machine that has VMware Server. The type of virtual machine must be compatible with VMware Server 1.*x*, because you will be running it in VMware Server 1.*x*. Choose the Workstation 5.x, VMware Server 1.x, Player 1.x option, as shown in Figure 4-50. If you need to enter alternate credentials to access the network location, you can click the Connect As button and enter your credentials, as shown in Figure 4-51, and then click OK. Click Next when you are finished with the name and location settings.

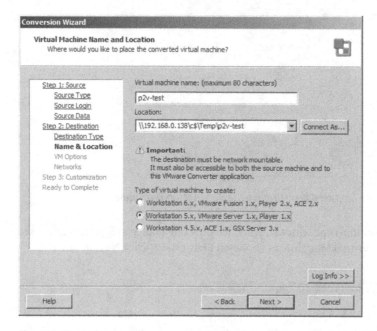

Figure 4-50. *Make sure the new virtual machine can be booted with VMware Server 1.x.*

Figure 4-51. *You can give alternate credentials for the network share, if necessary.*

11. In the VM Options window, select the option "Allocate all disk space now for better performance." Also, make sure the "Split disk into 2GB files" box is checked, as shown in Figure 4-52. This is needed for the VMDK to VHD Converter tool to function properly. Click Next.

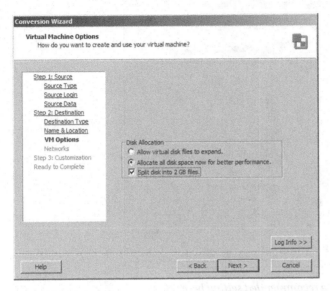

Figure 4-52. *It is important to specify 2GB files, or the VMDK to VHD conversion may not work.*

12. In the Networks window, shown in Figure 4-53, you can clear out any virtual network interface cards (NICs) that are listed here. You will not need them. Then click Next.

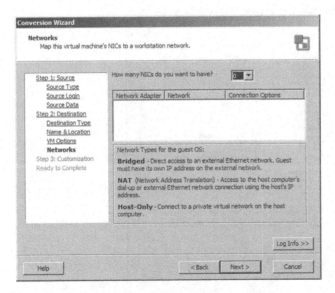

Figure 4-53. *Network interface cards are not necessary.*

13. You are now at the third step of the wizard, in which you can customize the guest operating system of the virtual machine. Check the "Remove all System Restore checkpoints (recommended)" box, as shown in Figure 4-54. Click Next.

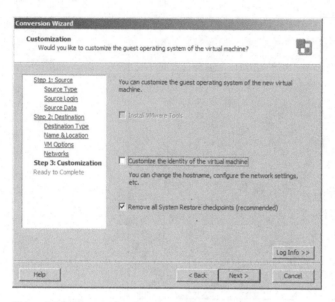

Figure 4-54. *Choose the recommended setting here.*

14. In the Ready to Complete window, look over the details on the right, as shown in Figure 4-55. Make sure they look correct, and then click Finish. You will see the main window, where you can view the progress of your conversion, as shown in Figure 4-56.

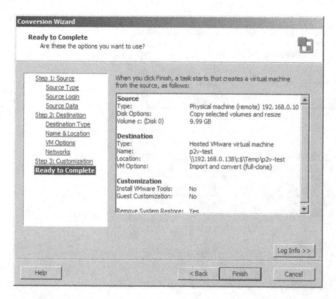

Figure 4-55. *Make sure everything looks correct before you click Finish.*

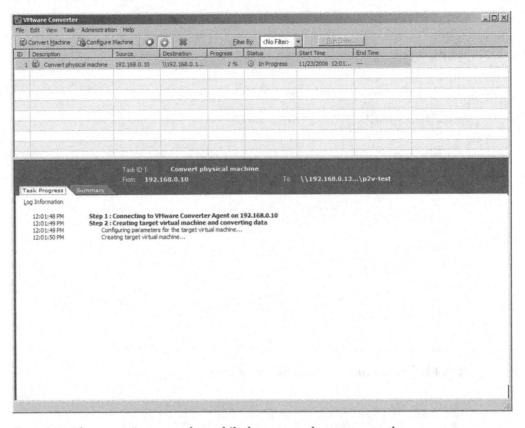

Figure 4-56. *The conversion may take a while, but you can keep an eye on the progress.*

After the conversion is complete, if you made a network share on the same machine that has VMware Server, you are all set. If it is on a different network share, you should copy the entire virtual machine folder from the network share to the system that has VMware Server installed for the best performance results.

Editing Virtual Machine Settings

Once the conversion is complete, the next task is to remove any unnecessary hardware devices from the virtual machine settings, as follows:

1. Open the VMware Server Console, as shown in Figure 4-57.

2. Select File ➤ Open. Click the Browse button and navigate to the folder that contains your converted virtual machine. Open the virtual machine configuration file (*.vmx), as shown in Figure 4-58.

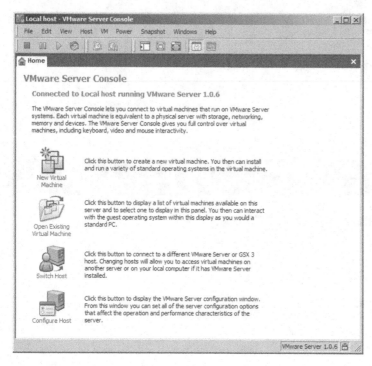

Figure 4-57. *The VMware Server Console main screen*

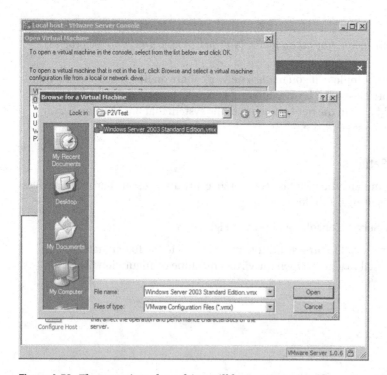

Figure 4-58. *The new virtual machine will have a *.vmx configuration file.*

3. You should see the new virtual machine in a tab in the VMware Server Console, as shown in Figure 4-59. Click "Edit virtual machine settings."

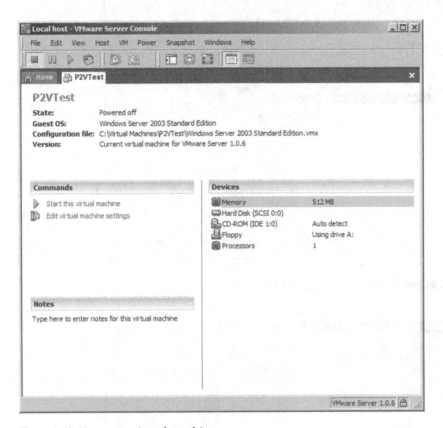

Figure 4-59. *Your new virtual machine*

4. You will see a list of hardware devices, as shown in Figure 4-60. Remove any extraneous hardware devices that are not needed. Some examples might be USB, parallel, and serial ports. These may show up after a P2V conversion with VMware vCenter Converter. Just highlight the hardware device and click Remove. All you really need to boot the virtual machine is the memory, processor, and hard disk, as shown in Figure 4-61. Click OK after you are finished removing devices.

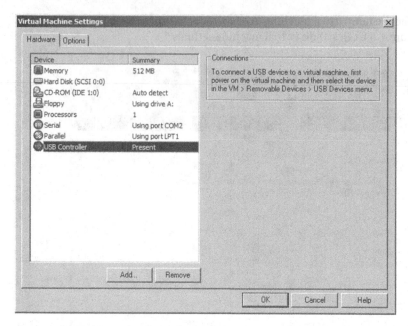

Figure 4-60. *Remove any unnecessary devices.*

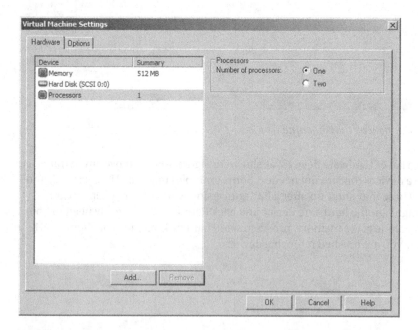

Figure 4-61. *These are the only devices needed for the virtual machine to boot.*

Booting the Virtual Machine

Once you have removed all of the unnecessary components, you are ready to boot the virtual machine.

1. Click the Play button (the green triangle) in the VMware Server Console toolbar, as shown in Figure 4-62.

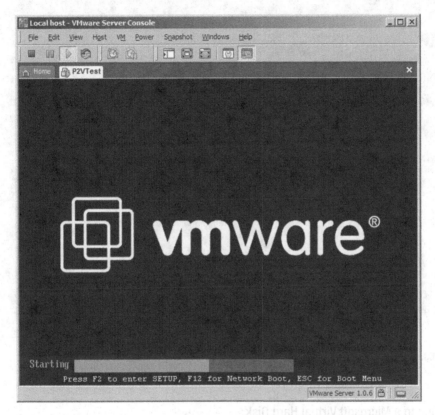

Figure 4-62. *Booting the new VMware virtual machine for the first time*

2. Once the virtual machine has booted to the logon window, press Ctrl+Alt+Ins to log in to the virtual machine, as shown in Figure 4-63. Log on using the local administrator account, since this virtual machine has no network access.

3. The first time you log on to this machine, it may require a reboot after it installs some drivers. After the reboot, just log on again as the local administrator.

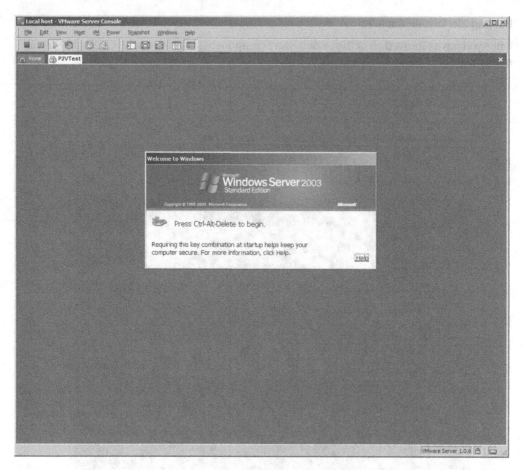

Figure 4-63. *Log on using Ctrl+Alt+Ins.*

Converting to a Microsoft Virtual Hard Disk

Now you need to do a little prep work to the virtual machine before it is ready to begin its journey to the Hyper-V system. The first concern is that VMware generally uses SCSI disks by default for server operating systems, and Hyper-V uses IDE system volumes. If you try to boot a Hyper-V virtual machine with the converted *.vhd file, you will most certainly get a Blue Screen of Death, with an Inaccessible Boot Device error.

You need to copy the appropriate IDE drivers into the %SystemRoot%\System32\Drivers folder. Then you need to merge the appropriate registry entries to tell Windows to look for the drivers when it boots. A Microsoft KB article, at http://support.microsoft.com/default.aspx?scid=kb%3ben-us%3b314082, deals with this situation. The registry file that you will be creating is in this KB article. (Note that the KB article states that this method is not supported by Microsoft.)

Follow these steps:

1. Open Notepad in your newly converted virtual machine that is running in VMware Server.

2. Copy the contents of the registry file that is in the Microsoft KB article and paste it into Notepad. Then save the file as `mergeide.reg`, as shown in Figure 4-64.

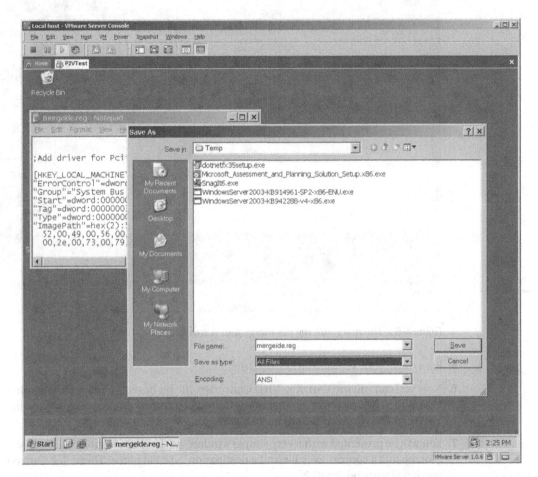

Figure 4-64. *The mergeide.reg file is necessary to enable the detection of IDE drivers.*

3. Copy the `Pciide.sys` file from the `%SystemRoot%\Driver Cache\I386\Driver.cab` file to the `%SystemRoot%\System32\Drivers` folder.

4. Double-click the `mergeide.reg` file you created to merge the appropriate registry entries into your system. Click Yes when the confirmation box appears. If all goes well, you will see a success message, as shown in Figure 4-65.

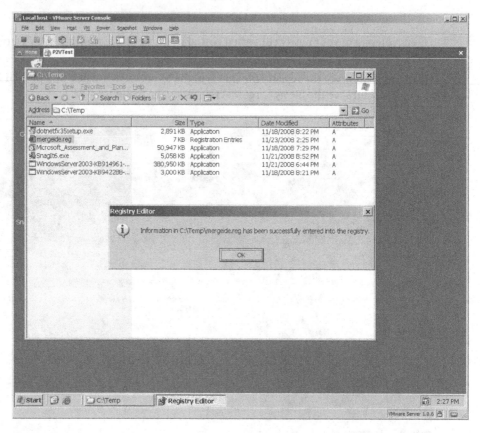

Figure 4-65. *The mergeide.reg file merge was a success.*

5. Shut down your VMware virtual machine.

6. Now you can run the VMDK to VHD Converter. (If you haven't already downloaded the VMDK to VHD Converter, do that now.) Go to the directory where you extracted the VMDK to VHD Converter and run Vmdk2Vhd.exe.

7. You will be presented with a very simple window, as shown in Figure 4-66. You need to give the tool a source .vmdk file and a destination .vhd file name. Then click Convert, and it will work on the disk.

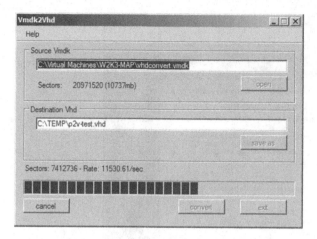

Figure 4-66. *Converting a .vmdk file to a .vhd file is very simple.*

8. Once the conversion is complete, copy the resulting `*.vhd` file to your Hyper-V system. If you are running Hyper-V on Windows Server 2008 Core, just copy the `*.vhd` file to a network share that you can map on the Windows Server 2008 Core system by typing `net use x: \\Server\share`. Then you can copy the `*.vhd` file to its final location on the Hyper-V server. The default path for virtual hard disks on Hyper-V is `C:\ProgramData\ Microsoft\Windows\Hyper-V\Virtual Hard Disks`.

9. Start up Hyper-V Manager and connect to your Hyper-V server.

10. Create a new virtual machine and attach the new `*.vhd` file to it to use as its boot disk.

Installing Integration Services

Once the virtual machine is created with all of the settings you need, you can start your new virtual machine and install Integration Services.

1. Start your new virtual machine and connect to it via a remote console using the Hyper-V Manager tool.

2. Once the virtual machine completely boots, log on with the local administrator account. When you first log on, the Found New Hardware Wizard may start, as shown in Figure 4-67. Just cancel this, because it will likely be related to VMware.

3. Wait a few minutes, and you will see the Systems Settings Change dialog box, as shown in Figure 4-68. This lets you know that Windows is finished installing new devices. Click Yes to restart your system.

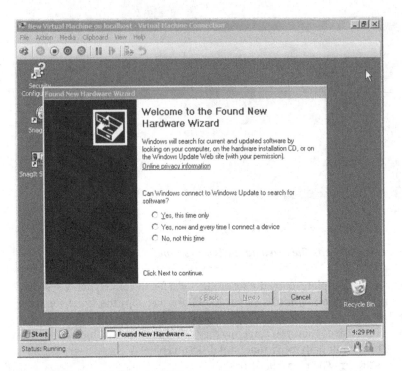

Figure 4-67. *Cancel this wizard if you see it.*

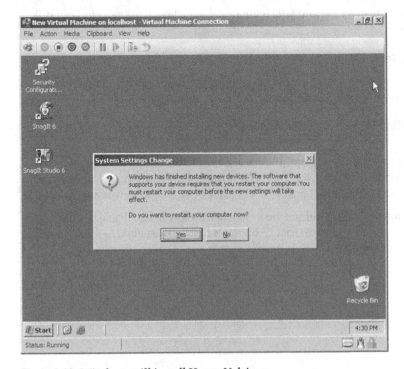

Figure 4-68. *Windows will install Hyper-V drivers.*

4. When your virtual machine is finished rebooting, log back on with the local administrator account.

5. To install Integration Services, select Action ➤ Insert Integration Services Setup Disk, as shown in Figure 4-69. Integration Services should begin installing, as shown in Figure 4-70.

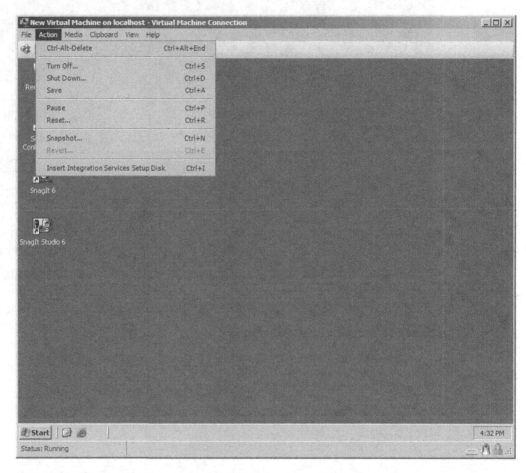

Figure 4-69. *Choosing the Insert Integration Services Setup Disk option*

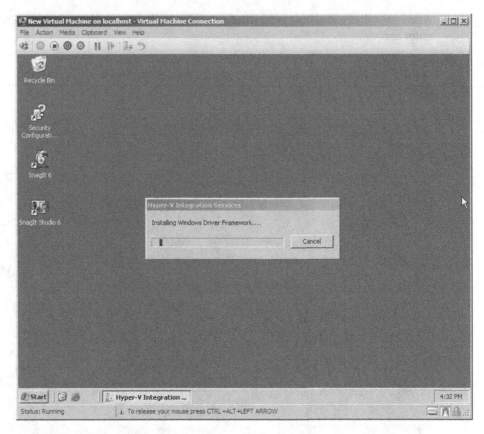

Figure 4-70. *Installing Integration Services*

6. After Integration Services installs, you will prompted to restart your system, as shown in Figure 4-71. Click Yes to do so.

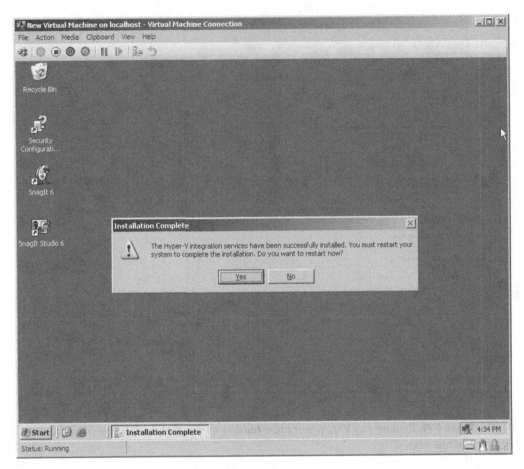

Figure 4-71. *After a reboot, Integration Services will be fully installed.*

Cleaning Up Your Virtual Machine

After the system restarts, you still have a bit more cleanup to do. You need to uninstall any devices that are left over from VMware, as well as any vendor-specific applications. These may include items like HP or Dell server management utilities.

1. Log in to the new virtual machine with the local administrator account.

2. Open a command prompt and type in the following:

   `set DEVMGR_SHOW_NONPRESENT_DEVICES=1`

   Then type in `DEVMGMT.MSC` and select Show hidden devices.

3. Device Manager will list some VMware devices, as shown in Figure 4-72. Uninstall any VMware devices that you see.

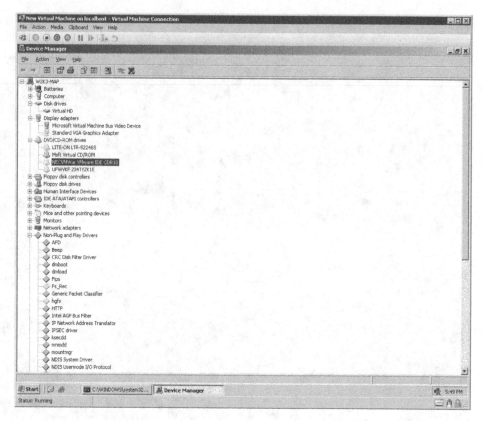

Figure 4-72. *Remove any VMware or other hidden devices that are left over from the physical machine.*

4. Look under SCSI and RAID Controllers. The LSI Logic controller is a VMware controller. You can safely uninstall it. (It should be grayed-out anyway.)

5. If you are going from a multiple-CPU physical machine to a single-CPU virtual machine, use the procedure outlined in the "Installing Single CPU Drivers" section earlier in the chapter to change the HAL drivers to the Uniprocessor driver.

6. Once you are finished cleaning up your virtual machine, shut it down. Look over the virtual machine settings, and make sure everything is correct.

Converting the Virtual Hard Disk to a Fixed Disk

You may also want to convert the *.vhd file you created to a fixed disk for performance reasons. To do this, follow these steps:

1. Choose the disk in Hyper-V Manager, as shown in Figure 4-73, and click Edit.

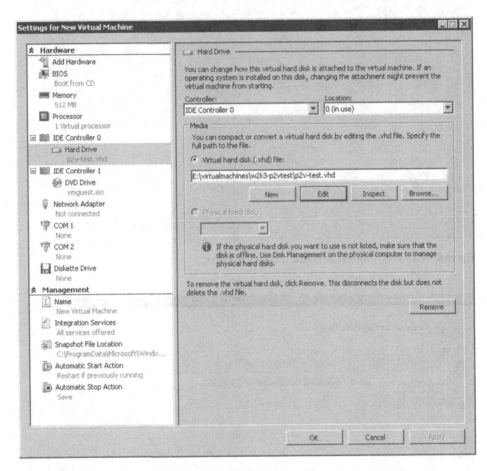

Figure 4-73. *Convert the *.vhd file to fixed for the best performance.*

2. In the Choose Action window, make sure that Convert is selected, as shown in Figure 4-74. Click Next to continue.

3. In the Convert Virtual Hard Disk window, browse to the location where you want to store the new fixed *.vhd file and type in a name for it, as shown in Figure 4-75. Click Next.

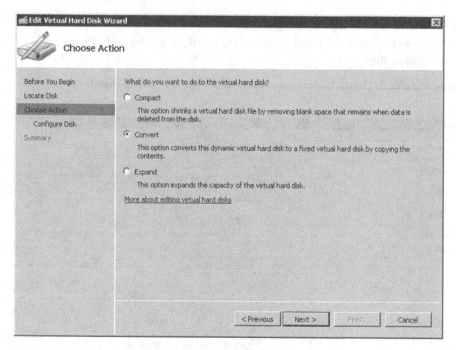

Figure 4-74. *Choose Convert to create a new fixed disk.*

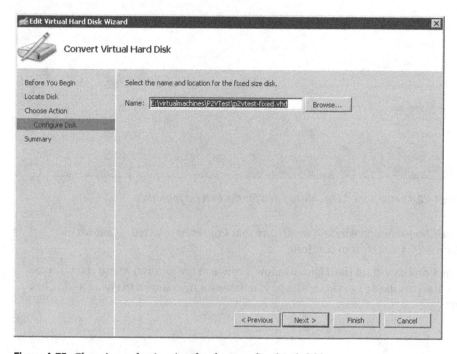

Figure 4-75. *Choosing a destination for the new fixed *.vhd file*

4. In the Completing the Edit Virtual Hard Disk Wizard window, make sure everything in the summary looks correct, as shown in Figure 4-76. Then click Finish. You should now see a progress bar for the conversion process. When it is finished, you will have a new fixed virtual disk file.

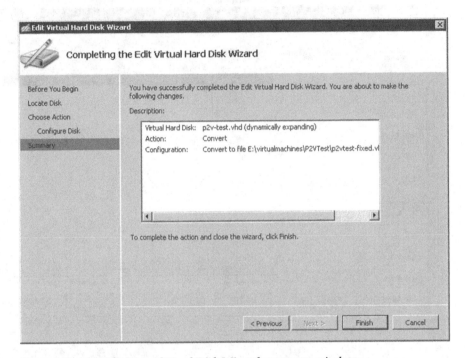

Figure 4-76. *The Edit Virtual Hard Disk Wizard summary window*

5. You need to point your virtual machine to the new disk. Go to the Settings for New Virtual Machine window, choose the hard disk, and browse to your new fixed virtual disk file to choose it, as shown in Figure 4-77. Click OK when you are finished to exit the virtual machine settings.

6. Once you are satisfied that the virtual machine is ready, start it up and log on with domain credentials (if it is a member of an Active Directory domain) to make sure everything works properly.

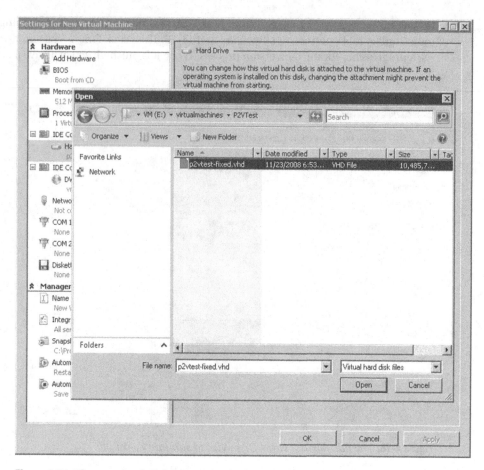

Figure 4-77. *The new fixed disk being attached to the virtual machine*

Congratulations! You have just converted a physical machine to a virtual machine without the use of VMM 2008.

VMM 2008 definitely offers a more straightforward approach for P2V conversions. However, if you do not have access to an VMM 2008 installation, it is good to know that there is more than one way to perform P2V conversions to Hyper-V.

Migrating Virtual Machines

The methods you just learned for P2V migrations will also work for migrating a virtual machine from one of the other server virtualization technologies (VMware Workstation, VMware Server, VMware ESX, Virtual PC, Virtual Server, XenServer, Virtual Iron, and so on) to a virtual machine that will run on a Hyper-V server. As mentioned at the beginning of this chapter, this is called V2V migration.

Just treat the source virtual machine as if it were a physical machine. The preparation steps and the cleanup steps will be the same, because they deal with the operating system instead of the underlying virtualization technology. This way, you have a proven method for performing conversions, no matter on which platform (physical or virtual) the machine resides.

Automating Migration Tasks

VMM 2008 does a great job of doing a straightforward P2V migration for a single host. However, you may want to do a P2V migration of multiple physical machines with similar parameters using VMM 2008. Going through the wizard each time would be time-consuming and an administrative pain. There is good news. Do you remember that View Script button at the end of the P2V conversion wizard? You did save that file, didn't you? If you didn't, run through the P2V conversion wizard again, as described earlier in the "Migrating Physical Servers Manually Using VMM 2008" section, and when you get to the end, click the View Script button. Save the file as *name*.p2v, where *name* is whatever you want to call the script. This gives you a good starting place to create a PowerShell script that you can run from the VMM 2008 server. You just need to modify it a bit to do multiple P2V conversions, instead of just one.

First, you need to do a bit of prep work on the physical machines that you will be converting.

Preparing the Physical Machines

If you go through the wizard, VMM 2008 will install a P2V agent on the source physical machine. You need to go through the VMM 2008 P2V wizard just far enough to let it install the agent on your target machine and scan the system. This will ensure that the target machine configuration is in the VMM 2008 database. The script will query the database for that information. This is only a few steps into the VMM 2008 P2V wizard, so it should not be that time-consuming. Perform steps 1 through 4 in the "Running the Conversion" section earlier in the chapter.

Next, create a text file (p2v.txt) that lists the computer names that you want to convert. There should be one computer name per line. Also create a text file (p2v-network.txt) with the MAC addresses of the network cards that you will be using to connect to the source physical machines. Make sure that line 1 in p2v.txt matches with line 1 in p2v-network.txt, line 2 in these files match, and so on. Save these files in the same directory as the script.

Modifying the P2V Wizard Script

Now you can modify the script that you saved earlier. The script doesn't need much modification. Look at the original script.

```
# Begin Code
# ----------------------------------------------------------------------
# Convert Physical Server (P2V) Wizard Script
# ----------------------------------------------------------------------
# Script generated on Monday, November 24, 2008 4:07:18 AM by Virtual Machine
# Manager
#
# For additional help on cmdlet usage, type get-help <cmdlet name>
# ----------------------------------------------------------------------

$Credential = get-credential

New-MachineConfig -VMMServer localhost ➡
-SourceComputerName "w2k3-dev" -Credential $Credential
```

```
$VMHost = Get-VMHost -VMMServer localhost | ➥
where {$_.Name -eq "HyperV-Dev.hyperv.int"}
$VirtualNetwork = Get-VirtualNetwork -VMMServer localhost ➥
| where {$_.ID -eq "d8149071-09d5-4df1-9fe0-a09844da87c9"}
$MachineConfig = Get-MachineConfig -VMMServer localhost | ➥
where {$_.Name -eq "w2k3-dev"}

New-P2V -VMMServer localhost -VMHost $VMHost -RunAsynchronously ➥
 -JobGroup 9d3d770f-fcbc-45ee-8390-3fd17deb2f59 ➥
-SourceNetworkConnectionID "00:0C:29:AE:4D:AE" ➥
-PhysicalAddress "00:0C:29:AE:4D:AE" -PhysicalAddressType Static ➥
 -VirtualNetwork $VirtualNetwork -MachineConfig $MachineConfig

$VMHost = Get-VMHost -VMMServer localhost | ➥
 where {$_.Name -eq "HyperV-Dev.hyperv.int"}
$MachineConfig = Get-MachineConfig -VMMServer localhost | ➥
 where {$_.Name -eq "w2k3-dev"}

New-P2V -VMMServer localhost -VMHost $VMHost -RunAsynchronously ➥
 -JobGroup 9d3d770f-fcbc-45ee-8390-3fd17deb2f59 ➥
-VolumeDeviceID "C" -Dynamic -IDE -Bus 0 -LUN 0 ➥
-MachineConfig $MachineConfig

$Credential = get-credential

$VMHost = Get-VMHost -VMMServer localhost | ➥
where {$_.Name -eq "HyperV-Dev.hyperv.int"}

$MachineConfig = Get-MachineConfig -VMMServer localhost | ➥
where {$_.Name -eq "w2k3-dev"}

New-P2V -Credential $Credential -VMMServer localhost ➥
-VMHost $VMHost -Path "e:\virtualmachines" -Owner "HYPERV\administrator" ➥
-RunAsynchronously -JobGroup 9d3d770f-fcbc-45ee-8390-3fd17deb2f59 ➥
-Trigger -Name "w2k3-dev" -MachineConfig $MachineConfig -CPUCount 1 ➥
-MemoryMB 512 -RunAsSystem -StartAction NeverAutoTurnOnVM -StopAction SaveVM

# End Code
```

Now, take a look at the modified script.

■ **Note** Any line with a # in front of it is a comment in PowerShell.

```
# Begin Code
# -------------------------------------------------------------------------------
# Convert Physical Server (P2V) Wizard Script
# -------------------------------------------------------------------------------
# Script generated on Monday, November 24, 2008 3:02:24 AM
#  by Virtual Machine Manager
# For additional help on cmdlet usage, type get-help <cmdlet name>
# -------------------------------------------------------------------------------

$Server = "hyperv-dev.hyperv.int"
$VMPath = "e:\virtualmachines"
$VMOwner = "hyperv\administrator"
$CPUCount = "1"
$VMMemory = "512"


#Initiate the variable used to go through the object array created with get-content


$a = 0


$b = 0


#Get the credentials needed for the P2V conversion
#Moved this out of the loop so that it only needs to be captured once

$Credential = get-credential

#Read the p2v.txt file to get the list of computers

get-content p2v.txt | Foreach-object {

#Get the $a line in the p2v.txt file

$strSourceComputer = (get-content p2v.txt)[$a]
$strSourceNIC = (get-content p2v-network.txt)[$b]

#Default P2V script that was produced by VMM 2008
New-MachineConfig -VMMServer localhost ➥
-SourceComputerName $strSourceComputer -Credential $Credential

$VMHost = Get-VMHost -VMMServer localhost | where {$_.Name -eq $Server}

$VirtualNetwork = Get-VirtualNetwork -VMMServer localhost | ➥
where {$_.ID -eq "d8149071-09d5-4df1-9fe0-a09844da87c9"}

$MachineConfig = Get-MachineConfig -VMMServer localhost | ➥
where {$_.Name -eq $strSourceComputer}
```

```
New-P2V -VMMServer localhost -VMHost $VMHost -RunAsynchronously ➥
-JobGroup a925f8e4-dae6-4db3-bf34-34a7cd7d4b2c ➥
-SourceNetworkConnectionID $strSourceNIC ➥
-PhysicalAddress $strSourceNIC -PhysicalAddressType Static ➥
-VirtualNetwork $VirtualNetwork -MachineConfig $MachineConfig

$VMHost = Get-VMHost -VMMServer localhost | where {$_.Name -eq "$Server"}

$MachineConfig = Get-MachineConfig -VMMServer localhost | ➥
where {$_.Name -eq $strSourceComputer}

New-P2V -VMMServer localhost -VMHost $VMHost -RunAsynchronously ➥
-JobGroup a925f8e4-dae6-4db3-bf34-34a7cd7d4b2c -VolumeDeviceID "C" ➥
-Fixed -IDE -Bus 0 -LUN 0 -MachineConfig $MachineConfig

$VMHost = Get-VMHost -VMMServer localhost | where {$_.Name -eq "$Server"}

$MachineConfig = Get-MachineConfig -VMMServer localhost | ➥
where {$_.Name -eq $strSourceComputer}

New-P2V -Credential $Credential -VMMServer localhost ➥
-VMHost $VMHost -Path $VMPath ➥
-Owner $VMOwner -RunAsynchronously ➥
-JobGroup a925f8e4-dae6-4db3-bf34-34a7cd7d4b2c ➥
-Trigger -Name $strSourceComputer -MachineConfig $MachineConfig ➥
-CPUCount $CPUCount -MemoryMB $VMMemory -RunAsSystem ➥
-StartAction NeverAutoTurnOnVM -StopAction ShutdownGuestOS

$a = $a+1

$b = $b+1

}
# End Code
```

The only real difference between the two scripts is that you are now reading the computer name and network connection information from text files, instead of having it hard-coded into the script. Also, the following variables that are used for P2V parameters are defined at the beginning of the script:

- $Server: The Hyper-V Server where the new virtual machine will be created

- $VMPath: The path for the virtual machine files when it is created

- $VMOwner: The owner of the new virtual machine

- $CPUCount: The number of virtual CPUs that will be assigned to the new virtual machine

- $VMMemory: The amount of memory assigned to the new virtual machine

This script and all the cmdlets contained in it need to be run from the PowerShell console that is launched from VMM 2008, as shown in Figure 4-78.

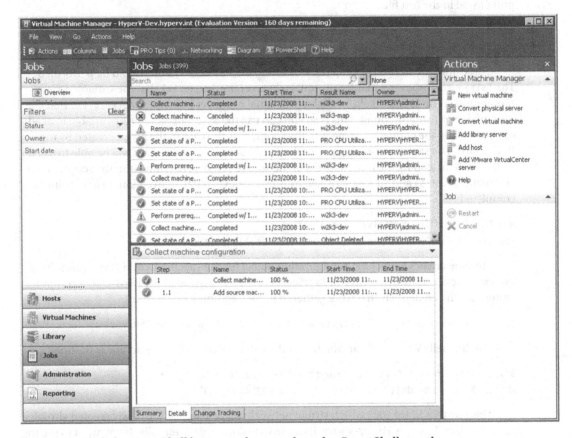

Figure 4-78. *Click the PowerShell button at the top to launch a PowerShell console.*

This allows you to loop through the computer names in the text file and perform a P2V conversion for each one.

Now, let's take a look at the modified script line by line.

```
$a = 0
```

This is a variable used to track the position in the p2v.txt file. Position 0 is line 1.

```
$b = 0
```

This is a variable used to track the position in the p2v-network.txt file. Position 0 is line 1.

```
$Credential = get-credential
```

This will pop up a window to ask for appropriate credentials to perform the P2V conversion. It was moved to the top, so the script will ask only once.

```
get-content p2v.txt | Foreach-object {
```

This line reads the contents of your text file and passes them on to a Foreach-object loop to do some processing. In other words, this script will do a P2V conversion "for each" computer listed in the text file.

```
$strSourceComputer = (get-content p2v.txt)[$a]
$strSourceNIC = (get-content p2v-network.txt)[$b]
```

These lines are needed to keep track of where the P2V conversion should be performed. The $strSourceComputer variable will equal whatever line in p2v.txt that the variable $a is representing. The $strSourceNIC variable will equal whatever line in p2v-network.txt that the variable $b is representing. This is so you can use the $strSourceComputer variable instead of hard-coding the computer name into the script, as is the case in the script created by the P2V wizard. The same reasoning goes for the $strSourceNIC variable. You will be able to use it instead of hard-coding the MAC address of the source physical machine into the script. At the end of the script, $a and $b are increased by one whenever a P2V conversion on a machine is completed.

```
New-MachineConfig -VMMServer localhost ➥
-SourceComputerName $strSourceComputer -Credential $Credential
```

This line creates a machine configuration object for the specified VMM 2008 server (in this case, localhost) with a source of $strSourceComputer (instead of the hard-coded computer name) and the credentials that were gathered in the beginning of the script.

```
$VMHost = Get-VMHost -VMMServer localhost | where {$_.Name -eq $Server}
```

This line tells VMM 2008 for which host the newly created virtual machine is destined.

```
$VirtualNetwork = Get-VirtualNetwork -VMMServer localhost | ➥
where {$_.ID -eq "d8149071-09d5-4df1-9fe0-a09844da87c9"}
```

This line tells VMM 2008 which virtual network will be used for the newly created virtual machine. The ID is how Hyper-V identifies the virtual network internally. If you want to see the IDs for all of the virtual networks, just run the Get-VirtualNetwork cmdlet from the VMM 2008 PowerShell console, as shown in Figure 4-79.

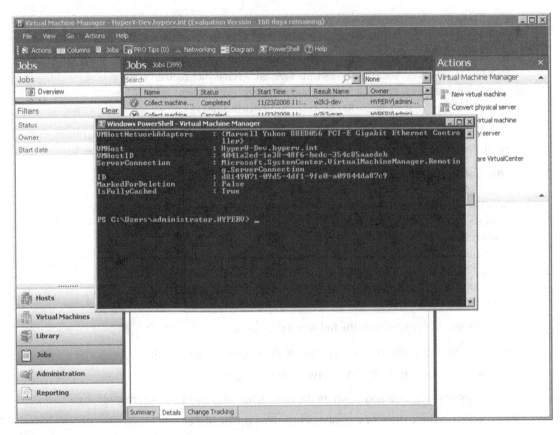

Figure 4-79. *The output of the Get-VirtualNetwork cmdlet*

```
$MachineConfig = Get-MachineConfig -VMMServer localhost | ➥
where {$_.Name -eq $strSourceComputer}
```

This line gets the physical machine information to use as a baseline to create the new
virtual machine.

```
New-P2V -VMMServer localhost -VMHost $VMHost -RunAsynchronously ➥
-JobGroup a925f8e4-dae6-4db3-bf34-34a7cd7d4b2c ➥
-SourceNetworkConnectionID $strSourceNIC ➥
-PhysicalAddress $strSourceNIC -PhysicalAddressType Static ➥
-VirtualNetwork $VirtualNetwork -MachineConfig $MachineConfig
```

This line creates the network parameters for the P2V conversion.

```
$VMHost = Get-VMHost -VMMServer localhost | where {$_.Name -eq $Server}
$MachineConfig = Get-MachineConfig -VMMServer localhost | ➥
where {$_.Name -eq $strSourceComputer}
```

These two lines are repeated to reset the $VMHost variable and the $MachineConfig variable. Notice that the $strSourceComputer variable is used again, instead of being hard-coded to a computer name.

```
New-P2V -VMMServer localhost -VMHost $VMHost -RunAsynchronously ➥
-JobGroup a925f8e4-dae6-4db3-bf34-34a7cd7d4b2c -VolumeDeviceID "C" ➥
-Fixed -IDE -Bus 0 -LUN 0 -MachineConfig $MachineConfig
```

This line creates the virtual disk parameters. As you can see, it takes some parameters, such as which volumes to convert (C:) and what type of virtual disk to create (Fixed).

```
$MachineConfig = Get-MachineConfig -VMMServer localhost | ➥
where {$_.Name -eq $strSourceComputer}
New-P2V -Credential $Credential -VMMServer localhost ➥
-VMHost $VMHost -Path $VMPath ➥
-Owner $VMOwner -RunAsynchronously ➥
-JobGroup a925f8e4-dae6-4db3-bf34-34a7cd7d4b2c ➥
-Trigger -Name $strSourceComputer -MachineConfig $MachineConfig ➥
-CPUCount $CPUCount -MemoryMB $VMMemory -RunAsSystem ➥
-StartAction NeverAutoTurnOnVM -StopAction ShutdownGuestOS
```

The New-P2V cmdlet uses the following parameters:

- Credential: The credentials given at the beginning of the script.

- VMMServer: The VMM 2008 server that you are using.

- VMHost: The host server where the new virtual machines will be created.

- Path: Where the new virtual machine files will be placed.

- Owner: The owner of the new virtual machines.

- RunAsynchronously: Ensures that the job runs asynchronously so you can perform other tasks while the conversions are being performed.

- JobGroup: A job group ID that is assigned so all of the gathered information in the script will run at the end of the script.

- Name: The name that will be given to the new virtual machine.

- MachineConfig: Gets the target new virtual machine's configuration.

- CPUCount: Sets the number of virtual CPUs that the new virtual machine will have.

- MemoryMB: Sets the amount of RAM that will be assigned to the new virtual machine.

- RunAsSystem: Tells the virtual machine to run using the system account on the target Hyper-V host server.

- StartAction: Defines the action for the virtual machine when the host server starts. In this case, it is set to never automatically turn on the virtual machine (NeverAutoTurnOnVM).

- StopAction: Defines the action for the virtual machine when the host server is shut down. In this case, it is set to shut down the guest operating system (ShutDownGuestOS).

Finally, with these last two lines, the rest of the parameters for the P2V conversion are defined. With each New-P2V command, VMM 2008 is actually adding parameters and items to the virtual machine it is creating.

```
$a = $a+1
$b = $b+1
}
```

These last three lines increment the $a and $b variables by one and close the Foreach-object loop. So, the script will perform a P2V conversion on each computer listed in the p2v.txt file. This can be accomplished because the $strSourceComputer variable holds whatever computer name the script happens to be working on from the text file.

Running the Script

To run this script, make sure that you set PowerShell to run scripts by opening the PowerShell console from VMM 2008 and running the following command:

```
Set-ExecutionPolicy Remote-Signed
```

Now you should just be able to run .\scriptname.ps1.

When the script first starts, you will be asked for your credentials, as shown in Figure 4-80.

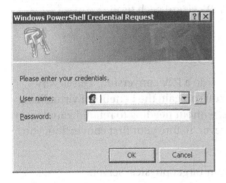

Figure 4-80. *You need to provide your credentials only once.*

After you enter the appropriate credentials, just let the script run. Keep in mind that the P2V conversions may take a while, as they are performed one at a time. You can view the progress in the VMM 2008 Jobs window, as shown in Figure 4-81.

	Name	Status	Start Time ▼	Result Name	Owner
▶	Collect machine configur...		0 % 11/24/2008 12:44:47 AM	w2k3-map	HYPERV\administrator
✓	Set state of a PRO tip	Completed	11/24/2008 12:29:42 AM	PRO CPU Utilization	HYPERV\HYPERV-DEV$
✓	Set state of a PRO tip	Completed	11/24/2008 12:29:39 AM	PRO CPU Utilization	HYPERV\HYPERV-DEV$
✓	Set state of a PRO tip	Completed	11/24/2008 12:23:56 AM	PRO CPU Utilization	HYPERV\HYPERV-DEV$
✓	Set state of a PRO tip	Completed	11/24/2008 12:23:49 AM	PRO CPU Utilization	HYPERV\HYPERV-DEV$
✓	Collect machine configuration	Completed	11/23/2008 11:22:02 PM	w2k3-dev	HYPERV\administrator
✗	Collect machine configuration	Canceled	11/23/2008 11:17:24 PM	w2k3-map	HYPERV\administrator
⚠	Remove source machine agent	Completed w/ Info	11/23/2008 11:16:39 PM	w2k3-dev	HYPERV\administrator
✓	Set state of a PRO tip	Completed	11/23/2008 11:07:43 PM	PRO CPU Utilization	HYPERV\HYPERV-DEV$
✓	Set state of a PRO tip	Completed	11/23/2008 11:07:40 PM	PRO CPU Utilization	HYPERV\HYPERV-DEV$
⚠	Perform prerequisites check f...	Completed w/ Info	11/23/2008 11:05:53 PM	w2k3-dev	HYPERV\administrator
✓	Collect machine configuration	Completed	11/23/2008 11:05:14 PM	w2k3-dev	HYPERV\administrator
✓	Set state of a PRO tip	Completed	11/23/2008 10:59:42 PM	PRO CPU Utilization	HYPERV\HYPERV-DEV$
✓	Set state of a PRO tip	Completed	11/23/2008 10:59:39 PM	PRO CPU Utilization	HYPERV\HYPERV-DEV$
⚠	Perform prerequisites check f...	Completed w/ Info	11/23/2008 10:53:50 PM	w2k3-dev	HYPERV\administrator
✓	Collect machine configuration	Completed	11/23/2008 10:52:11 PM	w2k3-dev	HYPERV\administrator
✓	Set state of a PRO tip	Completed	11/23/2008 10:39:40 PM	Object Deleted	HYPERV\HYPERV-DEV$
✓	Set state of a PRO tip	Completed	11/23/2008 10:39:39 PM	Object Deleted	HYPERV\HYPERV-DEV$
✗	Collect machine configuration	Failed	11/23/2008 10:27:57 PM	w2k3-dev	HYPERV\administrator

Figure 4-81. *The P2V conversions may take a while, but you can check on their progress in the Jobs window.*

When the script completes, you will have some brand-new virtual machines to clean up. At least you did not need to go through the VMM 2008 P2V wizard each time.

Summary

Sometimes the quickest route to virtualizing a server is to do a P2V conversion. This is very useful if you are trying to support legacy applications. You can gain the benefits of virtualizing a server so you can decommission the legacy hardware, without needing to rebuild your legacy server. There are several paths to accomplish this. However, before your first conversion, you should be sure to perform the following steps:

- Install the latest patches and service packs on your target physical servers.

- Check the disks on the target physical servers for errors.

- Defragment the disks on the target physical servers.

This will help to ensure a smooth conversion process. After these steps are performed, you have two general paths to a P2V conversion. The official Microsoft way is to use VMM 2008. This is the most straightforward route to a P2V conversion.

If your operating system is not supported for an VMM 2008 P2V, or you do not have access to VMM 2008, then you can use third-party tools for the P2V conversion. The third-party method discussed in this chapter involved the following general steps:

- Convert the physical server to a VMware Server 1.x virtual machine using VMware vCenter Converter 3.0.3.

- Convert the virtual hard disk of the VMware Server 1.x virtual machine (*.vmdk) to a Microsoft virtual hard disk (*.vhd) using the VMDK to VHD Converter tool.

- Create a new Hyper-V virtual machine and connect the converted *.vhd file to that virtual machine as the boot volume.

- Boot the Hyper-V virtual machine and perform any cleanup that is necessary.

With some planning and preparation, you should be able to convert many of your physical servers to virtual machines without the need to rebuild those servers. This can be accomplished with or without VMM 2008.

CHAPTER 5

■ ■ ■

Automating Hyper-V

After you've spent some time managing Hyper-V through the management console, you will eventually grow tired of clicking. In both the Hyper-V Manager and System Center Virtual Machine Manager (VMM) 2008, you will find that you perform some tasks repeatedly with the same result. After a fresh installation, you will notice that the same configurations are applied to your Hyper-V servers. At this point, you will want to start automating some of those boring, click-filled tasks.

We have basically two ways to automate Hyper-V with PowerShell: with VMM 2008 and without VMM 2008. VMM 2008 gives you the ability to run virtualization PowerShell cmdlets against it to manipulate Hyper-V hosts and virtual machines. Without VMM 2008, you can still manipulate Hyper-V hosts and virtual machines. However, you will be using Windows Management Instrumentation (WMI) inside your PowerShell scripts if you go that route.

In this chapter, we will first look at using WMI with PowerShell to manage a Hyper-V host machine. Then you will learn how to use PowerShell with VMM 2008 to perform the same management tasks.

Caution Most of the virtual machine manipulation discussed in this chapter requires that the virtual machine be turned off.

PowerShell and WMI

WMI is the tried-and-true method for managing pretty much anything related to Windows. If it is made by Microsoft and runs with or on Windows, chances are there is a way to manipulate it with WMI scripting. Hyper-V certainly is made by Microsoft, and WMI can definitely be used to manage aspects of Hyper-V. Let's start with the host server properties, and then look at virtual machine manipulation.

Manipulating Hyper-V Server Settings

You will probably want to make your Hyper-V system images deployed through Windows Deployment Services (WDS) as generic as possible, and do all of the configuration after the image is deployed. That can be tedious if you need to configure multiple Hyper-V hosts. It can also be error-prone. Instead, you can automate the process with a script, so that the results are consistent and repeatable.

The most common attributes you might want to change on the Hyper-V server are the default location for virtual machines and the default location for virtual hard disks. You may also want to set up an external virtual switch.

Changing the Default Virtual Machine and Virtual Disk Paths

The script that you will be writing in this section will use the following classes:

- Msvm_VirtualSystemManagementService: This class represents the virtualization service on a host system. In this script, the ModifyServiceSettings method of this class will be used to manipulate the settings on your Hyper-V server.

- Msvm_VirtualSystemManagementServiceSettingData: This class represents the settings for the virtualization service on a host system. However, the settings cannot be modified directly, so you must use Msvm_VirtualSystemManagementService. ModifyServiceSettings to actually modify the settings once you define them.

Note A good reference for all of the WMI classes available for Hyper-V can be found at http://msdn. microsoft.com/en-us/library/cc136986(VS.85).aspx.

The basic steps involved with changing the default paths of the virtual machine and virtual disk file locations are as follows:

1. Get an instance of the Msvm_VirtualSystemManagementService class to use later to modify the settings.

2. Get an instance of the Msvm_VirtualSystemManagementServiceSettingData class and set the parameters for the DefaultExternalDataRoot (virtual machine path) and the DefaultVirtualHardDiskPath (virtual disk path) properties.

3. Change the settings of the Hyper-V server with the ModifyServiceSettings method of the Msvm_VirtualSystemManagementService class.

You will use Scriptomatic for PowerShell to get the beginning of a WMI query that will allow you to change the settings on your Hyper-V servers. Begin by opening Scriptomatic for PowerShell, as shown in Figure 5-1.

You need one Hyper-V server to start exploring WMI. Enter the name of your target server in the text box at the bottom of the window, which contains LocalHost by default. Also, make sure you have administrator access, the Windows Firewall is open for WMI, and the WMI service is running on the target server. For the WMI namespace, choose root\virtualization. (The root\virtualization class will be available only when the Hyper-V role is enabled on your target server.) For the WMI class, select Msvm_VirtualSystemManagementServiceData.

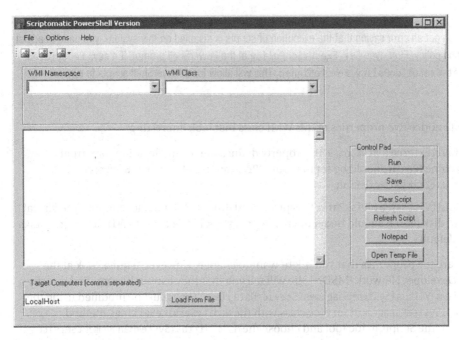

Figure 5-1. *The main Scriptomatic window*

You will notice that the Scriptomatic tool has already written a useful query in PowerShell for you, as shown in Figure 5-2. Click the Run button.

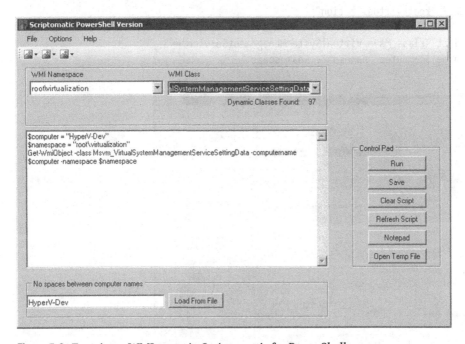

Figure 5-2. *Forming a WMI query in Scriptomatic for PowerShell*

> **Note** If you get an error saying that the execution of scripts is disabled on this system, you need to adjust your execution policy. First, type Get-ExecutionPolicy at the PowerShell prompt. If it says restricted, then type Set-ExecutionPolicy RemoteSigned. This will allow local PowerShell scripts to run.

You will notice two properties of this WMI class that look interesting:

- DefaultExternalDataRoot: This property defines the default location for virtual machine files. It should be set to <root>\ProgramData\Microsoft\Windows\Virtualization by default.

- DefaultVirtualHardDiskPath: This property defines the default location for the virtual hard disk files. It should be set to <root>\Users\Public\Documents\Virtual Hard Disks by default.

These are the properties that you might want to change. However, a quick look at the Microsoft Developer Network (MSDN) site will tell you that they cannot be modified directly using the Msvm_VirtualSystemManagementServiceData class. They must be modified using the Msvm_VirtualSystemManagementService class with the ModifyServiceSettings method.

Return to the Scriptomatic tool and choose the Msvm_VirtualSystemManagementService class. Scriptomatic will give you the beginning of a WMI query, as shown in Figure 5-3. Let's start by examining the base WMI query that Scriptomatic has provided.

```
$computer = "HyperV-Dev"

$namespace = "root\virtualization"

Get-WmiObject -class Msvm_VirtualSystemManagementService ➡
-computername $computer -namespace $namespace
```

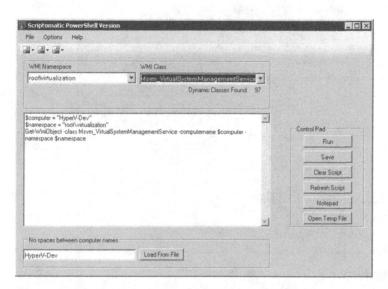

Figure 5-3. *The Msvm_VirtualSystemManagementService class in Scriptomatic*

The first line just defines the variable used to hold the computer name that you will run the query against. The second line defines the variable used to determine the WMI namespace that you will query. The third line actually does the work:

```
Get-WmiObject
```

This PowerShell cmdlet literally tells PowerShell to get a WMI object. In this case, three parameters go along with the cmdlet:

- `-class Msvm_VirtualSystemManagementService`: This tells PowerShell that the WMI object class will be `Msvm_VirtualSystemManagementService`.

- `-computername $computer`: This tells PowerShell that the computer name for the WMI query will be whatever is stored in the `$computer` variable.

- `-namespace $namespace`: This tells PowerShell that the namespace for the WMI query will be whatever is stored in the `$namespace` variable.

Now, if you run this simple query, it will not be very useful. It will basically just return a description of the `Msvm_VirtualSystemManagementService` class. You need to tell PowerShell to do something using a method of the `Msvm_VirtualSystemManagementService` class.

Let's modify the script a bit. The first thing you want to do is put the third line that does the query into a variable, so you can easily use a method on it later. This is simple. Make the third line look like this:

```
$query = Get-WmiObject -class Msvm_VirtualSystemManagementService ➥
-computername $computer -namespace $namespace
```

You just add a "`$query` = to the beginning of the line. Everything else remains the same.

Next, you need to use the `ModifyServiceSettings` method to change the two settings you are after. However, you need to do a little more work to define which settings you are modifying. You will do another query (assigned to a variable) to get the `Msvm_VirtualSystemManagementServiceData` class. Add the following line to the end of the script:

```
$querydata = Get-WmiObject -class Msvm_VirtualSystemManagementServiceSettingData ➥
 -computername $computer -namespace $namespace
```

This line gets the `Msvm_VirtualSystemManagementServiceSettingData` WMI class. As you can see, it is structured in the same way as the previous WMI query, with the same parameters.

Now you just need to define the properties that you want to change. Remember that the two properties you are interested in are `DefaultExternalDataRoot` and `DefaultVirtualHardDiskPath`. Add the following two lines to the bottom of your script:

```
$querydata.DefaultExternalDataRoot = "e:\virtualmachines"
```

```
$querydata.DefaultVirtualHardDiskPath = "e:\virtualdisks"
```

This is assuming that the path you want for your virtual machines is `e:\virtualmachines`, and the path you want for your virtual disks is `e:\virtualdisks`. You can change these lines to match the paths you want to use. When this script runs, the folders will be created, if they are not already in place on your Hyper-V system.

So far, you have told the new script what you want the `DefaultExternalDataRoot` and `DefaultVirtualHardDiskPath` values to be. Now you need to actually change the values using the `ModifyServiceSettings` method of the `Msvm_VirtualSystemManagementService` class. To do that, add the following line to the end of the script:

```
$query.ModifyServiceSettings($querydata.PSbase.GetText(1))
```

This line tells PowerShell to use the `ModifyServiceSettings` method with the input from the $querydata WMI query that you defined previously (along with the properties you defined). The generic syntax would be as follows:

```
Msvm_VirtualSystemManagementService.ModifyServiceSettings(SettingsData)
```

But what about the last part tacked on to the $querydata variable: PSbase.GetText(1)? Well, PowerShell adapts a standard view of many objects to make life easier for the user when viewing things through PowerShell. However, this means that sometimes things don't work as you would expect. To bypass the PowerShell adapter, you can use the `.PSbase` method. In this case, it allows you to use the WMI `GetText` method to get the `Msvm_VirtualSystemManagementServiceSettingData` WMI object as a string that the `ModifyServiceSettings` method can work with.

Let's take a look at the script so far.

```
$computer = "HyperV-Dev"

$namespace = "root\virtualization"

$query = Get-WmiObject -class Msvm_VirtualSystemManagementService ➥
-computername $computer -namespace $namespace

$querydata = Get-WmiObject -class Msvm_VirtualSystemManagementServiceSettingData ➥
-computername $computer -namespace $namespace

$querydata.DefaultExternalDataRoot = "e:\virtualmachines"

$querydata.DefaultVirtualHardDiskPath = "e:\virtualdisks"

$query.ModifyServiceSettings($querydata.PSbase.GetText(1))
```

The script stores two WMI queries in the variables $query (for the `Msvm_VirtualSystemManagementService` class) and $querydata (for the `Msvm_VirtualSystemManagementServiceSettingData` class). Then it defines the default path settings for the virtual machine and virtual disk files. Finally, it changes the default path settings to the appropriate values. All of this happens in seven lines of code—not bad.

However, there is still one last thing you could do to improve this script. The $computer variable is set to only one machine right now. You want to use this script on multiple Hyper-V systems, right? You could just change the computer name every time you want to run the script against a new Hyper-V system, but that is not very efficient.

What if you could have a list of all the Hyper-V systems that you want to run the script against and have that done automatically? Luckily, this is fairly easy to accomplish with PowerShell. You start by creating a text file with all of the Hyper-V System computer names (one on each line) that you want to run the script against. The following is an example of this text file:

```
HyperV1
HyperV2
HyperV3
```

Now you just need to add some code to your script so that it runs on each of the Hyper-V systems in the text file. This can be accomplished with four additional lines: two at the beginning of the script and two at the end. Here are the first two lines:

```
$a = 0

get-content HyperV_List.txt | ➥
Foreach-object {$computer = (get-content HyperV_List.txt)[$a]
```

This starts a `Foreach-object` loop that does something for each object in the text file `HyperV_List.txt`. In this case, the objects in `HyperV_List.txt` are the Hyper-V servers that you want the script to run against. The $a variable is used to keep track of which line of the text file the script is currently operating on: 0 is the first line, 1 is the second line, and so on.

The reality is that the `get-content` cmdlet puts the contents of the text file into an array, with each line being a position in the array. Line 1 is position 0, line 2 is position 1, and so on. So the line or array position that is being read at the time is put into the `$computer` variable. This is similar to the way the script started before. However, the computer name is now defined by a line in the text file, instead of being explicitly defined in the script itself. The `Foreach-object` { starts the loop. Everything inside the brackets ({ and }) is the action to be performed against each line of the text file.

Now, let's take a look at the last two lines.

```
$a = $a+1

}
```

The first of these lines increments the $a variable defined in the beginning by one, so that the `$computer` variable is reset to the next computer name in the text file. Finally, the bracket closes the `Foreach-object` loop.

The rest of the script is exactly the same.

```
$a = 0

get-content HyperV_List.txt | ➥
Foreach-object {$computer = (get-content HyperV_List.txt)[$a]

$namespace = "root\virtualization"

$query = Get-WmiObject -class Msvm_VirtualSystemManagementService ➥
-computername $computer -namespace $namespace

$querydata = Get-WmiObject -class Msvm_VirtualSystemManagementServiceSettingData ➥
-computername $computer -namespace $namespace

$querydata.DefaultExternalDataRoot = "e:\virtualmachines"
```

```
$querydata.DefaultVirtualHardDiskPath = "e:\virtualdisks"

$query.ModifyServiceSettings($querydata.PSbase.GetText(1))

$a = $a+1

}
```

You could run this script, and it would probably work. However, you would not be able to verify that it actually changed the default locations for the virtual machine and virtual hard disk unless you logged on to each Hyper-V system and checked the settings. Who has time for that? Let's modify the script so that it sends a notification when it completes and indicates whether or not it was successful.

A simple form of notification is e-mail, so you will use that. Remember that PowerShell has the .NET Framework at its disposal, so all you need to do is call a .NET object to send e-mail. The object that makes this happen is Net.Mail.SmtpClient. It just needs some parameters fed to it before it will work. Take a look at the following code snippet:

```
$emailFrom = "defaultpathscript@hyperv.int"
$emailTo = "hstagner@hyperv.int"
$subject = "Script Complete"
$body =  "The script completed successfully on: $scriptsucceed. ➡
The script did not complete on: $scriptfail."
$smtpServer = "smtp.hyperv.int"
$smtp = new-object Net.Mail.SmtpClient($smtpServer)
$smtp.Send($emailFrom, $emailTo, $subject, $body)
```

You should recognize the primary variables in this script as the parts of an e-mail message and the means to send it. $emailFrom is the From field; $emailTo is the To field; $subject is the Subject field; and $body is the Body field. You then define the server to use ($smtpServer), the SMTP client (Net.Mail.Smtpclient($smtpServer)), and the parameters to send the e-mail ($smtp.send($emailFrom, $emailTo, $subject, $body)). Those are the basic building blocks to send an e-mail message. You will just need to add parameters for your own environment. However, you may want your e-mail message to contain a bit more information than "The script completed successfully." That is where the variables $scriptsucceed and $scriptfail come in.

To get some more insight, let's go through the last section that you will add to your script line by line. The logic is a bit more complicated, but it is not difficult if you break it apart.

```
$a = 0
```

This should look familiar from earlier in the script. It is still used to keep track of your place in the text file, because you are going to perform a WMI query after the script runs to see what the values for DefaultExternalDataRoot and DefaultVirtualHardDiskPath are for each computer listed in the text file. This will confirm whether the script actually did its job.

```
function New-Array {,$args}
```

In order to keep track of which computers were successfully changed and which computers failed, you need to set up an array. A new function is created here to make sure that an array is explicitly created.

```
$scriptfail = New-Array ""
```

The $scriptfail variable will hold the names of the computers that fail when the script runs. It is initialized with a space character.

```
$scriptsucceed = New-Array ""
```

The $scriptsucceed variable will hold the names of the computers that succeed when the script runs. It is initialized with a space character.

```
get-content HyperV_List.txt | ➡
Foreach-object {$computer = (get-content HyperV_List.txt)[$a]
```

Just as earlier in the script, the actions will be contained in a Foreach-object loop that will end when it reaches the end of the text file.

```
$querydata = Get-WmiObject -class Msvm_VirtualSystemManagementServiceSettingData ➡
-computername $computer -namespace $namespace
```

This is the WMI query that is used to get the values of the DefaultExternalDataRoot and DefaultVirtualHardDiskPath properties.

```
if ((!($querydata.DefaultExternalDataRoot -eq "e:\virtualmachines")) ➡
-and (!($querydata.DefaultVirtualHardDiskPath -eq "e:\virtualdisks")))
```

This is the beginning of an if statement. The ! character stands for "not" in PowerShell. This conditional test is saying, "If DefaultExternalDataRoot does not equal e:\virtualmachines and DefaultVirtualHardDiskPath does not equal e:\virtualdisks, then do something."

```
{$scriptfail +=$computer}
```

If the condition (DefaultExternalDataRoot does not equal e:\virtualmachines and DefaultVirtualHarddiskPath does not equal e:\virtualdisks) evaluates to true, then the computer that is being tested at the time will be added to the $scriptfail array.

```
else {$scriptsucceed +=$computer}
```

Otherwise (else), if the condition (DefaultExternalDataRoot does not equal e:\virtual-machines and DefaultVirtualHarddiskPath does not equal e:\virtualdisks) evaluates to false, then the computer that is being tested at the time will be added to the $scriptsucceed array.

```
$a = $a+1

}
```

The last two lines increment the placeholder $a variable and end the loop action.

```
$emailFrom = "defaultpathscript@hyperv.int"
$emailTo = "hstagner@hyperv.int"
$subject = "Script Complete"
$body = "The script completed successfully on: $scriptsucceed. ➥
The script did not complete on: $scriptfail."
$smtpServer = "smtp.hyperv.int"
$smtp = new-object Net.Mail.SmtpClient($smtpServer)
$smtp.Send($emailFrom, $emailTo, $subject, $body)
```

Finally, the last section of code sets up the e-mail. Notice that the $scriptsucceed and $scriptfail variables are in the body of the e-mail. This will put the contents of those arrays into the body of the message, so that you can tell which systems succeeded and which ones failed.

In just a few lines of code, you have created a script that will change the default paths for virtual machine and hard disk files for multiple Hyper-V systems, and then notify you of the results. If you created this script in the Scriptomatic tool, you can use the Save button to save it as *yourscriptname*.ps1. Make sure you save the HyperV_List.txt file in the same directory as the script file. You can now run it from a PowerShell prompt. Alternatively, you can run it in a batch file with a line in the following form:

PowerShell *path\to\yourscriptname*.ps1

For example, the line might read as follows:

PowerShell c:\dev\hyper-v_settings.ps1

Just put this line in a text file and save it as *yourscriptname*.bat. Then you can run it outside the PowerShell prompt.

The following is the final script with comments included (comments begin with a # sign).

```
# Variable to keep track of your place in the HyperV_List.txt file.

$a = 0

# Set up the Foreach-object loop to act on each computer in the text file.

get-content HyperV_List.txt | ➥
Foreach-object {$computer = (get-content HyperV_List.txt)[$a]

# Define the namespace used for WMI queries

$namespace = "root\virtualization"

# Define the WMI query object to change Hyper-V server settings.

$query = Get-WmiObject -class Msvm_VirtualSystemManagementService ➥
-computername $computer -namespace $namespace

# Define the WMI query to get the Hyper-V server settings data.
```

```
$querydata = Get-WmiObject ➥
-class Msvm_VirtualSystemManagementServiceSettingData ➥
-computername $computer -namespace $namespace

# Set the value for the DefaultExternalDataRoot property.

$querydata.DefaultExternalDataRoot = "e:\virtualmachines"

# Set the value for the DefaultExternalHardDiskPath property.

$querydata.DefaultVirtualHardDiskPath = "e:\virtualdisks"

# Actually modify the default path settings.

$query.ModifyServiceSettings($querydata.PSbase.GetText(1))

# Increment the text file placeholder variable.

$a = $a+1

# End the Foreach loop action

}

# Variable to keep track of your place in the HyperV_List.txt file.

$a = 0

# Set up a function to explicitly define an array.

function New-Array {,$args}

# Set up a new $scriptfail array with a space character.

$scriptfail = New-Array ""

# Set up a new $scriptsucceed array with a space character.

$scriptsucceed = New-Array ""

# Set up the Foreach-object loop to act on each computer in the text file.

get-content HyperV_List.txt | ➥
Foreach-object {$computer = (get-content HyperV_List.txt)[$a]

# Define the WMI query to get the Hyper-V server settings data.

$querydata = Get-WmiObject -class Msvm_VirtualSystemManagementServiceSettingData ➥
-computername $computer -namespace $namespace
```

```
# If the path settings are not what is expected then add the computer name
# to the $scriptfail array.

if ((!($querydata.DefaultExternalDataRoot -eq "e:\virtualmachines")) ➥
-and (!($querydata.DefaultVirtualHardDiskPath -eq "e:\virtualdisks")))

{$scriptfail +=$computer}

# Else, add the computer name to the $scriptsucceed array.

else {$scriptsucceed +=$computer}

# Increment the text file placeholder variable.

$a = $a+1

# End the Foreach loop action

}

# Set up and send the script completed email.

$emailFrom = "defaultpathscript@hyperv.int"
$emailTo = "hstagner@hyperv.int"
$subject = "Script Complete"
$body =  "The script completed successfully on: $scriptsucceed. ➥
The script did not complete on: $scriptfail."
$smtpServer = "smtp.hyperv.int"
$smtp = new-object Net.Mail.SmtpClient($smtpServer)
$smtp.Send($emailFrom, $emailTo, $subject, $body)
```

Adding an External Virtual Switch to a Hyper-V Host Server

Another Hyper-V setting that you will probably want to set up after a fresh installation of the Hyper-V role is an external virtual switch. If you have one Hyper-V machine, setting this up through the Hyper-V Manager console is easy enough. However, this can get tedious if you have multiple machines to set up. Let's automate it.

To create an external virtual switch with PowerShell and WMI, you need to perform several steps. It's not as simple as a cmdlet that says Create-VirtualSwitch. However, it is manageable. The basic steps are as follows:

1. Create the switch.
2. Create the switch ports.
3. Get an external network interface card (NIC) to bind to the virtual switch.
4. Bring all the pieces together to configure the virtual switch as an external virtual switch.

In the Hyper-V Manager tool, these steps are completed in the background as soon as you add a new external network to the Hyper-V host in the Network Manager settings. The switch is created with the appropriate ports, and you choose an external NIC to which to bind the new switch. To accomplish this programmatically with PowerShell and WMI, you need to go through each step.

The following root\virtualization classes will be used in this script:

- Msvm_VirtualSwitchManagmentService: This class controls the global networking resources for the virtualization service. These resources include virtual switches, switch ports, and internal Ethernet ports. You will be using several methods with this class:

  - The CreateSwitch method will create a new virtual switch.

  - The CreateSwitchPort method will create a new switch port on the switch.

  - The SetupSwitch method will be used to set up the newly created virtual switch at the end of the script.

- Msvm_ExternalEthernetPort: This class represents a physical network adapter. You will be using this class to determine which physical network adapter will be bound to the newly created virtual switch.

Note The script used here is a modified version of the one created by the Windows Virtualization Team and included in *Hyper-V WMI Using PowerShell Scripts – Part 5* (http://blogs.technet.com/ virtualization/archive/2008/05/26/hyper-v-wmi-using-PowerShell-scripts-part-5.aspx).

Let's go through the steps by looking at the modified PowerShell code to create a switch on one Hyper-V server, line by line.

```
$Namespace = "root\virtualization"
```

This line is just a variable to hold the namespace for your WMI query.

```
$VirtualSwitchQuery = Get-WmiObject ➥
-Class "Msvm_VirtualSwitchManagementService" -Namespace $Namespace
```

This type of WMI query should look familiar if you read through the script shown in the previous section. The difference is that this time, you are using the Msvm_ VirtualSwitchManagementService class, which manages virtual switches in Hyper-V. The query is stored in the variable $VirtualSwitchQuery for use at the end of the script.

```
$ReturnObject = $VirtualSwitchQuery.CreateSwitch([guid]::NewGuid().ToString(), ➥
"Hyper-V External Switch", "1024","")
```

The CreateSwitch method is used here with some parameters to create the virtual switch. $ReturnObject is just a temporary variable used to hold the virtual switch object until it can be assigned to a permanent variable. The section [guid]::NewGuid().ToString() generates a GUID and turns it into a string. This GUID will be the internal name (the name that Hyper-V references) of the virtual switch. Hyper-V External Switch is the friendly name for the virtual switch. 1024 is the number of MAC addresses that the switch is capable of learning. Finally, the last parameter is the Authorization Manager (AzMan) scope name. In this case, the AzMan scope parameter is blank, because you will not be delegating permissions on this virtual switch to another user or group.

Note AzMan is a Microsoft technology that is used to handle role-based delegation of security in Windows applications. An AzMan scope is used to define is a set of roles, tasks, and operations. The scope can then be applied to the virtual machine to delegate permissions to the virtual machine. AzMan is covered in more detail in Chapter 9.

```
$CreatedSwitch = [WMI]$ReturnObject.CreatedVirtualSwitch
```

The permanent variable to hold the virtual switch that you created is $CreatedSwitch. The [WMI] preceding $ReturnObject.CreatedVirtualSwitch allows you to retrieve the created virtual switch as a WMI object.

```
$ReturnObject = $VirtualSwitchQuery.CreateSwitchPort($CreatedSwitch, ➥
 [guid]::NewGuid().ToString(), "InternalSwitchPort", "")
```

Again, the $ReturnObject variable is temporary. This time, you are using it to store the switch port that you are creating in this line using the CreateSwitchPort method. The parameters are the virtual switch on which the port is being created ($CreatedSwitch), the GUID, a friendly name, and the AzMan scope.

```
$InternalSwitchPort = [WMI]$ReturnObject.CreatedSwitchPort
```

The created switch port is then assigned to the variable $InternalSwitchPort.

```
$ReturnObject = $VirtualSwitchQuery.CreateSwitchPort($CreatedSwitch, ➥
 [guid]::NewGuid().ToString(), "ExternalSwitchPort", "")
```

You should start to see a pattern here. This time, you are creating an external switch port.

```
$ExternalSwitchPort = [WMI]$ReturnObject.CreatedSwitchPort
```

Again, the created switch port is stored in a variable ($ExternalSwitchPort).

```
$ExternalNic = Get-WmiObject -Class "Msvm_ExternalEthernetPort" ➥
-Namespace $Namespace | ➥
Where-Object -FilterScript ➥
{$_.ElementName -eq "Marvell Yukon 88E8056 PCI-E Gigabit Ethernet Controller"}
```

This line queries for the external physical NIC that you will use to bind to the virtual switch. This is what makes the virtual switch an external virtual switch. The first part before the pipe (|) should look familiar, because it is another WMI query. It uses a class of Msvm_ExternalEthernetPort to get all the external Ethernet ports on the particular Hyper-V machine. The trick here that narrows down the query to a particular NIC is the use of PowerShell piping and filtering. The WMI query is piped (using the | symbol) into the Where-Object cmdlet.

Where-Object has a parameter called -FilterScript, which applies whatever script snippet is inside the brackets that follow the -FilterScript parameter. In this case, you are selecting an external Ethernet port that has the property .ElementName equal to Marvell Yukon 88E8056 PCI-E Gigabit Ethernet Controller (the device name for one of the network connections on the Hyper-V server). This will work on multiple machines if the NIC that you want to bind to the virtual switch is the same on each machine, which is not that uncommon.

```
$VirtualSwitchQuery.SetupSwitch($ExternalSwitchPort, $InternalSwitchPort, ➥
$ExternalNic, [guid]::NewGuid().ToString(), "Hyper-V Internal Ethernet Port")
```

Finally, you bring it all together with this line. It uses the SetupSwitch method to configure the virtual switch that was created. The parameters are the external switch port ($ExternalSwitchPort), the internal switch port ($InternalSwitchPort), the external NIC ($ExternalNic), the GUID, and the friendly name.

To review, the following are the basic steps to add an external virtual switch to a Hyper-V server:

1. Get an instance of the Msvm_VirtualSwitchManagementService class.

2. Use the CreateSwitch method of the Msvm_VirtualSwitchManagementService class to create the virtual switch.

3. Use the CreateSwitchPort method of the Msvm_VirtualSwitchManagementService class to create the virtual switch ports.

4. Get an instance of the Msvm_ExternalEthernetPort class that will represent the target external physical NIC.

5. Configure the switch with all of these parameters using the SetupSwitch method of the Msvm_VirtualSwitchManagementService.

Configuring the Hyper-V Server Settings for Multiple Servers

As it is written now, the external virtual switch script will work on one system. Let's add it to the previous script so that the virtual machine path, virtual disk path, and the virtual switch are configured for each machine listed in a text file. The following is the final combined script with comments.

```
# Variable to keep track of your place in the HyperV_List.txt file.

$a = 0

# Define the namespace used for WMI queries

$Namespace = "root\virtualization"

# Set up the Foreach-object loop to act on each computer in the text file.

Get-Content HyperV_List.txt | ➥
Foreach-object {$Computer = (Get-Content HyperV_List.txt)[$a]
```

```
# Ping test to see if the target server is reachable.

$Ping = Get-WmiObject -Query "SELECT * FROM Win32_PingStatus ➥
WHERE Address = '$Computer'"

# If the target server is reachable through a ping, then go ahead with the script.

if ($Ping.StatusCode -eq 0)

{

# Define the WMI query object to change Hyper-V server settings.

$PathQuery = Get-WmiObject ➥
-Class "Msvm_VirtualSystemManagementService" ➥
-Computername $Computer -Namespace $Namespace

# Define the WMI query to get the Hyper-V server settings data.

$PathQueryData = Get-WmiObject -Class ➥
"Msvm_VirtualSystemManagementServiceSettingData" ➥
-Computername $Computer -Namespace $Namespace

# Set the value for the DefaultExternalDataRoot property.

$PathQueryData.DefaultExternalDataRoot = "e:\virtualmachines"

# Set the value for the DefaultExternalHardDiskPath property.

$PathQueryData.DefaultVirtualHardDiskPath = "e:\virtualdisks"

# Actually modify the default path settings.

$PathQuery.ModifyServiceSettings($PathQueryData.PSbase.GetText(1))


# WMI query used to set up the virtual switch.

$VirtualSwitchQuery = Get-WmiObject -Class "Msvm_VirtualSwitchManagementService" ➥
-Namespace $Namespace -ComputerName $Computer

# Create the virtual switch.

$ReturnObject = $VirtualSwitchQuery.CreateSwitch([guid]::NewGuid().ToString(), ➥
"Hyper-V External Switch", "1024","")

# Store the created switch as a WMI object for later use.
```

```
$CreatedSwitch = [WMI]$ReturnObject.CreatedVirtualSwitch

# Create the internal switch port.

$ReturnObject = $VirtualSwitchQuery.CreateSwitchPort($CreatedSwitch, ➥
 [guid]::NewGuid().ToString(), "InternalSwitchPort", "")

# Store the created internal switch port as a WMI object for later use.

$InternalSwitchPort = [WMI]$ReturnObject.CreatedSwitchPort

# Create the external switch port.

$ReturnObject = $VirtualSwitchQuery.CreateSwitchPort($CreatedSwitch, ➥
 [guid]::NewGuid().ToString(), "ExternalSwitchPort", "")

# Store the external switch port as a WMI object for later use.

$ExternalSwitchPort = [WMI]$ReturnObject.CreatedSwitchPort

# Query to get the external NIC that will be bound to the virtual switch.

$ExternalNic = Get-WmiObject -Class "Msvm_ExternalEthernetPort" ➥
-Namespace $Namespace -ComputerName $Computer | ➥
Where-Object -FilterScript ➥
{$_.ElementName -eq "Marvell Yukon 88E8056 PCI-E Gigabit Ethernet Controller"}

# Configure the switch using all of the WMI objects and the external NIC.

$VirtualSwitchQuery.SetupSwitch($ExternalSwitchPort, $InternalSwitchPort, ➥
$ExternalNic, [guid]::NewGuid().ToString(), "Hyper-V Internal Ethernet Port")

}

# Increment the computer list array variable by 1.

$a = $a+1

# End the Foreach loop action

}


# Variable to keep track of your place in the HyperV_List.txt file.

$a = 0
```

```
# Set up a function to explicitly define an array.

function New-Array {,$args}

# Set up a new $HostUnreachable array with a space character.

$HostUnreachable = New-Array ""

# Set up a new $PathFail array with a space character.

$PathFail = New-Array ""

# Set up a new $PathSucceed array with a space character.

$PathSucceed = New-Array ""

# Set up a new $SwitchSucceed array with a space character.

$Switchsucceed = New-Array ""

# Set up a new $SwitchFail array with a space character.

$SwitchFail = New-Array ""

# Set up the Foreach-object loop to act on each computer in the text file.

Get-Content HyperV_List.txt | ➡
Foreach-object {$Computer = (Get-Content HyperV_List.txt)[$a]

# Ping test to see if the target server is reachable.

$Ping = Get-WmiObject ➡
-Query "SELECT * FROM Win32_PingStatus WHERE Address = '$Computer'"

# If the target server is reachable through a ping, then go ahead with the script.
# Else, store the computer name that the script is working on in the
# $HostUnreachable array.

if ($Ping.StatusCode -eq 0)

{

# Define the WMI query to get the Hyper-V server settings data.

$PathQueryData = Get-WmiObject -Class ➡
 Msvm_VirtualSystemManagementServiceSettingData ➡
-Computername $Computer -Namespace $Namespace
```

```
# Define the WMI query to see if the target server has a NIC
# bound to a virtual switch.

$SwitchQueryData = Get-WmiObject ➥
-Class Msvm_ExternalEthernetPort -Computername $Computer ➥
-Namespace $Namespace | Where-Object -Filterscript {$_.IsBound -eq "True"}

# If the path settings are not what is expected, then add the computer name
# to the $ScriptFail array.

if ((!($PathQueryData.DefaultExternalDataRoot -eq "e:\virtualmachines")) ➥
-and (!($PathQueryData.DefaultVirtualHardDiskPath -eq "e:\virtualdisks")))

{$PathFail +=$Computer}

# Else, add the computername to the $ScriptSucceed array.

else

{$PathSucceed +=$Computer}

# If the target server does not have a NIC bound to a virtual switch,
# add the computer name to the $SwitchFail array.

if ($SwitchQueryData -eq $null)

{$SwitchFail +=$Computer}

# Else add the computer name to the $SwitchSucceed array.

else

{$SwitchSucceed +=$Computer}

# Increment the text file placeholder variable.

}

# If the target server is reachable through a ping, then go ahead with the script.
# Else, store the computer name that the script is working on in the
# $HostUnreachable array.

else

{$HostUnreachable +=$Computer}

# Increment the computer list array variable by 1.
```

```
$a = $a+1

# End the Foreach loop action

}

# Set up and send the script completed email.

$EmailFrom = "hypervsetup@hyperv.int"
$EmailTo = "hstagner@hyperv.int"
$Subject = "Script Complete"
$Body = "The following hosts were unreachable: $HostUnreachable
The file paths were successfully changed on: $PathSucceed.
The file paths were not successfully changed on: $PathFail.

The external virtual switches were successfully created on: $SwitchSucceed.
The external virtual switches were not successfully created on: $SwitchFail.
"
$SmtpServer = "smtp.hyperv.int"
$Smtp = new-object Net.Mail.SmtpClient($smtpServer)
$Smtp.Send($emailFrom, $emailTo, $subject, $body)
```

For the most part, the two scripts have not been modified much. They have just been combined into one script to take care of both tasks. However, a couple changes make the script more robust. First, take a look at the following two lines:

```
$Ping = Get-WmiObject -Query "SELECT * FROM Win32_PingStatus ➥
WHERE Address = '$Computer'"

if ($Ping.StatusCode -eq 0)
```

These lines add a bit more error handling to the script. It's basically a ping test. You can see that a WMI query is initiated to select the Win32_PingStatus class for the computer that the script is working on at the time. A StatusCode property of 0 for the Win32_PingStatus class means that the ping was successful. You want to add this if statement so that you can make sure that the system on which you are trying to run the script can be reached over the network. These two lines also appear in the last section of the script where the script actions are verified. If the host is unreachable, it is added to an array that is used to send out the final e-mail. This e-mail will let you know of any hosts that are unreachable.

The other lines that were added verify that the external virtual switch was actually created on the target Hyper-V servers. Take a look at the WMI query:

```
$SwitchQueryData = Get-WmiObject -Class Msvm_ExternalEthernetPort ➥
-Computername $Computer -Namespace $Namespace | ➥
Where-Object -Filterscript {$_.IsBound -eq "True"}
```

This WMI query looks for any external Ethernet port (Msvm_ExternalEthernetPort) that is bound (the property IsBound) to a virtual switch. This query is paired with this if statement:

```
if ($SwitchQueryData -eq $null)

{$SwitchFail +=$Computer}

else

{$SwitchSucceed +=$Computer}
```

If there aren't any external Ethernet ports bound to a virtual switch, then add the computer name to the $SwitchFail array that will be used in the final e-mail. Otherwise (else), add the computer name to the $SwitchSucceed array that will be used in the final e-mail. With these few lines, and the combination of the two scripts, you have created a more comprehensive Hyper-V configuration script.

Manipulating Virtual Machine Resources

Now that your Hyper-V servers are installed, you can actually start creating and managing virtual machines on your systems. You can even automate this with PowerShell and WMI. In the next sections, you will learn how to programmatically manipulate the four core resources (disk, memory, processors, and network) for your virtual machines using PowerShell and WMI.

Virtual Disk Resource

Before you can manipulate or attach a virtual disk to a virtual machine, you need to create a virtual disk. This is actually quite simple. Consider the following short script:

```
$VDiskService = Get-Wmiobject -Class "Msvm_ImageManagementService" ➥
-Namespace "root\virtualization"

$VDiskService.CreateFixedVirtualHardDisk("e:\virtualdisks\test.vhd", 10GB)
```

These two lines will create a fixed disk with a size of 10GB. The first line should look familiar. It's just a WMI query to get the Msvm_ImageManagementService class, which is responsible for storage-related items in Hyper-V. Then the CreateFixedVirtualHardDisk method of the Msvm_ImageManagementService class is used to create a fixed virtual disk with the following parameters:

- The path is e:\virtualdisks\test.vhd.

- The size is 10GB.

To create a dynamic virtual disk file (*.vhd), use the CreateDynamicVirtualHardDisk method instead, as follows:

```
$VDiskService = Get-Wmiobject -Class "Msvm_ImageManagementService" ➥
-Namespace "root\virtualization"

$VDiskService.CreateDynamicVirtualHardDisk("e:\virtualdisks\test.vhd", 10GB)
```

Finally, to create a differencing disk, use the `CreateDifferencingVirtualHardDisk` method:

```
$VDiskPath = "e:\virtualdisks\test-delta.vhd"

$VDiskParent = "e:\virtualdisks\test.vhd"

$VDiskService = Get-Wmiobject -Class "Msvm_ImageManagementService" ➥
-Namespace "root\virtualization"

$VDiskService.CreateDifferencingVirtualHardDisk($VDiskPath, $VDiskParent)
```

The `CreateDynamicVirtualHardDisk` method takes two parameters: the path to the new disk and a parent disk, since you are creating a differencing disk based on a parent disk.

Adding a virtual disk to an existing virtual machine is a little more complicated. The script that adds a virtual disk to an existing virtual machine uses the following root\virtualization methods:

- `Msvm_VirtualSystemManagementService`: This class represents the virtualization service on a host system. In this case, the `AddVirtualSystemResources` method of this class will be used to add the disk to the virtual machine.

- `Msvm_ComputerSystem`: This class represents a virtual machine. It will be used to get the target virtual machine to which the disk will be attached.

- `Msvm_VirtualSystemSettingData`: This class represents the settings for a virtual machine. You will use this in combination with `Msvm_SettingsDefineState` to get the current settings of a virtual machine.

- `Msvm_SettingsDefineState`: This class associates an instance of the `Msvm_ComputerSystem` class with an instance of the `Msvm_VirtualSystemSettingData` class to get the current settings of a virtual machine.

- `Msvm_ResourceAllocationSettingData`: This class represents the current allocation state of a virtual resource. This is used to get an IDE controller that is attached to the target virtual machine.

- `Msvm_ResourceAllocationSettingData`: This class is used to establish that the IDE controller (instance of `Msvm_ResourceAllocationSettingData`) is a part of the `Msvm_ResourceAllocationSettingData` for the target virtual machine.

- `Msvm_AllocationCapabilities`: This class is used to define the range of capabilities that a virtual resource can have. In this case, you are using it to get an instance of the `Microsoft Synthetic Disk Drive` resource subtype.

- `Msvm_SettingsDefineCapabilites`: This class is used to establish a link between the `Msvm_AllocationCapabilities` instance and the default settings for a resource. In this case, it is used to get a default instance of the `Microsoft Virtual Hard Disk`.

The following are the basic steps for attaching a virtual disk to an existing virtual machine:

1. Get the Msvm_VirtualSystemManagementService object (this does all of the work when you attach the disk).

2. Get all of the parameters that the Msvm_VirtualSystemManagementService object needs to add a resource (*.vhd) to the existing virtual machine. These include the target virtual machine, the type of resource (*.vhd), and any parameters that the resource needs (IDE controller address and IDE controller port address).

3. Once all of these requirements are gathered, the virtual disk can be added to the target virtual machine using the AddVirtualSystemResources method.

Let's take a look at the script that I modified.

```
$VHD = "e:\virtualdisks\test.vhd"

$GuestVM = "W2K3-Map"

$Namespace = "root\virtualization"

$Computer = "HyperV-Dev"

$VMService = Get-WmiObject -class "Msvm_VirtualSystemManagementService" ➥
-namespace $Namespace -ComputerName $Computer

$VM = Get-WmiObject -Namespace $Namespace -ComputerName $Computer ➥
-Query "Select * From Msvm_ComputerSystem Where ElementName='$GuestVM'"

$VMSettingData = Get-WmiObject -Namespace $Namespace ➥
-Query "Associators of {$VM} Where ResultClass=Msvm_VirtualSystemSettingData ➥
 AssocClass=Msvm_SettingsDefineState"

$VMIDEController = (Get-WmiObject -Namespace $Namespace ➥
-Query "Associators of {$VMSettingData} ➥
Where ResultClass=Msvm_ResourceAllocationSettingData ➥
 AssocClass=Msvm_VirtualSystemSettingDataComponent" | ➥
where-object -FilterScript {$_.ResourceSubType ➥
-eq "Microsoft Emulated IDE Controller" -and $_.Address -eq 0})

$DiskAllocationSetting = Get-WmiObject -Namespace $Namespace ➥
-Query "SELECT * FROM Msvm_AllocationCapabilities ➥
WHERE ResourceSubType = 'Microsoft Synthetic Disk Drive'"

$DefaultDiskDrive = (Get-WmiObject -Namespace $Namespace ➥
-Query "Associators of {$DiskAllocationSetting} ➥
Where ResultClass=Msvm_ResourceAllocationSettingData ➥
 AssocClass=Msvm_SettingsDefineCapabilities" | ➥
where-object -FilterScript {$_.InstanceID -like "*Default"})
```

```
$DefaultDiskDrive.Parent = $VMIDEController.__Path

$DefaultDiskDrive.Address = 1

$NewDiskDrive = ($VMService.AddVirtualSystemResources($VM.__Path, ➥
 $DefaultDiskDrive.PSBase.GetText(1))).NewResources

$DiskAllocationSetting = Get-WmiObject -Namespace $Namespace ➥
-Query "SELECT * FROM Msvm_AllocationCapabilities ➥
WHERE ResourceSubType = 'Microsoft Virtual Hard Disk'"

$DefaultHardDisk = (Get-WmiObject -Namespace $Namespace ➥
-Query "Associators of {$DiskAllocationSetting} ➥
Where ResultClass=Msvm_ResourceAllocationSettingData ➥
 AssocClass=Msvm_SettingsDefineCapabilities" | ➥
where-object -FilterScript {$_.InstanceID -like "*Default"})

$DefaultHardDisk.Parent = $NewDiskDrive

$DefaultHardDisk.Connection = $VHD

$VMService.AddVirtualSystemResources($VM.__Path, $DefaultHardDisk.PSBase.GetText(1))
```

■Note This script is based on one by Taylor Brown, posted on his blog (http://blogs.msdn.com/ taylorb/archive/2008/10/13/pdc-teaser-attaching-a-vhd-to-a-virtual-machine.aspx).

This script may look intimidating, so let's break it down line by line.

```
$VHD = "e:\virtualdisks\test.vhd"
$GuestVM = "W2K3-Map"
$Namespace = "root\virtualization"
$Computer = "."
```

These first few lines just define some variables that will be needed later in the script. The $VHD variable defines the *.vhd file that will be added to the virtual machine. The $GuestVM variable defines the virtual machine that you will be working with in the script. The $Namespace variable defines the namespace for the WMI queries. Finally, $Computer defines the Hyper-V host server that you will be working with.

```
$VMService = Get-WmiObject -class "Msvm_VirtualSystemManagementService" ➥
-namespace $Namespace -ComputerName $Computer
```

This line is just a WMI query to get an instance of the Msvm_VirtualSystemManagmentService class. This class controls defining, modifying, and deleting virtual systems.

```
$VM = Get-WmiObject -Namespace $Namespace ➥
-ComputerName $Computer -Query "Select * From Msvm_ComputerSystem ➥
Where ElementName='$GuestVM'"
```

This line is another WMI query that gets an instance of the Msvm_ComputerSystem class (the actual virtual machine object) that has the name of the virtual machine you defined with the $GuestVM variable.

```
$VMSettingData = Get-WmiObject -Namespace $Namespace ➥
-Query "Associators of {$VM} ➥
Where ResultClass=Msvm_VirtualSystemSettingData ➥
AssocClass=Msvm_SettingsDefineState"
```

This line uses a WMI Associators of statement, which associates a source class with a result class. In this case, you are associating the Msvm_VirtualSystemSettingData class with the virtual machine object that you queried for in the previous line. Finally, the AssocClass=Msvm_SettingsDefineState part is getting the current settings that apply to the Msvm_VirtualSystemSettingData instance that is associated with the $VM object. So, there are three links in this query chain. You are getting the current state of the VirtualSystemSettingData for the $VM object.

```
$VMIDEController = (Get-WmiObject -Namespace $Namespace ➥
-Query "Associators of {$VMSettingData} ➥
Where ResultClass=Msvm_ResourceAllocationSettingData ➥
 AssocClass=Msvm_VirtualSystemSettingDataComponent" | ➥
where-object -FilterScript {$_.ResourceSubType ➥
-eq "Microsoft Emulated IDE Controller" -and $_.Address -eq 0})
```

As you can see, the script is starting to build the pieces necessary to define a resource (a virtual hard disk in this case) for a particular virtual machine. This line defines an instance of a virtual IDE controller using an Associators of statement again. The part from the Get-WMIObject statement to the | symbol queries for a particular VirtualSystemSettingDataComponent of the ResourceAllocationSettingData for the $VMSettingData object defined in the previous line. This is piped (|) into a filter that looks for a ResourceSubType of Microsoft Emulated IDE Controller whose address is 0. This query is getting the first (address 0) virtual IDE controller of the target virtual machine and storing it in the $VMIDEController variable. The Msvm_ResourceAllocationSettingData class defines the resource allocation settings (disk, memory, processor, and network) for virtual systems.

```
$DiskAllocationSetting = Get-WmiObject -Namespace $Namespace ➥
-Query "SELECT * FROM Msvm_AllocationCapabilities ➥
WHERE ResourceSubType = 'Microsoft Synthetic Disk Drive'"
```

The Msvm_AllocationCapabilities class defines the supported capabilities of a virtual resource. In this query, you are getting the Microsoft Synthetic Disk Drive resource subtype and assigning it to the $DiskAllocationSetting variable.

```
$DefaultDiskDrive = (Get-WmiObject -Namespace $Namespace ➥
-Query "Associators of {$DiskAllocationSetting} ➥
Where ResultClass=Msvm_ResourceAllocationSettingData ➥
 AssocClass=Msvm_SettingsDefineCapabilities" | ➥
where-object -FilterScript {$_.InstanceID -like "*Default"})
```

The `Msvm_ResourceAllocationSettingData` class is associated with the `Msvm_AllocationCapabilities` class to describe the minimum, maximum, default, and incremental values for a particular resource's allocation. The `Msvm_ResourceAllocationSettingData` class provides a link between the `Msvm_AllocationCapabilities` class object and the minimum, maximum, default, and incremental values for a particular resource. Here, another `Associators of` statement is used. Taking the filter at the end of this line into account, the `Associators of` statement is looking for the default value of the `Microsoft Synthetic Disk Drive` as defined in the `Msvm_ResourceAllocationSettingData` class.

```
$DefaultDiskDrive.Parent = $VMIDEController.__Path
$DefaultDiskDrive.Address = 1
```

These two lines define the virtual IDE controller and address to which the virtual disk will attach. The `Parent` property is defined by placing the WMI `Path` (which includes the GUID of the particular virtual IDE controller) of the `$VMIDEController` object that was created earlier into the `Parent` property of the `$DefaultDiskDrive` object. Then the `Address` property of the `$DefaultDiskDrive` object is set to 1.

```
$NewDiskDrive = ($VMService.AddVirtualSystemResources($VM.__Path, ➥
 $DefaultDiskDrive.PSBase.GetText(1))).NewResources
```

This line uses the `AddVirtualSystemResources` method of the `Msvm_VirtualSystemManagmentService` class to define the new disk drive that will be added to the target virtual machine and the settings data that is associated with that resource using the `.NewResources` portion of the line. The two parameters defined when using the `AddVirtualSystemResources` method in this case are the affected virtual machine (`$VM.__Path`) and the resource to be added (`$DefaultDiskDrive`). This reference to the new disk drive is stored in the `$NewDiskDrive` variable.

```
$DiskAllocationSetting = Get-WmiObject -Namespace $Namespace ➥
-Query "SELECT * FROM Msvm_AllocationCapabilities ➥
WHERE ResourceSubType = 'Microsoft Virtual Hard Disk'"
```

This line uses the `$DiskAllocationSetting` variable again to get the `Microsoft Virtual Hard Disk` resource subtype.

```
$DefaultHardDisk = (Get-WmiObject -Namespace $Namespace ➥
-Query "Associators of {$DiskAllocationSetting} ➥
Where ResultClass=Msvm_ResourceAllocationSettingData ➥
 AssocClass=Msvm_SettingsDefineCapabilities" | ➥
where-object -FilterScript {$_.InstanceID -like "*Default"})
```

This line gets the default `Microsoft Virtual Hard Disk` instance and stores it in the `$DefaulHardDisk` variable.

```
$DefaultHardDisk.Parent = $NewDiskDrive
$DefaultHardDisk.Connection = $VHD
```

These two lines serve the same purpose as the other two lines they resemble. They define some properties for the `$DefaultHardDisk` object that was queried for earlier in the script. The `Parent` property is set to the `$NewDiskDrive` object. The `Connection` property is set to whatever is defined in the `$VHD` variable.

```
$VMService.AddVirtualSystemResources($VM.__Path, $DefaultHardDisk.PSBase.GetText(1))
```

Finally, the AddVirtualSystemResources method of the Msvm_VirtualSystemManagementService class is used to add the $DefaultHardDisk object to the target virtual machine.

Now you know how to create different types of virtual disks and add them to an existing virtual machine. Let's move on to the virtual machine's memory resource.

Memory Resource

By default, a memory resource is added to a virtual machine when it is created. However, you can still manipulate the amount of memory that is assigned to a particular virtual machine. As it turns out, you can use some of the same techniques that are in the script that adds a virtual disk to a virtual machine.

The script to manipulate virtual machine memory will use the following root\ virtualization classes:

- Msvm_VirtualSystemManagementService: This class represents the virtualization service on a host system. In this case, the ModifyVirtualSystemResources method of this class will be used to adjust the memory settings for a virtual machine.

- Msvm_ComputerSystem: This class represents a virtual machine. It will be used to get the target virtual machine that will have its memory adjusted.

- Msvm_VirtualSystemSettingData: This class represents the settings for a virtual machine. You will use this in combination with Msvm_SettingsDefineState to get the current settings of a virtual machine.

- Msvm_MemorySettingData: This class represents the currently configured state of the target virtual machine's memory.

- Msvm_VirtualSystemSettingDataComponent: This class is used to establish that the memory is a part of the Msvm_MemorySettingData. It is used to get an instance of the Microsoft Virtual Machine Memory resource subtype.

The following are the basic steps to adjust the memory settings on a virtual machine:

1. Get an instance of the Msvm_VirtualSystemManagementService class to use to modify the settings later in the script.

2. Get an instance of the Msvm_ComputerSystem class that will represent the target virtual machine.

3. Get an instance of the Msvm_VirtualSystemSettingData class that represents the current settings of the virtual machine.

4. Get an instance of the virtual machine's Microsoft Virtual Machine Memory component by using the Msvm_MemorySettingData class.

5. Set the properties (VirtualQuantity, Reservation, and Limit) for the virtual machine's memory to the desired values.

6. Modify the memory settings using the ModifyVirtualSystemResources method of the Msvm_VirtualSystemManagementService class.

Now, let's take a look at the script.

```
$GuestVM = "W2K3-Map"

$Namespace = "root\virtualization"

$Computer = "HyperV-Dev"

$VMService = Get-WmiObject -class "Msvm_VirtualSystemManagementService" ➥
-namespace $Namespace -ComputerName $Computer

$VM = Get-WmiObject -Namespace $Namespace -ComputerName $Computer ➥
-Query "Select * From Msvm_ComputerSystem ➥
Where ElementName='$GuestVM'"

$VMSettingData = Get-WmiObject -Namespace $Namespace ➥
-Query "Associators of {$VM} ➥
Where ResultClass=Msvm_VirtualSystemSettingData ➥
AssocClass=Msvm_SettingsDefineState"

$Vmem = (Get-WmiObject -Namespace $Namespace ➥
-Query "Associators of {$VMSettingData} ➥
Where ResultClass=Msvm_MemorySettingData ➥
 AssocClass=Msvm_VirtualSystemSettingDataComponent" | ➥
where-object -FilterScript {$_.ResourceSubType ➥
-eq "Microsoft Virtual Machine Memory"})

$Vmem.VirtualQuantity = [string]2048
$Vmem.Reservation = [string]2048
$Vmem.Limit = [string]2048


$VMService.ModifyVirtualSystemResources($VM.__Path, $Vmem.PSBase.GetText(1))
```

Let's break it down line by line.

```
$GuestVM = "W2K3-Map"
$Namespace = "root\virtualization"
$Computer = "HyperV-Dev"
```

These first three lines just set up some variables that will be used later in the script. $GuestVM is the target virtual machine. $Namespace is the WMI namespace that will be used. $Computer is the Hyper-V server that the script will be run against.

```
$VMService = Get-WmiObject -class "Msvm_VirtualSystemManagementService" ➥
-namespace $Namespace -ComputerName $Computer
```

This line gets the Msvm_VirtualSystemManagmentService class that will be used later to modify the memory settings for the target virtual machine.

```
$VM = Get-WmiObject -Namespace $Namespace -ComputerName $Computer ➥
-Query "Select * From Msvm_ComputerSystem ➥
Where ElementName='$GuestVM'"
```

This line gets the target virtual machine instance so that it can be manipulated later.

```
$VMSettingData = Get-WmiObject -Namespace $Namespace ➥
-Query "Associators of {$VM} ➥
Where ResultClass=Msvm_VirtualSystemSettingData ➥
AssocClass=Msvm_SettingsDefineState"
```

This line gets the current settings of the target virtual machine instance by using an Associators of WMI statement.

```
$Vmem = (Get-WmiObject -Namespace $Namespace ➥
-Query "Associators of {$VMSettingData} ➥
Where ResultClass=Msvm_MemorySettingData ➥
 AssocClass=Msvm_VirtualSystemSettingDataComponent" | ➥
where-object -FilterScript {$_.ResourceSubType ➥
-eq "Microsoft Virtual Machine Memory"})
```

This is where the script starts to differ from the previous disk allocation script. The disk allocation script used the generic Msvm_ResourceAllocationSettingData class, whereas this script uses the specific Msvm_MemorySettingData class. However, they both are essentially performing the same type of task. This line gets the instance of the Microsoft Virtual Machine Memory component settings that are associated with the target virtual machine.

```
$Vmem.VirtualQuantity = [string]2048
$Vmem.Reservation = [string]2048
$Vmem.Limit = [string]2048
```

These three lines set the parameters for the Microsoft Virtual Machine Memory component retrieved in the previous line. All three properties (VirtualQuantity, Reservation, and Limit) must be set to the desired amount of memory in megabytes. In this case, it is set to 2048MB, or 2GB, of memory.

```
$VMService.ModifyVirtualSystemResources($VM.__Path, $Vmem.PSBase.GetText(1))
```

Finally, this line uses the ModifyVirtualSystemResources method of the Msvm_VirtualSystemManagementService class to modify the memory setting of the target virtual machine. The first parameter of the method is the target virtual machine. The second parameter is the ResourceSettingData. In this case, the only setting data is the MemorySettingData.

Now that you know how to modify the memory setting data for a virtual machine, let's move on to the processor setting data for a virtual machine.

Processor Resource

The process for manipulating virtual processors on a target virtual machine is very similar to that for manipulating virtual machine memory, as described in the previous section. You will start to see a pattern emerge the more you work with WMI, PowerShell, and Hyper-V, so once you learn how to manipulate one setting of a virtual machine, it becomes easier to figure out how to manipulate other virtual machine settings with PowerShell and WMI.

Actually, to manipulate the virtual processors that are assigned to a particular virtual machine, you can use the memory script presented in the previous section, with just two changes: modify one variable name and one of the objects referenced.

The processor script will use the following root\virtualization classes:

- Msvm_VirtualSystemManagementService: This class represents the virtualization service on a host system. In this case, the ModifyVirtualSystemResources method of this class will be used to adjust the processor settings for a virtual machine.

- Msvm_ComputerSystem: This class represents a virtual machine. It will be used to get the target virtual machine that will have its processors adjusted.

- Msvm_VirtualSystemSettingData: This class represents the settings for a virtual machine. You will use this in combination with Msvm_SettingsDefineState to get the current settings of a virtual machine.

- Msvm_MemorySettingData: This class represents the currently configured state of the target virtual machine's processor.

- Msvm_VirtualSystemSettingDataComponent: This class is used to establish that the processor is a part of the Msvm_MemorySettingData. It is used to get an instance of the Microsoft Processor resource subtype.

The following are the basic steps to adjust the processor settings on a virtual machine:

1. Get an instance of the Msvm_VirtualSystemManagementService class to use to modify the settings later in the script.

2. Get an instance of the Msvm_ComputerSystem class that will represent the target virtual machine.

3. Get an instance of the Msvm_VirtualSystemSettingData class that represents the current settings of the virtual machine.

4. Get an instance of the virtual machine's Microsoft Processor component by using the Msvm_ProcessorSettingData class.

5. Set the properties (VirtualQuantity, Reservation, Limit, and Weight) for the virtual machine's processor to the desired values.

6. Modify the processor settings using the ModifyVirtualSystemResources method of the Msvm_VirtualSystemManagementService class.

The following is the complete script:

```
$GuestVM = "W2K3-Map"

$Namespace = "root\virtualization"

$Computer = "HyperV-Dev"

$VMService = Get-WmiObject -class "Msvm_VirtualSystemManagementService" ➥
-namespace $Namespace -ComputerName $Computer

$VM = Get-WmiObject -Namespace $Namespace -ComputerName $Computer ➥
-Query "Select * From Msvm_ComputerSystem Where ElementName='$GuestVM'"
```

```
$VMSettingData = Get-WmiObject -Namespace $Namespace ➥
-Query "Associators of {$VM} ➥
Where ResultClass=Msvm_VirtualSystemSettingData ➥
AssocClass=Msvm_SettingsDefineState"➥

$Vproc = (Get-WmiObject -Namespace $Namespace ➥
-Query "Associators of {$VMSettingData} ➥
Where ResultClass=Msvm_ProcessorSettingData ➥
 AssocClass=Msvm_VirtualSystemSettingDataComponent" | ➥
where-object -FilterScript {$_.ResourceSubType -eq "Microsoft Processor"})

$Vproc.VirtualQuantity = [string]1

$Vproc.Reservation = [string]0

$Vproc.Limit = [string]100000

$Vproc.Weight = [string]100

$VMService.ModifyVirtualSystemResources($VM.__Path, $Vproc.PSBase.GetText(1))
```

The majority of the script is the same as the memory script. Of course, you are interested in the processor settings in this case, so you use this line:

```
$Vproc = (Get-WmiObject -Namespace $Namespace ➥
-Query "Associators of {$VMSettingData} ➥
Where ResultClass=Msvm_ProcessorSettingData ➥
 AssocClass=Msvm_VirtualSystemSettingDataComponent" | ➥
where-object -FilterScript {$_.ResourceSubType -eq "Microsoft Processor"})
```

Here, you are getting an Msvm_ProcessorSettingData object instead of an Msvm_MemorySettingData object. As a result, the ResourceSubType you are looking for is now Microsoft Processor.

The Msvm_ProcessorSettingData class also has some different properties to manipulate:

```
$Vproc.VirtualQuantity = [string]1
$Vproc.Reservation = [string]0
$Vproc.Limit = [string]100000
$Vproc.Weight = [string]100
```

These four lines represent the settings for four properties that you might be interested in adjusting. VirtualQuantity is the number of virtual processors that you want to have assigned to the virtual machine. Reservation, Limit, and Weight are the Reserve, Limit, and Weight settings that you can view in the Hyper-V Manager tool. These are the only major differences in this script compared with the previous memory script.

Network Resource

When we talk about network resources for a virtual machine, we are referring to a virtual NIC connected to a virtual switch. You can create a virtual NIC and add it to a virtual machine. However, it is not until you connect that virtual NIC to a virtual switch that it becomes useful.

The script to manipulate network resource settings will use the following root\ virtualization classes:

- Msvm_SyntheticEthernetPortSettingData: This class represents the currently configured state of a synthetic Ethernet adapter. It is used to get a default instance of a synthetic Ethernet adapter.

- Msvm_ComputerSystem: This class represents a virtual machine. This will be used to get the target virtual machine that will have the NICs added to it.

- Msvm_VirtualSwitchManagementService: This class controls the global networking resources for the virtualization service. These resources include virtual switches, switch ports, and internal Ethernet ports. The CreateSwitchPort method will create a new switch port on the switch.

- Msvm_VirtualSystemManagementService: This class represents the virtualization service on a host system. In this case, the AddVirtualSystemResources method of this class will be used to add the NICs to the virtual machine.

- Msvm_VirtualSwitch: This class represents a virtual switch. It is used here to get the instance of the target virtual switch to connect the virtual NICs.

Here are the basic steps involved in adding NICs to a virtual machine:

1. Get a default instance of the Msvm_SyntheticEthernetPortSettingData to use to create the new virtual NICs later in the script.

2. Get the instance of the Msvm_ComputerSystem class that represents your target virtual machine.

3. Get an instance of the Msvm_VirtualSwitchManagementService that will be used to create the virtual switch ports later in the script.

4. Get an instance of the Msvm_VirtualSystemManagementService class that will be used to add the virtual NICs to the virtual machine at the end of the script.

5. Get an instance of the Msvm_VirtualSwitch class that represents your target virtual switch.

6. Create two ports (one for each NIC) on the virtual switch using the CreateSwitchPort method of the Msvm_VirtualSwitchManagementService class.

7. Create two new virtual NICs (one static and one dynamic) by using the Clone method to clone the default instance of the Msvm_SyntheticEthernetPortSettingData class you got earlier.

8. Set the parameters for each of the virtual NICs.

9. Add each virtual NIC to the virtual machine using the AddVirtualSystemResources method of the Msvm_VirtualSystemManagementService class.

The following networking script creates two virtual NICs (one static and one dynamic), attaches those NICs to a virtual switch (already created), and adds those NICs to an existing virtual machine:

```
$GuestVM = "W2K3-Map"
$Namespace = "root\virtualization"
$Computer = "HyperV-Dev"
$VSwitchName = "Hyper-V External Switch"
$VSwitchPortName = "VMPort"
$VNicGUID1 = [GUID]::NewGUID().ToString()
$VNicGUID2 = [GUID]::NewGUID().ToString()

$DefaultNIC = Get-WmiObject -Namespace $Namespace ➡
-Class Msvm_SyntheticEthernetPortSettingData | ➡
Where-Object -FilterScript {$_.InstanceID -like "*Default*"}

$VM = Get-WmiObject -Namespace $Namespace -ComputerName $Computer ➡
-Query "Select * From Msvm_ComputerSystem Where ElementName='$GuestVM'"

$VSwitchQuery = Get-WmiObject ➡
-Class "Msvm_VirtualSwitchManagementService" -Namespace $Namespace

$VMService = Get-WmiObject -class "Msvm_VirtualSystemManagementService" ➡
-namespace $Namespace -ComputerName $Computer

$VSwitch = Get-WmiObject -Namespace $Namespace ➡
-Query "Select * From Msvm_VirtualSwitch ➡
Where ElementName='$VSwitchName'"

$ReturnObject = $VSwitchQuery.CreateSwitchPort ➡
($VSwitch, [guid]::NewGuid().ToString(), $VSwitchPortName, "")

$NewSwitchPort1 = $ReturnObject.CreatedSwitchPort

$ReturnObject = $VSwitchQuery.CreateSwitchPort ➡
($VSwitch, [guid]::NewGuid().ToString(), $VSwitchPortName, "")

$NewSwitchPort2 = $ReturnObject.CreatedSwitchPort

$StaticNIC = $DefaultNIC.psbase.Clone()
$StaticNIC.VirtualSystemIdentifiers = "{$VNicGUID1}"
$StaticNIC.StaticMacAddress = $true
$StaticNIC.Address = "00155D9290FF"
$StaticNIC.Connection = $NewSwitchPort1

$DynamicNIC = $DefaultNIC.psbase.Clone()
$DynamicNIC.VirtualSystemIdentifiers = "{$VNicGUID2}"
$DynamicNIC.Connection = $NewSwitchPort2
```

```
$VMService.AddVirtualSystemResources($VM.__Path, $StaticNIC.PSBase.GetText(1))
$VMService.AddVirtualSystemResources($VM.__Path, $DynamicNIC.PSBase.GetText(1))
```

Once again, let's break this script into smaller sections to see what it does.

```
$GuestVM = "W2K3-Map"
$Namespace = "root\virtualization"
$Computer = "HyperV-Dev"
$VSwitchName = "Hyper-V External Switch"
$VSwitchPortName = "VMPort"
$VNicGUID1 = [GUID]::NewGUID().ToString()
$VNicGUID2 = [GUID]::NewGUID().ToString()
```

This first section just defines some variables that will be used later in the script. $GuestVM is the target virtual machine; $Namespace is the WMI namespace; $Computer is the target Hyper-V server; $VSwitchname is the name of the virtual switch where the virtual NICs will attach; and $VSwitchPortName is a friendly port name for the virtual switch ports that you will create in the script. Finally, the last two variables, $VNicGUID1 and $VNicGUID2, are the GUIDs that the created virtual NICs will use.

■Note Remember that Hyper-V uses GUIDs to identify components internally. The friendly names are just for the administrators' benefit.

```
$DefaultNIC = Get-WmiObject -Namespace $Namespace ➥
-Class Msvm_SyntheticEthernetPortSettingData | Where-Object ➥
-FilterScript {$_.InstanceID -like "*Default*"}

$VM = Get-WmiObject -Namespace $Namespace -ComputerName $Computer ➥
-Query "Select * From Msvm_ComputerSystem Where ElementName='$GuestVM'"

$VSwitchQuery = Get-WmiObject -Class "Msvm_VirtualSwitchManagementService" ➥
-Namespace $Namespace

$VMService = Get-WmiObject -class "Msvm_VirtualSystemManagementService" ➥
-namespace $Namespace -ComputerName $Computer

$VSwitch = Get-WmiObject -Namespace $Namespace ➥
-Query "Select * From Msvm_VirtualSwitch ➥
Where ElementName='$VSwitchName'"
```

This next section consists of some standard WMI queries. They should look familiar from some of the previous scripts in this chapter. $DefaultNIC gets an instance of a default virtual NIC, which belongs to the Msvm_SyntheticEthernetPortSettingData class. $VM gets an instance of your target virtual machine. $VSwitchQuery gets an instance of the Msvm_VirtualSwitchManagementService class that will be used to create new switch ports for the virtual NICs. $VMService gets an instance of the Msvm_VirtualSystemManagementService class that will be used to add the virtual NIC resources to the target virtual machine. Finally, $VSwitch gets an instance of the target virtual switch (the one to which you will be adding ports).

```
$ReturnObject = $VSwitchQuery.CreateSwitchPort ➥
($VSwitch, [guid]::NewGuid().ToString(), $VSwitchPortName, "")

$NewSwitchPort1 = $ReturnObject.CreatedSwitchPort

$ReturnObject = $VSwitchQuery.CreateSwitchPort ➥
($VSwitch, [guid]::NewGuid().ToString(), $VSwitchPortName, "")

$NewSwitchPort2 = $ReturnObject.CreatedSwitchPort
```

This section is where the two virtual switch ports are actually created for the virtual NICs. This code is the same as that used in the script that created an entire virtual switch, presented in the "Adding an External Virtual Switch to a Hyper-V Host Server" section earlier in the chapter. A temporary variable ($ReturnObject) is used to store the result of the CreateSwitchPort job. The CreateSwitchPort method takes four parameters: the target virtual switch ($VSwitch), a new GUID, a friendly name for the switch port ($VSwitchPortName), and the AzMan scope (blank in this case). Finally, the new switch port instances are stored in the $NewSwitchPort1 and $NewSwitchPort2 variables.

```
$StaticNIC = $DefaultNIC.psbase.Clone()
$StaticNIC.VirtualSystemIdentifiers = "{$VNicGUID1}"
$StaticNIC.StaticMacAddress = $true
$StaticNIC.Address = "00155D9290FF"
$StaticNIC.Connection = $NewSwitchPort1

$DynamicNIC = $DefaultNIC.psbase.Clone()
$DynamicNIC.VirtualSystemIdentifiers = "{$VNicGUID2}"
$DynamicNIC.Connection = $NewSwitchPort2
```

This section actually sets up the two virtual NICs. Each is a clone of the default virtual NIC instance. For demonstration purposes, this script creates a static NIC and dynamic NIC. Each has a property called VirtualSystemIdentifiers that is defined with a GUID. They also have a Connection property that is defined by the $NewSwitchPort1 and $NewSwitchPort2 instances defined earlier in the script. This property connects the virtual NICs to the target ports on the target virtual switch.

The static NIC ($StaticNIC) has some additional property settings. The StaticMacAddress property can be either $true or $false. In this case, it is set to $true, making it a static NIC. Since it is a static NIC, a MAC address needs to be assigned to it. This is defined in the Address property as 00155D9290FF.

```
$VMService.AddVirtualSystemResources($VM.__Path, $StaticNIC.PSBase.GetText(1))

$VMService.AddVirtualSystemResources($VM.__Path, $DynamicNIC.PSBase.GetText(1))
```

Finally, all of the properties of the two new virtual NICs are defined, and the target virtual machine ($VM) is chosen.

All that is left is to add the virtual NICs to the target virtual machine ($VM). This is accomplished by using the AddVirtualSystemResources method of the Msvm_ VirtualSystemManagementService class that was defined earlier ($VMService). This is done once for each NIC. The method takes two parameters: the target virtual machine instance ($VM.__Path) and the item to add ($StaticNIC.PSBase.GetText(1) and $DynamicNIC.PSBase. GetText(1)). Again, PSBase is used in both cases to get the raw object data without using PowerShell's view of the WMI object.

Congratulations! You have just scripted the addition of virtual NICs to an existing virtual machine.

Creating a Virtual Machine

Now that you have learned how to create, modify, and add resources to a virtual machine, you can automate the creation of a virtual machine with all of its resources added. The following script does just that.

```
$VMName = "TestVM"
$Namespace = "root\virtualization"
$Computer = "HyperV-Dev"
$VHD = "e:\virtualdisks\test.vhd"
$VHDSize = "10GB"
$VSwitchName = "Hyper-V External Switch"
$VSwitchPortName = "TestPort"
$VNicAddress = "00155D9290FF"

$VMService = Get-WmiObject -class "Msvm_VirtualSystemManagementService"
-namespace $Namespace -ComputerName $Computer

# Assign a name to the new Virtual Machine#####

$VMGlobalSettingClass = ➥
 [WMIClass]"\\$Computer\root\virtualization:Msvm_VirtualSystemGlobalSettingData"

$NewVMGS = $VMGlobalSettingClass.psbase.CreateInstance()

while ($NewVMGS.psbase.Properties -eq $null) {}

$NewVMGS.psbase.Properties.Item("ElementName").value = $VMName

# Create Virtual Disk#######################

$VDiskService = Get-Wmiobject -Class "Msvm_ImageManagementService" ➥
-Namespace "root\virtualization"

$DiskCreate = $VDiskService.CreateFixedVirtualHardDisk($VHD, 10GB)
$DiskJob = [WMI]$DiskCreate.job

while (($DiskJob.JobState -eq "2") -or ($DiskJob.JobState -eq "3")
-or ($DiskJob.JobState -eq "4")) {Start-Sleep -m 100
```

```
$DiskJob = [WMI]$DiskCreate.job}

# Create NIC############################

$DefaultNIC = Get-WmiObject -Namespace $Namespace ➡
-Class Msvm_SyntheticEthernetPortSettingData | ➡
Where-Object -FilterScript {$_.InstanceID -like "*Default*"}

$GUID1 = [GUID]::NewGUID().ToString()
$GUID2 = [GUID]::NewGUID().ToString()

$VSwitchQuery = Get-WmiObject ➡
-Class "Msvm_VirtualSwitchManagementService" -Namespace $Namespace

$VMService = Get-WmiObject -class "Msvm_VirtualSystemManagementService" ➡
-namespace $Namespace -ComputerName $Computer

$VSwitch = Get-WmiObject -Namespace $Namespace ➡
-Query "Select * From Msvm_VirtualSwitch Where ElementName='$VSwitchName'"

$ReturnObject = $VSwitchQuery.CreateSwitchPort➡
($VSwitch, [guid]::NewGuid().ToString(), $VSwitchPortName, "")
$NewSwitchPort1 = $ReturnObject.CreatedSwitchPort

$ReturnObject = $VSwitchQuery.CreateSwitchPort➡
($VSwitch, [guid]::NewGuid().ToString(), $VSwitchPortName, "")
$NewSwitchPort2 = $ReturnObject.CreatedSwitchPort

$StaticNIC = $DefaultNIC.psbase.Clone()
$StaticNIC.VirtualSystemIdentifiers = "{$GUID1}"
$StaticNIC.StaticMacAddress = $true
$StaticNIC.Address = $VNicAddress
$StaticNIC.Connection = $NewSwitchPort1

$DynamicNIC = $DefaultNIC.psbase.Clone()
$DynamicNIC.VirtualSystemIdentifiers = "{$GUID2}"
$DynamicNIC.Connection = $NewSwitchPort2

# Add the NIC resources to the Resource Allocation Settings Data Array#

$VMRASD = @()

$VMRASD += $StaticNic.psbase.gettext(1)
$VMRASD += $DynamicNic.psbase.gettext(1)

# Create the Virtual Machine
$VMService.DefineVirtualSystem($NewVMGS.psbase.GetText(1), $VMRASD)
```

```
# Add the Disk to the new Virtual Machine############################################

$VM = Get-WmiObject -Namespace $Namespace -ComputerName $Computer ➥
-Query "Select * From Msvm_ComputerSystem Where ElementName='$VMName'"

$VMSettingData = Get-WmiObject -Namespace $Namespace ➥
-Query "Associators of {$VM} ➥
Where ResultClass=Msvm_VirtualSystemSettingData ➥
AssocClass=Msvm_SettingsDefineState"

$VMIDEController = (Get-WmiObject -Namespace $Namespace ➥
-Query "Associators of {$VMSettingData} Where ➥
ResultClass=Msvm_ResourceAllocationSettingData ➥
AssocClass=Msvm_VirtualSystemSettingDataComponent" | ➥
where-object -FilterScript {$_.ResourceSubType ➥
-eq "Microsoft Emulated IDE Controller" -and $_.Address -eq 0})

$DiskAllocationSetting = Get-WmiObject -Namespace $Namespace ➥
-Query "SELECT * FROM Msvm_AllocationCapabilities ➥
WHERE ResourceSubType = 'Microsoft Synthetic Disk Drive'"➥
$DefaultDiskDrive = (Get-WmiObject -Namespace $Namespace ➥
-Query "Associators of {$DiskAllocationSetting} ➥
Where ResultClass=Msvm_ResourceAllocationSettingData ➥
 AssocClass=Msvm_SettingsDefineCapabilities" | ➥
where-object -FilterScript {$_.InstanceID -like "*Default"})

$DefaultDiskDrive.Parent = $VMIDEController.__Path

$DefaultDiskDrive.Address = 0

$NewDiskDrive = ($VMService.AddVirtualSystemResources($VM.__Path, ➥
 $DefaultDiskDrive.PSBase.GetText(1))).NewResources

$DiskAllocationSetting = Get-WmiObject -Namespace $Namespace ➥
-Query "SELECT * FROM Msvm_AllocationCapabilities ➥
WHERE ResourceSubType = 'Microsoft Virtual Hard Disk'" ➥

$DefaultHardDisk = (Get-WmiObject -Namespace $Namespace ➥
-Query "Associators of {$DiskAllocationSetting} ➥
Where ResultClass=Msvm_ResourceAllocationSettingData ➥
 AssocClass=Msvm_SettingsDefineCapabilities" | ➥
where-object -FilterScript {$_.InstanceID -like "*Default"})

$DefaultHardDisk.Parent = $NewDiskDrive
$DefaultHardDisk.Connection = $VHD

$VMService.AddVirtualSystemResources($VM.__Path, $DefaultHardDisk.PSBase.GetText(1))
```

```
# Add DVD Drive#####################################

$DVDAllocationSetting = Get-WmiObject -Namespace $Namespace ➥
-Query "SELECT * FROM Msvm_AllocationCapabilities ➥
WHERE ResourceSubType = 'Microsoft Synthetic DVD Drive'"

$DefaultDVDDrive = (Get-WmiObject -Namespace $Namespace ➥
-Query "Associators of {$DVDAllocationSetting} ➥
Where ResultClass=Msvm_ResourceAllocationSettingData ➥
 AssocClass=Msvm_SettingsDefineCapabilities" |
where-object -FilterScript {$_.InstanceID -like "*Default"})

$DefaultDVDDrive.Parent = $VMIDEController.__Path

$DefaultDVDDrive.Address = 1

$NewDVDDrive = $DefaultDVDDrive.psbase.Clone()

$VMService.AddVirtualSystemResources($VM.__PATH, $NewDVDDrive.psbase.Gettext(1))
```

The individual sections of the script are similar to the smaller resource scripts that you have seen so far in this chapter. However, this script includes a few new items that bring it together. First is the virtual machine name assignment:

```
# Assign a name to the new Virtual Machine#################

$VMGlobalSettingClass = ➥
[WMIClass]"\\$Computer\root\virtualization:Msvm_VirtualSystemGlobalSettingData"

$NewVMGS = $VMGlobalSettingClass.psbase.CreateInstance()

while ($NewVMGS.psbase.Properties -eq $null) {}

$NewVMGS.psbase.Properties.Item("ElementName").value = $VMName
```

Global settings are the settings of a virtual machine that do not change when a snapshot of the virtual machine is taken. One of those settings is the virtual machine name. This section of code creates a new instance of the Msvm_VirtualSystemGlobalSettingData class using the CreateInstance method. Then it waits for the new instance to be populated with properties.

```
while ($NewVMGS.psbase.Properties -eq $null) {}
```

Finally, it assigns the virtual machine name ($VMName, which was defined at the beginning of the script) to the ElementName property.

The next new section adds the NIC resources to a resource allocation settings data array ($VMRASD):

```
# Add the NIC resources to the Resource Allocation Settings Data Array#

$VMRASD = @()
```

```
$VMRASD += $StaticNic.psbase.gettext(1)
$VMRASD += $DynamicNic.psbase.gettext(1)

#Create the Virtual Machine
$VMService.DefineVirtualSystem($NewVMGS.psbase.GetText(1), $VMRASD)
```

When a virtual machine is created using the DefineVirtualSystem method, you can define the global settings ($NewVMGS) for the virtual machine. You can also define the resources that the virtual machine will have using a resource allocation settings data array ($VMRASD). You'll probably notice that the hard disk was not added to this array. That is because the hard disk is added to one of the virtual IDE ports of the virtual machine. Because these ports do not exist until the virtual machine is created, the hard disk is added after the creation.

The last new item in this script is the addition of a DVD drive.

```
# Add DVD Drive##########################################

$DVDAllocationSetting = Get-WmiObject -Namespace $Namespace ➥
-Query "SELECT * FROM Msvm_AllocationCapabilities ➥
WHERE ResourceSubType = 'Microsoft Synthetic DVD Drive'"

$DefaultDVDDrive = (Get-WmiObject -Namespace $Namespace ➥
-Query "Associators of {$DVDAllocationSetting} ➥
Where ResultClass=Msvm_ResourceAllocationSettingData ➥
 AssocClass=Msvm_SettingsDefineCapabilities" | ➥
where-object -FilterScript {$_.InstanceID -like "*Default"})

$DefaultDVDDrive.Parent = $VMIDEController.__Path

$DefaultDVDDrive.Address = 1

$NewDVDDrive = $DefaultDVDDrive.psbase.Clone()

$VMService.AddVirtualSystemResources($VM.__PATH, $NewDVDDrive.psbase.Gettext(1))
```

Much of this section is similar to adding a virtual hard disk to a virtual machine. The allocation setting data ($DVDAllocationSetting) is a Microsoft Synthetic DVD Drive. Then the default settings of the Microsoft Synthetic DVD Drive instance are stored in the $DefaultDVDDrive variable. The IDE controller and IDE controller address are changed to reflect this specific scenario. Next, the new DVD drive instance ($NewDVDDrive) is created by cloning the default instance. Finally, the DVD drive resource is added to the virtual machine.

With this script, you can now programmatically create a new virtual machine on a Hyper-V system. The script can easily be modified to create multiple virtual machines, provide reporting, or whatever else you would like to add.

So far, you have learned that you can manage almost every aspect of a Hyper-V system with PowerShell and WMI. You've seen that certain patterns can be reused in your scripts. Still, WMI can be verbose and unwieldy. Thankfully, if you invest in VMM 2008 to manage your Hyper-V infrastructure, automating Hyper-V is even easier.

VMM 2008 and PowerShell

VMM 2008 is built from the ground up to take advantage of PowerShell when performing management tasks. Actually, just about every task that is performed in VMM 2008 is performed by a PowerShell cmdlet. In some cases, PowerShell cmdlets allow you to use a single command to do what may take several lines of WMI code. For example, the New-VirtualSwitch cmdlet will create a new virtual switch on a Hyper-V host. In this sense, PowerShell cmdlets are more like command-line tools than traditional scripting constructs.

As an example, consider creating a new virtual machine. In the wizard's Summary window, shown in Figure 5-4, you can click the View Script button to see the following PowerShell code, which is actually performing the task of creating the virtual machine:

```
# ------------------------------------------------------------------------------
# New Virtual Machine Script
# ------------------------------------------------------------------------------
# Script generated on Sunday, December 21, 2008 4:33:08 AM
# by Virtual Machine Manager
#
# For additional help on cmdlet usage, type get-help <cmdlet name>
# ------------------------------------------------------------------------------

New-VirtualNetworkAdapter -VMMServer localhost ➡
-JobGroup 556774c5-c019-4122-bfbc-60c23c15846a ➡
-PhysicalAddressType Dynamic ➡
-VirtualNetwork "Hyper-V External Switch" -VLanEnabled $false ➡

New-VirtualDVDDrive -VMMServer localhost ➡
-JobGroup 556774c5-c019-4122-bfbc-60c23c15846a -Bus 1 -LUN 0

$CPUType = Get-CPUType -VMMServer localhost | ➡
where {$_.Name -eq "1.20 GHz Athlon MP"}

New-HardwareProfile -VMMServer localhost -Owner "HYPERV\administrator" ➡
-CPUType $CPUType -Name "Profile8f5786fa-8278-4585-be3c-9e196ec2cbfe" ➡
-Description "Profile used to create a VM/Template" -CPUCount 1 ➡
-MemoryMB 2048 -RelativeWeight 100 -HighlyAvailable $false ➡
-NumLock $false -BootOrder "CD", "IdeHardDrive", "PxeBoot", "Floppy" ➡
-LimitCPUFunctionality $false -JobGroup 556774c5-c019-4122-bfbc-60c23c15846a

New-VirtualDiskDrive -VMMServer localhost -IDE -Bus 0 -LUN 0 ➡
-JobGroup 556774c5-c019-4122-bfbc-60c23c15846a -Size 40960 -Dynamic ➡
-Filename "Test-VM2_disk_1"

$VMHost = Get-VMHost -VMMServer localhost | ➡
where {$_.Name -eq "hyperv-dev.hyperv.int"}➡
$HardwareProfile = Get-HardwareProfile -VMMServer localhost | ➡
where {$_.Name -eq "Profile8f5786fa-8278-4585-be3c-9e196ec2cbfe"}➡
$OperatingSystem = Get-OperatingSystem -VMMServer localhost | ➡
where {$_.Name -eq "Windows Server 2003 Enterprise x64 Edition"}
```

```
New-VM -VMMServer localhost -Name "Test-VM2" -Description ""➥
-Owner "HYPERV\administrator" -VMHost $VMHost ➥
-Path "e:\virtualmachines" -HardwareProfile $HardwareProfile ➥
-JobGroup 556774c5-c019-4122-bfbc-60c23c15846a -RunAsynchronously ➥
-OperatingSystem $OperatingSystem -RunAsSystem ➥
-StartAction NeverAutoTurnOnVM -StopAction SaveVM
```

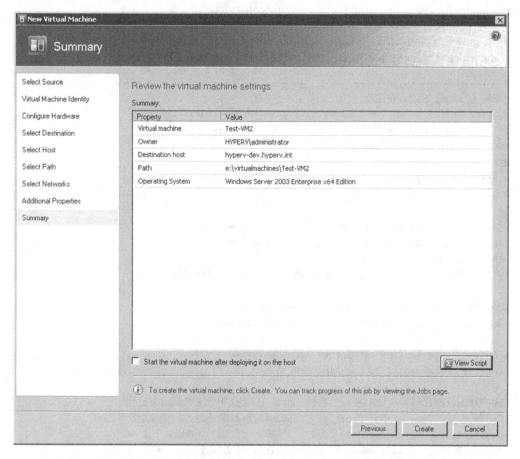

Figure 5-4. *You can click the View Script button to see the PowerShell code behind this action.*

You do not see any trace of WMI in the code. This is because all of the actions are performed by the VMM 2008 PowerShell cmdlets. To use these cmdlets, you need to install the VMM 2008 Administrator console (as described in Chapter 3) on the computer that you will be using to run these scripts.

Let's go through some of the same tasks that you performed with WMI to see how much easier they are to do with the VMM 2008 PowerShell interface. Keep in mind that these scripts should be run from the VMM 2008 PowerShell console, shown in Figure 5-5, accessed by clicking the PowerShell button in the Administrator console.

Figure 5-5. *The VMM 2008 PowerShell console*

■**Tip** You can get help on using the cmdlets included with VMM 2008 by typing `help about_VMM` from the PowerShell console.

Manipulating Hyper-V Server Settings

A setting that you will probably want to change on your Hyper-V hosts is the location of the virtual machines. This can be accomplished on a single host with three lines of code:

```
Get-VMMServer -ComputerName "hyperv-dev2.hyperv.int"

$VMHost = Get-VMHost -ComputerName "hyperv-dev"

Set-VMHost -VMHost $VMHost -VMPaths "e:\virtualmachines"
```

This script is fairly straightforward. The first line gets the VMM server that will be used. The second line gets the Hyper-V host that will be modified. The third line brings it all together by using the Set-VMHost cmdlet. The -VMHost parameter is the Hyper-V host stored in the $VMHost variable from line 2. The -VMPaths parameter defines the new path for the virtual machine files (e:\virtualmachines). Pretty easy, right?

This script can easily be modified to accept a text file to specify multiple Hyper-V hosts to change, as follows:

```
$a = 0

get-content HyperV_List.txt | ➥
Foreach-object {$computer = (get-content HyperV_List.txt)[$a]
```

```
Get-VMMServer -ComputerName "hyperv-dev2.hyperv.int"

$VMHost = Get-VMHost -ComputerName $computer

Set-VMHost -VMHost $VMHost -VMPaths "e:\virtualmachines"

$a = $a+1
```

}

Just make sure the HyperV_List.txt file is stored in the same directory as the one from which you run the script.

You can monitor the success of the script by looking at the Jobs window in VMM 2008, as shown in Figure 5-6.

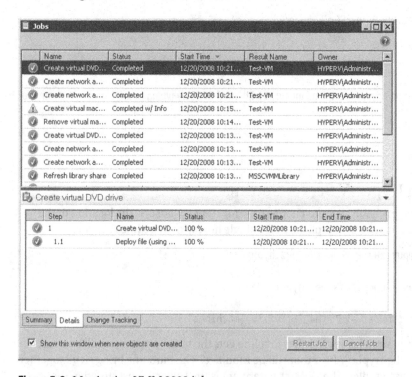

Figure 5-6. *Monitoring VMM 2008 jobs*

The other common setting for Hyper-V hosts is the addition of a new virtual network. Let's take a look at the script for creating the most difficult type of virtual network: an external virtual network.

```
Get-VMMServer -ComputerName "HyperV-Dev2.hyperv.int"

$VMHost = Get-VMHost -ComputerName "hyperv-dev.hyperv.int"
```

```
$HostAdapter = Get-VMHostNetworkAdapter ➥
-VMHost $VMHost ➥
-Name "Marvell Yukon 88E8056 PCI-E Gigabit Ethernet Controller"

New-VirtualNetwork -Name "Hyper-V External Switch" -VMHost $VMHost ➥
-VMHostNetworkAdapter $HostAdapter
```

As you can see, with VMM 2008, creating an external virtual network can be achieved with four lines of code. The first line gets the VMM server that will be used. The second line gets the Hyper-V host that will be modified. The third line gets the physical NIC on the Hyper-V host that will be attached to the virtual network. Finally, all of these are brought together using the New-VirtualNetwork cmdlet. The name of the new virtual network is Hyper-V External Switch. The Hyper-V host that will be modified was stored in the $VMHost variable on the second line. The physical NIC that will be used as the external port was stored in the $HostAdapter variable in the third line. This same action took about ten lines of code and some WMI queries without VMM 2008. With one line, the New-VirtualNetwork cmdlet creates the virtual switch, creates the virtual switch ports, and binds the external NIC.

Manipulating Virtual Machine Resources

Now that your Hyper-V hosts are configured, you can start manipulating virtual machine resources. Let's start with disks.

Disk Resource

The following script creates a virtual hard disk (*.vhd) and adds it to an existing virtual machine.

```
Get-VMMServer -Computername "HyperV-Dev2.hyperv.int"

$VM = Get-VM -Name "Test-VM"

New-VirtualDiskDrive -VM $VM -Fixed ➥
-Filename "e:\virtualdisks\Test_Disk.vhd" -IDE ➥
-Size 10240 -Bus 0 -LUN 1
```

This script is a mere three lines. The first line gets the VMM server to use (you can see that this is pretty standard by now). The second line gets the virtual machine to which the disk will be attached. The third line uses the New-VirtualDiskDrive cmdlet to create the new virtual disk drive attached to e:\virtualdisks\Test_Disk.vhd (a fixed *.vhd file with a size of 10240MB) on IDE controller 0 (-Bus 0) and address 1 (-LUN 1).

Now that the disk resources are taken care of, let's move on to memory resources.

Memory Resource

The following is the script to adjust the memory on a virtual machine. Keep in mind that the virtual machine must be shut off for this to work.

```
Get-VMMServer -ComputerName "HyperV-Dev2.hyperv.int"

$VM = Get-VM -Name "Test-VM"

Set-VM -VM $VM -MemoryMB 1024
```

You should recognize the first two lines by now. The cmdlet that does all of the work is Set-VM. The MemoryMB parameter is fairly self-explanatory. The value is the new value for the amount of RAM that the virtual machine will use, in megabytes (1024 in this case).

That brings us to configuring the processor resources.

Processor Resource

Here is the script for adding a second processor to a virtual machine:

```
Get-VMMServer -ComputerName "HyperV-Dev2.hyperv.int"

$VM = Get-VM -Name "Test-VM"

Set-VM -VM $VM -CPUCount 2
```

You should start to see a pattern by now. Most of these scripts are three or four lines long. The first few lines get the VMM server and the specific details (virtual machine, NIC, host server, and so on). The Set-VM cmdlet is the star in this script as well. All that is required is the CPUCount parameter, which has been set to 2. If you wanted four processors assigned to the virtual machine, you would set this value to 4.

Let's move on to the final of the core four resources.

Network Resource

As with the previous tasks, it is relatively easy to add virtual NICs to a virtual machine using VMM 2008 cmdlets. Here is the script:

```
Get-VMMServer -ComputerName "hyperv-dev2.hyperv.int"

$VM = Get-VM -Name "Test-VM"

$VNetwork = "Hyper-V External Switch"

New-VirtualNetworkAdapter -VirtualNetwork $VNetwork -VM $VM

New-VirtualNetworkAdapter -VM $VM ➥
-VirtualNetwork $VNetwork -PhysicalAddress "00-15-5D-92-90-FF" ➥
-PhysicalAddressType "Static"
```

The first two lines should look familiar. You need to get the VMM server and the target virtual machine. The third line stores the name of the external network to which the newly created virtual NICs will attach. The work in this script is performed on the fourth and fifth lines by the New-VirtualNetworkAdapter cmdlet.

This script creates and attaches two virtual NICs to the virtual machine. The first virtual NIC that is created on the fourth line uses a dynamic MAC address. The second virtual NIC on the last line is set to a static MAC address (00-15-5D-92-90-FF). By default, this will create two emulated virtual NICs. If you want to create synthetic NICs instead, just use the -Synthetic parameter with the New-VirtualNetworkAdapter cmdlet, as follows:

```
New-VirtualNetworkAdapter -VirtualNetwork $VNetwork -Synthetic -VM $VM
```

Creating a Virtual Machine

Now that the four core resources are taken care of, you can create an entire virtual machine with the appropriate resources assigned to it. This is easy in PowerShell with VMM 2008. For this next example, copy the Test_Disk.vhd file (or whatever *.vhd file you want to attach to your virtual machine) to the VMM 2008 Library share folder. Here is the script:

```
$VHD = Get-VirtualHardDisk | where {$_.Name -eq "Test_Disk.vhd"}

$VMPath = "e:\virtualmachines"

$VMHost = Get-VMHost | where {$_.Name -eq "hyperv-dev.hyperv.int"}

New-VM -Name "Test-VM" -VirtualHardDisk $VHD -VMHost $VMHost -Path $VMPath

$VNetwork = "Hyper-V External Switch"

$VM = Get-VM -Name "Test-VM"

New-VirtualNetworkAdapter -VirtualNetwork $VNetwork -VM $VM

New-VirtualNetworkAdapter -VM $VM -VirtualNetwork $VNetwork ➡
-PhysicalAddress "00-15-5D-92-90-FF" -PhysicalAddressType "Static"

New-VirtualDVDDrive -VM $VM -Bus 0 -LUN 1
```

Most of this is the same as in the smaller scripts that modified individual core resources. The first line defines the *.vhd file that will be attached to the virtual machine from the VMM 2008 Library. The second line defines the path in which the virtual machine will be created. The third line defines the Hyper-V host server on which the virtual machine will be created. Then the New-VM cmdlet is used with all of those parameters to actually create the new virtual machine. After the virtual machine is created, two NICs and a DVD drive are added. If you wanted to prestage an operating system for creating new virtual machines, you would just have to make sure an operating system prepared with Sysprep is installed on the Test_Disk. vhd virtual disk.

Congratulations! You have automated the creation of a virtual machine using VMM 2008 and PowerShell.

Summary

This chapter covered a lot of Hyper-V automation techniques using PowerShell. First, you saw how to modify some Hyper-V server settings using PowerShell and WMI. Then the four core resources were created, modified, and added to existing virtual machines using some of the same techniques. Finally, you created a full virtual machine using PowerShell and WMI. The next section covered the same topics using VMM 2008 and PowerShell. You saw that this approach is less complex and requires less code and research.

The bottom line is that Hyper-V can be automated with or without VMM 2008. WMI is a very powerful tool for managing many aspects of Windows operating systems, including Hyper-V. However, if you have implemented or plan to implement VMM 2008, it will make automation through PowerShell much easier.

CHAPTER 6

■■■

Monitoring Hyper-V and VM Performance

What is the most important component of a virtual infrastructure? I'll give you a hint: it's nothing technical. It's the users. As IT administrators, server engineers, infrastructure architects, and the like, we may have a tendency to forget about the users. After all, we are surrounded by incredibly cool technology, and that's why we got into this field in the first place. Users can get very cranky (rightfully so) if they notice that the IT resources given to them are not meeting their expectations. And if the users are unhappy, the IT team is going to be very unhappy.

Users expect predictable, stable performance. To achieve this, you need to have performance metrics in place. Capturing performance trends over time also helps you to architect your virtual infrastructure for the future. Those metrics need to be measured against a baseline periodically, so resources can be adjusted accordingly. This is how to set user expectations as far as performance is concerned.

Although monitoring server performance is an important part of systems management, it is sometimes overlooked, as businesses demand that IT teams implement more resources with less expense more quickly. This approach can lead to implementing first and asking questions later. While you may get away with this on a single application, file, or print server that is utilizing only 5% to 7% of its available resources, it will not work for virtualized workloads.

Host resources are quickly taken by virtual machines in a virtualization system. This is a good thing, because it means that the host server is being utilized with the greatest efficiency that Hyper-V will allow. That also means that resources must be scrutinized more closely, because resource contention among the virtual machines is bound to happen at some point.

Fortunately, Windows Server 2008 comes with some tools that administrators can use to monitor the performance of any Windows Server 2008 system, whether or not it is using Hyper-V. This chapter describes how to take advantage of those tools.

Using the Reliability and Performance Monitoring Tool

As discussed in previous chapters, four core resources create the foundation for IT services (especially in virtual environments): processor, disk, network, and memory. So, it makes sense that performance monitoring, especially in virtual environments, is concerned with these four resources.

In previous versions of Windows Server, the tools to get a good picture of overall system performance with regard to the four core resources were fragmented. You had Performance Monitor, System Monitor, and Server Performance Advisor (available as an add-on component). It was difficult to get a good view of what was going on with performance and system stability with these separate tools. In Windows Server 2008, these tools have been combined into a comprehensive supertool called Reliability and Performance Monitor. The tool is available locally, or it can connect to a remote computer (useful if you are using the recommended Windows Server 2008 Core installation of Hyper-V).

To get started with the Reliability and Performance Monitor tool, select Start ➤ Administrative Tools ➤ Reliability and Performance Monitor. You will see something useful right away: a dashboard of the four core resources, as shown in Figure 6-1. At a glance, you can see real-time system activity.

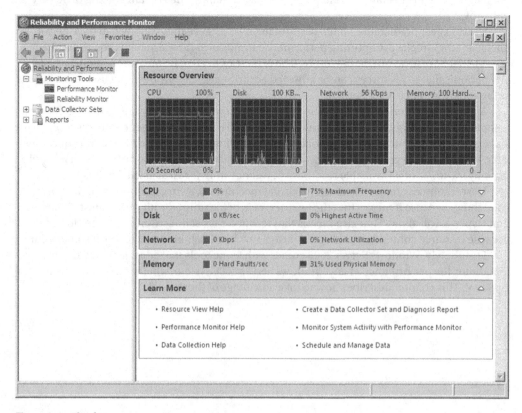

Figure 6-1. *The four core resources overview*

Below the four performance charts are sections for each of the four core resources. To the right of these sections are drop-down arrows that, when clicked, reveal processes that are using that particular core resource. For example, if you want to see which process is taking the most disk I/O, you can simply look at the Disk drop-down list, as shown in Figure 6-2.

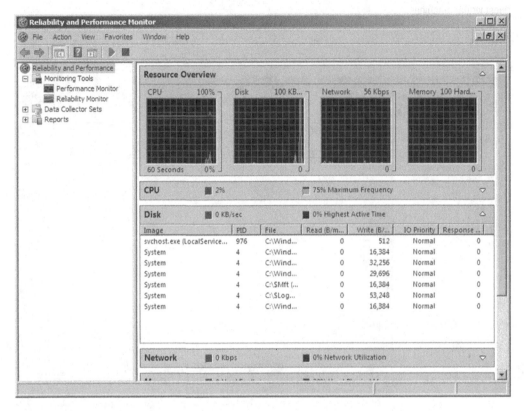

Figure 6-2. *Individual disk processes*

This is a great tool to get a bird's eye view at what may be a resource bottleneck. However, if you want to dive deeper to get a specific metric, you will need to use the Performance Monitor section.

Adding Counters

The Performance Monitor section of Reliability and Performance Monitor is like the Performance Monitor tool that you may be used to from previous versions of Windows Server. To get to it, just select the Performance Monitor section in the tree view in the left pane of the main Reliability and Performance Monitoring window, as shown in Figure 6-3.

Caution Performance Monitor may not give accurate results when used inside a virtual machine. The virtualization-specific counters for processor utilization discussed in the "Creating a Baseline of Your Virtual Environment" section later in this chapter should be used from the Hyper-V host, instead of from inside the guest virtual machine.

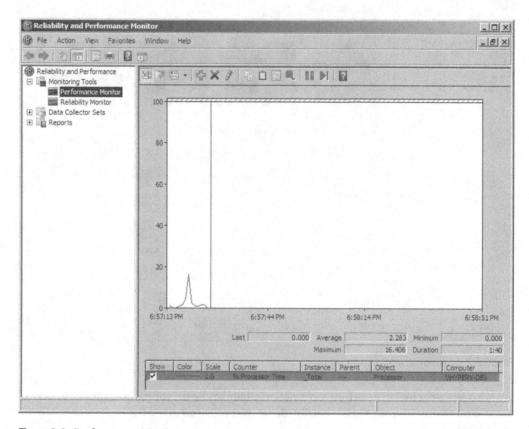

Figure 6-3. *Performance Monitor*

This is where you can add very specific performance metrics called *counters*. To add counters, just click the green plus button at the top of the window. In the Add Counters dialog box that appears, navigate to the category of interest, select the appropriate counter, and then click the Add button, as shown in Figure 6-4. You can continue to add other counters in this manner. Click OK when you are finished adding counters.

After you've added the counters, they can be viewed in real time in a line graph, histogram, or report view by clicking the corresponding button in the toolbar (for example, click the button with a picture of a graph to view a line graph). Figure 6-5 shows an example of a line graph of some logical disk read and disk write times.

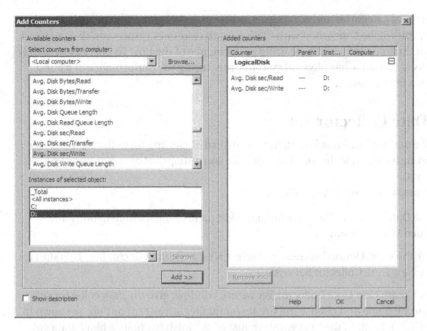

Figure 6-4. *Adding counters to Performance Monitor*

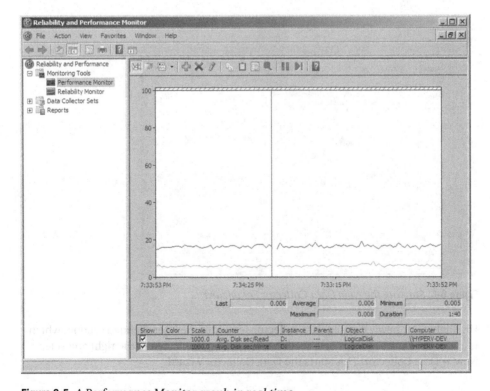

Figure 6-5. *A Performance Monitor graph in real time*

A dizzying array of categories and counters is available for Windows Server 2008. Don't panic. In general, you will be concerned with the four core resources (processor, disk, network, and memory). But do note that while measuring performance of the host Hyper-V system may be what you are used to with other physical systems, measuring the performance of a guest virtual machine is a little different.

Creating a Data Collector Set

If you want to save performance results to a log file instead of viewing them in real time, you can do so by creating a data collector set. This will give you a snapshot of performance results that you can analyze.

Follow these steps to create a data collector set:

1. Expand the Data Collector Sets section in the left pane of the main Reliability and Performance Monitor window.

2. Right-click the User-Defined section and select New ➤ Data Collector Set. This starts the Create New Data Collector Set wizard.

3. In the first Create New Data Collector Set wizard window, give the data collector set an appropriate name and choose the Create manually (Advanced) option, as shown in Figure 6-6. Click Next. In the next window, just click Finish to create a blank data collector set.

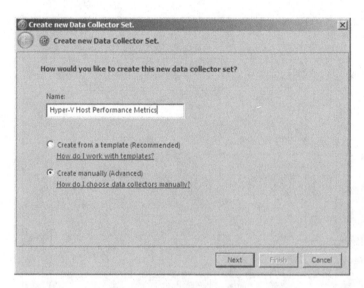

Figure 6-6. *Starting the New Data Collector Set wizard*

4. Highlight your newly created data collector set under the User-Defined section, which is under the Data Collector Sets section. Click in the blank area to the right and select New ➤ Data Collector. This starts the Data Collector wizard.

5. In the first Data Collector wizard window, select "Performance counter data collector" and give it an appropriate name, as shown in Figure 6-7. Click Next to continue.

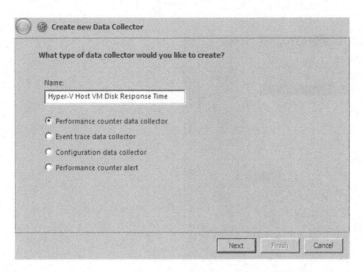

Figure 6-7. *Naming the Data Collector Set*

6. In the next window, you choose your performance counters, as shown in Figure 6-8. Click Add and select the appropriate performance counters. Then choose your sample interval. Click Next when you are finished adding counters.

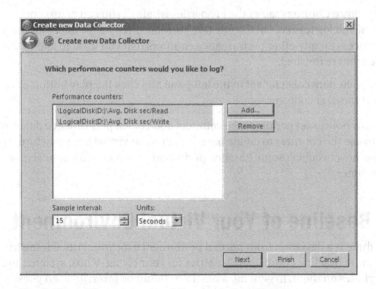

Figure 6-8. *Adding counters to the new data collector set*

7. In the next window, select Open Properties for this Data Collector, and then click Finish. This will bring up the Properties window for the data collector, as shown in Figure 6-9.

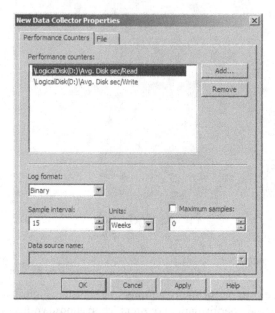

Figure 6-9. *The data collector set properties*

8. On the Performance Counters tab of the Properties window, you can adjust your sample interval and log format. On the File tab, you can specify a file name for the log. Repeat this process for any other performance counters that you want to add to the set. Click OK when you're finished.

9. Highlight your new data collector set in the left pane and click the play button in the toolbar to start the data collector set.

Now that you know how to set performance counters and collect performance data from them, let's see how to use the counters to create baselines for your virtual infrastructure. The next section describes how to collect some baseline performance statistics for your Hyper-V hosts and virtual machines.

Creating a Baseline of Your Virtual Environment

You cannot know if there is a deviation from normal performance for your virtual infrastructure if you do not capture baseline performance metrics for your Hyper-V host systems and the guest virtual machines on them. In general, a baseline should be taken for each guest virtual machine and the underlying Hyper-V host whenever a new guest virtual machine is added. You can then compare your previous baseline to the current baseline to see if the system, as a whole, is adversely affected by the additional load introduced by the new guest virtual machine.

Baselines should contain a representative sample of performance data, covering off-hours and peak hours for the systems involved. So, what performance metrics should you consider measuring? Specific applications like Microsoft Exchange Server and SQL Server will have different suggestions for which metrics are important based on vendor recommendations. However, in general, you should focus on the four core resources of processor, disk, network, and memory.

Processor Performance Metrics

Measuring processor performance in a guest virtual machine is different from measuring processor performance in a physical machine. There are some considerations to take into account because of the way that processor resources are assigned to a guest virtual machine in Hyper-V.

First, since Hyper-V schedules the processor time for guest virtual machines in the form of processor threads, the processor time for guests will be spread over the available processors in a host. However, the guest cannot exceed the processor capacity assigned to the virtual machine. So, if a guest virtual machine is assigned two processors, it will take advantage of only two processors on the Hyper-V host at any one time. Processing time is distributed in a round-robin fashion for the guest virtual machines running on the Hyper-V host.

Typically, the \Processor(*)\% Processor Time metric would be used to measure processor performance. However, this is not an accurate portrayal of the processor utilization in a guest virtual machine. Since processing time is distributed in a round-robin fashion for the guest virtual machines, the processor utilization metric for \Processor(*)\% Processor Time is a value that is relative to the number of virtual processors assigned to a particular guest virtual machine. For example, in a two-processor system, each virtual processor in a guest virtual machine will attempt to use 50% of each physical processor. So, a virtual machine that is assigned one virtual processor on a four-processor host system will be utilizing only 25% of the total host system's capacity, even when the virtual processor is utilized at 100%.

Also, there are basically three partitions in a Hyper-V installation: the parent partition (where Windows Server 2008 resides), the root partition (where the actual hypervisor resides), and the child partitions (where the guest virtual machines reside). Processor I/O happens between the child partitions and the root partition; this I/O is never passed to the parent partition. So, when you measure Processor(*)\% Processor Time, it is actually taking a measurement of the parent partition, which should really not be utilized much at all. The hypervisor is doing all of the processor scheduling work for the virtual machines.

Due to these considerations, specific processor performance counters exist for Hyper-V and Hyper-V guests. One is for measuring performance of the Hyper-V system as a whole. This is the \Hyper-V Hypervisor Logical Processor(_Total)\% Total Run Time counter, which measures the percentage of time that the processor is running the host and guest virtual machines. You don't want to let this counter get above 60% to 75% consistently. Anything above 75% means that the host processors are being overutilized.

If the \Hyper-V Hypervisor Logical Processor(_Total)\% Total Run Time metric for the host is at a reasonable level and a guest virtual machine is still having performance issues, there are processor metrics for the guests as well. One of the most important counters to look at in this case is \Hyper-V Hypervisor Virtual Processor(*)\% Total Run Time. This counter will let you see which virtual processor is taking the most processing time. If this particular counter is consistently high (75% to 100%), you may consider disabling any unneeded roles and services on the particular guest virtual machine that is having trouble. You may also want to consider adding another virtual processor to the virtual machine in question.

A good general baseline for processor resources in a virtual infrastructure should include the following counters:

- \Hyper-V Hypervisor Logical Processor(_Total)\% Total Run Time for the Hyper-V host system

- \Hyper-V Hypervisor Virtual Processor(*)\% Total Run Time for each guest virtual machine

---

Tip If you want to put a processing load on a virtual machine to see how it is going to affect the host system (make sure it is not a production system), you can do this easily with the Windows calculator. Just open `Calc.exe` in scientific mode. Type in 99999 and hit the n! button to calculate a factorial of 99999. This will take a very long time and generate a load on the processor. You can cancel the calculation when you are finished with your testing.

Disk Performance Metrics

Two counters provide a good indicator of disk performance on both the host Hyper-V machine and the guest virtual machines: \Logical Disk(*)\Avg. sec/Read and \Logical Disk(*)\Avg. sec/ Write. These counters measure the amount of time it takes for the operating system to respond to read and write operations. They show accurate values on both the host and guest operating systems. As a general guideline, you will want these values to be under 15 ms to 20 ms. Anything greater than 25 ms may have a performance impact on the host and the virtual machines. The \Logical Disk(*)\Avg. sec/Read and \Logical Disk(*)\Avg. sec/Write counters can also be used to test disk performance in a guest virtual machine.

If the disk is direct-attached storage, another disk performance counter you should look at is the \PhysicalDisk\Average Disk Queue Length performance counter. (This counter should be ignored if the disk is on a storage area network, or SAN.) This counter indicates the average number of read and write operations that were queued during the sample interval. This value should be, at most, two times the number of physical spindles assigned to the disk, or it should be 1 if the disk is a single disk.

A good baseline for disk resources should include the following counters:

- Logical Disk(*)\Avg. sec/Read for the Hyper-V host system and each guest virtual machine

- \Logical Disk(*)\Avg. sec/Write for the Hyper-V host system and each guest virtual machine

- \PhysicalDisk\Average Disk Queue Length for the host system if the disk is direct-attached storage

Network Performance Metrics

You will probably see a pattern for performance benchmarking appearing at this point. You need to capture performance statistics for both the Hyper-V host and the guest virtual machines. This also applies to capturing network utilization metrics. The two counters of interest for the Hyper-V host are \Network Interface(*)\Bytes Total/sec and \Network Interface(*)\Output Queue Length.

The \Network Interface(*)\Bytes Total/sec counter will help you determine the percentage of network utilization on the host after a little math. Take the following steps to calculate the percentage of network utilization:

1. Multiply the value of the \Network Interface(*)\Bytes Total/sec counter by 8 to get bits.

2. Multiply the bits value by 100.

3. Divide the previous value by the network adapter's current bandwidth.

This will give you the percentage of network utilization for a particular network adapter on the host. Less than 40% of the network adapter's available bandwidth being utilized is considered healthy. Anywhere between 41% and 65% indicates that you should monitor the network utilization more closely. Performance of your Hyper-V system and its virtual machines may be adversely affected if the network utilization is between 65% and 100%, depending on the applications that you are running on your virtual machines. (If you know that a network utilization of over 65% is normal for your workload, you can adjust the monitoring to a more appropriate level.)

The \Network Interface(*)\Output Queue Length counter measures the number of threads that are waiting on the network adapter. Ideally, this value should be 0. If it is consistently sitting between 1 and 2, you should monitor this metric more closely. If the value is over 2, then the network may be a bottleneck. This can most commonly be attributed to poor network latency or high collision rates. To correct this, you may want to add more physical network adapters to the Hyper-V host computer and bind one of those adapters to guest virtual machines. For example, you could have some of your virtual machines use one physical adapter and some of your virtual machines use another physical adapter. This way, the load is split between the two adapters.

■**Note** If you are going to split the load of your virtual machines between two physical network adapters, you need to create a virtual network for each physical adapter, because Hyper-V does not have any NIC-teaming capabilities.

Output queue length may also be affected by high processor utilization. This may cause the processor to be too busy to process network packets. If this is the case, you may also want to check the processor utilization of the host or guest virtual machines by using the guidelines presented earlier in the "Processor Performance Metrics" section. Once you find out which guest is utilizing the host processor resources heavily, you can investigate inside the guest virtual machine to see which process might be taking the majority of the processor resources.

Another recommendation is to make sure the Message Transfer Unit (MTU) sizes match for both the physical network adapters on the Hyper-V host and the virtual network adapters assigned to the guest virtual machines. The default MTU for Windows is 1500, so your host and Windows guests should match if you have not changed the MTU.

If you want to identify which virtual network adapters are utilizing the most bandwidth, use the \Hyper-V Virtual Network Adapter(*)\Bytes/sec performance counter. Just see which virtual network adapters have the highest value for this performance counter.

A good baseline for network utilization should include the following counters:

- \Network Interface(*)\Bytes Total/sec for the Hyper-V host system

- \Network Interface(*)\Output Queue Length for the Hyper-V host system

- \Hyper-V Virtual Network Adapter(*)\Bytes/sec for each guest virtual machine

Memory Performance Metrics

Two questions should be answered where memory is concerned:

- How much memory is available?

- How much is the swap file being used?

Windows Server 2008 provides two counters to help you answer these questions.

To find out how much memory is available to the Hyper-V host, use the \Memory\ Available MBytes counter. This value will be the amount of free memory in megabytes. You should have between 10% and 20% of your total memory free. In other words, you should not allocate any more than 90% of your available memory on your Hyper-V host.

When sizing your Hyper-V host, use the following formula as a guideline:

(2GB of memory for the Hyper-V parent partition and operating system)
+ total of assigned RAM per virtual machine
+ 32MB of RAM per 1GB of RAM assigned to each virtual machine

For example, let's say that you have two virtual machines on your Hyper-V host. One virtual machine needs 1GB of RAM, and the other virtual machine needs 2GB of RAM. The formula should look like this:

$$2GB + 3GB + (32MB \times 3) = 5.09375GB \text{ of RAM}$$

The Hyper-V host should have at least 5.09375GB of RAM. Realistically, this translates into a host server with at least 6GB of RAM, if you are going to run only those two virtual machines on the host server.

The other counter that you will want to keep an eye on is \Memory\Pages/sec. This counter measures the rate at which pages are read from or written to the disk. If this is too high, it could indicate bad blocks of memory or not enough memory available. For a healthy system, this value should be 500 or less. If the value is between 500 and 1000, you should monitor this counter closely. If the value is greater than 1000, performance will be adversely affected. Consider either adding more memory to the Hyper-V host server or replacing a bad memory stick.

These same counters can be used in guest virtual machines to measure memory performance.

A good baseline for memory should include the following counters:

- \Memory\Available MBytes for both the Hyper-V host system and the guest virtual machines.

- \Memory\Pages/sec counters for both the Hyper-V host system and the guest virtual machines

Now that you understand how to collect performance monitor baselines the manual way, let's see how to automate this collection.

Automating Performance Monitoring

The four core resources should be measured under very little load, medium load, and peak load. Once you have decided on the counters to use, they should be set up in a baseline data collector set so the log files can be easily collected, as shown in Figure 6-10.

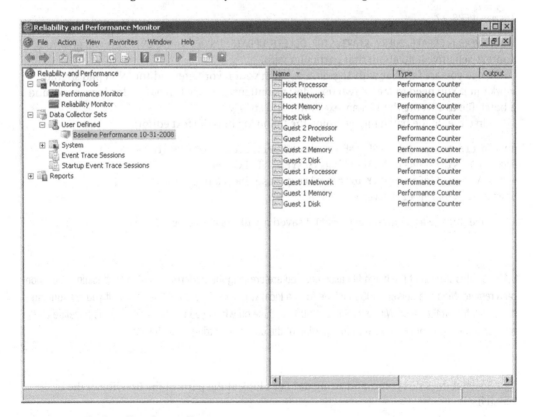

Figure 6-10. *The baseline data collector set*

Creating a baseline can be quite time-consuming. This is especially true when you have multiple Hyper-V hosts with several guest virtual machines to monitor.

So, how can you automate collection of Performance Monitor baselines? In previous chapters, I've shown you how to use PowerShell to automate many tasks. However, I am a pragmatist, so I tend to favor solutions that are simple to implement and do the job as intended. In this case, a text file and a two-line batch file beat PowerShell in simplicity, and this approach "just works."

This method uses a utility called logman.exe to set up and start your baseline collection. Before you create the batch file, take a second to familiarize yourself with logman.exe, which should already be installed on Windows Server 2008. Open a command prompt on your Windows Server 2008 machine by selecting Start ➤ Run, typing cmd, and pressing Enter. At the command prompt, type logman /?. This will show you the general usage and options for logman.exe. The logman command takes the following form:

```
logman VERB <collection_name> [options]
```

In this case, you will be using the CREATE verb. If you want to get more information about a particular verb, just type the following:

```
logman VERB /?
```

where VERB is CREATE, QUERY, START, STOP, DELETE, UPDATE, IMPORT, or EXPORT. This will give you context-sensitive help about that particular verb.

Once you are familiar with logman.exe, open your favorite text editor (Notepad should work fine). You need to create two text files: a configuration file (*.config) for logman.exe and a batch file to execute the logman.exe command string.

First, create the batch file by typing the following into the text editor:

```
logman create counter BASELINE -s <YourHyperVServer> -f bincirc ➡
-max 500 -si 2 --v -o "c:\perflogs\SERVERBASELINE" ➡
-cf "\\<YourFileServer>\<YourShare>\host_baseline.config"
logman -s <YourHyperVServer> start BASELINE
```

Save this file as a batch file (*.bat). I saved my file as baseline.bat.

Note This version of the batch file assumes you are creating the Performance Monitor baseline collection on a remote Windows Server 2008 machine from a local Windows Server 2008 machine. If you are running this batch file on the same Windows Server 2008 machine on which you will be collecting the baseline counters, omit the -s <YourHyperVServer> portion of the command string on both lines.

So what does this command string do? Let's look at the parts of the first line of the batch file.

```
-logman create counter BASELINE
```

This creates a counter collection called BASELINE.

```
--s <YourHyperVServer>
```

This connects to a remote Hyper-V server.

```
-f bincirc -max 500 -si 2
```

This creates a circular (overwriting) binary log file with a maximum size of 500MB. It also sets the collection interval at 2 hours, so some meaningful statistics can be collected over 24 hours without overwriting important data.

```
--v -o "c:\perflogs\SERVERBASELINE"
```

This command turns off the versioning information and sets the output location for the log file to c:\perflogs\SERVERBASELINE. The output could also be set to a file share if you prefer.

```
-cf "\\<YourFileServer>\<YourShare>\host_baseline.config"
```

This command tells logman.exe where to find the configuration file. The configuration file, which you'll create next, will hold the names of the performance counters that will be used when creating the baseline collection.

```
logman -s <YourHyperVServer> start BASELINE
```

Finally, this command connects to the remote system where the baseline counters will be collected and starts the BASELINE collection.

Note If your server is rebooted, you will need to run logman -s <YourHyperVServer> start BASELINE again, because it will not start automatically when the server starts.

The configuration file (*.config) tells logman.exe which performance counters to use to create the collection. To create it, enter the following in your text editor:

```
"\Hyper-V Hypervisor Logical Processor(_Total)\% Total Run Time"
"\Logical Disk(*)\Avg. Disk sec/Read"
"\Logical Disk(*)\Avg. Disk sec/Write"
"\PhysicalDisk\Average Disk Queue Length"
"\Network Interface(*)\Bytes Total/sec"
"\Network Interface(*)\Output Queue Length"
"\Memory\Available MBytes"
"\Memory\Pages/sec"
```

For this example, save the file as host_baseline.config and store it on a file share. With the configuration file and the batch file, you now have a predictable, repeatable process to collect baseline performance counter data on a Hyper-V server. Just adjust the specific details to suit your environment. Double-click the batch file to start the performance counter collection on the specified Hyper-V server.

Summary

Measuring performance for your virtual infrastructure is an important part of managing your virtual system. When you are running a single physical server, that server may have more resources than it needs. However, when you are running multiple virtual machines on a host server, you need to manage performance carefully.

While there may be performance tweaks that can be used for different applications, a general baseline of the four core resources (disk, memory, processor, and network) is a good starting point for a new virtual infrastructure. To manage performance and track trends, you should follow these general steps:

- Gather baseline performance statistics for your Hyper-V hosts and virtual machines under low, medium, and high workloads.

- Save those baseline statistics so you can compare their results with newer statistics.

- Periodically gather performance statistics for your Hyper-V hosts and virtual machines so you can track performance trends against the baseline.

- Add more resources to your virtual infrastructure if it becomes necessary.

Following these general steps will help to ensure that you have predictable, stable performance for your virtual infrastructure. Over time, you will begin to see certain trends with different workloads. If you can recognize the trends, you can size your virtual infrastructure capacity more appropriately in the future.

As your virtual infrastructure grows, you may also want to consider using System Center Virtual Machine Manager 2008 (VMM 2008) with System Center Operations Manager 2007 (SCOM 2007) reporting to get a better view of resource utilization trends in your infrastructure. Chapter 3 covers VMM 2008 and SCOM 2007 integration.

CHAPTER 7

■■■

Creating Highly Available Hyper-V Systems

One of the initial advantages of any server virtualization platform is physical server consolidation. Server virtualization gives you the ability to run many guest virtual machines on one physical server. However, if that physical server fails, your virtual machines on that server will be unavailable until the physical server is brought back online. This risk can usually be tolerated in a lab environment; however, in a production environment, you will need more availability.

Different businesses can take on different levels of risk when it comes to system availability. How fault-tolerant you want to make your Hyper-V system is up to you. This chapter provides an overview of the options available.

Server Hardware

Protection against server hardware failure starts with the server that you choose to run Hyper-V. The following are some general recommendations when choosing the host server and setting it up in your datacenter.

Power

Here are some recommendations for your server's power supply and power distribution units (PDUs):

- Make sure the server has at least two power supplies, and keep a spare power supply in stock on the shelf.

- If possible, make sure that each power supply is plugged into a PDU, which is plugged into a separate uninterruptible power supply (UPS).

- If possible, purchase metered PDUs so you can see the load on the PDU. Some PDUs even offer Simple Network Management Protocol (SNMP), so you can monitor their status.

- If you are using two PDUs, you should load each PDU to only around 40% of its power capacity. This is because when each power supply is active in a server, it shares a portion of the load (for two power supplies, that would be 50% each). If a power supply should fail on a server, the other power supply would take up 100% of the load, increasing the load on the PDU.

Network Adapters

The following are recommendations for your server's network interface cards (NICs):

- Microsoft does not support NIC teaming for Hyper-V. However, NICs can be teamed in the parent Windows Server 2008 partition using vendor-supplied drivers and utilities. Consult your NIC vendor for teaming configuration recommendations (especially if you need to configure teaming in Windows Server 2008 Core). There are usually three modes of NIC teaming:

  - *Fail-on-fault*: One NIC is active, and the other is standby. If the active NIC fails, the other NIC takes over with the same MAC address.

  - *Load balance*: Both NICs are active. This will give you the throughput of both NICs for any data that is sent from the NICs. You will still receive data on only one NIC.

  - *Switch-assisted load balance*: This requires configuration on a switch to be aware of the NIC team. This enables the server to gain the full throughput of both NICs when sending and receiving data.

- If you are going to use NIC teaming, try to team two physical NICs, rather than two ports on a dual-port NIC. This way, if a PCI slot fails, the entire NIC team will not fail with it.

- Keep an appropriate number of spare NICs in stock in case you need to replace a NIC quickly.

Direct-Attached Storage

If your server uses direct-attached storage, here are some recommendations:

- You should use hardware RAID level 1 (mirrored drives) for the operating system partition.

- You should use at least hardware RAID level 5. If your storage budget allows the use of RAID level 10 (or 1+0), consider it for superior drive failure protection.

- Keep an appropriate number of spare SCSI or SAS adapters in stock, in case you need to replace an adapter quickly.

Storage Area Network Redundancy

A storage area network (SAN) is a network designed to provide access to attached storage devices. The two most common ways to utilize a SAN today are by using the Fibre-Channel or Internet SCSI (iSCSI) protocol. Both the Fibre-Channel and iSCSI protocols are wrappers for SCSI commands so that they can be transferred over the SAN. The iSCSI protocol transports SCSI commands over a standard Ethernet network.

When a server uses Fibre-Channel to connect to storage on the network, a host bus adapter (HBA) inside the server is used to connect to the storage via fiber-optic (most common) or copper cabling. When a server uses the iSCSI protocol, an iSCSI HBA or an iSCSI software initiator that runs in the operating system can be used. If a server is using a software initiator for iSCSI, then standard NICs can be used for the iSCSI network connectivity.

When deploying a SAN for use on any server, you should consider the following best practices for redundancy:

- Dedicate two HBAs or NICs for SAN connectivity and configure them so they connect to two different storage switches (Fibre-Channel or Ethernet).

- Configure your storage switches to connect to two different storage ports on your storage array.

- Multipath input/output (MPIO) drivers make the redundant connections possible. Make sure your storage vendor and operating system support MPIO. Windows Server 2008 has built-in MPIO drivers that provide this functionality when the storage vendor supports the Windows MPIO driver specification.

- Configuring multipath redundancy differs depending on the storage vendor you use. Consult your vendor documentation for details on configuring MPIO.

- When using a SAN, traditional RAID levels can be used within the array. However, a few vendors may offer some other form of RAID level redundancy that is specific to the vendor. Consult your storage vendor for RAID option support.

Server Application Availability with Failover Clustering

Some server applications have built-in redundancy capabilities. Domain Name Service (DNS) replication, Active Directory replication, Microsoft Exchange Server 2007 continuous replication, and SQL Server database mirroring and database replication are a few examples of techniques that applications use to provide redundancy. However, if an application does not have built-in redundancy, you will need to find some other means to ensure availability in case of a failure. Many third-party solutions provide redundancy on a subset of applications, but you may find the redundancy capabilities of Windows Server 2008 better fit your needs.

If you are running your applications on Windows guest virtual machines, you can make the virtual machines themselves highly available by using Microsoft failover clustering. Failover clustering is available on Windows Server 2008 Enterprise and Datacenter editions.

> ■**Note** Even if an application has built-in redundancy, you may still want to enable Microsoft failover clustering for your virtual machines. In some cases, clustering may be easier to manage and cost less in licensing than using the built-in application redundancy features.

Your Hyper-V hosts can be made cluster-aware, so that the cluster will failover your virtual machines. If one node in the cluster fails, the virtual machines will start up on the other node. This way, you do not need to set up any third-party tools, or even Microsoft failover clustering, in your virtual machines to provide a level of redundancy, if you can tolerate a couple of minutes of downtime for your virtual machine.

Microsoft failover clustering will also let you take advantage of a feature in Hyper-V called *quick migration*. With quick migration, you can briefly pause a virtual machine on one Hyper-V host and continue the operation of a virtual machine on another Hyper-V host.

> ■**Note** Quick migration is not the same as a *live migration*. Live migration does not pause the virtual machine, but keeps it running while it transitions to another host. Hyper-V does not yet support live migration, although it should provide this support in the next version of Hyper-V.

This section covers setting up a failover cluster for the Hyper-V host to make virtual machines highly available. If you need a bit more redundancy than a Hyper-V failover cluster provides, you can also set up a failover cluster between two virtual machines, using the techniques described here.

First, you should know what a failover cluster does. Then you can plan your failover clustering deployment.

How Failover Clustering Works

A *cluster* is a set of computers (nodes) that are presented to the user as one physical computer (virtual cluster server) on the network. The user will establish a connection to the virtual cluster server, instead of on the individual nodes in the cluster.

A virtual cluster server in Windows Server 2008 failover clustering can contain the following items:

- *Resource*: This can be a service, application, IP address, disk, or network name. Within a cluster, these resources are grouped into service and application groups.

- *Client access point*: This is the network name and IP address of the virtual cluster server.

- *Quorum*: The quorum is the brains of the cluster. It contains the cluster configuration. It also contains the current status of each node, resource, service and application group, and network in the cluster. The cluster quorum can be stored on either a disk (called a *witness disk*) or file share (called a *witness file share*).

The node status in failover clusters is determined by a cluster heartbeat. A *heartbeat* is a form of internode communication that happens in the failover cluster. When a node becomes unavailable, the failover cluster will initiate a failover of the service and application groups to another node in the cluster. When service is restored, the failover cluster can be configured to allow the service and application groups to failback to the original server. However, this is not the default behavior.

Windows Server 2008 failover clustering has four types of quorum models:

Node Majority. This model is meant for clusters with an odd number of nodes. In this model, as long as the majority of nodes is still available, the cluster will remain online.

Node and Disk Majority. This model is designed for an even number of nodes that all have access to the same shared disk. It uses the number of available nodes and the witness disk to determine if a cluster can remain online. As long as the witness disk remains available and at least half of the nodes are still available, the cluster is kept online. The quorum data is kept on a shared disk that is accessible to each node in the cluster (the witness disk). If the witness disk becomes unavailable, the cluster can continue to function if the majority of nodes are still available.

Node and File Share Majority. This model behaves in a similar fashion to the Node and Disk Majority quorum model. The difference is that the quorum is stored on a witness file share instead of a disk. If the file share is available and at least half of the nodes are still available, the cluster remains online. If the file share becomes inaccessible, the cluster will remain online as long as the majority of the nodes are still available.

No Majority: Disk Only. As long as the witness disk is available, all of the nodes except one can fail, and the cluster will remain online. The nodes are not used as a deciding factor. This model is recommended only in a test scenario, as the witness disk becomes a single point of failure.

Planning Failover Clustering Deployment

Now that you are familiar with how a failover cluster works, you can start planning the deployment of failover clustering on your Hyper-V host. For the failover cluster to be completely supported by Microsoft, you should follow these guidelines:

- All of the hardware components in your system must be marked as "Certified for Windows Server 2008."

- If you use a network adapter for iSCSI connectivity, it should be a separate, dedicated network adapter that is connected to a separate, dedicated network switch. Also, the iSCSI network adapter cannot be teamed.

- Your iSCSI target must support persistent reservations.

- HBAs used for shared storage have the following requirements:
  - They must have matching firmware revisions and drivers.
  - They must use Storport device drivers.
  - They must support the SCSI-3 standard.
- In general, identical hardware, drivers, and firmware should be used for each node in the failover cluster. Hyper-V failover clusters have a requirement for identical processors for each node in the cluster.

Keep these requirements in mind for a production system.

■Note In past versions of Windows, Microsoft maintained a clustering hardware compatibility list (HCL). This is no longer the case for Windows Server 2008 failover clustering.

If you would like to test and become more familiar with the capabilities of a failover cluster before deployment to a production system, you may be able to build a failover cluster with hardware that is not "Certified for Windows Server 2008." But be aware that Microsoft will probably not fully support such a system.

Configuring a Hyper-V Failover Cluster

Let's walk through configuring a two-node failover cluster on Windows Server 2008 Enterprise Core to protect four separate virtual machines with iSCSI storage (connected via the Microsoft iSCSI initiator). This example will use the Node and Disk Majority quorum model (when everything is preconfigured, the Create Cluster Wizard will use this model automatically).

■Note If you want to take advantage of the quick migration capabilities of Hyper-V, you need to store each virtual machine on a separate LUN, if you are going to format the LUN with NTFS. The only other alternative is to use a third-party clustered file system, such as Sanbolic's Melio FS. For more information about Melio FS, visit http://www.sanbolic.com/melioFS.htm.

First, you need to document some information, such as IP addresses and logical unit numbers (LUNs). Table 7-1 shows the items you should document and the values used for this example.

Table 7-1. *Cluster Setup Information*

Item	Value
Node 1 hostname	hyperv-dev
Node 2 hostname	hyperv-dev2
hyperv-dev public IP address	192.168.0.20
hyperv-dev iSCSI IP address	192.168.1.20
hyperv-dev heartbeat IP address	192.168.2.20
hyperv-dev2 public IP address	192.168.0.30
hyperv-dev2 iSCSI IP address	192.168.1.30
hyperv-dev2 heartbeat IP address	192.168.2.30
iSCSI target portal IP address	192.168.1.40
Domain user account	hyperv\clusteradmin
LUN for VM1	VM1
LUN for VM2	VM2
LUN for VM3	VM3
LUN for VM4	VM4
LUN for quorum	Quorum
Service and application group for VM1	Test-VM1
Service and application group for VM2	Test-VM2
Service and application group for VM3	Test-VM3
Service and application group for VM4	Test-VM4

■**Note** The domain user account is the account used to run the Failover Cluster Management tool. The account can be any user account that has administrator rights on the cluster nodes.

Configuring the Nodes Initially

Your first task is to perform the initial configuration of your Windows Server 2008 Core nodes. (Chapter 9 provides details on the initial configuration of Windows Server 2008 Enterprise Core.)

For the initial configuration, follow these steps:

1. Configure your node hostnames.

2. Configure your node IP addresses.

3. Rename your interfaces to their intended use. For example, you might rename the interface that will be used for the heartbeat network to Heartbeat. The iSCSI network could be iSCSI. The public network could be Public. To rename an interface, enter the following at the command line:

```
netsh interface set interface name = "<InterfaceName>" newname = "<NewName>"
```

<InterfaceName> is the existing name of the network interface. *<NewName>* is the new name that you want to assign to the interface.

4. Join your nodes to the domain.

5. Enable the Hyper-V role on each node.

6. Configure Hyper-V to be ready for your virtual machines.

You need at least one NIC dedicated to external virtual machine network traffic. This NIC should not be any of the NICs you are using for your cluster (public, iSCSI, or heartbeat).

Now that the initial configuration is taken care of, you can attach the iSCSI storage to each of the cluster nodes. You can do this in two ways: by using the Storage Explorer administrative tool on another Windows Vista or full installation of Windows Server 2008, or by using iscsicli. exe at the command line. For both methods, you first need to start the iSCSI service.

Starting the iSCSI Service

Before you can attach the iSCSI storage to a cluster node, you should complete the following steps:

1. Open the Windows Firewall for iSCSI initiator traffic with the following command:

```
netsh advfirewall firewall set rule group="iSCSI Service" new enable=yes
```

2. Configure the iSCSI service to start automatically on each node, as follows:

```
sc config msiSCSI start= auto
```

3. Start the service with sc.exe, a command-line tool for Windows that will allow you to manage services, as follows:

```
net start msiscsi
```

Caution Make sure your LUNs can be seen only by the nodes in the cluster—whether you are using Fibre-Channel or iSCSI.

Connecting to iSCSI Storage Using Storage Explorer

After you complete the steps in the preceding section, you can use Storage Explorer to connect each host server to the iSCSI targets by using the following steps:

1. Open Storage Explorer by selecting Start ➤ Administrative Tools ➤ Storage Explorer.

2. Click Connect to in the Actions pane to open the Connect To dialog box. Choose the host you will add the iSCSI storage to, as shown in Figure 7-1.

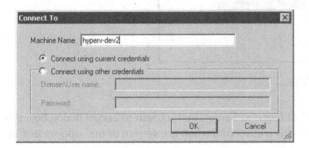

Figure 7-1. *Connecting to your Hyper-V host*

3. Expand the Servers node until you can select the iSCSI initiator that is on your chosen Hyper-V host server, as shown in Figure 7-2.

Figure 7-2. *Selecting the iSCSI initiator*

4. Click Add Portal in the center pane. In the Add Target Portal dialog box, type in the IP address or DNS name of your iSCSI target portal, as shown in Figure 7-3. Click OK.

Figure 7-3. *Adding your iSCSI target portal*

5. Right-click Storage Explorer at the top of the navigation pane and select Refresh SAN view to see your changes.

6. Expand the iSCSI initiator node in the navigation pane to see the LUNs that are now presented through the iSCSI target portal, as shown in Figure 7-4.

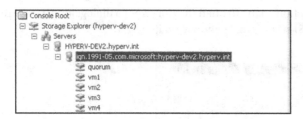

Figure 7-4. *Viewing the LUNs*

7. Right-click a LUN and select Login to Target. In the Login to Target dialog box, select the "Automatically restore this connection when the system boots" option, as shown in Figure 7-5. Click OK.

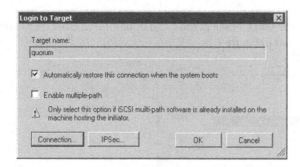

Figure 7-5. *Logging in to a target LUN*

8. Repeat step 7 for each LUN that you need to connect to the Hyper-V host server.

Connecting to iSCSI Storage Using iscsicli.exe

After you complete the steps outlined earlier in the "Starting the iSCSI Service" section, you can use iscsicli.exe to connect to the iSCSI storage.

■**Note** Using iscsicli.exe works for a single iSCSI connection. If you need to set up multiple paths, it is best to use Storage Explorer to configure your iSCSI connectivity and multipathing.

Follow these steps to use `iscsicli.exe`:

1. Add the target portal (the iSCSI storage array):

    `iscsicli QAddTargetPortal 192.168.1.40`

2. List the available targets:

    `iscsicli ListTargets`

    Figure 7-6 shows an example of the output of this command.

Figure 7-6. *The result of the iscsi ListTargets command*

3. Log on to the appropriate target:

    `iscsicli QloginTarget <target_iqn>`

    `<target_iqn>` is the IQN identifier for your target. This is the identifier that is listed with the `ListTargets` command. You should see a prompt similar to the one shown in Figure 7-7.

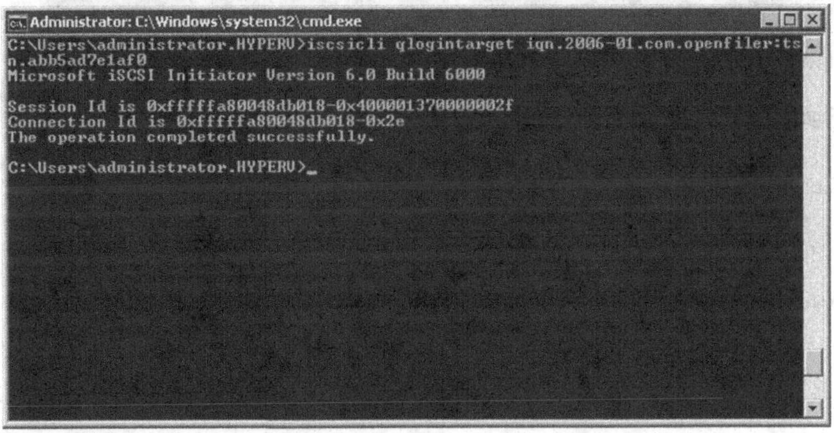

Figure 7-7. *The details of the target login*

4. Create a persistent login to the target so you don't need to manually log in after each reboot:

```
iscsicli PersistentLoginTarget <target_iqn> T * * * * * * * * * * * * * * * 0
```

This command needs a little more explanation because of the unfriendly syntax. The generic command is as follows:

```
iscsicli PersistentLoginTarget <target_iqn> <Report_To_PNP> ➥
<Target_Portal_Address> <TCP_Port_Number_Of_Target_Portal> * * * ➥
<Login_Flags> * * * * * <Username> <Password> <Authtype> * <Mapping_Count>
```

<Report_To_PNP> is the parameter that decides if the LUNs will be exposed to the operating system as a storage device. A value of T (or t) sets this as true. The rest of the asterisks indicate the default settings of parameters. The last 0 is for the *<Mapping_ Count>* parameter. It indicates that no mappings are specified and no further parameters are required.

5. Confirm that the list of persistent targets is correct:

```
iscsicli ListPersistentTargets
```

Figure 7-8 shows an example of the output of this command.

Figure 7-8. *The target is now persistent.*

6. Confirm that all of your LUNs from the target are listed:

```
iscsicli ReportTargetMappings
```

You should get results similar to those shown in Figure 7-9.

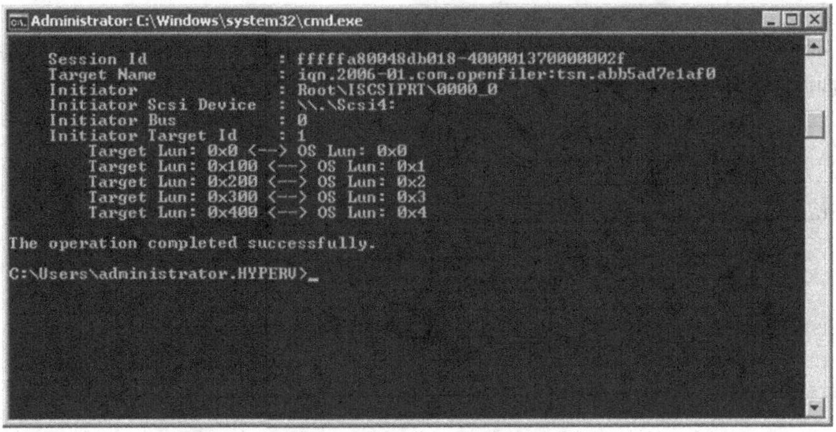

Figure 7-9. *The available LUNs on the persistent target*

For this example, there are actually five LUNs: one for each of the four virtual machines and a quorum LUN.

At this point, your LUNs are available to your node (although they are offline at the moment). You need to repeat the preceding steps for each node in your cluster.

■**Note** For a complete iscsicli.exe reference, see the Microsoft iSCSI Software Initiator User Guide at http://www.microsoft.com/downloads/details.aspx?familyid=12cb3c1a-15d6-4585-b385-befd1319f825&displaylang=en.

Preparing the LUNs Using Diskpart

After the LUNs have been persistently attached to each node in your cluster, shut down all except for one of your nodes. Now you can configure the disks on that active node either by using diskpart.exe on that node or by using the Disk Management tool remotely. Here, we'll look at using diskpart.exe, a command-line utility for managing disks in Windows, since you are probably already familiar with the Disk Management tool.

■**Note** To use Disk Management remotely, you need the Remote Management and Remote Volume Management firewall groups open on your management computer.

The disks should be configured as basic disks. A single partition should span the entire disk. The following instructions outline how to configure the disks from the command line.

Note Although `diskpart.exe` is a command-line tool, currently there is no easy way to script the steps for configuring the disks on node.

1. Start `diskpart.exe`:

   `diskpart`

2. List the disks:

   `list disk`

   In this example, there are five disks. Each of them is listed as offline, as shown in Figure 7-10.

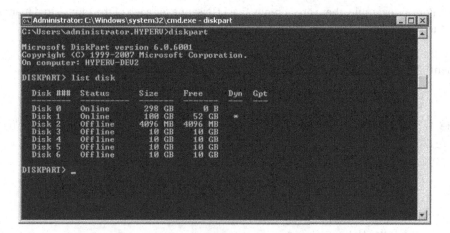

Figure 7-10. *Five offline disks need to be configured.*

3. Bring the disks online. This must be done one disk at a time.

   a. Select the disk:

   `select disk <DiskNumber>`

   `<DiskNumber>` is number of the disk that is shown by the `list disk` command. For example, choose disk 2 by entering `select disk 2`.

   b. Bring the selected disk online:

   `online disk`

   Figure 7-11 shows the result.

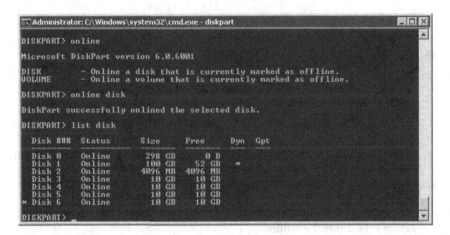

Figure 7-11. *Putting the selected disk online*

    c. Repeat steps a and b to bring each disk online.

4. Make sure that all of the disks are now online:

```
list disk
```

Figure 7-12 shows that all the disks are online.

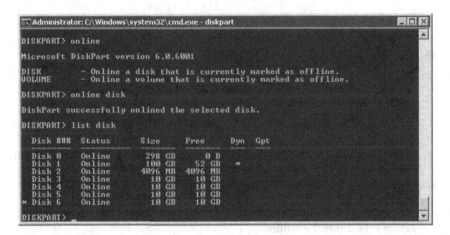

Figure 7-12. *Verify that all of the disks are now online.*

5. At this point, even though the disks are online, they will be read-only to protect them from being written to by multiple computers. Clear the read-only attribute on each disk.

   a. Select the disk:

```
select disk <DiskNumber>
```

   b. Clear the read-only attribute on the disk:

```
attributes disk clear readonly
```

Figure 7-13 shows the result.

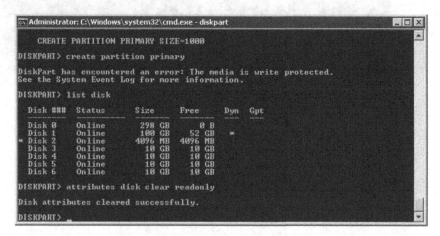

Figure 7-13. *You need to clear the read-only attribute before you can continue.*

   c. Repeat steps a and b for each disk.

6. Create a partition on each disk.

   a. Select the disk:

```
select disk <DiskNumber>
```

   b. Make sure there are no partitions currently on the disk (to ensure you have the right disk):

```
list partition
```

Figure 7-14 shows the output.

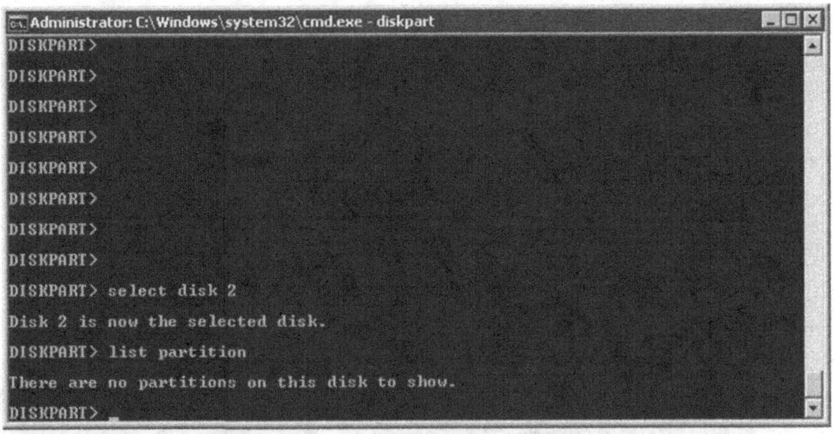

Figure 7-14. *Make sure there are no partitions on the disk before you begin.*

c. Create a partition on the disk:

```
create partition primary
```

d. Verify that the partition was created:

```
list partition
```

Figure 7-15 shows the output.

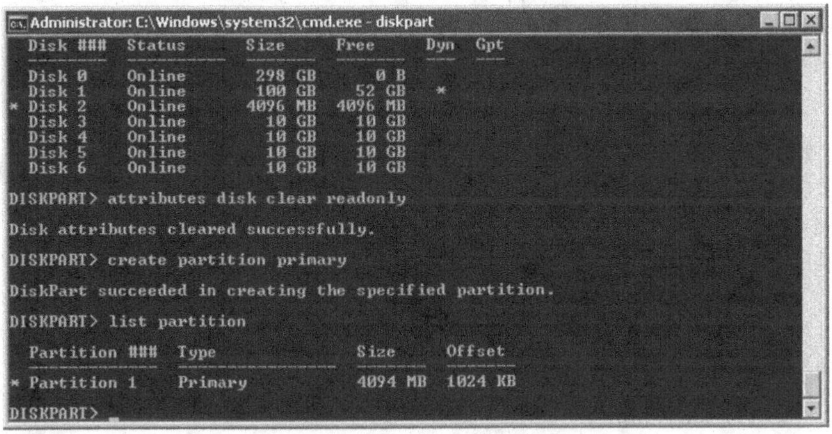

Figure 7-15. *A new partition was created on the disk.*

e. Repeat steps a–d for each disk.

7. Format the partitions you just created.

   a. Select the disk:

```
select disk <DiskNumber>
```

   b. Select the partition:

```
select partition <PartitionNumber>
```

Figure 7-16 shows that the partition is selected.

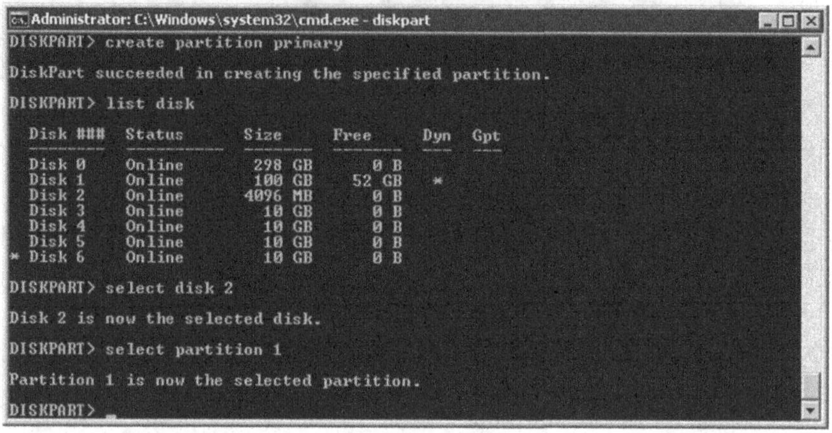

Figure 7-16. *Select the appropriate partition to format.*

   c. Format the partition:

```
format fs=ntfs label=<DiskLabel>
```

`<DiskLabel>` is the label you want to assign to the disk. For example, for the quorum disk in this example, assign the disk label of `Quorum`.

   d. Wait for the format to complete.

   e. Repeat steps a–d for the other partitions that you need to format on the other disks, being careful to name them appropriately.

8. Assign drive letters to the formatted volumes.

   a. List the volumes:

```
list volume
```

Figure 7-17 shows the output.

Administrator: Command Prompt - diskpart
DISKPART> list volume
Volume ### Ltr Label Fs Type Size Status Info
Volume 0 E KRMSXVOL_EN UDF DVD-ROM 2542 MB Healthy
Volume 1 C NTFS Partition 146 GB Healthy System
Volume 2 D Data NTFS Partition 152 GB Healthy
* Volume 3 Quorum NTFS Partition 4094 MB Healthy
Volume 4 VM1 NTFS Partition 10 GB Healthy
Volume 5 VM2 NTFS Partition 10 GB Healthy
Volume 6 VM3 NTFS Partition 10 GB Healthy
Volume 7 VM4 NTFS Partition 10 GB Healthy
DISKPART> _

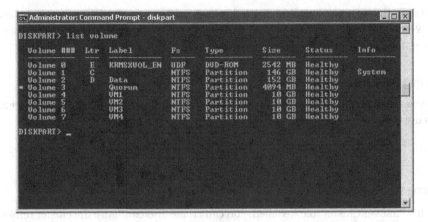

Figure 7-17. *List the volumes so that you can select the appropriate volume.*

- **b.** Select the appropriate volume:

```
select volume <VolumeNumber>
```

- **c.** Assign a drive letter to the volume:

```
assign letter=<L>
```

<*L*> is the letter you want to assign. For example, you can assign the `Quorum` volume the letter `Q`. If you do not select a letter, the next available letter will be used.

- **d.** Repeat steps b and c for each formatted volume.

9. List the volumes again to make sure they are all configured with NTFS partitions and drive letters:

```
list volume
```

Figure 7-18 shows the result.

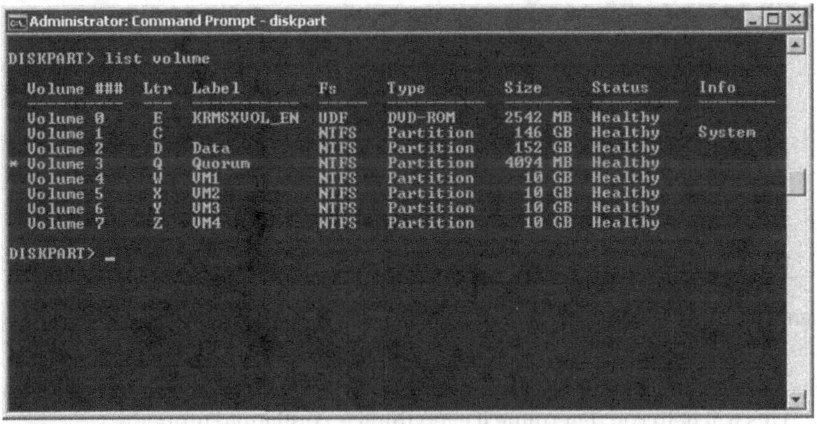

Administrator: Command Prompt - diskpart
DISKPART> list volume
Volume ### Ltr Label Fs Type Size Status Info
Volume 0 E KRMSXVOL_EN UDF DVD-ROM 2542 MB Healthy
Volume 1 C NTFS Partition 146 GB Healthy System
Volume 2 D Data NTFS Partition 152 GB Healthy
* Volume 3 Q Quorum NTFS Partition 4094 MB Healthy
Volume 4 W VM1 NTFS Partition 10 GB Healthy
Volume 5 X VM2 NTFS Partition 10 GB Healthy
Volume 6 Y VM3 NTFS Partition 10 GB Healthy
Volume 7 Z VM4 NTFS Partition 10 GB Healthy
DISKPART> _

Figure 7-18. *Verify that all of the volumes are formatted.*

If everything looks good, shut down this node and start each of the other nodes one at a time. Verify that the disks are available in the other nodes. If necessary, bring the disks online on each node and change the drive letters to match.

Installing the Failover Cluster Role

Now you are ready to install the Failover Cluster role on each node. To do this, start each node. Then use ocsetup on each node as follows:

```
ocsetup FailoverCluster-Core
```

Creating the Failover Cluster

With the Failover Cluster role installed, you can create and configure the cluster remotely using the Failover Cluster Management tool, as follows:

1. Log on to the management computer as a user with administrator rights on the nodes, and then open the Failover Cluster Management tool by selecting Start ➤ Administrative Tools ➤ Failover Cluster Management.

2. Click Create a Cluster in the Actions pane.

3. Click Next in the Before You Begin window.

4. In the Select Servers window, select the servers you will use for nodes in the cluster, as shown in Figure 7-19.

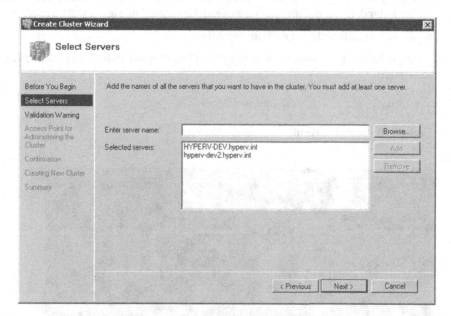

Figure 7-19. *Select the servers that will participate as nodes in the cluster.*

5. Select Yes in the Validation Warning window to run the Validate a Configuration wizard. This will help you determine if everything is configured properly.

6. Click Next in the Before You Begin window of the Validate a Configuration wizard.

7. In the Testing Options window, choose to run all the tests.

8. On the Confirmation page, click Next to start the validation test.

Note Not all of the validation test will pass if you are just setting up a test scenario. That is OK. The cluster may still work. It is just unlikely that Microsoft will fully support the configuration.

---

9. When the validation test is complete, click the View Report button to view the complete test report, as shown in Figure 7-20.

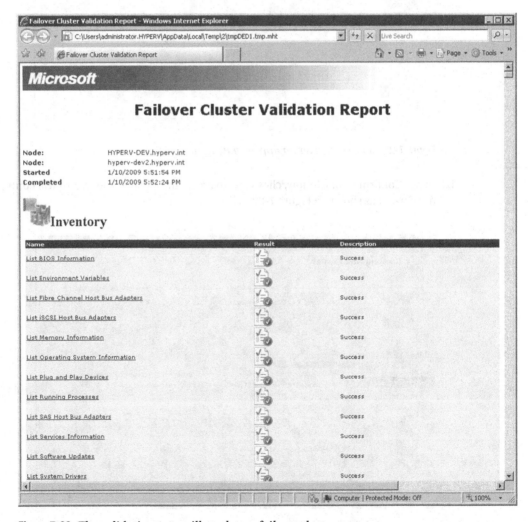

Figure 7-20. *The validation tests will produce a failover cluster report.*

10. When you are finished, click Finish to return to the Create Cluster Wizard and continue.

11. In the Access Point for Administering the Cluster window, give the cluster an appropriate name, as shown in Figure 7-21.

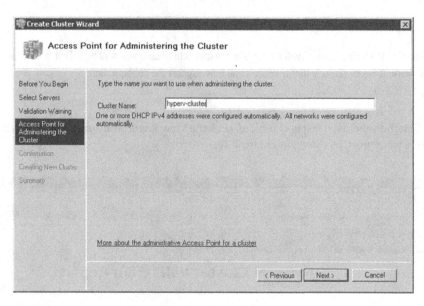

Figure 7-21. *Give the cluster an appropriate name.*

12. In the Confirmation window, click Next to create the cluster. The wizard will configure the cluster, as shown in Figure 7-22.

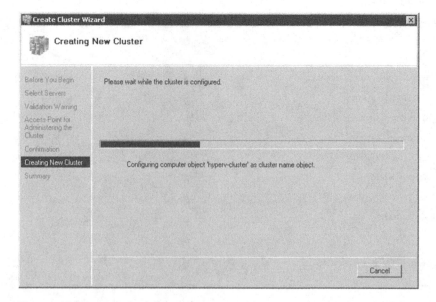

Figure 7-22. *Creating the failover cluster*

13. In the Summary window, review the cluster settings, as shown in Figure 7-23. Then click Finish to close the Create Cluster Wizard.

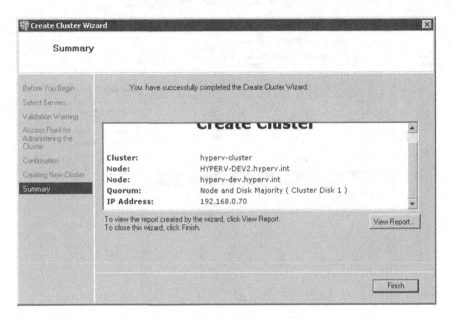

Figure 7-23. *Review the cluster settings on the Summary page.*

When the cluster configuration is finished, the cluster should be automatically configured and online. If you did the proper preparation, the correct quorum model will be selected as well.

Viewing and Adjusting Cluster Settings

You can view and adjust the cluster settings in the Failover Cluster Management tool. To see the node status, select the node under Nodes in the navigation pane, as shown in Figure 7-24.

Select Storage in the navigation pane to view your storage status and see the status of the witness disk, as shown in Figure 7-25.

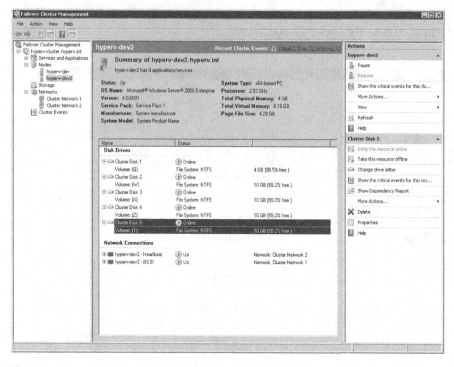

Figure 7-24. *Hyperv-dev2 has control of the cluster resources.*

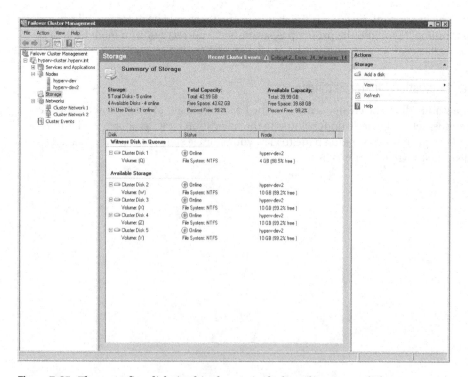

Figure 7-25. *There are five disks in this cluster, including the witness disk.*

Select Network in the navigation pane to view the status of your networks, as shown in Figure 7-26. You can rename a network to something more appropriate by right-clicking the network and selecting Rename.

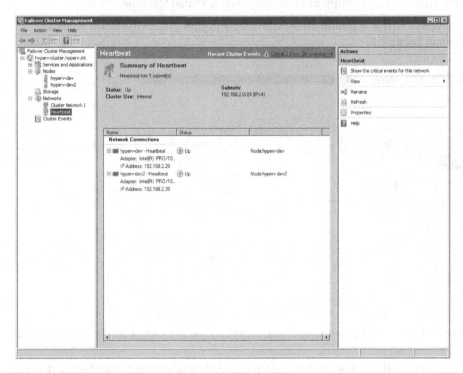

Figure 7-26. *The private heartbeat network for the cluster*

Configuring Hyper-V for Failover Clustering

When you are ready to configure Hyper-V for failover clustering, follow these steps:

1. In the Hyper-V Manager tool, for each virtual machine that you want to protect, set the automatic start action for the virtual machine to nothing. This is because the cluster will now handle the start actions of the virtual machines, not the individual Hyper-V host.

2. In the Failover Cluster Management tool, select Services and Applications in the navigation pane.

■**Note** When you configure failover clustering on Hyper-V, you are configuring failover clustering for individual virtual machines, not the Hyper-V host itself. So, you configure clustering per virtual machine instead of all the virtual machines on a host. In order for the virtual machines to failover, you need to initially deploy them on shared storage. For this example, I have already deployed virtual machines on the VM1, VM2, VM3, and VM4 disks.

---

3. Select Configure a Service or Application in the Actions pane.

4. In the Before You Begin window, click Next.

5. In the Select Service or Application window, select Virtual Machine.

6. In the Select Virtual Machine window, choose the appropriate virtual machines, as shown in Figure 7-27.

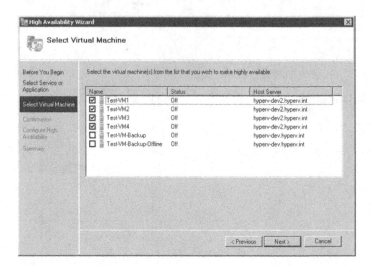

Figure 7-27. *Selecting the virtual machines that you want to protect with the failover cluster*

7. In the Confirmation window, click Next to create the application groups for the virtual machines.

8. In the Summary window, shown in Figure 7-28, click Finish.

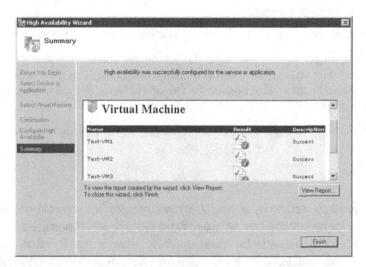

Figure 7-28. *The virtual machines are now protected successfully.*

9. Your virtual machines will be listed under Applications and Services in the navigation pane. You will probably want to rename them to something other than Virtual Machine.

    a. Select the virtual machine in the navigation pane and view its details to see the virtual machine name, as shown in Figure 7-29.

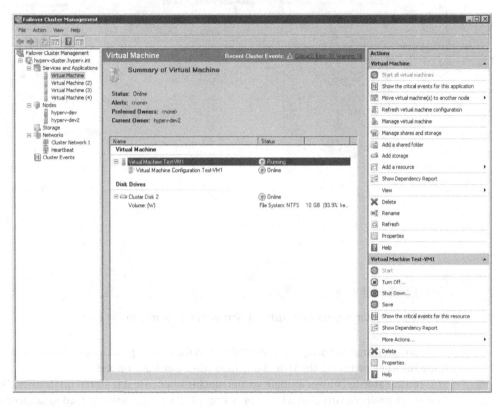

Figure 7-29. *You may want to rename your virtual machines to something more appropriate.*

    b. Right-click Virtual Machine in the navigation pane and select Rename to rename it to the proper virtual machine name.

Now, your virtual machines are protected with failover clustering.

Using Quick Migration

If you want to test the failover of a virtual machine, just right-click the appropriate virtual machine in the navigation pane, select "Move virtual machine(s) to another node," and choose the appropriate node, as shown in Figure 7-30. This is also known as a *quick migration*.

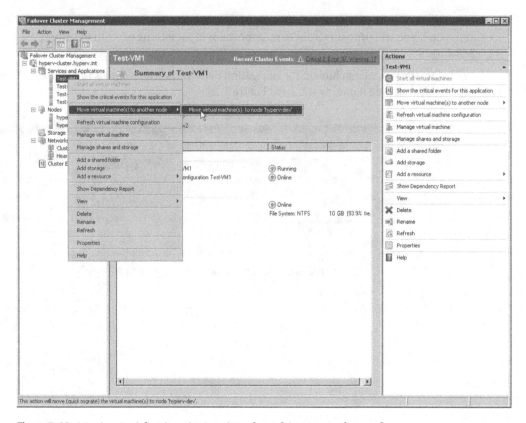

Figure 7-30. *Moving (quick migrating) a virtual machine to another node*

You can watch the progress of the failover in the results pane in the middle of the window. If the failover succeeded, the virtual machine will come back online.

You are able to failover a single virtual machine because it is stored on its own LUN. If there were multiple virtual machines on a single LUN, they would all need to failover at the same time, because only a single node can have control of an NTFS volume at once.

Setting Failover Properties

To set failover properties on a protected virtual machine, right-click it in the navigation pane of the Failover Cluster Management tool and choose Properties. On the General tab, shown in Figure 7-31, you can choose a preferred host for the virtual machine.

On the Failover tab, shown in Figure 7-32, you can choose the failover policy for the virtual machine. Failback is disabled by default. You can turn on failback and adjust the schedule that the failback will use. You can also choose the failover threshold for the virtual machine by adjusting the number of times a failure can happen in the specified period of time.

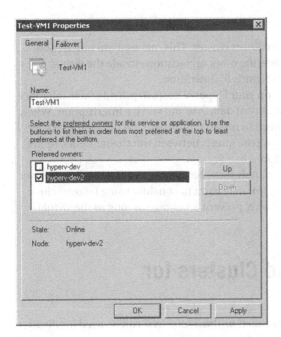

Figure 7-31. *You can select a preferred host for each virtual machine that is protected.*

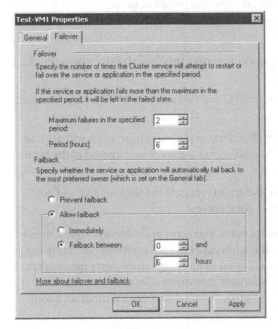

Figure 7-32. *Choose if you want the virtual machine to failback. The default setting is to prevent failback.*

Failover Clustering Notes

Now your virtual machines are protected by a failover cluster. This makes them much more fault-tolerant. It also reduces the need for clustering other applications inside the virtual machines, if your business can tolerate a few seconds of downtime.

However, when failover clustering is used on your Hyper-V hosts to provide fault-tolerance for your virtual machines, there is still a possibility of data loss and service interruption. When a Hyper-V host fails, the virtual machine will need to restart (automatically) on another Hyper-V host in the cluster. Also, as stated earlier, moving the guests between the cluster nodes (quick migration) will cause a brief service interruption.

If you are running an application that absolutely must have more availability than failover clustering for your Hyper-V hosts can provide, you may want to consider using failover clustering inside your guest virtual machines. This may prevent an outage as long as the virtual machines are on separate Hyper-V hosts.

Geographically Dispersed Clusters for Disaster Recovery

Geographically dispersed clusters (sometimes called *multisite clusters*) can be used for disaster recovery. Multisite clusters are typically set up so that some nodes are in one datacenter and other nodes are in other geographically dispersed datacenters. This ensures that a datacenter failure does not interrupt your infrastructure for an extended period of time.

When planning for multisite clusters to protect a Hyper-V infrastructure, you should take the following items into consideration:

- You will need to use the Node Majority quorum model (no shared disk), which should be used with an odd number of nodes.

- You will need to have a very redundant, reliable wide area network (WAN) link between the datacenters.

- Actions like DNS lookups for the cluster IP address and cluster heartbeats will need to be monitored closely, because they will occur across the WAN link instead of the local area network (LAN).

- You will need to have a third-party mechanism to replicate the witness disk and any other data (virtual machines) to the other datacenters.

Since the point of geoclustering is disaster recovery, you want to avoid any single points of failure. This is why there is no shared disk. So, the main concern with multisite clusters is replicating the data between the datacenters. You will need to find some third-party mechanism to perform this replication. Currently, three of Microsoft's partners offer products that will replicate the data disks between the datacenters for the cluster. For more information about these products, visit the partner's web sites:

- Double-Take Software: http://www.doubletake.com/english/products/geocluster/Pages/default.aspx

- SteelEye Technology: http://www.steeleye.com/products/windows/

- Neverfail: http://www.neverfailgroup.com/products/app-modules/clusterprotector.aspx

Summary

Building a fault-tolerant virtualization platform requires up-front planning and design work. The foundation of the virtual infrastructure is the host server. Start by choosing fault-tolerant components for your host. Then move on to setting up failover clusters for your Hyper-V servers.

To achieve fault tolerance for the host server hardware, keep in mind some of these best practices:

- Use redundant power supplies connected to redundant power paths.

- Team your NICs in the parent partition if possible.

- Use RAID-level fault-tolerance protection for your storage.

- Use redundant HBAs, switches, and storage ports when designing your SAN connectivity.

When you are ready to configure a failover cluster, design with these best practices in mind:

- Make sure you use "Certified for Windows Server 2008" hardware components.

- Use dedicated network connections for storage if you are using an iSCSI initiator.

- Make the entire path to your storage array on the SAN redundant.

- To use Microsoft failover clustering with Hyper-V to its fullest potential, store each virtual machine on a separate LUN.

CHAPTER 8

■ ■ ■

Protecting Your Virtual Machines

Virtual machines provide a tremendous amount of flexibility for your infrastructure. Since they exist as a series of files, they can be cloned, copied, and moved fairly easily. They can be exported to another Hyper-V host if you need to migrate to a new datacenter. However, they also share some other attributes of files that are not so advantageous: they can be deleted accidentally, become corrupt, or be lost due to a hard drive malfunction. This is why a backup strategy for your virtual machines is very important and should be included in any virtualization design plan. This is just as crucial in the virtual world as it is in the physical world. This chapter will discuss some different strategies for backing up virtual machines.

Virtual Machine Backup Strategies

Many different backup products are available to add value to your backup plan. The myriad of options can overwhelm even the most seasoned IT professionals. However, no matter which options you choose, you are really using one of two approaches to backing up your virtual machines: backing up the data inside the virtual machine or backing up the virtual machine files outside the virtual machine.

How often you perform the backups will depend on your business' tolerance for data loss. System volumes typically do not need to be backed up as often as data volumes. This is why the two are usually stored on separate disks or partitions.

So, which strategy is best? Should you treat the virtual machine just like a physical server, and have a backup agent inside the virtual machine do the work? Should you leverage the fact that the virtual machines are just a series of files and perform the backup on the files themselves, outside the virtual machine? The answers to these questions depend on your situation.

Several considerations must be taken into account. The first is host resources—specifically, processor resources. Backing up the host server once is far more efficient than backing up data stored in each virtual machine using an agent inside each virtual machine. Using an agent inside each virtual machine means that each virtual machine will require processing time while the backup for that virtual machine is occurring. So, as far as processing time goes, backing up the virtual machine files is the better choice. Backing up the virtual machine files also gives you the flexibility to either quickly restore the virtual machine or to restore a subset of files that were stored in the virtual machine. An agent-based backup typically gives you only the option for file restoration.

Another consideration is backup management. Would you rather manage the backup for a single host server or manage the backup of all the virtual machines that are hosted on that server? Doing a single backup of the host server is certainly the option that involves less management effort.

So far, the odds are in favor of the option to back up the virtual machine files by utilizing a single backup job on the host. However, this may not always be possible, due to one more consideration: system downtime. Does your environment afford you the downtime necessary to back up your servers offline? In many environments, the answer to this question is a resounding "No!"

Additionally, some virtual machines do not support Volume Shadow Copy Service (VSS) backups. As you'll learn later in this chapter, VSS allows you to back up a running system using snapshots. Some virtual machines may not meet all the criteria for an online Hyper-V host backup, even if they support VSS backups. In order to back up a running virtual machine in Hyper-V, the guest virtual machine must support VSS and have Integration Services installed and running. Guest operating systems such as Windows XP and Windows 2000 cannot be backed up while running, so they will be placed in a saved state temporarily while a backup is taking place. This takes them offline during the backup.

A mix of backup strategies must often be used to cover the whole environment. Also, some virtual machines may need a different backup strategy depending on the applications they are hosting. For example, SQL Server and Exchange Server servers would likely be backed up more often than infrastructure servers that host Dynamic Host Configuration Protocol (DHCP), Domain Name Service (DNS), or domain controller services.

Finally, there is the question of restoration. A backup is only as good as its ability to restore your data. Is your goal to restore an entire Hyper-V server? Is your goal to restore a single virtual machine? Is your goal to restore a single file from a single virtual machine? How long do you want to allow the restoration to take? All of these questions must be addressed in your backup strategy.

This chapter will cover the backup options so you can make the best decision for your environment. But before you can decide on a backup strategy, you need to know which files make up your virtual machine and how those files will affect the restoration of service to your business.

Anatomy of a Virtual Machine

A Hyper-V virtual machine is actually made of several different files. Table 8-1 lists those files, their purpose, and whether they are needed to restore the virtual machine.

Table 8-1. *Virtual Machine Files*

File Extension	Purpose	Needed to Restore Service?
*.vhd	Virtual hard disk	Yes
*.avhd	Differencing disk for snapshots	No
*.xml	Virtual machine configuration	No
*.bin	Stores virtual machine's RAM when paused or during a snapshot	No
*.vsv	Stores information about the virtual machine's current state when paused or during a snapshot	No

Actually, none of the virtual machine files are really necessary if you just want to rebuild a server from scratch. However, that is a worst-case scenario, which you would rather avoid if possible.

Aside from the worst-case scenario, to restore the functionality of a virtual machine, you just need the *.vhd files (or *.vhd and *.avhd files if you have implemented differencing disks). If you have these files, you can create a new virtual machine using them as the hard disks.

■**Caution** Creating a new virtual machine and attaching the disk may not be appropriate in all circumstances. For example, you should never use this method to restore domain controllers, due to replication problems that this might cause.

However, it sure would be nice if you had all of the virtual machine files, allowing you to completely restore the virtual machine with as little administrative overhead as possible. With that in mind, you want to aim for backing up the files necessary to completely restore the virtual machine. If that is not possible (perhaps some of the files have been corrupted), your next best option is to just create a new virtual machine and attach your *.vhd files to it.

Backing Up Virtual Machines with Hyper-V Manager

I am a huge proponent of using the tools that are at your immediate disposal to accomplish a task whenever possible. The first tool that comes to mind for backing up virtual machines is the import/export functionality built into Hyper-V.

■**Note** The virtual machine must be offline (shut down) when you export it. Therefore, using the import/export method for backup will work only if you have a sufficient downtime window for the virtual machine in question.

Since this backup method requires downtime for the target virtual machine, it is best used for creating backups of virtual machines that host relatively static data that does not change much. Some examples of this type of virtual machine would be an application server that does not host any data or a file server for which you can perform a nightly backup without disrupting users.

First, let's take a look at where the virtual machine files are actually stored. The following are the default file locations for virtual machines:

- Virtual disks: C:\ProgramData\Microsoft\Windows\Hyper-V\Virtual Hard Disks

- Snapshots: C:\ProgramData\Microsoft\Windows\Hyper-V\Snaphots

- Configuration files: C:\ProgramData\Microsoft\Windows\Hyper-V

This is far from ideal when you are trying to manage backups of multiple virtual machines. The recommendation is to choose a different path to store the virtual machine in when it is created. Or you could add a different default path for virtual machines on the Hyper-V host. That way, all of the files are kept in the same folder structure.

If you follow the advice of creating a different default path for your virtual machines, you will have a much easier time keeping track of the file locations. Let's take a virtual machine file path of D:\virtualmachines as an example. Suppose you have a virtual machine named Test-VM-Backup that you would like to export. Take a look in the D:\virtualmachines directory. You should see the following folder structure:

- D:\virtualmachines\Test-VM-Backup: This subfolder holds all of the virtual machine files and folders.

- D:\virtualmachines\Test-VM-Backup\Virtual Hard Disks*.vhd: These are the virtual hard disk files. You will have one for each virtual hard disk that is attached to the virtual machine.

- D:\virtualmachines\Test-VM-Backup\Virtual Machines: This subfolder holds the configuration (*VirtualMachineGUID*.xml) file and another folder.

- D:\virtualmachines\Test-VM-Backup\Virtual Machines*VirtualMachineGUID*.xml: This is the virtual machine's configuration file.

- D:\virtualmachines\Test-VM-Backup\Virtual Machines*VirtualMachineGUID*: This subfolder holds the *VirtualMachineGUID*.bin and *VirtualMachineGUID*.vsv files when the virtual machine is powered on.

- D:\virtualmachines\Test-VM-Backup\SnapShots: This subfolder will exist only if you have any snapshots of the virtual machine (or checkpoint in the case of System Center Virtual Machine Manager 2008). This folder holds snapshot data for the virtual machine (including the *.avhd, *.xml, *.bin, and *.vsv files).

■**Note** This backup method will back up only the data that is stored on a *.vhd file with the virtual machine. It will not back up the data that is stored on pass-through disks.

Exporting a Virtual Machine

Now that you are familiar with what you will be exporting, let's actually export a virtual machine.

Open the Hyper-V Manager tool and select the virtual machine that you want to export. Apply or delete any snapshots that are attached to the virtual machine before you export it. This just makes the backup cleaner. (Snapshots were not meant to be used long term anyway.) After the snapshots have been cleaned up, make sure the virtual machine is shut down. Next, right-click the virtual machine and choose Export. This will bring up the Export Virtual Machine dialog box, which simply asks for an export path, as shown in Figure 8-1.

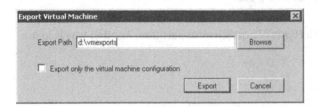

Figure 8-1. *Exporting a virtual machine*

You should use a local path if you have the space. Later, you can move the exported virtual machine folder structure to a remote location. Using a local path will ensure that you do not have an interruption in the export process due to a network failure. When you are finished choosing your path, click the Export button. You will see the progress of the export in the Hyper-V Manager window, as shown in Figure 8-2.

Figure 8-2. *Export progress*

After the export, you should see the virtual machine folder structure stored in the export path. This has all of the virtual machine files. You will notice a couple of differences if you look in the folders:

- The *VirtualMachineGUID*.xml file has been replaced by a *VirtualMachineGUID*.exp file.

- There is an additional file at the root of the folder structure named config.xml.

These files are used when you import the virtual machine. The *VirtualMachineGUID*.exp file is actually the virtual machine configuration file.

Now that you have a copy of the virtual machine, you can move the virtual machine folder and its contents to another location. In fact, you should make at least one other copy of this virtual machine folder every time you back it up. When you need to import the virtual machine, the files will be used by the virtual machine and cannot be imported again. After the import, the *VirtualMachineGUID*.exp file is changed back into the *VirtualMachineGUID*.xml file, so you cannot reimport the virtual machine until you export it again.

At this point, you can do the following with these exported files:

- Restore a virtual disk by replacing the virtual disk files in a virtual machine's folder with the backup copies.

- Mount the backup copy of a virtual disk file and just recover a single file or set of files through normal file-copying procedures.

- Recover the entire virtual machine by importing it.

Mounting the Virtual Hard Disk File

There are a couple of ways to mount a .vhd file. One is to use Windows Management Instrumentation (WMI) to mount the file on a Hyper-V host's parent partition. Another way is to use VHDMount.exe.

Mounting the VHD with WMI

Mounting the *.vhd file with WMI is relatively easy. The actual mounting can be accomplished with the following script.

Note This script is meant to be run locally on a Hyper-V server. This is a problem if you want to run the script on a Hyper-V server that has a Windows Server 2008 Core installation as its parent partition. Power-Shell does not work on Windows Server 2008 Core installations. You should create a management server (a full installation of Windows Server 2008) with the Hyper-V role enabled to perform tasks like mounting a .vhd file.

```
#Get the vhd path from the user

$VHDPath = Read-Host "Enter the path to the VHD you want to mount"

$Namespace = "root\virtualization"

#Get the MSVM_ImageManagementService via WMI.

$VHDService = Get-WMIobject -Class "Msvm_ImageManagementService" ➥
-Namespace $Namespace -Computername "."

#Mount the VHD

$VHDService.Mount($VHDName)
```

Let's see what this script does line by line.

```
$VHDPath = Read-Host "Enter the path to the VHD you want to mount"
```

This line stores whatever you type in the PowerShell prompt in the $VHDName variable. This is where you type in the path to the *.vhd file that you want to mount. This is most likely a network location, unless you have copied the *.vhd file to the local server.

```
$Namespace = "root\virtualization"
```

This line just stores the WMI namespace that will be used in the WMI query.

```
$VHDService = Get-WMIobject -Class "Msvm_ImageManagementService" ➡
-Namespace $Namespace -Computername "."
```

This line is the WMI query that gets an instance of the "Msvm_ImageManagementService" class that can be used to mount the *.vhd file.

```
$VHDService.Mount($VHDName)
```

Finally, this line uses the Mount method of the Msvm_ImageManagementService class to mount the *.vhd file.

The *.vhd file will be mounted as an offline disk. So, you just need to open the Disk Management tool on the server on which the disk is mounted and bring the disk online. To do this, open Server Manager on your target server and choose Storage ➤ Disk Management. You should see a new offline disk. Right-click the disk and select Online, as shown in Figure 8-3.

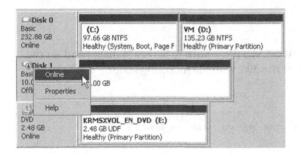

Figure 8-3. *Bringing a disk online using Disk Management*

After the disk is online, you can access it through Windows Explorer, as shown in Figure 8-4, so you can copy any important files that you need to restore.

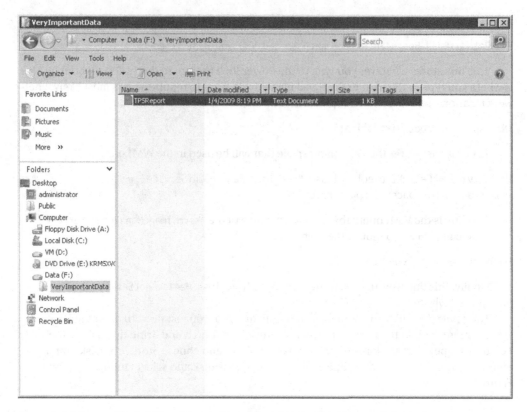

Figure 8-4. *Mounted *.vhd file with very important data to recover*

When you are finished with the mounted `*.vhd` file, return to Server Manager and set the disk back to Offline. Then you can unmount the disk with the following script.

```
#Get the vhd path from the user

$VHDPath = Read-Host "Enter the path to the VHD you want to mount"

$Namespace = "root\virtualization"

#Get the MSVM_ImageManagementService via WMI.

$VHDService = Get-WMIobject -Class "Msvm_ImageManagementService" ➥
-Namespace $Namespace -Computername "."

#Mount the VHD

$VHDService.Unmount($VHDName)
```

This script uses the Unmount method of the Msvm_ImageManagementService to unmount the `*.vhd` file. The rest of the script is the same as the one to mount the file.

Mounting the VHD with VHDMount.exe

VHDMount.exe is a utility that comes with Microsoft Virtual Server 2005 Release 2 (R2) Service Pack 1 (SP1). This is a free download from Microsoft, available from http://technet.microsoft.com/en-us/bb738033.aspx#.

Note If you just want to install the VHDMount.exe utility, you can do a custom install of Windows Server 2005 R2 SP1 and choose to install only the VHDMount.exe utility.

The default installation location for the VHDMount utility is %Program Files%\Microsoft Virtual Server\Vhdmount. If you open a command prompt and run VHDMount.exe, you will see all of the options for this utility. The following is the basic command to mount a *.vhd file so that you can copy files:

```
vhdmount /m <Path to VHD>
```

Note VHDMount.exe does not support mounting *.vhd files from a UNC path or a network drive. So, you will need to have a local copy of the *.vhd file that you are trying to mount.

This tells VHDMount to mount the *.vhd file and attempt to mount all of the volumes on that particular *.vhd file. Now you can access the mounted *.vhd disk through Windows Explorer.

Note When the *.vhd file is mounted using the default mounting method, a differencing disk is created in the current user's temporary folder, so that any changes are written to it instead of the original disk. This is best practice, so you don't write changes to the backup disk. If you want to override this behavior, you can use the following command: vhdmount /m /f <Path to VHD>.

When you are finished with the mounted *.vhd disk, you can unmount it using the following command:

```
vhdmount /u /d <Path to VHD>
```

This tells VHDMount to unmount the *.vhd file and discard all the changes that were made to the differencing disk.

Importing an Entire Virtual Machine

If you need to restore an entire virtual machine, you can import an exported backup of your target virtual machine. To prepare for the imported virtual machine, you need to do the following tasks:

- Delete the existing virtual machine from the Hyper-V server by right-clicking the virtual machine and selecting Delete from the menu.

- Delete or move the existing virtual machine's folder.

- Copy the backup virtual machine's folder to the original location of the virtual machine you are trying to restore. For example, if your original virtual machine named Test-VM-Backup was stored in D:\virtualmachines\Test-VM-Backup, you need to copy the exported Test-VM-Backup folder to D:\virtualmachines.

Caution If you want the virtual machine to be restored exactly as it was when the backup was taken, you will need to delete the existing virtual machine before you import the backup copy. Make sure that you absolutely need to restore the entire virtual machine before proceeding. Also, make sure you have a second copy of the backup virtual machine that you want to import, because you will not be able to reimport the same virtual machine again.

Once everything is prepared, open Hyper-V Manager and click Import Virtual Machine. You will see the Import Virtual Machine dialog box, as shown in Figure 8-5. Type in or browse to the path of your root virtual machine folder (it should have been copied to its original location by you prior to this step). Select the check box to "Reuse old virtual machine IDs." Then click Import to import the virtual machine. Since no copying takes place, this should happen relatively quickly.

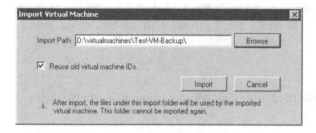

Figure 8-5. *Importing a virtual machine*

After the import, you can start your virtual machine. You may need to bring some of your data virtual disks back online if they are in offline mode. You can do this using the Disk Management tool, as described earlier. You may also need to rejoin the Active Directory domain if the virtual machine backup is older than the computer password reset policy on the Active Directory domain. After those items are taken care of, your virtual machine should be back in production.

How the Volume Shadow Copy Service Works

Before we discuss how virtual machines can be backed up with Windows Server Backup and with System Center Data Protection Manager 2007, you need a quick primer on Microsoft's volume shadow copy technology. It plays an important role when backing up virtual machines with either of these Microsoft utilities, providing the underlying backup infrastructure for Windows operating systems after Windows 2000.

Volume shadow copy technology consists of several components, including the following:

- Volume Shadow Copy Service (VSS)
- Requestor
- Writer
- Provider
- Source volume
- Storage volume

VSS is the component that coordinates all of the other components to create shadow copies (point-in-time copies of a volume). The basic process is as follows:

1. A requestor (such as backup software) will request that a shadow copy be taken of certain data.

2. A provider will satisfy the request to create a shadow copy by working with an application-specific writer if needed.

3. The application-specific writer (like a VSS writer for Hyper-V, SQL Server, or Exchange Server) will assist in coordinating the shadow copy to make sure the application is quiesced so a consistent shadow copy can be taken of the volume (this usually happens in a number of milliseconds).

4. A shadow copy is created. The source volume is the original volume, and the storage volume is the volume that holds the shadow copy data.

When a VSS-compatible backup product backs up data, it is really backing up the shadow copy that it has requested to be created. This is how virtual machines that support VSS can be backed up while they are still online.

The Hyper-V writer provided by Windows Server Backup and Data Protection Manager uses a technique called a *referential VSS query* to actually tell any application-specific VSS writers inside the guest virtual machines (SQL Server, Exchange Server, and so on) to quiesce the application. When the applications inside the guest virtual machines are quiesced, the guest reports back to the Hyper-V writer. At this point, the volume shadow copy can be made. Then the backup software will create a backup using the volume shadow copy.

Now that you have a high-level overview of how VSS works with Hyper-V, let's see how it can be utilized by Windows Server Backup.

Backing Up Virtual Machines with Windows Server Backup

Windows Server 2008 comes with Windows Server Backup. Under the right circumstances, Windows Server Backup will even allow you to back up your running virtual machines.

Windows Server Backup Considerations

Before you choose to use Windows Server Backup to backup your virtual machines, you need to consider the following:

- Windows Server Backup is a volume-based backup solution. You can back up only entire volumes. You cannot choose to back up certain files or folders. You cannot automatically restore individual virtual machines using the Windows Server Backup restore function (unless the virtual machine is on a volume by itself).

- If any of your virtual machines contain dynamic disks (the operating system type of dynamic disk, not the Hyper-V type of virtual disk), VSS will not be used to back up the virtual machine. In this case, you would need to back up the contents of the virtual machine just as you would back up a physical system or perform an offline backup of the virtual machine files.

- If any of your virtual machines do not support VSS (for example, Linux, Windows NT, Windows 2000, and Windows XP systems do not support VSS), they will enter a saved state (interrupting service) while a snapshot is taken of the volume. They will return to normal service after the snapshot is taken. This behavior will also occur in virtual machines that do not have Integration Services installed and the Backup (Volume Snapshot) selection is not checked in the virtual machine's Management settings. You may want to store these virtual machines on a separate volume.

- Windows Server Backup does not support backing up to a tape drive. You will need to back up the files created by Windows Server Backup using some other solution. Later, you can transfer the backed-up files to tape for offsite storage.

- Windows Server Backup does not support scheduling a backup to a network share. Also, performing a one-time backup to a network share will overwrite any existing backups for the Hyper-V host. This ultimately makes Windows Server Backup less than ideal for a permanent main backup solution. However, it can still be useful for emergency or one-time backups.

- Windows Server Backup does not support backing up an Exchange Server system. If you need to back up an Exchange Server system, you should use an Exchange-aware backup application like System Center Data Protection Manager, as discussed later in this chapter.

In summary, for a virtual machine to fully support VSS backup using Windows Server Backup to back up the Hyper-V volume, the following items are required:

- The virtual machine's operating system must be Windows Server 2003 or greater (Windows 2000 and Windows XP do not support VSS).

- There cannot be any dynamic disks inside the virtual machine.

- The Hyper-V Integration Services must be installed for the virtual machine and the Backup (Volume Snapshot) option must be checked under the virtual machine's Hardware configuration.

Given those considerations, here are a couple of recommendations to get the most out of Windows Server Backup when backing up Hyper-V virtual machines.

- Keep your fully VSS-supported virtual machines on a separate volume from those that do not support VSS.

- If you want the ability to automatically restore an individual virtual machine, store each virtual machine on a separate volume. This is actually a recommendation you may be using anyway if you are taking advantage of quick migration.

- If you want to use Windows Server Backup as a primary backup solution, you should consider dedicating a disk attached to a storage area network (SAN), such as iSCSI or Fibre-Channel, to the Hyper-V server to use as backup storage. This way, the disks are not actually in the server and can be attached to another server in case the Hyper-V server fails.

Before you can use Windows Server Backup, you need to install it and take care of a few other preparations. So, let's get started.

Preparing to Use Windows Server Backup

You can install Windows Server Backup through either Server Manager or a Windows Server 2008 Core command prompt.

To use Server Manager, from your Hyper-V server, start Server Manager, select Features in the navigation pane, and then click Add Features. In the Features list, select Windows Server Backup and Command-Line Tools, as shown in Figure 8-6. Click Next, and then click Install.

If you are using a Windows Server 2008 Core system, open a command prompt and type in the following:

```
start /w ocsetup WindowsServerBackup
```

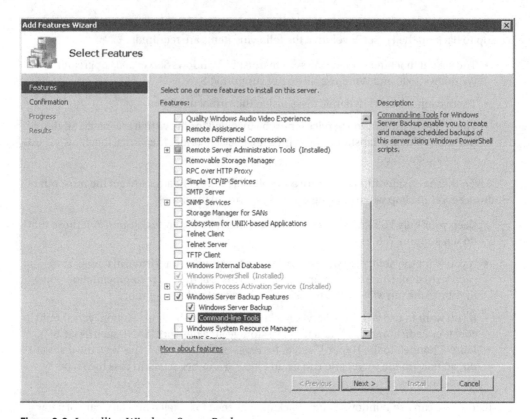

Figure 8-6. *Installing Windows Server Backup*

When the installation finishes, you are almost ready to start using Windows Server Backup for Hyper-V. You just need to make sure a hotfix is installed and create a registry entry.

Download and install KB956697, if it is not already installed. This fixes an issue with VSS backups in Windows Server Backup, where VSS was not used for any of the backup when a single corrupt virtual machine file was accessed during a backup. To install the KB956697 hotfix on a Windows Server 2008 Core system, just type the following at the command prompt:

```
wusa.exe Windows6.0-KB956697-x64.msu
```

Next, create a registry entry to register the Hyper-V VSS writer with Windows Server Backup. The VSS writer for Hyper-V will allow the integration of VSS on the Hyper-V server with VSS inside the guest virtual machines to properly back up the virtual machines while they are running. To create the registry entry, open Regedit and create the following key:

```
HKEY_LOCAL_MACHINE\Software\Microsoft\Windows NT
\CurrentVersion\WindowsServerBackup\ ➥
Application Support\{66841CD4-6DED-4F4B-8F17-FD23F8DDC3DE}
```

Then you need to create a string value in that key with the following attributes:

Name: Application Identifier

Type: REG_SZ

Data: Hyper-V

Figure 8-7 shows the new registry entry.

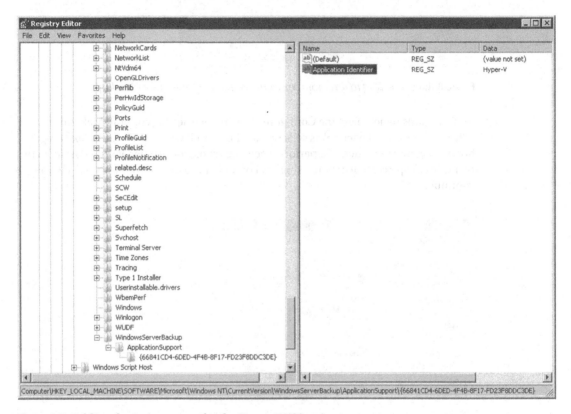

Figure 8-7. *Adding the registry entry for the Hyper-V VSS writer*

Creating a Backup with Windows Server Backup

When you are ready to use Windows Server Backup to back up your virtual machines, follow these steps:

1. Select Start ➤ Administrative Tools ➤ Windows Server Backup.

2. You can choose to back up the local server or a remote computer. To back up a Hyper-V server, choose the "Connect to another computer" option in the Actions pane.

3. In the Computer Chooser window, select the Another computer option and type in the name of the computer that you want to connect to, as shown in Figure 8-8.

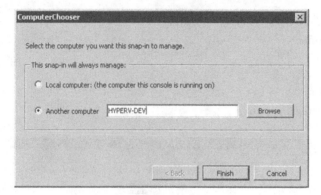

Figure 8-8. *Connecting to a remote computer with Windows Server Backup*

4. In the Actions pane, select the Configure Performance Settings option. Make sure "Always perform full backup" is selected, as shown in Figure 8-9. This will take longer, but will not have as much of a performance impact on your Hyper-V server as an incremental backup, which leaves the shadow copies behind on the volume. Click OK to continue.

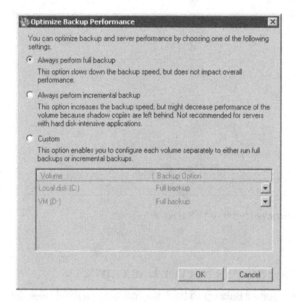

Figure 8-9. *Optimizing backup performance in Windows Server Backup*

5. You can choose to create a backup schedule or backup once. If you want to use Windows Server Backup as your primary backup solution, you will probably want to do a regular backup of your virtual machines, so choose the Backup schedule option in the Actions pane.

6. The Backup Schedule Wizard starts. Click Next in the first window.

7. In the Select Backup Configuration window, your choices are Custom and Full Server, as shown in Figure 8-10. If you want to capture all of the volumes on the Hyper-V server, choose the Full Server option. If you want to exclude some volumes, select the Custom option. Click Next.

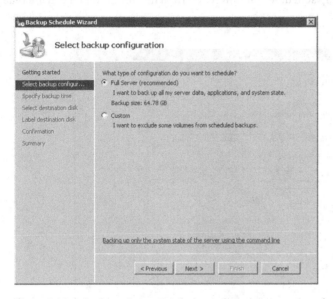

Figure 8-10. *Windows Server Backup configuration*

8. If you chose to do a custom backup, you will see the Select Backup Items window, as shown in Figure 8-11. Here, you can choose the volumes that you want to include in the backup. Click Next after making your selections.

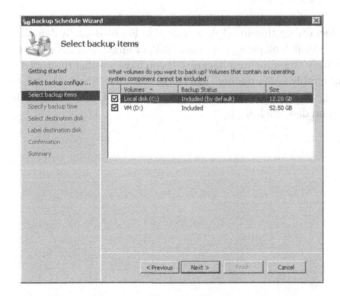

Figure 8-11. *Selecting your backup volumes*

9. In the next window, you can choose to run daily backups or to perform backups more than once daily, as shown in Figure 8-12. You may want to perform backups more than once a day (if it is feasible) on systems that have files that change often. Keep in mind that this backup job is for the entire volume, so you will need to plan accordingly if you want different backup schedules for different virtual machines. When you are ready to continue, click Next.

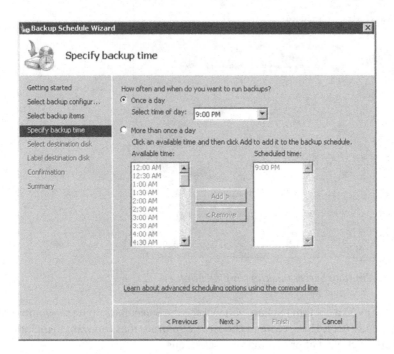

Figure 8-12. *Selecting the backup time*

10. Now you need to select the destination disk, as shown in Figure 8-13. By default, Windows Server Backup will look for any external, USB, or Firewire attached disks. This is not the most likely target for your backups. If you have another internal disk you would like to use (preferably SAN-attached, like iSCSI), click the "Show all available disks" button to choose an internal disk, as shown in Figure 8-14. After you've selected your backup destination disk, click Next.

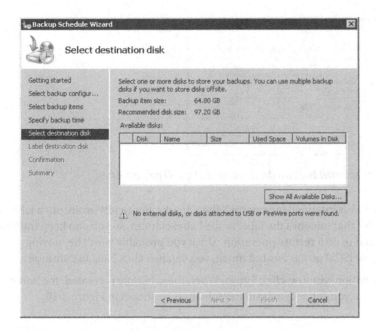

Figure 8-13. *Selecting the destination disk*

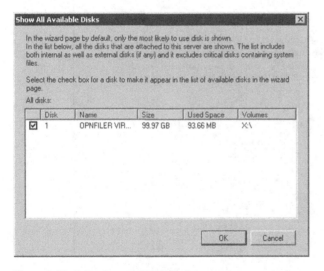

Figure 8-14. *Selecting an iSCSI disk*

11. You will see a warning letting you know that the chosen disk will be formatted and
    dedicated to performing backups, as shown in Figure 8-15. The chosen disk will also
    no longer be visible in Windows Explorer. If you are satisfied with this, click Yes to
    continue.

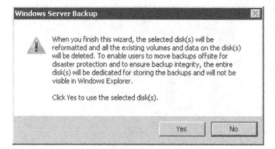

Figure 8-15. *The selected backup destination disks will be formatted.*

12. The next window is intended for external disks. It asks you to physically put a label on the backup disk that matches the label in the Label column, so you can keep track of it later if you need to do a restore operation. Since you probably won't be moving your internal disks or iSCSI arrays around much, you can just click Next to continue.

13. In the Confirmation window, click Finish. When the schedule is created, the Summary window will give you some details on the schedule, as shown in Figure 8-16.

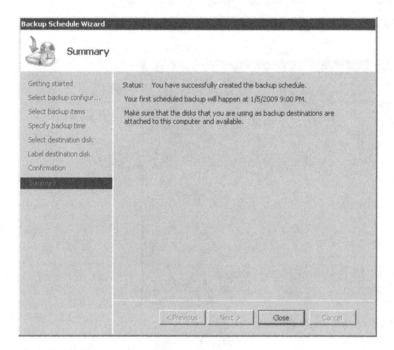

Figure 8-16. *Backup schedule summary*

Your backup is now scheduled.

If you ever need to do a one-time emergency backup of a virtual machine volume, you can use the Backup Once option in the Actions pane of Windows Server Backup. After you select this option, choose Different Options in the first wizard window. The rest of the configuration is similar to that outlined in the previous steps (minus the ability to schedule the backup), with a few key differences. If you choose to do a custom backup, you can select to exclude the system volume in the Select Backup Items window, as shown in Figure 8-17.

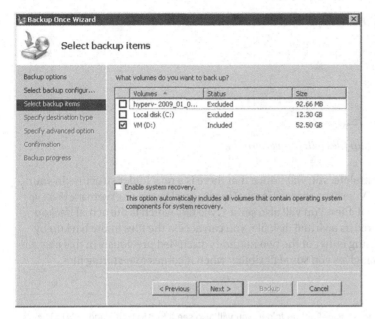

Figure 8-17. *Selecting the volumes to back up one time*

Also, there is a Specify Destination Type window, where you can specify a remote share, if you would like, as shown in Figure 8-18.

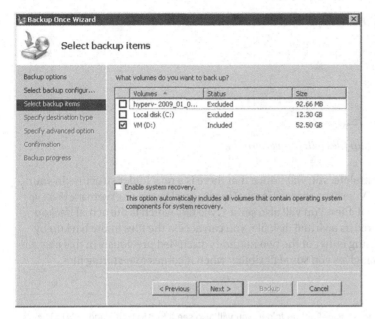

Figure 8-18. *Backing up to a remote shared folder*

Note that when you select a remote destination for the backup, if there is a backup already there, it will be overwritten. You will see the warning shown in Figure 8-19.

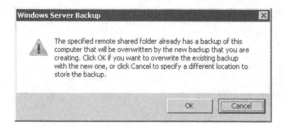

Figure 8-19. *The existing backup files will be overwritten.*

When the backup is complete, you will notice that there is a new folder structure in your remote share. If you look in \\Server\share\WindowsImageBackup\hyperv-servername\Backup *Date*, you will see various XML files. You will also see a *.vhd file, which is the actual backup file. Since the backup is stored as a virtual disk file, you can access the files in the backup by mounting the virtual disk using either of the two methods discussed previously in this chapter (WMI or VHDMount.exe). That gives you some flexibility when it comes to restoring files.

■**Note** At the root of the WindowsImageBackup folder, you will also see a MediaID file and a Catalog directory with the GlobalCatalog and BackupGlobalCatalog files. These files are used by Windows Server Backup to keep track of what files belong to a particular backup.

Restoring a Backup with Windows Server Backup

If you want to restore a volume that contains virtual machines, Windows Server Backup can do this for you.

■**Caution** When you restore the virtual machine volume through Windows Server Backup, the existing virtual machines on the target volume will be turned off and deleted. Make sure you are OK with this before you initiate a restore operation.

To restore from a backup, follow these steps:

1. Start Windows Server Backup and select Recover.

2. In the first Recovery Wizard window, choose Another Server if you will be recovering files from a network share. For the location type, select Remote Shared Folder. Click Next.

3. In the Specify Remote Folder window, type the path to your backup share. Click Next.

4. Next, you need to enter credentials that have access to the backup files on the share. Click Next.

5. You are prompted to select the backup date. The calendar will show dates on which backups occurred in bold type, as shown in Figure 8-20. Select the appropriate date, and then click Next to continue.

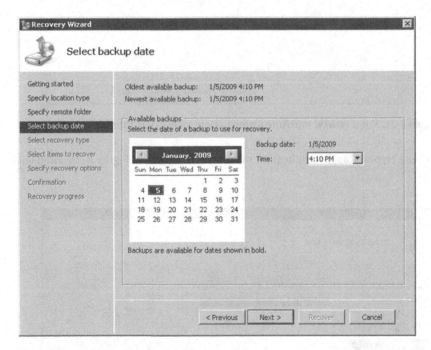

Figure 8-20. *Selecting the backup date to restore*

6. In the Select Recovery Type window, choose Applications, as shown in Figure 8-21. This allows you to recover the virtual machine volume using the registered Hyper-V VSS writer. Click Next.

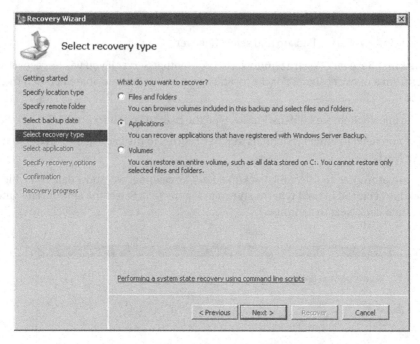

Figure 8-21. *For a virtual machine restore, the recovery type should be Applications.*

7. Choose Hyper-V as the application to recover, as shown in Figure 8-22. Then click Next.

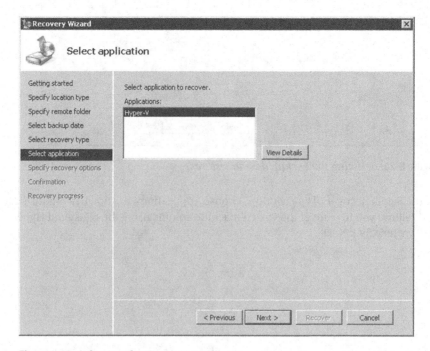

Figure 8-22. *Selecting the Hyper-V application restore.*

8. The Recover to Original Location option is selected by default. Click Next to accept it and continue.

9. The Confirmation window appears, as shown in Figure 8-23. Click the Recover button to start the recovery. You can watch the recovery progress, as shown in Figure 8-24.

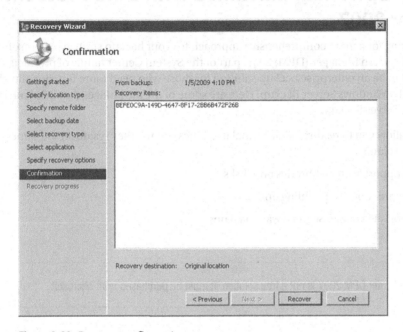

Figure 8-23. *Restore confirmation*

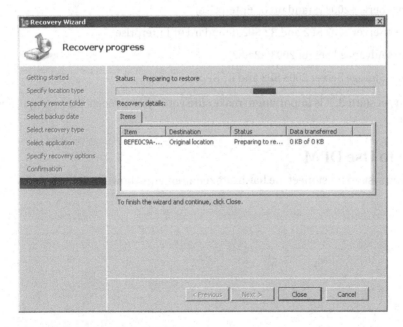

Figure 8-24. *Restoration progress*

After the recovery finishes, any virtual machine that was hosted on that volume should be restored. You just need to start the virtual machines.

Backing Up Virtual Machines with Data Protection Manager 2007

If you are looking for a more comprehensive approach for your backup strategy, Microsoft offers Data Protection Manager (DPM) 2007, part of the System Center family of products. DPM is meant to be an enterprise backup solution for those who need more functionality than that provided by Windows Server Backup. Here are some of the advantages that DPM offers over Windows Server Backup:

- It will allow you to restore single virtual machines, even if they reside on the same source volume.
- It has support for tape libraries and disks.
- It has more robust scheduling options.
- It supports Exchange Server-aware backups.

Note System Center DPM 2007 is not a free solution. It must be purchased from Microsoft.

DPM can be installed on the following operating systems.

- Windows Server 2008 (Standard or Enterprise)
- Windows Server 2003 SP2 and R2 SP2 (Standard or Enterprise)
- Windows Advanced Server 2003 R2 SP2
- Windows Storage Server 2003 SP2 and R2 SP2

Before you get started, it is important to make sure your system meets the prerequisites for using DPM.

Preparing to Use DPM

To use DPM, you system must meet the hardware requirements shown in Table 8-2.

Table 8-2. *DPM Hardware Requirements*

Component	Minimum Requirement	Recommended
Processor	1GHz or faster	2.33GHz Quad-Core
Memory	2GB	4GB
Page file	1.5 × amount of RAM + 0.2% of recovery point volumes	
Disk space for DPM	2–3GB	2–3GB
Disk space for storage pool	1.5 × the data protected	2–3 × the data protected

DPM also has some software prerequisites. The following software will be installed with DPM on Windows Server 2008, if it is not already configured:

- .NET Framework 2.0

- Internet Information Services (IIS) 7.0

- SQL Server 2005 Standard SP2 Workstation Components

- SQL Server 2005 Standard SP2 with Reporting Services

Since you are going to be protecting Hyper-V servers with DPM, you also need the following updates:

- DPM 2007 SP1 (http://technet.microsoft.com/en-us/dpm/dd296757.aspx)

- KB951308, only for clusters (http://go.microsoft.com/fwlink/?LinkID=132733)

- KB959962, for the host system and guest virtual machines (http://support.microsoft.com/default.aspx?scid=kb;EN-US;959962)

- KB960038, for the host system (http://support.microsoft.com/kb/960038/en-us)

Once you have all of your software and updates installed, you can prepare the DPM server for installation.

As noted, DPM comes with SQL Server 2005 Standard SP2. However, you can use a remote SQL Server instance if you would like. If you are going to use a remote database, you need to run sqlprep.msi on the server hosting the database. You can find sqlprep.msi in the DPM2007\msi\SQLprep folder on the product DVD or in the setup directory.

You will also need to install Single Instance Storage on your Windows Server 2008 server. Issue the following command at the command prompt:

```
start /wait ocsetup.exe SIS-Limited /quiet /norestart
```

After the installation completes, you need to restart your server. Now you are ready to install the DPM server.

Installing the DPM Server

Follow these steps to install DPM:

1. From the DPM installation window, choose Install Data Protection Manager. Read and agree to the license agreement, and then click OK.

2. Click Next in the Welcome window. If everything is OK in the prerequisites check, click Next to continue.

3. In the Product Registration window, enter an appropriate name and company, and then click Next to continue.

4. The Installation Settings window appears, as shown in Figure 8-25. You can choose a different installation path if you would like. You can also choose to use an existing SQL Server instance or have DPM install SQL Server 2005 from the installation DVD and set up its own instance. Click Next after making your choices.

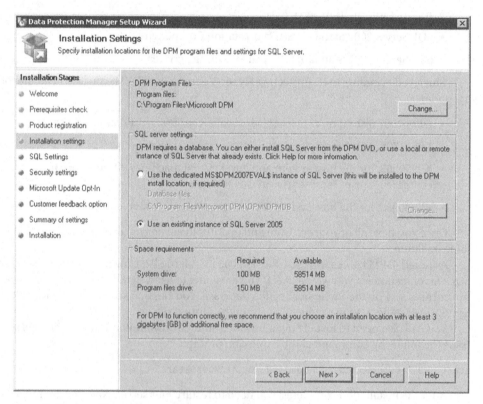

Figure 8-25. *Installing DPM on an existing SQL Server instance*

5. If you chose to use an existing SQL Server instance, you will see the SQL Settings window, as shown in Figure 8-26. Enter the appropriate SQL Server instance and credentials so the DPM installation can create the necessary database. Click Next to continue.

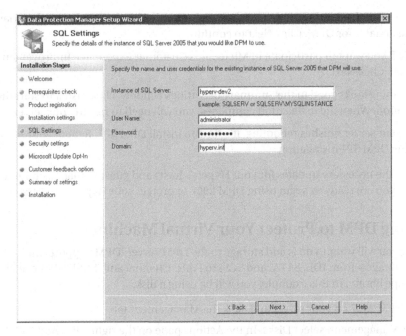

Figure 8-26. *Entering the credentials for the SQL Server database creation*

6. In the Security Settings window, shown in Figure 8-27, enter passwords for the two local service accounts that DPM will set up to run the SQL Service and generate reports. Click Next.

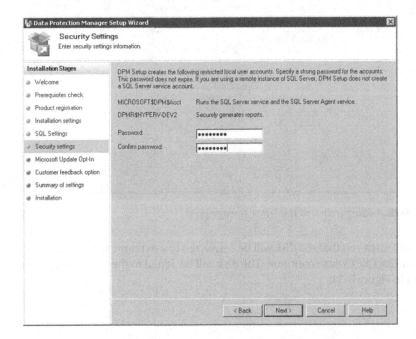

Figure 8-27. *Setting the password for the local SQL service accounts*

7. The Microsoft Update Opt-In window appears. Decide if you want Microsoft Update to handle updates for DPM. Click Next to continue.

8. Decide if you want to participate in Microsoft's Customer Experience Improvement Program. Click Next.

9. If everything looks good in the Summary of Settings window, click Install to start the installation. When the installation completes, you will need to restart your server.

10. When your server finishes rebooting, it's time to install DPM SP1. Reboot your server after the DPM SP1 installation.

Once all of the necessary updates for your Hyper-V hosts and guest virtual machines have been installed, you are ready to begin using DPM 2007 to protect your Hyper-V servers.

Configuring DPM to Protect Your Virtual Machines

The first thing you will want to do is add storage to the DPM server. DPM supports multiple forms of disk storage—from IDE, SATA, and SCSI to Fibre-Channel and iSCSI. DPM can also back up to a tape library. In this example, you will be using a disk.

1. Open DPM 2007 on your server and click the Management tab.

2. Under Management, select Disks. In the Actions pane on the right, click Add. DPM will list any available disks that are on the server, as shown in Figure 8-28. Click OK to add the disk.

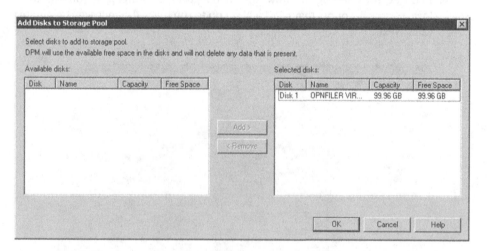

Figure 8-28. *Adding a disk to the DPM storage pool*

3. DPM will warn you that the disk will be converted to a dynamic disk, as shown in Figure 8-29. Click Yes to continue. The disk will be added to the DPM storage pool, as shown in Figure 8-30.

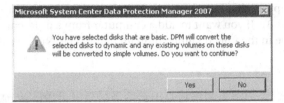

Figure 8-29. *The disks will be changed to dynamic once they are added to the storage pool.*

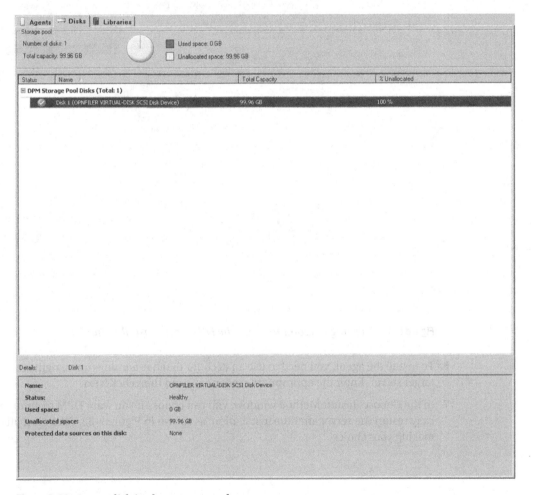

Figure 8-30. *A new disk in the storage pool*

4. Next, you need to install the DPM agents on your Hyper-V hosts. To do this, click
    Agents under the Management tab. Click Install in the Actions pane. This will start the
    Protection Agent Installation Wizard.

5. In the first window, any computer that is in the same domain as the DPM server is listed, as shown in Figure 8-31. If you want to add a computer from a different domain, you will need to type in the fully qualified domain name (FQDN). Click Next to continue.

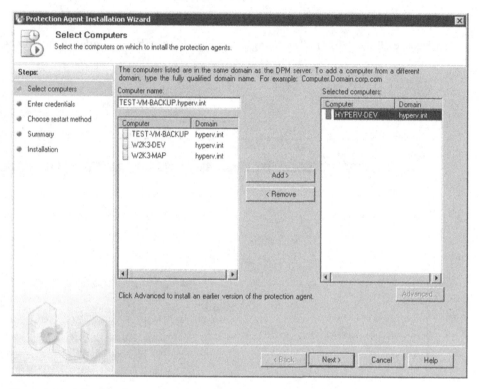

Figure 8-31. *Selecting the computers for the DPM agent installation*

6. To install the agent, you need to use an account that has administrative rights on the target server. Enter the appropriate credentials, and then click Next.

7. In the Choose Restart Method window, you can choose if you want DPM to automatically restart the server after the installation, as shown in Figure 8-32. Click Next after making your choice.

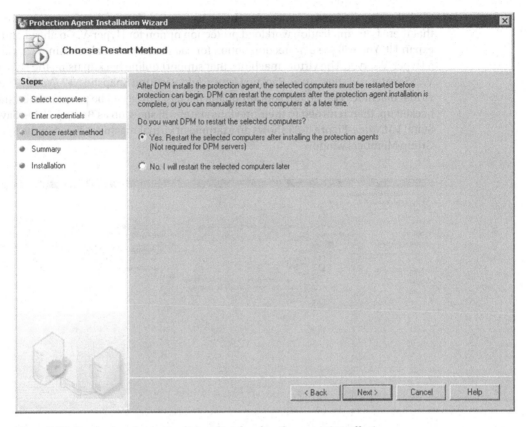

Figure 8-32. *Restarting the server immediately after the agent installation*

8. Click Install in the Summary window to begin the agent installation.

9. After the agent is installed, either restart your target server manually or wait for the server to restart. When the target server finishes restarting, make sure the agent status is reporting as OK in the DPM console under the Management/Agents tab.

Creating a Protection Group

To start protecting your Hyper-V servers, you need to create a protection group for them, as follows:

1. Open DPM 2007 on your server and click the Protection tab. In the Actions pane, click Create Protection Group.

2. The Create New Protection Group wizard starts. Click Next in the Welcome window.

3. Click the plus symbol (+) next to the Hyper-V servers that you want to protect. Notice that there is an application workload protection option for Hyper-V. Go ahead and expand it. You will see a protection option for each of your virtual machines that are on a Hyper-V server. The virtual machines that support online backup using the Hyper-V VSS writer will show up as Backup Using Child Partition Snapshot*VMName*. The virtual machines that do not support online backup (these will be put in a saved state, backed up, then returned to their previous state) will show up as Backup Using Saved State*VMName*. Figure 8-33 shows an example of virtual machines listed in the Select Group Members window.

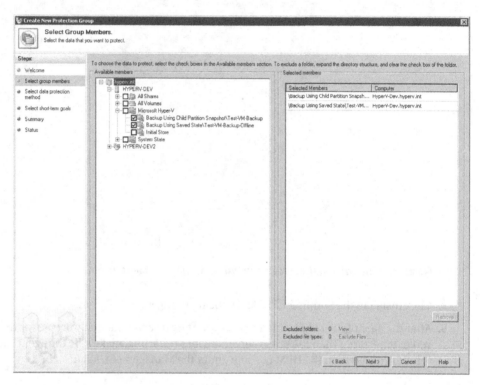

Figure 8-33. *Choosing your virtual machines to back up*

4. You can already see one of the advantages of using DPM over the built-in Windows Backup Server. You can choose to protect virtual machines with separate protection groups, even if the virtual machines reside on the same volume. Go ahead and select the virtual machines that you want to protect. You could also protect the Hyper-V server itself if you would like. Click Next when you are ready to continue.

5. In the Select Data Protection Method window, you can give the protection group a name. You can also decide if you want long-term or short-term protection. Since this example is using disk, choose short-term protection using disk, as shown in Figure 8-34.

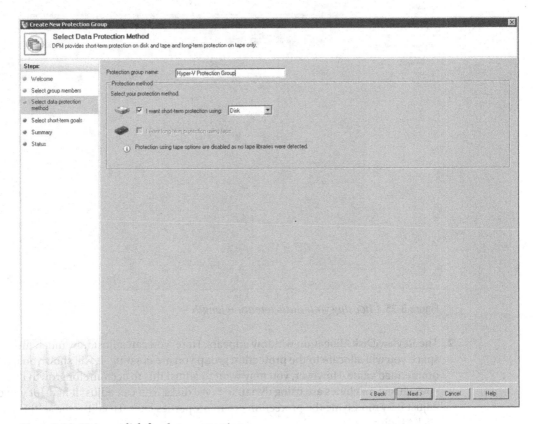

Figure 8-34. *Using a disk for data protection*

6. In the Select Short-Term Goals window, you can decide how many days you want to retain the backup, as shown in Figure 8-35. DPM uses Express Full Backups to quickly recover application data (from SQL Server, Exchange Server, and so on). You can adjust the schedule for these backups by clicking the Modify button. When you are ready to continue, click Next.

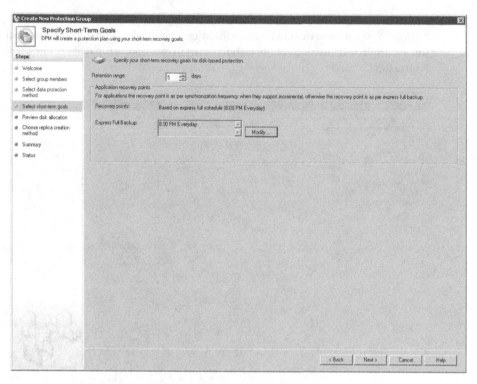

Figure 8-35. *Choosing your data-retention length*

7. The Review Disk Allocation window appears. Here, you can adjust how much disk space you will allocate to the protection group you are creating. It will show you a recommended value. However, you may want to adjust this to account for growth if any of your virtual machines are using dynamic *.vhd disks. You can adjust it here, or you can adjust it by modifying the protection group properties later. To adjust the settings now, click Modify.

8. You will see the options to adjust the replica volume and the recovery point volume sizes, as shown in Figure 8-36. A replica volume holds the replica for the protected data source (the virtual machine in this case). Once a replica is made for the protected data source, only incremental changes are synchronized with the DPM server. A recovery point volume contains shadow copies and recovery points for the protected data source (the virtual machine). Adjust the settings as desired. Click OK, and then click Next.

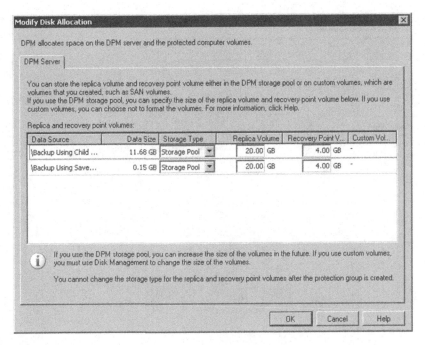

Figure 8-36. *Adjusting the replica and recovery point volume storage allocation*

Note Take note of the recovery point volume sizes. Remember that the page file for the DPM server should be adjusted to the recommended 1.5 times the amount of RAM in the DPM server plus 0.2% the size of the total size of all the recovery point volumes combined. For example, if the combined size for all of your recovery point volumes is 2TB, you should add about 4GB to the page file size on the DPM server.

---

9. In the Choose Replica Creation Method window, you can select to have DPM create the replica of the source data now or at a scheduled time, as shown in Figure 8-37. You can also choose to manually copy over the replica data from removable media if you want more control over the data copy. Make sure that your virtual machines can support an online backup or you are ready for some downtime before you copy the replica data using any of these methods. Click Next to continue.

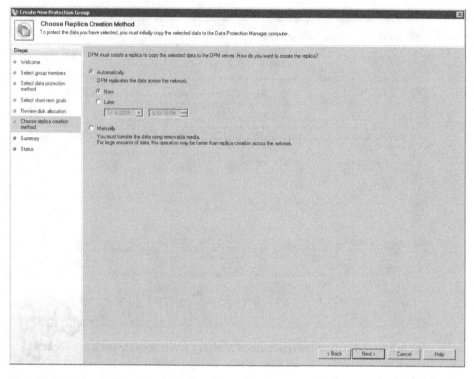

Figure 8-37. *Choosing how the initial replica data will be created*

Note The procedure for manual replica data copying to import data into DPM depends on the backup method used to copy the replica data. Keep in mind that the directory structure, timestamps, and security permissions on the replica data match the source data.

10. In the Summary window, click the Create Group button to create your new protection group. You can view the group creation status, as shown in Figure 8-38.

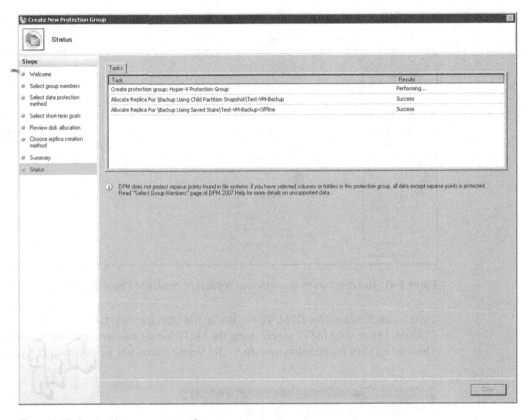

Figure 8-38. *Protection group creation status*

Now that your Hyper-V virtual machines are being protected by DPM, you can manage backups as follows:

- View your protection group status in the Protection tab of the DPM console, as shown in Figure 8-39.

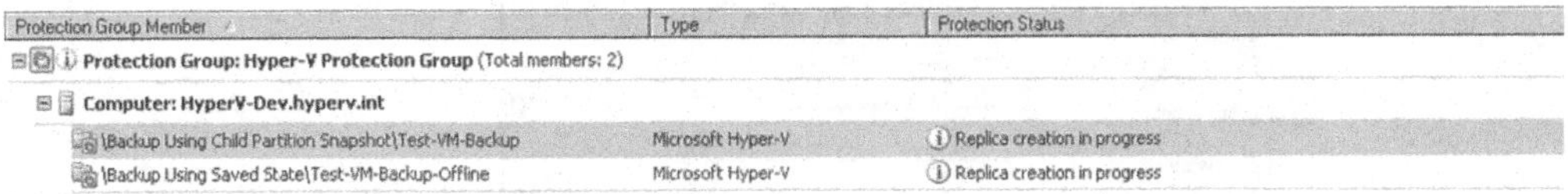

Protection Group Member	Type	Protection Status
⊟📦ⓘ **Protection Group: Hyper-V Protection Group** (Total members: 2)		
⊟📄 **Computer: HyperV-Dev.hyperv.int**		
📄 \Backup Using Child Partition Snapshot\Test-VM-Backup	Microsoft Hyper-V	ⓘ Replica creation in progress
📄 \Backup Using Saved State\Test-VM-Backup-Offline	Microsoft Hyper-V	ⓘ Replica creation in progress

Figure 8-39. *Viewing the virtual machines in your new protection group*

- Monitor alerts and jobs in the Monitoring tab, as shown in Figure 8-40.

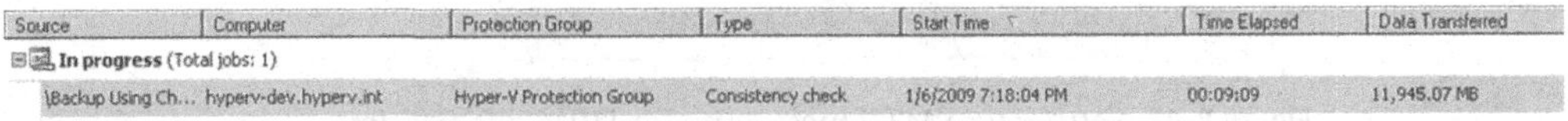

Source	Computer	Protection Group	Type	Start Time	Time Elapsed	Data Transferred
⊟🖳 **In progress** (Total jobs: 1)						
\Backup Using Ch...	hyperv-dev.hyperv.int	Hyper-V Protection Group	Consistency check	1/6/2009 7:18:04 PM	00:09:09	11,945.07 MB

Figure 8-40. *Monitoring DPM jobs*

• Run different reports in the Reporting tab, as shown in Figure 8-41.

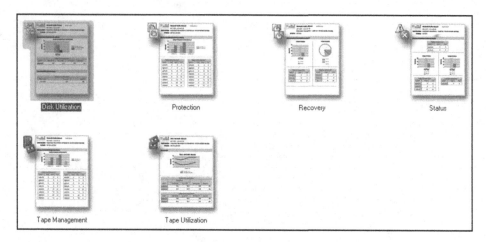

Figure 8-41. *You can run many different reports in the DPM Reporting tab.*

• Turn on notifications for DPM. To do this, in the Management tab's Action pane, click Options. Set up your SMTP server using the SMTP Server tab, as shown in Figure 8-42. Then set up your notification options in the Notifications tab, as shown in Figure 8-43.

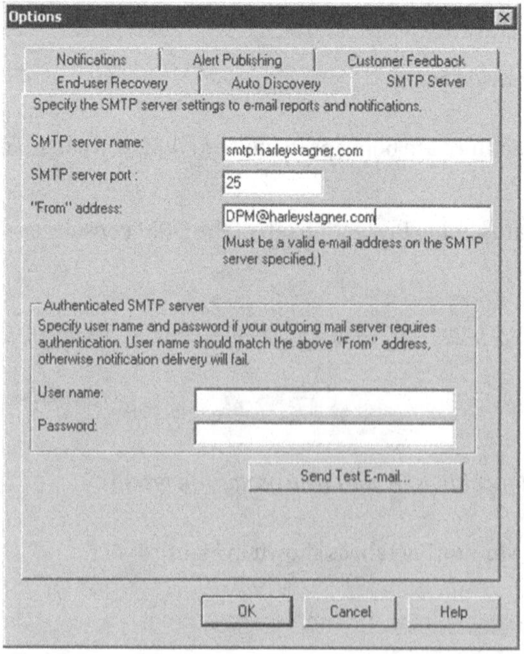

Figure 8-42. *Setting up SMTP messaging for DPM notifications*

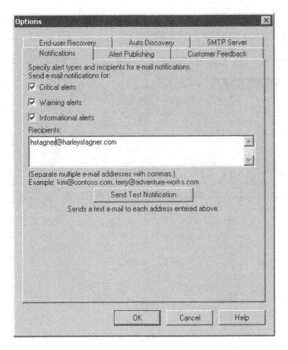

Figure 8-43. *Selecting the recipients for notification messages*

Recovering Protected Data

At some point, you may need to recover one of your virtual machines using DPM. Here's how:

1. Start DPM and click the Recovery tab. Drill down to the protected item that you want to recover, as shown in Figure 8-44.

■**Caution** DPM will turn off and delete any virtual machines that you are recovering to the original Hyper-V server. Make sure you are OK with this before you continue.

Figure 8-44. *Selecting the virtual machine that you want to recover*

2. Use the calendar to select the appropriate recovery points. Dates with available recovery points will appear in bold type, as shown in Figure 8-45.

Figure 8-45. *Selecting your recovery point*

3. After you have selected the appropriate item to recover, click Recover in the Actions pane.

4. The Recovery Wizard starts. In the first window, review the recovery selection to make sure it is correct, and then click Next.

5. Select your recovery type. You can recover to the original location, copy the files to a network share (useful if you want to mount the *.vhd and recover a certain file from the virtual machine), or copy the data to a tape, as shown in Figure 8-46.

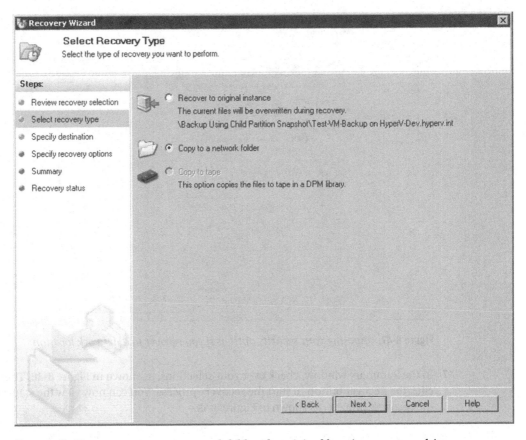

Figure 8-46. *You can recover to a network folder, the original location, or a tape drive.*

6. If you chose to restore the data to a network location, click Next to browse and choose a location from a server that has the DPM agent installed. Then in the Recovery Options window, you can choose to apply the security settings of either the original data or the destination server, as shown in Figure 8-47. You can also choose to perform a SAN-based recovery using hardware snapshots if you have configured this feature with DPM. If you chose to restore the data to the original location, you will just see the SAN-based recovery option. Click Next when you're ready to continue.

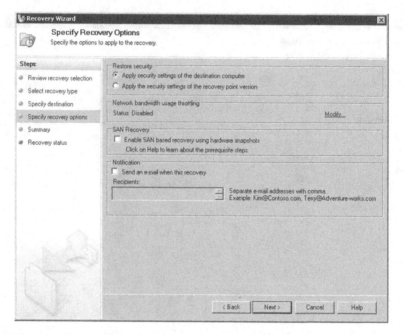

Figure 8-47. *Choosing your security options if you recover to a network location*

7. In the Summary window, check over your selections, as shown in Figure 8-48. Then click the Recover button to start the recovery process. You can now view the status of the recovery process, as shown in Figure 8-49.

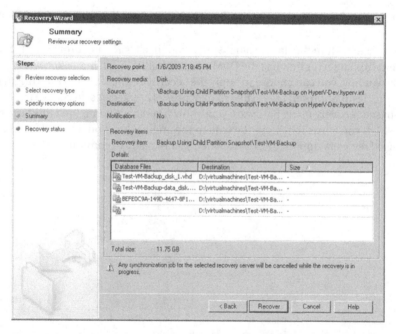

Figure 8-48. *Check over your recovery items before you click Recover.*

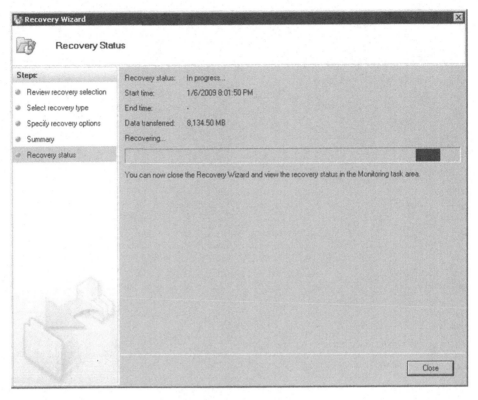

Figure 8-49. *You can view the status of the recovery.*

After the recovery, you can power on your virtual machine.

Summary

Protecting virtual machines is a crucial part of your virtual infrastructure planning. There are a few free or built-in tools that you can use for emergency backups or small environments. You can use the import/export functionality of Hyper-V for emergency backups. You can schedule backups for your virtual machines using Windows Server Backup. However, you can schedule a backup to only a disk that is presented to the server as a local disk or a removable disk. For larger environments, Microsoft offers a more robust solution in DPM 2007. Both Windows Server Backup and DPM 2007 are capable of performing online virtual machine backups by utilizing a Hyper-V VSS writer.

Whatever backup solution you choose, you should consider how you want to restore your data. If you want to restore a subset of folders and files that were stored on your virtual machine, you can mount the *.vhd file using WMI and Hyper-V or VHDMount.exe. If you want to restore an entire virtual machine, any of the backup options will work.

Sometimes, you need to treat the virtual machine like a physical computer and install a backup agent inside the virtual machine. This is true in cases where a virtual machine connects to an iSCSI volume or uses a pass-through disk. Ultimately, a combination of many of the backup techniques discussed in this chapter may provide the greatest protection scheme.

CHAPTER 9

∎∎∎

Securing Your Virtual Infrastructure

In many ways, securing your virtual infrastructure is no different than securing your physical infrastructure. It uses the same security concepts, such as the principle of least privilege.

Obviously, securing your virtual infrastructure should not be taken lightly. When you deploy virtual machines, you are putting a lot of trust in the virtualization platform that is hosted on physical servers. Those servers may hold almost your entire network infrastructure.

This chapter will set you on the right path to securing your virtual infrastructure, from the beginning of your Hyper-V host setup to the delegation of managing the hosts and virtual machines.

Hyper-V Host Setup

Security for a virtual infrastructure starts when you deploy your first host server. After all, the host server is carrying a lot of your infrastructure. If it were compromised in some way, you could be looking at some extended downtime for your infrastructure. Let's go through some steps you may consider when setting up your Hyper-V host server.

The first decision to make is whether you will deploy Hyper-V on a Windows Server 2008 Core installation. If you want to start off with a more secure system, you will choose to use a Core installation. Windows Server 2008 Core will also have better performance. Yes, it is different. Yes, it has a learning curve if you are used to working with other Windows Server versions. However, it has a smaller footprint on your host hardware. This means it has a smaller attack surface. This decision also has the added benefit of using fewer host resources.

Once you configure your Windows Server 2008 Core system installation for remote administration, you can use nearly all of the graphical user interface (GUI) tools to manage the installation remotely. This brings us to the next recommendation.

As tempting as it may be to turn off the Windows Firewall, you should leave it on. The Windows Firewall is another line of defense for your host server.

With those two recommendations in mind, let's go through a sample configuration for a Windows Server 2008 Core installation. First, you need to familiarize yourself with some of the most common commands and tools you will be using.

Reviewing the Configuration and Management Utilities

The following utilities are commonly used to set up your Hyper-V hosts running on a Windows Server 2008 Core system:

- `netsh`
- `netdom`
- `net`
- `start`
- `oclist.exe`
- `ocsetup.exe`
- `pkgmgr.exe`
- `slmgr.vbs`
- `scregedit.wsf`
- `wusa.exe`

These are discussed in the following sections, as well as the use of piping. Additionally, Table 9-1 lists some miscellaneous commands that you will need when you are administering your Windows Server 2008 Core system.

Table 9-1. *Some Useful Commands for Windows 2008 Core Administration*

Command	Purpose
shutdown	Shut down or restart the server
logoff	Log off the server
control intl.cpl	Open the Control Panel applet to change regional and language options
control timedate.cpl	Open the Control Panel applet to change the date and time

netsh

`netsh.exe` is a command-line scripting utility for Windows that has been included since Windows 2000. It is used to configure network settings. It is absolutely necessary to familiarize yourself with this tool in Windows Server 2008 Core.

You can use `netsh` in interactive mode, or you can script the `netsh` commands in a batch file. To start `netsh` in interactive mode, simply type `netsh` at the command prompt. Your prompt will change to `netsh>`. Then you need to change to a context by typing in the context name for the item you want to configure.

`netsh` operates in different contexts, depending on which item you want to configure. For a list of the contexts, you can access the `netsh` help by typing the following at the command line:

`netsh /?`

This will give you a list of options and contexts for `netsh`. If you want to learn more about a certain command or context, just type the following command:

```
netsh <context> /?
```

From there, you can keep drilling down through the context commands with the help switch (/?):

```
netsh <context> <command> /?
```

For example, if you want to see information about the firewall context, type the following:

```
netsh firewall /?
```

Then, if you want to see more information about the add command within the firewall context, type the following:

```
netsh firewall add /?
```

You can use this method to drill down as far as you want into a context.

Table 9-2 lists the contexts available in netsh on Windows Server 2008 and how to enter them.

Table 9-2. *Windows Server 2008 netsh Contexts*

Context	Command to Enter
Dynamic Host Configuration Protocol (DHCP) client	dhcpclient
DHCP server	dhcp
Health Registration Authority (HRA)	nap hra
Hypertext Transfer Protocol (HTTP)	http
Interface (IPv4 and IPv6)	interface
Internet Authentication Service (IAS)[a]	nps
Internet Protocol security	ipsec
Network Access Protection (NAP) client	nap
Network Bridge	bridge
Network Input Output (NETIO)	netio
Network Policy Server (NPS)	nps
Remote Access	ras
Routing	routing
Remote Procedure Call (RPC)	rpc
Windows Firewall	firewall
Windows Firewall with Advanced Security	advfirewall
Windows HTTP (WinHTTP)	winhttp
Windows Internet Name Service (WINS)	wins
Windows Sockets (WINSOCK)	winsock
Wired Local Area Network (LAN)	lan
Wireless LAN	wlan

[a] *IAS is renamed to Network Policy Server.*

The specific `netsh` commands that you will be using will be covered in the sections about configuring your Windows Server 2008 Core with Hyper-V installation later in this chapter.

netdom

`netdom` is a utility that allows administrators to manage Active Directory domains and trusts from the command prompt.

To see all the commands available for `netdom`, type the following at the command prompt:

```
netdom help
```

If you are interested in learning more about a specific command, type the following:

```
netdom help <command>
```

or

```
netdom <command> /help
```

You will use `netdom` primarily to change the computer name of your Hyper-V host and to have your Hyper-V host join the domain. To rename the computer, use this command:

```
netdom renamecomputer <Machine> /NewName:<NewName>
```

<Machine> is the current computer name (you can use `localhost`). *<NewName>* is the new computer name.

To join the computer to the domain, use this command:

```
netdom join <ComputerName> /domain:<DomainName> /userd:<UserName> /passwordd:*
```

<ComputerName> is your computer name. *<DomainName>* is the domain you want to join. *<UserName>* is the username you will use to join the computer to the domain.

net

`net` is an older utility used to manage network-related settings on Windows systems. To see the list of commands available for `net`, type the following at the command prompt:

```
net help
```

For additional help on any of the `net` commands, type the following:

```
net help <command>
```

You will commonly use `net` to stop and start services or connect to a network share. To start and stop a service, use these commands:

```
net start <ServiceName>

net stop <ServiceName>
```

<ServiceName> is the name of the service you want to start or stop.

To add a particular user to a local group, use this command:

```
net localgroup <GroupName> /add <DomainName>\<UserName>
```

<GroupName> is the name of the local group to which you want to add the user. *<DomainName>* is the domain name for the user, and *<UserName>* is the name of the user that you want to add to the group.

To map a drive, use this command:

```
net use <DriveLetter> \\<ServerName>\<ShareName>
```

This will map a drive using the *<DriveLetter>* specified to the UNC path (*<ServerName>**<ShareName>*).

start

The start command is used to start programs. This is usually in the form of start *<ProgramPath>*. However, start does have some options that you can use. To see the list of options and usage information, just type the following at the command line:

```
start /?
```

The most common option that you will use with the start command is /wait, which starts the application and waits for it to terminate. This will help you determine when the particular application is finished processing a request.

oclist.exe and ocsetup.exe

The oclist and ocsetup utilities are used together to install and verify roles and features in a Windows Server 2008 Core system. Their usage is pretty straightforward.

If you want to see a list of roles and features available on your Windows Server 2008 Core installation, just type this:

```
oclist
```

This will also tell you if the role or feature is installed.

To see the options for the ocsetup command, type this:

```
ocsetup /?
```

If you want to install a role or feature, enter the following command:

```
start /wait ocsetup <Role or Feature Name>
```

Note Feature and role names are always case-sensitive.

To uninstall a role or feature, use this command:

```
start /wait ocsetup <Role or Feature Name> /uninstall
```

For example, if you want to install the Hyper-V role, type the following:

```
start /wait ocsetup Microsoft-Hyper-V
```

You can use the start command with the /wait option so you can tell when the feature or role is finished installing. Otherwise, the ocsetup command returns to the command prompt immediately, and the role or feature is installed in the background.

pkgmgr.exe

pkgmgr is the Windows Package Manager utility. You can also use this to install roles and features.

To install a role or feature, type the following:

```
start /w pkgmgr.exe -iu:<Role or Feature Name>
```

To uninstall a role or feature, use this command:

```
start /w pkgmgr.exe -uu:<Role or Feature Name>
```

To uninstall a particular package, type this:

```
start /w pkgmgr /up:<Package>
```

If you want to see all of the available options for pkgmgr, use its help command:

```
pkgmgr /?
```

slmgr.vbs

The slmgr.vbs script is the Windows Software License Manager tool. It is most commonly used to activate Windows, as follows:

```
slmgr.vbs -ato
```

If you want to install a license (such as an enterprise volume license), use this command:

```
slmgr.vbs -ipk <ProductKey>
```

<ProductKey> is the product key for your new license. This will replace any existing license that is on the system.

To see the additional options available for slmgr.vbs, type the following:

```
slmgr.vbs
```

scregedit.wsf

The scregedit.wsf script can manage many of the registry settings of a Windows Server 2008 Core system. This script is most commonly used to enable Remote Desktop on a Windows Server 2008 Core installation, as follows:

```
scregedit.wsf /AR 0
```

The following are some of the other settings that the `scregedit.wsf` script can manage:

- Enable automatic updates (disable with a value of 1 instead of 4):

```
scregedit.wsf /AU 4
```

- Enable remote desktop connections from Windows versions older than Windows Vista and Windows Server 2008

```
scregedit.wsf /CS 0
```

- Configure DNS SRV record priority:

```
scregedit.wsf /DP <value>
```

- Configure DNS SRV record weight:

```
scregedit.wsf /DW <value>
```

- Allow remote management of the IP Security Monitor:

```
scregedit.wsf /IM 1
```

To find out more about the other registry settings you can manage, type the following at the command prompt:

```
scregedit.wsf /?
```

wusa.exe

`wusa.exe` is the Windows Update Stand-alone Installer. It is used to install Windows updates. All you need to do is download and copy the update to your Windows Server Core installation, and then type the following:

```
wusa.exe <PackageName> /quiet
```

For example, if you want to install Windows Server Core 2008 and enable Hyper-V, you'll want the update available for the Hyper-V role (KB950050). To install this, type the following:

```
wusa.exe Windows6.0-KB950050-x64.msu /quiet
```

Piping

Piping is a useful technique for finding more granular information at the command prompt. Piping is done by using the pipe symbol (|). You can try it out by piping the output of a `help` command to the `more` command, like this:

```
net help use | more
```

This will allow you to scroll through the help text, instead of having it whiz by in the command prompt window.

Here's another example of how piping can be very useful at the command line:

```
oclist | find "Installed" | find /v "Not Installed"
```

This command uses the output of `oclist` with the `find` command (a text-searching utility that comes with Windows), searching for the text "Installed." The output of the `find` `"Installed"` command is piped to another `find` query, which uses the `/v` option to exclude the text "Not Installed" from the results. The final output gives you only the roles and features that are installed on the server.

Configuring the Initial Network Settings

After you have installed Windows Server 2008 Core and logged on for the first time, you are presented with a command prompt. Now you can start configuring your system.

Configuring the IP Address, Subnet, Default Gateway, and DNS Settings

To set your network settings, first get the interface IDs:

```
netsh interface ipv4 show interfaces
```

Note the number shown in the `Idx` column of the results. You will use this number to configure the desired network adapter(s).

Next, configure the static IP address, subnet, and default gateway for your network adapter(s):

```
netsh interface ipv4 set address name="<ID>" ➥
source=static address=<StaticIP> mask=<SubnetMask> gateway=<DefaultGateway>
```

where:

- `<ID>` is the `Idx` number shown in the results of the `show interfaces` command.

- `<StaticIP>` is your desired static IP address.

- `<SubnetMask>` is your desired subnet mask.

- `<DefaultGateway>` is the desired default gateway.

Next, configure the DNS settings for your network adapter(s):

```
netsh interface ipv4 add dnsserver name="<ID>" address=<DNSIP>index=1
```

Again, `<ID>` is the `Idx` number for this network adapter. `<DNSIP>` is the IP address of your DNS server. Repeat this step for every DNS server that you want to add, incrementing the index number by one each time.

Setting the Time and Date

To set the time and date, open the Date/Time Control Panel applet, as follows:

```
control timedate.cpl
```

From here, you can adjust the appropriate settings.

Setting the Computer Name

If you need to set the computer name, first rename the computer:

```
netdom renamecomputer <Machine> /NewName:<NewName>
```

<Machine> is the current name for your computer (you can use `localhost` here). *<NewName>* is the new name.

After you've renamed the computer, restart it:

```
shutdown /r /t 0
```

Joining an Active Directory Domain

To join the computer to an Active Directory domain, first use the `netdom join` command:

```
netdom join <ComputerName> /domain:<DomainName> /userd:<UserName> /passwordd:*
```

<ComputerName> is your computer name, *<DomainName>* is the name of the domain you are joining, and *<UserName>* is a domain user account that has permission to join a computer to the domain.

Enter the password for the user you specified when prompted.

You can now add a domain account to the local Administrators group, if necessary:

```
net localgroup administrators /add <DomainName>\<UserName>
```

<DomainName> is the name of the domain you just joined, and *<UserName>* is the user account that you want to add to the Administrators group.

Then restart the computer:

```
shutdown /r /t 0
```

You can now activate the server when it finishes rebooting:

```
slmgr.vbs -ato
```

Configuring Remote Administration

At this point, you can begin to configure remote administration for your server. Before you do, you should be familiar with the different ways you can remotely administer your Windows Server 2008 Core system. You can use one of the following methods:

- Remote Desktop

- Windows Remote Management (WinRM)

- Microsoft Management Console (MMC) tools

You will probably use a combination of at least two of these methods to remotely administer your Windows Server 2008 Core server.

Enabling Remote Desktop

Remote Desktop on Windows Server 2008 is configured to negotiate encryption with the client. Also, starting with Remote Desktop Client version 6.1 (Windows Vista SP1 and Windows XP SP3), you can utilize Network Level Authentication (NLA) when connecting to a Remote Desktop session that supports it. NLA completes the user authentication before the Remote Desktop Protocol (RDP) session is established. This uses fewer resources on the server that you are establishing an RDP session with, and is more secure than previous versions of RDP.

If you will be connecting with a client that does not support NLA, you can set the Remote Desktop properties of your Windows Server 2008 Core server to use the old authentication method (before RDP version 6.1). However, you should try to use an NLA-capable client on Windows XP SP3, Windows Vista SP1, and Windows Server 2008 full installation systems for the best security. Remote Desktop on a Windows Server 2008 Core installation supports only one concurrent user connection.

To enable Remote Desktop on your Windows Server 2008 Core installation, enter the following at the command prompt:

```
SCregEdit.wsf /AR 0
```

If you ever want to disable Remote Desktop, use a 1 instead of a 0 in the SCregEdit.wsf command.

Next, open the Windows Firewall for Remote Desktop access:

```
Netsh advfirewall firewall set rule group="Remote Desktop" ➥
new enable=yes remoteip=<context>
```

The *<context>* can be a single IP address, a subnet, or any (to allow any remote IP address for Remote Desktop). The best security practice is to at least limit the Remote Desktop access to a certain subnet.

You can also restrict the users that have access to a Remote Desktop session, as follows:

```
net localgroup "Remote Desktop Users" /add <DomainName>\<UserName>
```

<DomainName> is the name of the domain for the user account, and *<UserName>* is the user account that you want to add to the Remote Desktop Users group.

If you need to allow a client that does not support NLA to access a Remote Desktop session on you Windows Server 2008 Core system, type the following:

```
SCregEdit.wsf /CS 0
```

■**Caution** The SCregEdit.wsf /CS 0 setting is less secure than using the NLA method.

Enabling WinRM

WinRM is Microsoft's implementation of WS-Management, a protocol for managing applications, servers, and other network devices. WinRM uses fewer network resources than a full-blown RDP session (and you will get only a command prompt in an RDP session anyway).

WinRM is web-based, and is actually the server listener component. Windows Remote Shell (WinRS) is the client component that you use to connect to the WinRS server. If you are in the same Active Directory domain as the server you are trying to connect to, the communication is encrypted using the Negotiate or Kerberos Security Service Provider (SSP).

■**Caution** WinRM is potentially less secure than RDP, because it listens on port 80, and firewalls are often configured to let port 80 traffic through.

To check if WinRM is already enabled on your Windows Server 2008 Core system, enter the following at the command line:

```
WinRM enumerate winrm/config/listener
```

Nothing will be returned if there is no listener enabled.

To enable WinRM's default port 80 listener, enter the following at the command line:

```
WinRM quickconfig
```

Press Y to continue. The following will display if the configuration of WinRM was successful:

```
WinRM has been updated for remote management. WinRM service type changed to delayed
auto start. WinRM service started. Created a WinRM listener on HTTP://* to accept
WS-Man requests to any IP on this machine.
```

Now you can get a remote command prompt on your Windows Server 2008 Core system by typing the following from another Windows Vista or Windows Server 2008 system's command prompt:

```
winrs -r:<ServerName> cmd.exe
```

<ServerName> is the name of the server to which you want to connect.

If you find an unauthorized WinRM listener on one of your servers, you can disable it with the following command at the Windows Server 2008 Core command prompt:

```
WinRM delete winrm/config/listener?IPAddress=*+Transport=HTTP
```

Enabling Remote MMC Management

You can also manage your Windows Server 2008 Core system remotely using MMC tools (like Hyper-V Manager) from a Windows Vista SP1 or Windows Server 2008 full installation. To do this, you need to enable an exception for remote administration in the Windows Firewall by typing the following at the command prompt:

```
Netsh advfirewall firewall set rule group="Remote Administration" ➡
new enable=yes remoteip=<context>
```

The <context> can be a single IP address, a subnet, or any (to allow any remote IP address for remote administration). The best security practice is to at least limit the remote administration access to a certain subnet.

Installing the Hyper-V Role on Windows Server 2008 Core

Now that your remote administration is set up, you can connect remotely to your Windows Server 2008 Core installation to perform the rest of the Hyper-V setup.

To begin this process, perform the following steps at the command line:

1. Make sure you have the KB950050 update installed on your server to update from the release candidate of Hyper-V to the RTM version of Hyper-V if you need to do so. Issue the following command to check:

```
wmic qfe list
```

This will list the updates that you have installed on your system. If you do not have it, download it from the following URL:

```
http://www.microsoft.com/downloads/details.aspx?FamilyId=
F3AB3D4B-63C8-4424-A738-BADED34D24ED&displaylang=en
```

2. Copy the update file (and any other updates you want to install) to a network share that is accessible from your Hyper-V server.

3. Map a drive to the network share:

```
net use <DriveLetter> \\<ServerName>\<ShareName>
```

<DriveLetter> is the letter you want to use for the mapped drive (for example, x:), *<ServerName>* is the name of the server that hosts the network share, and *<ShareName>* is the name of the share on the server.

4. Copy any update files to the Hyper-V server:

```
copy <Source> <Destination>
```

<Source> is the source file path, and *<Destination>* is the destination file path, as in this example:

```
copy x:\Windows6.0-KB950050-x64.msu c:\temp\Windows6.0-KB950050-x64.msu
```

5. Install the updates on the server:

```
wusa.exe <UpdateName> /quiet
```

<UpdateName> is the name of the *.msu file that you need to install, as in this example:

```
wusa.exe Windows6.0-KB950050-x64.msu /quiet
```

6. Enable the Hyper-V role:

```
start /w ocsetup Microsoft-Hyper-V
```

7. Reboot the server:

```
shutdown /r /t 0
```

Allowing Scripting

If you want to be able to do any WMI scripting remotely on your Hyper-V Server, you need to enable an exception for this in the Windows Firewall. To do so, type the following at the command prompt of your Hyper-V server:

```
netsh advfirewall firewall set rule ➥
group="Windows Management Instrumentation (WMI)" ➥
new enable=yes remoteip=<context>
```

The *<context>* can be a single IP address, a subnet, or any (to allow any remote IP address for WMI). The best security practice is to at least limit the WMI access to a certain subnet.

Removing Source Packages

For those who are extra paranoid, it is also possible to remove the source packages for features and roles on your Hyper-V server. You might consider removing packages if you are sure you will not need them. Ideally, your Hyper-V server should be used for only Hyper-V. Removing packages will ensure that any other roles and services cannot be installed, and will free up some disk space on your Hyper-V server.

■**Caution** The process of removing the features and roles cannot be reversed. Your only option if you want to use a feature or role that has been removed later is to reinstall the operating system. Be absolutely sure you do not want to use a role or feature before you remove the source package!

To remove the package, issue the following command at the command line:

```
pkgmgr /up:<Package>
```

<Package> is the name of the package that you want to remove. The package names take the following form:

```
Microsoft-<PackageDescription>~31bf3856ad364e35~<Architecture>~~<Version>
```

<PackageDescription> can be any of the following:

- `Windows-BLB-Package`
- `Windows-DFSN-ServerCore`
- `Windows-DFSR-ServerEdition-Package`
- `Windows-DhcpServerCore-Package`
- `Windows-DirectoryServices-ADAM-SrvFnd-Package`
- `Windows-DirectoryServices-DomainController-SrvFnd-Package`
- `Windows-DNS-Server-Core-Role-Package`
- `Windows-FailoverCluster-Core-Package`

- Windows-FileReplication-Package
- Windows-IIS-WebServer-Core-Package
- Windows-Internet-Naming-Service-SC-Package
- Windows-MultipathIo-Package
- Windows-NetworkLoadBalancingHeadlessServer-Package
- Windows-NFS-ServerFoundation-Package
- Windows-Printing-ServerCore-Package
- Windows-QWAVE-Package
- Windows-RemovableStorageManagementCore-Package
- Windows-SecureStartup-OC-Package
- Windows-SNMP-SC-Package
- Windows-SUA-Core-Package
- Windows-Telnet-Client-Package
- Windows-ServerCore-EA-IME-Package
- Windows-ServerCore-EA-Fonts-Package

<Architecture> can be either x86 or amd64. *<Version>* is the version of Windows Server 2008 you are running. The RTM version of Windows Server 2008 is 6.0.6001.18000. The following is an example of a full package name on a Hyper-V host (amd64):

```
Microsoft-Windows-IIS-WebServer-Core-Package~31bf3856ad364e35~amd64~~6.0.6001.18000
```

Repeat this command for each package that you want to remove. When you are finished, reboot the server:

```
shutdown /r /t 0
```

Wait approximately 30 minutes for the disk cleanup to occur.

Now, if you type oclist, the packages you removed will not show up in the list, and you won't be able to install them.

Enabling Windows Update on Your Windows Server 2008 System

If you are not using Windows Server Update Service, Systems Management Server, group policy, or some other patch management solution to patch your servers, then you should use Windows Update to patch them. To enable Windows Update on a Windows Server 2008 Core installation, enter the following command at the command prompt:

```
cscript SCregEdit.wsf /AU 4
```

Then stop the Windows Update service:

```
Net stop wuauserv
```

And finally, restart the Windows Update service:

```
Net start wuauserv
```

This will enable Windows Update for automatic updates using the default of a download and installation at 3 a.m. This is not ideal in many environments. You can adjust the Windows Update settings after it has been enabled by using group policy or by editing the registry. To adjust the registry settings associated with Windows Update, open Regedit:

```
regedit
```

Then navigate to the following registry key:

```
HKEY_LOCAL_MACHINE\SOFTWARE\Microsoft\Windows\CurrentVersion\
WindowsUpdate\Auto Update
```

Adjust the scheduled install day using the `ScheduleInstallDay` REG_DWORD value. This value is 0 for every day, or 1 through 7 for a day of the week, starting with Sunday as 1.

Adjust the scheduled installation time using the `ScheduledInstallTime` REG_DWORD value. This value can be from 0 to 23, as it is in a 24-hour clock format.

■**Caution** Even when you adjust these settings, your server will still reboot (if necessary) after an installation. It is probably best to handle patch installation with a patch management system, such as Windows Server Update Service or Systems Management Server, if you want to avoid rebooting.

Congratulations! You have configured your Windows Server 2008 Core installation with the Hyper-V role in a secure manner, while still allowing the flexibility for remote administration and scripting. Now you just need to configure Hyper-V for your environment.

Hyper-V Network Security

The following are some best practices when configuring Hyper-V. These suggestions will help with Hyper-V security and stability:

Use a separate physical NIC for Hyper-V management. Use a different physical NIC port for your virtual machines and your Hyper-V management. Then you can set different network security policies for your virtual machines than you have for your Hyper-V host. This way, your virtual machine traffic is isolated from your host server. If your virtual machines are on the same physical NIC as your host server, the host server can see all the network traffic on the virtual machines.

Isolate iSCSI storage. If you are going to use iSCSI attached storage on the host, keep it isolated on a separate physical NIC and separate subnet. This gives better performance, because if iSCSI traffic is dedicated to a physical NIC and on its own subnet, no other network traffic will be able to interfere with the iSCSI traffic. It also provides better security, because there is no possibility that iSCSI traffic can be seen by any other virtual machines.

A simple example of why it is not a good idea to put virtual machines on the same physical NIC as your Hyper-V management NIC can be shown with a Wireshark (a packet capturing utility) packet capture running on the Hyper-V host (192.168.0.20). By default, switched networks are point-to-point. This means that a network device can see only network packets destined for it or broadcast packets. In the example shown in Figure 9-1, it looks like a user using a virtual machine (192.168.0.60) on the Hyper-V host logged on to an FTP server. You can plainly see that the username is hstagner and the password is password. Neither the source nor the destination is the Hyper-V host, so it really has no business seeing those packets. This is just a simple example. The Hyper-V host could just as easily see other types of network traffic of any virtual machine bound to the same physical NIC as the management NIC. If this virtual machine were on a different physical NIC, the traffic shown in Figure 9-1 would not be visible to the Hyper-V host or any other virtual machine on that physical NIC.

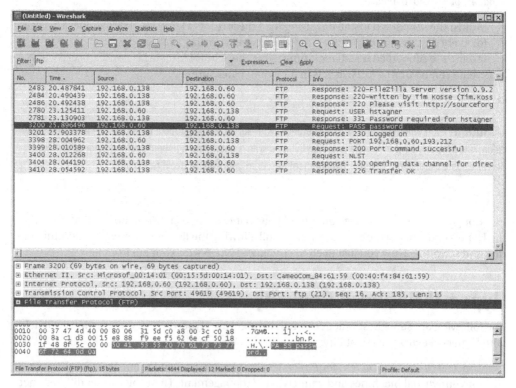

Figure 9-1. *A host Wireshark capture of an FTP session initiated from a virtual machine*

■**Note** Currently, it is not possible to install a functioning intrusion detection system (IDS) or intrusion prevention system (IPS) in a virtual machine on the Hyper-V host so you can protect the virtual network(s) inside the host. IDS and IPS systems rely on the ability to be attached to a switch port that has been set to monitoring mode (or promiscuous mode). A switch port in monitoring mode allows the device connected to it to see all of the network traffic on the switch (even the point-to-point traffic). Hyper-V does not currently support monitoring mode for a virtual switch port, although this support may be added in the future.

Hyper-V Manager Security

If you have not deployed System Center Virtual Machine Manager (VMM) 2008, delegating administration for your Hyper-V virtual machines is possible, but it requires a bit of work. There are two parts to the delegation:

- Set up your scope, tasks, roles, and role assignments using the Authorization Manager (AzMan) MMC tool.

- Assign a scope to a virtual machine using WMI scripting.

Hyper-V Manager configuration was covered in Chapter 1. Here, we'll look at the basic steps for using AzMan and an example of a WMI script for assigning scope to a virtual machine.

Using Authorization Manager

AzMan is a role-based security architecture for Windows. It has two basic parts: a runtime component implemented by `azroles.dll` and an administration console called `azman.msc` (an MMC). You will use `azman.msc` to configure Hyper-V for delegated administration. This administration console comes with Windows Server 2000 SP4, Windows Server 2003, Windows Vista SP1, and Windows Server 2008.

Before you can start delegating administration of your virtual machines with AzMan, you need to be familiar with the following terms:

Operation: A low-level permission in an application. Some examples of operations in Hyper-V are Reconfigure Virtual Machine, Create Virtual Switch Port, and Change VLAN Configuration on Port. Operations form the foundation for role-based access control.

Policy: The data that AzMan uses for the role-based access control. This is in the form of an XML file that can be edited with `azman.msc` or via scripting.

Role: A set of groups or users that can perform a subset of operations that are assigned to them.

Authorization store: The repository for the authorization policy. It can be stored in a XML file, Active Directory, or a SQL database. In this case, you will be modifying an XML-file based authorization store for Hyper-V.

Scope: A set of resources that have a common access-control policy. Examples of scopes are Human Resources and Development.

Task: A logical group of operations. For example, a task to monitor virtual machines might include the operations Read Service Configuration, View External Ethernet Ports, View Internal Ethernet Ports, View LAN Endpoints, View Switch Ports, View Switches, View Virtual Switch Management Service, and View LAN Settings.

Role definition: The list of operations that a user can perform within the assigned role.

Role assignment: The list of users that can perform the operations listed in the role definition.

Virtualization administrator: Any user that has local administrator permission on the Hyper-V server's parent partition. The local administrator on the Hyper-V server can control all delegated role-based access.

To use AzMan to set role-based permissions, follow this procedure:

1. Open the AzMan administration console on your management workstation or server by selecting Start ➤ Run and typing in azman.msc. As the message in the opening window says (see Figure 9-2), to get started, you need to open an authorization store.

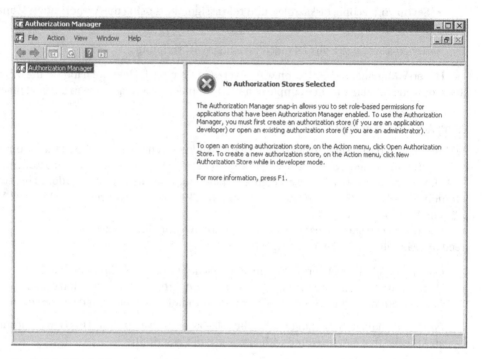

Figure 9-2. *The AzMan screen before a store is added*

2. To open an authorization store, select Action ➤ Open Authorization Store. The default path to the authorization store for Hyper-V is c:\programdata\microsoft\windows\hyper-v\initialstore.xml on the Hyper-V server that you are configuring for role-based security. So, your path should be the hidden c$ share on your remote Hyper-V server, such as \\hyperv-dev\c$\programdata\microsoft\windows\hyper-v\initialstore.xml, as shown in Figure 9-3. Click OK to open the authorization store.

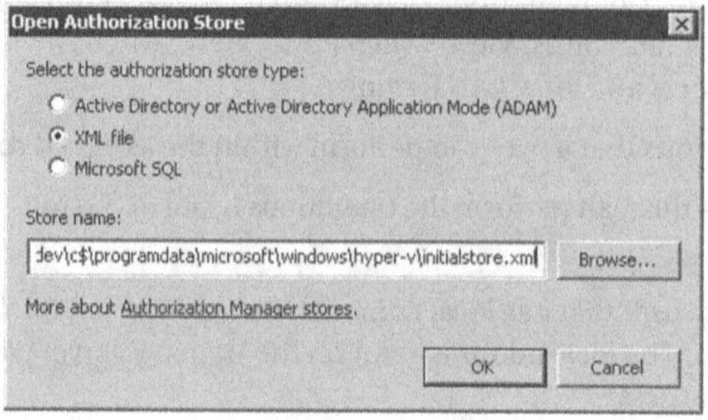

Figure 9-3. *Selecting the XML file store for Hyper-V*

Caution You might want to make a backup copy of the default `initialstore.xml` file before you modify it, because everything you do in `azman.msc` takes effect immediately.

3. The authorization store for that Hyper-V server will be loaded. Expand each of the items in the navigation pane on the left. You will see that AzMan provides the following:

   - A default scope (Hyper-V services): This is an application scope and is also the root scope for Hyper-V.

   - A default role definition (Administrator): The administrator can perform all of the operations available to Hyper-V.

   - A default role assignment (Administrator), as shown in Figure 9-4: The `BuiltIn\Administrators` group is a member of this role assignment.

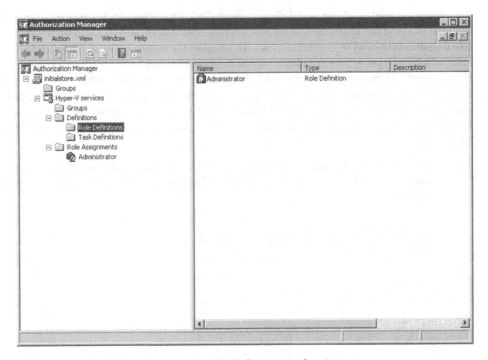

Figure 9-4. *The default Administrator role definition and assignment*

4. You need to decide your scope. Some examples of scopes are Human Resources, Production, and Development. The scope can be based on geography, department, or organizational function, as a few examples. This is a business decision that you will need to make. To create your new scope, right-click Hyper-V services in the navigation pane and choose New Scope. Give the new scope a name and description, as shown in Figure 9-5. Rather than use multiple words for a scope (like "Human Resources"), you should combine the words into a form without spaces, to make scripting easier later (like "HumanResources"). Click OK when you are finished.

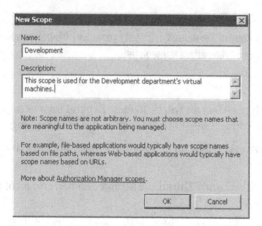

Figure 9-5. *Defining a new scope*

Now you could go ahead and define a role and add operations to it. However, it might be better in the long run to define tasks (collections of operations), so you can assign those in role definitions instead of individual tasks. This makes life easier, because performing a high-level action in Hyper-V (like creating a virtual machine) involves many different operations. If you have them grouped into tasks, it becomes easier to create role definitions by defining tasks instead of individual operations. Microsoft has provided some suggested task definition names with the operations required to accomplish the task in Appendix A of the Technet Hyper-V Planning and Deployment Guide (`http://technet.microsoft.com/en-us/library/dd282980.aspx`).

5. To create a task definition, right-click Task Definitions in the navigation pane and select New Task Definition. Give the task definition an appropriate name and description, as shown in Figure 9-6.

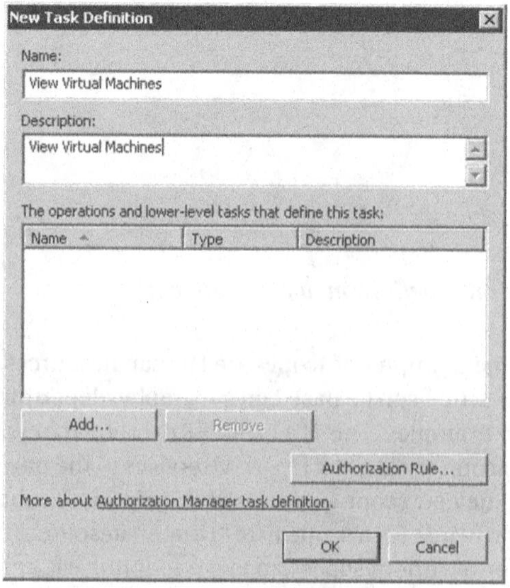

Figure 9-6. *Naming a new task*

6. Click the Add button to add operations to the task definition. If this is the first task you are creating, you'll see a warning letting you know that there are no tasks available to add. Just click OK to continue, because you will be adding operations, not tasks.

7. Click the Operations tab and choose the appropriate operations for the task that you are creating, as shown in Figure 9-7. For example, the View Virtual Machines task would have the operations Allow Output from Virtual Machine, Read Service Configuration, and View Virtual Machine Configuration. Click OK to continue.

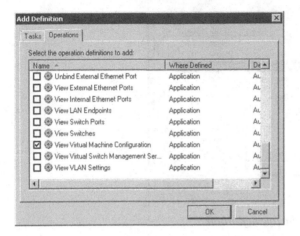

Figure 9-7. *Adding operations to the task definition*

8. Repeat steps 5 through 7 for each task that you want to create.

9. After your tasks are created, you can create a new role definition. To do this, right-click Role Definitions in the navigation pane and choose New Role Definition. Enter an appropriate name and description for the role definition, as shown in Figure 9-8.

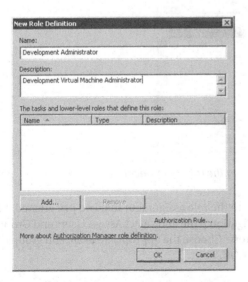

Figure 9-8. *Naming the new role definition*

10. When you are ready to add tasks, click the Add button. Click the Tasks tab to select your tasks, as shown in Figure 9-9. For example, you might assign the Development Administrator all of the virtual machine-related tasks to manage the development virtual machines, but not the Hyper-V server itself. When you are finished assigning tasks, click OK twice.

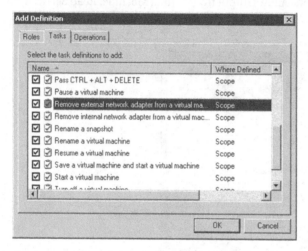

Figure 9-9. *Adding tasks to the role definition*

11. To create a new role assignment to assign your users and group to the new role, right-click Role Assignments in the navigation pane and choose New Role Assignment. Choose the role you just created, as shown in Figure 9-10, and then click OK.

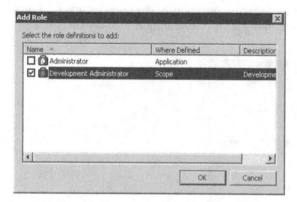

Figure 9-10. *Adding the role definition to the role assignment*

12. Now you can assign users or groups to the role assignment that you just created. Right-click the role assignment in the navigation pane and select Assign Users and Groups ➤ From Windows and Active Directory. Choose the appropriate users and groups, as shown in Figure 9-11, and then click OK.

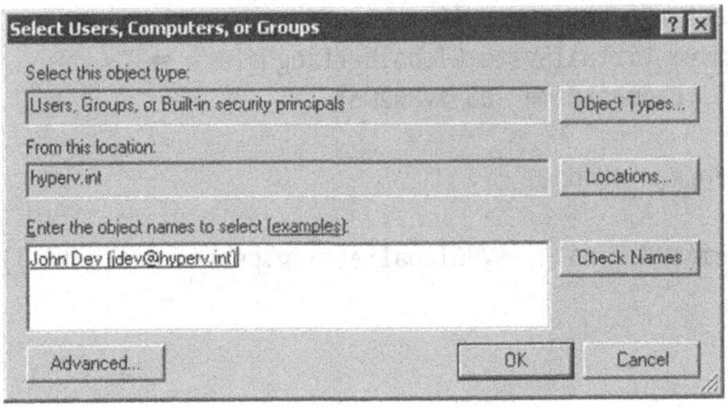

Figure 9-11. *Adding a user account to the role assignment*

Now that you have created your roles assignments in azman.msc, you need to assign the scopes to the virtual machines that you want to delegate. There is no way to do this in the Hyper-V Manager console. It can only be scripted through WMI.

Assigning Scopes to Virtual Machines

Before you can script the virtual machine scope assignments using WMI, you need to make sure that WMI access to your Hyper-V server is open, as follows:

```
netsh advfirewall firewall set rule ➥
group="Windows Management Instrumentation (WMI)" ➥
new enable=yes remoteip=<context>
```

The <context> can be a single IP address, a subnet, or any (to allow any remote IP address for WMI). The best security practice is to at least limit the WMI access to a certain subnet.

The following PowerShell script accomplishes the scope assignments:

```
$Namespace = "root\virtualization"
$Computer = Read-Host "Enter the Hyper-V server that you want to connect to"
$VMName = Read-Host ➥
"Enter the Virtual machine that you would like to assign the scope to"
$Scope = Read-Host ➥
"Enter the scope name that you would like to assign to the virtual machine"

$VM_Service = Get-WmiObject -ComputerName $Computer ➥
-Namespace $Namespace -Class Msvm_VirtualSystemManagementService

$VM = Get-WmiObject -ComputerName $Computer ➥
-Namespace $Namespace -Class Msvm_ComputerSystem | ➥
Where-Object -FilterScript {$_.ElementName -eq $VMName}

Get-Wmiobject -ComputerName $Computer ➥
-Namespace $Namespace -Class Msvm_ComputerSystem | ➥
Where-Object -FilterScript {$_.ElementName -eq $VMName} | ForEach-Object {
if ( $VMName -ne $Null)
{
```

```
$VMGlobalSetting = Get-Wmiobject -ComputerName $Computer ➡
-Namespace $Namespace -Class Msvm_VirtualSystemGlobalSettingData | ➡
Where-Object -FilterScript { $_.ElementName -eq $VMName}

$VMGlobalSetting.ScopeOfResidence = $Scope

$VM_Service.ModifyVirtualSystem($VM.__PATH, $VMGlobalSetting.psbase.Gettext(1))

}

}
```

Let's look at this script line by line.

```
$Namespace = "root\virtualization"

$Computer = Read-Host "Enter the Hyper-V server that you want to connect to"

$VMName = Read-Host ➡
"Enter the Virtual machine that you would like to assign the scope to"

$Scope = Read-Host ➡
"Enter the scope name that you would like to assign to the virtual machine"
```

These first four lines just define four variables. $Namespace is the namespace used for the WMI queries in this script (root\virtualization). $Computer, $VMName, and $Scope take user input from the command line for the name of the Hyper-V host, the name of the target virtual machine, and the name of the scope you want to assign, respectively.

```
$VM_Service = Get-WmiObject -ComputerName $Computer ➡
-Namespace $Namespace -Class Msvm_VirtualSystemManagementService
```

This line gets an instance of the Msvm_VirtualSystemManagementService class so it can be used to modify the target virtual machine later in the script.

```
$VM = Get-WmiObject -ComputerName $Computer ➡
-Namespace $Namespace -Class Msvm_ComputerSystem | ➡
Where-Object -FilterScript {$_.ElementName -eq $VMName}
```

This line gets the instance of the Msvm_ComputerSystem class that has an element name of $VMname (this is what the user enters at the beginning of the script).

```
Get-Wmiobject -ComputerName $Computer ➡
-Namespace $Namespace -Class Msvm_ComputerSystem | ➡
Where-Object -FilterScript {$_.ElementName -eq $VMName}
```

This is the same as the preceding line, except this time, you are going to use it for the processing portion of the script by piping it into the line following it.

```
ForEach-Object {
if ( $VM -ne $Null)
{
```

These lines say that ForEach-Object from the preceding WMI query, do something. That something is conditional with an if statement. If $VM (the virtual machine instance with the name defined earlier in the script) does not equal $Null, do something.

```
$VMGlobalSetting = Get-Wmiobject -ComputerName $Computer ➥
-Namespace $Namespace -Class Msvm_VirtualSystemGlobalSettingData | ➥
Where-Object -FilterScript { $_.ElementName -eq $VMName}

$VMGlobalSetting.ScopeOfResidence = $Scope

$VM_Service.ModifyVirtualSystem($VM.__PATH, $VMGlobalSetting.psbase.Gettext(1))
```

These few lines are the workhorse of the script. $VMGlobalSetting is the instance of the Msvm_VirtualSystemGlobalSettingData class that has the ElementName of $VMName (defined at the beginning of the script). Then the property ScopeOfResidence on the instance $VMGlobalSetting is assigned a value of $Scope (the scope name defined by the user in the beginning of the script). Finally, the virtual machine is modified using the ModifyVirtualSystem method of the Msvm_VirtualSystemManagementService class. The last two brackets in the script just close the ForEach loop and if statement.

So, to review, the steps to delegate administration of your virtual machines without VMM 2008 are as follows:

1. Set up your scope, tasks, roles, and role assignments using azman.msc. The default path of the authorization store is c:\programdata\microsoft\windows\hyper-v\initialstore.xml.

2. Assign a scope to a virtual machine using WMI scripting.

■**Caution** Since the intitialstore.xml file is the authorization store for your Hyper-V server, it is protected only by NTFS permissions. Make sure those permissions are appropriate. Also, be sure to periodically back up the initialstore.xml file in case of file corruption.

VMM 2008 Security

When you decide to deploy VMM 2008, the delegation in initialstore.xml for any Hyper-V hosts that are under VMM 2008 management will no longer function. You will need to set up delegation in VMM 2008. Thankfully, delegation of access is much easier in VMM 2008 than it is in Hyper-V Manager. Using the VMM 2008 Administrator console is covered in Chapter 3. Refer back to that chapter if you need a refresher.

Take the following steps to set up delegation with VMM 2008:

1. In the VMM Administrator console, create a new host group to hold the hosts and virtual machines that will be delegated. An example of a host group name might be Development.

2. Place any hosts that you want to delegate in the host group you just created.

3. Go to the Administration view and select User Roles. Click New User in the Actions pane.

4. If you want to delegate only virtual machine actions to the group or user, then follow the steps for creating a Self-Service user role outlined in Chapter 3. If you want to delegate the administration of an entire Hyper-V host or set of hosts to a user or group, choose the Delegated Administrator role type in the General window, as shown in Figure 9-12.

Note In order for Self-Service delegation to work, the VMM Self-Service Portal must be installed somewhere in your infrastructure. Installing the Self-Service Portal is covered in Chapter 3.

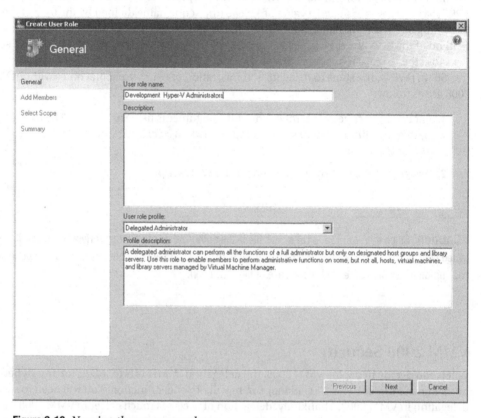

Figure 9-12. *Naming the new user role*

5. In the Add Members window, shown in Figure 9-13, add the appropriate users or groups for delegation.

6. In the Select Scope window, select the host group that you created earlier, as well as any libraries you want to allow the user role to access, as shown in Figure 9-14.

7. Verify your settings in the Summary window. Then click the Create button to create the user role.

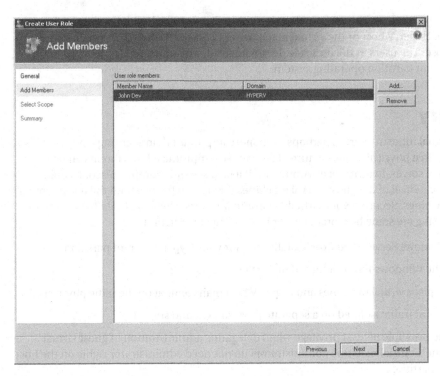

Figure 9-13. *Adding a user to the new user role*

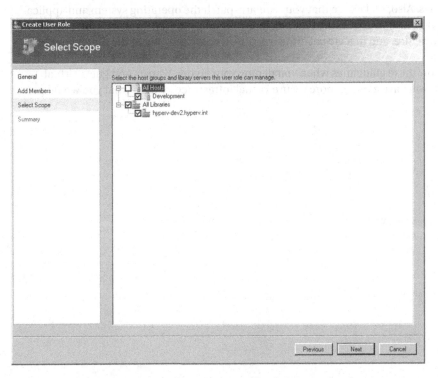

Figure 9-14. *Selecting the scope of management for the new user role*

That's all there is to it. The users in that user role will now be delegated to either administer the entire Hyper-V host or the virtual machines on a host, depending on which user role type you choose. The users in the user role do not need administrator rights on the Hyper-V host server parent partition operating system.

Summary

Securing a virtual infrastructure is perhaps even more important than securing a physical infrastructure. In a physical infrastructure, if a server is compromised, the threat can be isolated on the one server. In a virtual environment, if a host server is compromised, it could potentially threaten all of the guest virtual machines that are on the host and the data store on the virtual machines. Securing your virtual environment starts when you build the host server.

The following are some best practices for Hyper-V host configuration:

- Use Windows Server 2008 Core installations for your Hyper-V parent partition.

- Keep the Windows Firewall turned on for your Hyper-V hosts.

- Do not place virtual machines and Hyper-V host management on the same physical NIC.

- Keep iSCSI traffic isolated on a separate physical NIC and subnet.

- Use the principle of least privilege when delegating administration of guest virtual machines. Virtual machine administrators do not need administrator rights on the host parent partition.

You should also follow some of the security guidelines mentioned here for your guest virtual machines. Also, make sure that you regularly patch the operating system and applications on your host and your guest virtual machines. A compromised guest can still be a threat to your infrastructure, and in a virtual infrastructure, it could also starve the other guests of a host resources.

If you follow these guidelines when you deploy your Hyper-V hosts and guest virtual machines, you will have a much more secure virtual infrastructure than what you would get out of the box.

APPENDIX

■ ■ ■

A Preview of Windows Server 2008 R2 Hyper-V with Live Migration

As it stands today, Hyper-V is a capable platform for building your virtual infrastructure. However, there is always room for improvement in any product. The following are some of the exciting enhancements that will be in the next version of Hyper-V included with Windows Server 2008 Release 2 (R2):

- The ability to add and remove storage from virtual machines while they are running (available if Hyper-V Integration Services is installed on the virtual machine)

- Support for up to 32 physical processor cores

- Support for Intel extended page tables (EPTs) and AMD nested page tables (NPTs) in processors that include this functionality

---

■**Note** When a virtual machine is running, the guest operating system maps out memory pages inside the virtual machine. The hypervisor addresses and stores those memory pages in physical RAM. Because the memory addresses that the guest operating system knows about and the addresses that are in physical RAM usually do not match, the hypervisor must translate the retrieval and updating of pages in RAM. EPT and NPT do the translating for the hypervisor, so overall performance can be increased.

- The ability to perform a live migration (a migration while the virtual machine is running with no interruption of service) of a virtual machine from one host to another

- A clustered file system that enables all the hosts in a failover cluster to share a volume simultaneously

- Enhanced networking that includes support for jumbo frames in virtual machine guests

---

■Note The features discussed here are from a Beta version of Windows Server 2008 R2 (available from `http://www.microsoft.com/downloads/details.aspx?FamilyID=85cfe4c9-34de-477c-b5ca-75edae3d57c5&displaylang=en`). They are subject to change when Windows Server 2008 R2 is released to manufacturing (RTM).

Of all these features, the one that I am the most excited about is live migration, and this appendix focuses on that feature.

Live Migration

Live migration refers to the ability to move a running virtual machine from one Hyper-V host to another Hyper-V host without service interruption. It can bring a lot of flexibility to your virtual infrastructure.

One of the major features that makes live migration possible in this future release is Clustered Shared Volumes (CSV). CSV acts as a distributed-access file system. This means that it can be accessed by more than one host at a time (read and write). It is similar to a clustered file system, but is built on NTFS, and not a new file system. So, with just the selection of a single check box, you can enable CSV.

The fact that multiple hosts can access CSV at the same time is what really unlocks the live migration capability of Hyper-V. To better understand why, let's take a look at what happens during a quick migration (discussed in Chapter 7 of this book) in the current release of Windows Server 2008 with Hyper-V:

- An administrator issues a quick migration command for a virtual machine.

- The virtual machine is put into a saved state.

- The logical unit number (LUN) that the virtual machine resides on is failed over to another Hyper-V node in a failover cluster.

- Once the LUN is brought online on the other Hyper-V cluster, the virtual machine is restored to a running state.

Although this process takes only a few seconds, it does cause a service interruption. The main cause for the service interruption in quick migration is the LUN failover. Since only one Hyper-V node can have access to a LUN at a time, the virtual machine must be put into a saved state so the LUN can failover, and the virtual machine can be brought back up gracefully on the other node. A one-to-one ratio of virtual machine to LUN must be maintained if you need to use quick migration in the current release of Hyper-V, because failover happens at the LUN level, rather than the virtual machine level.

Now, let's take a look at the general process for live migration with Hyper-V on Windows Server 2008 R2 Beta 1.

- An administrator issues a live migration command for a virtual machine.

- An initial bitmap copy of the virtual machine's memory is copied over to the destination host.

- Changes (deltas) to the memory pages are logged during the initial memory copy.

- The virtual machine is put into a paused state briefly (not noticeable from a user standpoint), so the smaller deltas can be copied to the new destination host.

- The destination host assumes control of the virtual machine and takes it out of a paused state, without any service interruption.

There is a lot more going on under the hood, but these five steps give a good overview of what is happening. The important detail to notice here is that the migration happens at the virtual machine level, because there was no need for a LUN failover. Each host in the cluster has access to CSV at the same time. Any virtual machine that is stored on CSV is eligible for live migration. This also means that you no longer need to maintain a virtual machine to LUN ratio of one to one.

Here, you will learn how to configure live migration so you can see for yourself the flexibility that this new feature can bring to your virtual infrastructure.

Note Live migration cannot be used for unplanned downtime without any interruption, because the source host must still be functioning to start the live migration process.

Configuring Live Migration

The basic steps involved in configuring and using the new live migration feature of Hyper-V R2 are as follows:

- Configure and verify the functionality of your Hyper-V failover cluster.

- Enable and configure CSV. This requires the Enterprise or Datacenter version of Windows Server 2008 R2 Beta 1.

- Deploy a virtual machine on CSV.

- Test the live migration for the virtual machine.

Configuring and verifying the functionality of a Hyper-V failover cluster is covered in Chapter 7 of this book. Refer to that chapter for details on setting up a failover cluster. Once the failover cluster is set up, follow these steps to configure live migration:

1. Open the Failover Cluster Management tool by selecting Start ➤ Administrative Tools ➤ Failover Cluster Management on Windows Server 2008 or Windows Vista.

2. Once you have connected to your cluster, click Enable Clustered Shared Volumes in the Actions pane, as shown in Figure A-1.

Figure A-1. *Choose Enable Cluster Shared Volumes from the Actions pane of the Failover Cluster Management tool.*

3. The Enable Cluster Shared Volumes window appears, as shown in Figure A-2. This warns you that the CSV feature should be used only for Hyper-V clusters. No other data should be stored on CSV. Click the check box to accept the terms and restrictions.

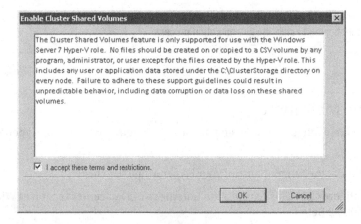

Figure A-2. *CSV terms and restrictions*

4. Now you just need to add a volume to the cluster. (The CSV feature allows you to store multiple virtual machines on the same LUN, so this example uses a single volume.) Right-click Cluster Shared Volumes in the navigation pane on the left and select Add Storage. Select the volume that you want to add to CSV, as shown in Figure A-3, and then click OK.

Figure A-3. *Choosing a volume for CSV*

5. Select Cluster Shared Volumes in the navigation pane, and you will see your CSV volume. When CSV is enabled, a new namespace, `C:\ClusterStorage`, is created on each node in the cluster for these volumes. Notice that your new CSV volume is in the `C:\ClusterStorage\Volume1` path on each node, as shown in Figure A-4.

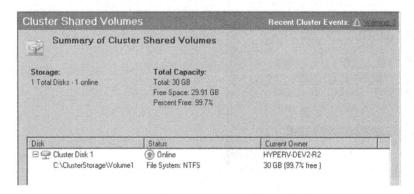

Figure A-4. *The Clustered Shared Volume path*

6. For your virtual machines to be capable of a live migration, you need to deploy them into the `C:\ClusteredStorage\Volume1` path by selecting that path in the Specify Name and Location section of the New Virtual Machine Wizard in Hyper-V Manager, as shown in Figure A-5. (See Chapter 1 of this book for details on using the Hyper-V Manager tool.)

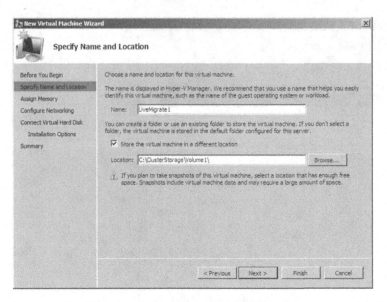

Figure A-5. *Deploying your virtual machine on CSV*

7. Once your virtual machines are deployed and made fault-tolerant (refer to Chapter 7 for details on how to deploy a fault-tolerant virtual machine), you need to choose the network that will be used for the live migration. This is done on a per-virtual machine basis. To do this, right-click your virtual machine under Services and Applications in the navigation pane in the Failover Cluster Management tool and choose Properties. Click the Network for Live Migration tab, and choose the network that you will use for live migration traffic (this includes a memory bitmap of the virtual machine sent from one host to another), as shown in Figure A-6.

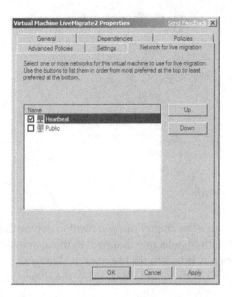

Figure A-6. *Choosing the network for live migration traffic*

Note As a best practice, the live migration network should be a separate physical network.

Performing a Live Migration

To perform a live migration for a virtual machine, just select the virtual machine. Then click "Live migrate this virtual machine to" in the Actions pane of the Failover Cluster Management tool and choose the host to which to migrate the virtual machine, as shown in Figure A-7.

Figure A-7. *Starting the live migration process*

To verify the current owner of the virtual machine before or after a live migration, select the appropriate virtual machine resource group under the Services and Applications section in the navigation pane. Look for the current owner in the Summary section of the results pane in the middle of the window, as shown in Figure A-8.

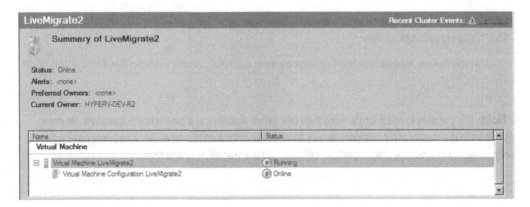

Figure A-8. *Verifying the current owner of the virtual machine*

PowerShell and Failover Clustering

In Windows Server 2008 R2, you can control some aspects of failover clustering through Windows PowerShell. To use this feature, open the Failover Cluster PowerShell Management tool from a Windows Server 2008 R2 full installation that has the failover cluster feature installed. This tool can be accessed from the Start ➤ Administrative Tools menu.

Once the PowerShell window is open, to get a list of all the cmdlets available for failover clustering, type the following:

```
Get-Command -Module FailoverClusters
```

To get syntax help for any of the cmdlets, use this command:

```
Get-Help <CmdletName> -Full
```

This will give the full help as well as some examples for the cmdlet.

If you want to start the live migration of a virtual machine with PowerShell, you can do so using these cmdlets. Here is an example:

```
Get-Cluster "<ClusterName>" | Move-ClusterVirtualMachineRole ➡
-Name "<VMGroupName>" -Node "<DestinationNodeName>"
```

where:

- <ClusterName> is the name of the cluster you want to work with.

- <VMGroupName> is the name of the virtual machine resource group.

- <DestinationNodeName> is the name of the destination node that the virtual machine will move to.

Let's examine what is happening in this single-line PowerShell command. It begins like this:

```
Get-Cluster "<ClusterName>"
```

This connects to the cluster you will be working with. This is then piped to the rest of the command:

```
Move-ClusterVirtualMachineRole -Name "<VMGroupName>" ➡
-Node "<DestinationNodeName>"
```

This moves the virtual machine resource group from its current node to the destination node.

Note It is possible to live migrate more than one virtual machine at a time using PowerShell. However, each host in the cluster can participate in only a single live migration at a time. So, if you only have a two-node cluster, you would be able to perform only a single live migration at one time.

Summary

Some exciting new features and improvements are coming to Hyper-V with Windows Server 2008 R2. CSV and live migration are two very welcome additions. They will bring the following benefits to your virtual infrastructure:

- You can migrate virtual machines without service interruption.

- You no longer need to maintain a one-to-one virtual machine to LUN mapping ratio.

- You get a more reasonable maintenance window due to the ability to migrate virtual machines without user interruption.

While not specifically announced, I believe that live migration will also unlock some other interesting abilities for your virtual infrastructure. The future may hold dynamic load balancing among Hyper-V hosts. Also, when integrated with System Center Virtual Machine Manager PRO Tips (covered in Chapter 3 of this book), live migration could enable your virtual infrastructure to make intelligent placement or migration decisions for your virtual machines, without user interruption.

Whatever the future may hold, it is an exciting time to use server virtualization technology. Microsoft's first bare-metal hypervisor is a good start for your virtual infrastructure needs. It looks like the future release is right on track to provide even more enterprise-class capabilities for your virtual infrastructure.

Index

You Need the Companion eBook

Your purchase of this book entitles you to buy the companion PDF-version eBook for only $10. Take the weightless companion with you anywhere.

We believe this Apress title will prove so indispensable that you'll want to carry it with you everywhere, which is why we are offering the companion eBook (in PDF format) for $10 to customers who purchase this book now. Convenient and fully searchable, the PDF version of any content-rich, page-heavy Apress book makes a valuable addition to your programming library. You can easily find and copy code—or perform examples by quickly toggling between instructions and the application. Even simultaneously tackling a donut, diet soda, and complex code becomes simplified with hands-free eBooks!

Once you purchase your book, getting the $10 companion eBook is simple:

❶ Visit **www.apress.com/promo/tendollars/**.

❷ Complete a basic registration form to receive a randomly generated question about this title.

❸ Answer the question correctly in 60 seconds, and you will receive a promotional code to redeem for the $10.00 eBook.

eBookshop

Apress®
THE EXPERT'S VOICE™

2855 TELEGRAPH AVENUE │ SUITE 600 │ BERKELEY, CA 94705

Offer valid through 10/09.